John Calvin's Perspectival Anthropology

American Academy of Religion Academy Series

edited by
Susan Thistlethwaite

Number 52
John Calvin's Perspectival Anthropology
by
Mary Potter Engel

Mary Potter Engel

JOHN CALVIN'S PERSPECTIVAL ANTHROPOLOGY

Scholars Press
Atlanta, Georgia

John Calvin's Perspectival Anthropology

by
Mary Potter Engel

© 1988
American Academy of Religion

Library of Congress Cataloging-in-Publication Data

Engel, Mary Potter.
  John Calvin's perspectival anthropology / by Mary Potter Engel.
      p.   cm.—(American Academy of Religion academy series ; no.
52)
    Bibliography: p.
    ISBN 1-555-40159-7 (alk. paper).   ISBN 1-555-40217-8 (pbk. : alk.
paper)
    1. Calvin, Jean, 1509–1564—Contributions in anthropology.   2. Man
(Christian theology)—History of doctrines—16th century.
I. Title. II. Series.
BT701.2.E54   1988
233—dc19   87-37678
                                                                              CIP

Printed in the United States of America
on acid-free paper

TABLE OF CONTENTS

PREFACE

This is not the dissertation I set out to write. The original title of this study was to be *Three Renaissance Portraits of Humankind: Calvin's Anthropology in Relation to the Anthropology of the Florentine Platonists.* I planned to investigate the relation between Calvin's "Reformation" anthropology and the "Renaissance" anthropologies of Marsilio Ficino and Pico della Mirandola for three reasons: (1) to ascertain the truth of Roy Battenhouse's claim that Calvin's anthropology evidenced a "subterranean dependence" on the anthropologies of Ficino and Pico;[1] (2) to see if I could help to clarify Calvin's relationship to humanism, so widely debated among Calvin scholars for so many years; and (3) to attempt to contribute to the ongoing Renaissance/Reformation research by focusing on a particular issue in specific authors. With these as my questions and goals I went digging in Calvin's texts. Given my preliminary research on Calvin's relation to humanism and the characteristics of Renaissance anthropologies, I had a hunch that I would find a more complicated anthropology in Calvin's theology than previously described in the literature. What I did not know was that I would discover an anthropological complex so intricate a separate argument would be necessary to describe, analyze, and defend it. Hence, I postponed the original research project in order to write the following essay on Calvin's distinctive perspectival anthropology. Now that this has been accomplished, I hope to return to my original plan of investigating the relationship among the anthropologies of Calvin, Ficino, and Pico.

Note

/1/ Roy Battenhouse, "The Doctrine of Man in Calvin and Renaissance Platonism," *Journal of the History of Ideas* 9 (1948): 470.

INTRODUCTION

In 1954 the renowned historian and Calvin scholar J. T. McNeill summarized the history of Calvin interpretation by noting that "Calvin formerly stirred debate because people agreed or disagreed with his teaching. Recently, men have been in disagreement over what his teaching was."[1] Thirty years later this observation remains a true and tidy characterization of Calvin research, especially for two specific areas of Calvin studies: the doctrine of humankind and the problem of Calvin's relation to humanism. A definitive analysis or even a general consensus has yet to appear in both of these areas.

Calvin's anthropology has been one of the doctrines most neglected by scholars. Aside from T. F. Torrance's *Calvin's Doctrine of Man*, no full-length study of Calvin's doctrine of humankind has been published.[2] One reason for this may be that although most Calvin scholars would readily agree with Gerd Babelotzsky that there is an "implicit anthropology" in Calvin's theology, it is Calvin's theocentrism which has drawn the most attention and praise.[3] In fact, most of the references to the intimate connection Calvin draws between God-knowledge and self-knowledge in the opening sentences of the *Institutes* are made somewhat hastily on the way to discussions of the more substantive and important "theological" doctrines such as Christology, Soteriology, or Pneumatology.[4] For this reason the significance of Calvin's pairing of God-knowledge and self-knowledge has not been properly understood or appreciated. In Calvin's view, self-knowledge is at the center of the heavenly philosophy or Reformed theology. Anthropology, then, is neither an afterword nor a second-class doctrine in his thought, but rather a constant and primary focus. If one neglects Calvin's anthropology, therefore, one fails to understand a fundamental and pervasive element of his entire theology.[5] It is the intent of this study to contribute to the understanding of Calvin's theology by providing a thorough description and analysis of his anthropology.

When Calvin's anthropology has been studied in the past, it

has given rise to conflict and confusion paralleling the conflict and confusion among scholars over the structure of Calvin's theology. The problem of the structure of Calvin's theology has plagued scholars since Alexander Schweizer and Ferdinand Christian Baur named predestination as the central dogma of Calvin's theology in the mid-nineteenth century.[6] As François Wendel notes, this position was repeated without verification by historians and theologians for three quarters of a century.[7] Then, in 1922, Hermann Bauke published *Die Probleme der Theologie Calvins*, in which he argued persuasively that there is no one idea or doctrinal premise from which all other doctrines are deduced in Calvin, but that the coherence of his theology lay in three formal principles: rationalism, *complexio oppositorum*, and biblicism.[8] Having been warned against over-systematizing Calvin's theology, scholars writing after 1922 adopted one of two positions. They either nodded in Bauke's direction before going on to specify what they considered to be the "heart" or "inspiration" of Calvin's thought. Or they concluded that there was finally no system or definite structure in his theology. The first held a special attraction for theologians influenced by Neo-orthodoxy, many of whom found the doctrine of faith, the majesty of God, or Christology to be at the center of Calvin's theology.[9] Quite different central features were discovered by theologians more influenced by existentialism than Barth, as for example Gilbert Rist's "existential knowledge of God" and Sandra Rudnick's "voluntarist presupposition."[10] Recently, theologians have begun to emphasize the centrality of the Augustinian theme of God as the give of every good gift.[11] The second alternative reflects a hardening of Bauke's original thesis. It is now common to find theologians and historians arguing that there is neither a thematic core nor a consistent formal structure in Calvin's theology. Representatives attribute the alleged lack of consistency to various causes, but all agree that Calvin's theology is, in some sense or some place, finally contradictory.[12]

Summary evaluations of Calvin's anthropology are as diverse as those of his theology. For many years his anthropology was characterized as a pessimistic view of humankind focusing on the absolute submission of the human creature to the almighty power of God and the total depravity of the sinner before God the righteous judge. Recently this thesis has been challenged by a more optimistic counter-thesis emphasizing the contribution of Calvin to the modern understanding of human freedom and dignity. More recently still a compromise thesis of contradiction, which argues that Calvin's anthropology has no single focus or emphasis because it is a realistic anthropology reflecting the contradictory anthropologies of the scriptures, has been proposed.[14] In other words, just as Bauke discovered the "problem of Calvin's theology" in the twenties, in the seventies and eighties scholars are discovering the "problem of Calvin's anthropology."

It is the primary intent of this study to contribute to greater understanding of the "problem of Calvin's anthropology" by offering a new interpretation of his view of humankind that moves beyond the thesis of pessimism, the counter-thesis of optimism, and the compromise thesis of contradiction. This interpretation is based on my thesis of perspectivalism, which is described and defended in the following chapters. A brief statement of the thesis of perspectivalism follows here.

Calvin's anthropology is an intricate complex of a wide variety of assertions and judgments about humankind, each one reflecting a different theological perspective. Many of these assertions and judgments support the thesis of pessimism; many the counter-thesis of optimism. Some are undeniably contradictory to one another, supporting the thesis of contradiction. All of these assertions and judgments, however, are held together by a determinable set of distinct theological perspectives which I refer to as the "dynamic perspectival structure of Calvin's anthropology." The overall impression one is left with is that for Calvin the human creature is such a complex reality that only a complex, dynamic model of interpretation is adequate to understand it. Just as the phenomenon of light requires both the wave and particle theory to be described accurately, so the existence of human beings requires different perspectives that are *at once* contradictory and complementary to be described accurately.

The task of the following essay, then, is twofold: to demonstrate that Calvin's anthropology contains such a definite and constant set of shifting perspectives that are contradictory yet complementary; and, to persuade the reader that using this set of perspectives as an interpretive tool helps to make sense out of Calvin's disparate anthropological statements. Two clarifications are necessary at this point. First, my intent is *not* to argue that Calvin intentionally created or deliberately used the dynamic perspectival structure I describe in his anthropology. I found no evidence to support this claim; and, my argument for the existence of this complex structure in his anthropology does not rest upon such a claim. Second, my intent is *not* to prove that the prior theses for interpreting Calvin's

anthropology are invalid. On the contrary, the thesis of perspectivalism verifies the observations and clarifies the conclusions of the
thesis of pessimism, the counter-thesis of optimism, and the compromise thesis of contradiction. I do argue, throughout, however, for
the greater adequacy of the thesis of perspectivalism in interpreting
Calvin's anthropology on the basis of two criteria: its capacity to
make sense out of more texts than either the thesis of pessimism or
the thesis of optimism; and, its greater specificity about the structural context of the contradictions embedded in Calvin's anthropology than the thesis of contradiction. If the latter argument
proves unsuccessful, I hope at the very least to have convinced the
reader that the thesis of perspectivalism offers an alternative interpretation of Calvin's often perplexing anthropology, an alternative
that may provoke new understandings.

The set of theological perspectives present in Calvin's anthropology will be described generally, both in terms of its basic
structure and dynamic functioning, in chapter 1. The remaining
chapters support the analysis of chapter 1 by analyzing the set of
shifting perspectives as it appears in Calvin's discussion of specific
anthropological issues, namely: (a) the problem of the loss and/or
retention of the *imago dei* after the fall (chapter 2), (b) the problem of
the rejection and/or use of reason in human affairs (chapter 3), (c) the
problem of the denial of human freedom and/or the emphasis on
human responsibility (chapter 4), and (d) the problem of the immortality of the soul and/or the resurrection of the body (chapter 5).
Each of these issues has been selected because it has been identified
as a particularly problematic area of Calvin's anthropology. It is my
hope that using the thesis of perspectivalism to interpret each of
them will bring greater clarity to these individual aspects of Calvin's
anthropology as well as to the whole.

Notes

/1/ John T. McNeill, *The History and Character of Calvinism* (New York:
Oxford University Press, 1954), p. 202.
/2/ T. F. Torrance, *Calvin's Doctrine of Man* (London: Lutterworth Press,
1952). Several works contain chapters or sections that are devoted to Cal-
vin's anthropology: Charles Partee's *Calvin and Classical Philosophy*
(Leiden: E. J. Brill, 1977) contains a chapter entitled "Soul and Body in
Anthropology," pp. 51–65; Sandra Dell Rudnick's *From Created to Creator:
Conceptions of Human Nature and Authority in Sixteenth Century England*
(Ann Arbor: University Microfilms, 1963) treats Calvin's anthropology in

some detail in the opening of her work; André Biéler's *La pensée économique et sociale de Calvin* (Geneva: Georg et Cie, 1961) contains a brief but helpful summary of Calvin's anthropology entitled "Esquisse d'une anthropologie et d'une sociologie théologique," pp. 184–265; and Carla Calvetti's *La Filosofia di Giovanni Calvino* (Milan: Societá Editrice "Vita et Pensiero," 1955) discusses certain anthropological assumptions of Calvin throughout the first chapter; and Gerd Babelotzky's entire work, *Platonische Bilder und Gedankengänge in Calvins Lehre vom Menschen* (Wiesbaden: Franz Steiner Verlag, 1977) [hereafter referred to as *Platonische Bilder*] focuses on Calvin's teaching on humankind, though from the limited point of view of its use of Platonic images.

/3/ Babelotzky, *Platonische Bilder*, pp. 77–78. Babelotzsky also expresses the need to render this implicit anthropology more explicit.

/4/ The famous sentence of the *Institutes of the Christian Religion* 1.1.1 reads: "Tota fere sapientiae nostrae summa, quae vera demum ac solida sapientia censeri debeat, duabus partibus constat, Dei cognitione et nostri," *Calvini opera selecta* [hereafter referred to as *OS*], ed. Peter Barth and Wilhelm Niesel, 5 vols (Monachii: Kaiser Verlag, 1926–36), 3:31. For an example of the common view that Calvin is not interested in humankind, but in God, See Reinhold Hedtke, *Erziehung durch die Kirche bei Calvin: Der Unterweisungs- und Erziehungsauftrag der Kircher und seine anthropologischen und theologischen Grundlagen* (Heidelberg: Quelle und Meyer, 1969).

/5/ In sermon 43 on Job 11 Calvin makes a lengthy statement about the importance of self-knowledge which is very similar to Petrarch's version of Augustine's famous sentence on self-knowledge. Calvin says: "If a person knows all things, yet understands nothing, is he wise? For example, a man applies himself to the study of letters, good conscience, etc., and yet he is foolish, senseless, as to what concerns himself," *Ioannis Calvini opera quae supersunt omnia*, ed. Wilhelm Baum, Edward Cunitz, and Edward Reuss, 59 vols. (Brunsvigae: C. A. Schwetscke, 1863–1900), vols. 29–87: *Corpus Reformatorum*, 33: 539 [hereafter referred to as *CO*]. Petrarch's quotation of Augustine's statement and his use of the image may be found in "Ascent of Mont Ventoux" in *The Renaissance Philosophy of Man*, ed. Ernst Cassirer (Chicago: University of Chicago Press, 1948), p. 44. Augustine's original statement is found in the *Confessions* 10. 8: "I am lost in wonder when I consider this problem. It bewilders me. Yet men go out and gaze in astonishment at high mountains, the huge waves of the sea, the broad reaches of the rivers, the ocean that encircles the earth, or the stars in their course. But they pay no attention to themselves," trans. R. S. Pine (Harmondsworth: Penguin, 1976), p. 216. For a discussion of the understanding of self-knowledge and the relation between God-knowledge and self-knowledge in this day, see Josef Bohatec's *Budé und Calvin: Studien zur Gedankenwelt des französischen Frühhumanismus* (Graz: Böhlau, 1950), chapter 2. The remainder of this investigation will indirectly show the importance of self-knowledge to Calvin and the way it is to be understood.

/6/ Alexander Schweizer, *Die Glaubenslehre der evangelische-reformierten Kirche dargestellt und den Quellen belegt*, 2 vols. (Zurich: Orell, Fussli, 1944–47), 1:8; Ferdinand Christian Baur, *Lehrbuch der christlichen*

Dogmengeschichte (Tübingen: Fues, 1858), pp. 279–84.

/7/   François Wendel, *Calvin: Sources et évolution de sa pensée religieuse* (Paris: Presses Universitaires de France, 1950), pp. 200–201. See p. 200, n. 100 of his book for a list of all texts that have repeated this view.

/8/   Hermann Bauke, *Dei Probleme der Theologie Calvins* (Leipzig: Hinrichs'schen, 1922), p. 20.

/9/   Williston Walker, *John Calvin: The Organiser of Reformed Protestantism, 1509–64,* (New York: Schocken Books, 1969), pp. 138, 148 and Paul Tillich, *A History of Christian Thought,* ed. Carl Braaten (New York: Harper & Row, 1968), p. 263 speak of the agency or reality and the majesty of God respectively as the center of Calvin's theology. Peter Brunner sees the doctrine of faith as central in *Vom Glauben bei Calvin* (Tübingen: Mohr, 1925). T. F. Torrance states "That takes us to the heart of Calvin's doctrine of man, which he insists, again and again, we can formulate truly *only* from the standpoint of the grace of God in Jesus Christ," *Calvin's Doctrine of Man,* p. 18. (Emphasis mine.) This focus on the Christology of Calvin's theology has had the greatest popularity. Wilhelm Niesel concludes in *The Theology of Calvin,* trans. Harold Knight (Philadelphia: Westminster Press, 1956, that it is Christology which controls both the form and content of Calvin's theology even though there is no one axiom from which all is deduced, pp. 246–50. François Wendel is quite circumspect in his conclusion, maintaining that the doctrine of Jesus Christ is one of the dominant preoccupations of Calvin but not a central systematic idea from which all else is deduced, *Calvin: Sources,* pp. 274–75. More recently, Gerrish has made a similar claim to Wendel's, saying that "Although Christology may not be the structural center of Calvin's 'system,' . . . 'Christocentrism' [is] at least a characteristic habit of Calvin's thought—a habit which determined both his theology and his conception of reform," *Reformers in Profile* (Philadelphia: Fortress Press, 1967), p. 144. While these more circumspect claims about Calvin's Christology are accurate, they will be clarified by the analysis of this study.

/10/   Gilbert Rist, "Modernité de la méthode théologique de Calvin." *Revue de Théologie et de Philosophie* 18 (1968): 23; Rudnick, *From Created to Creator,* p. 51. She claims this is the heart of Calvin's theology and that his emphasis on the historicity of humankind must be noted as well.

/11/   Ronald Wallace's *Calvin's Doctrine of the Christian Life* (Grand Rapids: Wm. B. Eerdmans, 1952) stresses this theme throughout, though he does not make a major statement about the structure or coherence of Calvin's theology. See Garret Wilterdink's "Irresistible Grace and the Fatherhood of God in Calvin's Theology" (Ph.D dissertation, University of Chicago, 1974), also.

/12/   For example, John Leith, in his "Calvin's Theological Method and the Ambiguities in his Theology," in *Reformation Studies,* ed. F. H. Littell (Richmond: John Knox, 1962), pp. 108, 110, 113, ascribes the ambiguities to Calvin's eclecticism; Jack Forstman, *Word and Spirit: Calvin's Doctrine of Biblical Authority* (Stanford: University Press, 1962), p. 36, to his exegetical techniques; Richard Stauffer, "Dieu, la création et la providence dans l'oeuvre homilétique de Calvin," *La Revue Réformée* 27–28 (1976–77): 196–207, finds no doctrinal homogeneity in the sermons of Calvin and no Christological center, a fact which he also attributes to Calvin's radical biblicism, pp. 201–3. Wendel stresses that Calvin's doctrinal system does not compare in rigor to that of Aristotle or Aquinas and attributes this fact to Calvin's biblical foundation also, which would not allow rigid philosophical or rational constructions, *Calvin: Sources*, p. 273. His conclusion is relatively common: "[L]e système de Calvin n'est pas un système ferme, élaboré, à partir d'une idée centrale, mais qu'il englobe successivement toute une série de notions bibliques dont quelquesunes sont difficilement conciliables en logique," ibid., p. 274. My point in response to such views of Calvin's theology is that although his "system" does not lend itself to a rigid rational analysis, it is definitely consistent due to the employment of shifting perspectives. Furthermore, this perspectival approach cannot simply be referred to as "biblicism" or "Christocentrism."

/13/   There are many examples of this. For one, see Augustin Renaudet's claim that Calvin attempted to rub out vainglory in people as the Jansenists did in his *Humanisme et Renaissance* (Geneva: Librairie E. Droz, 1958), pp. 40–41.

/14/   Specific problems of interpretation will be discussed in detail in chapters 2 through 5. For now we will simply note the claims of a few scholars to have found "inconsistencies" or "contradictions" in Calvin's anthropology: Torrance suggests that there may be no way to reconcile Calvin's views on the erasure and disfigurement of the *imago dei* (*Calvin's Doctrine of Man*, p. 93); Leith claims that Calvin's view of the soul and body and immortality and resurrection exhibit inconsistencies ("Calvin's Theological Method," pp. 108, 110); Wallace points to the confusion in Calvin's theology concerning the natural law and knowledge of the law in Christ (*Calvin's Doctrine of the Christian Life*, p. 148).

CHAPTER 1

THE DYNAMIC PERSPECTIVAL STRUCTURE OF CALVIN'S ANTHROPOLOGY

> No matter what subject is under considera-
> tion, making certain distinctions usually
> sheds a great deal of light on it.
> *Concerning Scandals*

The Distinction Between the Perspective of Humankind and the Perspective of God

In my view the solution to the "problem of Calvin's anthropology" does not lie in any one logical premise, doctrine, or
theme. This does not imply, however, that his anthropology lacks a
unifying structure or order. Bauke argued that the unity of Calvin's
theology lies not in any external arrangement but in a set of ordering
principles: rationalism, *complexio oppositorum*, and biblicism.[1]
Similarly, the coherence of Calvin's anthropology lies in its dynamic
perspectival structure, a structure determined by a distinction between the perspective of God and the perspective of humankind as
it operates in both the doctrines of creation and redemption. In this
chapter the distinction itself and its variations will be outlined. In
subsequent chapters I will demonstrate how the distinction in its
variations operates in the doctrines of the *imago dei*, reason and
revelation, providence and freedom, and immortality and resurrection.

Pervading all Calvin's comments on humankind is a basic
distinction between the perspective of God and the perspective of
humankind. Each of these perspectives represents a different vantage point for viewing and evaluating the human creature and leads
to different knowledge about the self. The perspective of God is an

absolute perspective. When one assumes the position of God in the universe, all of reality, including human beings, appears in stark contrast to the divine being. In fact, from this vantage point, God and humankind appear to be either mutually exclusive of one another or in contradiction to one another. Also, from this perspective, human beings appear not as unique individuals but as parts of an undifferentiated mass. This absolute perspective is distinct from the relative perspective of humankind. When one assumes the position of a human being in the midst of the universe, all of reality, including human beings, appears as related though differentiated. In fact, from this vantage point, God and humankind appear to be intimately related to one another. Also, from this perspective human beings appear as unique individuals with varying and comparative degrees of skills and gifts. This basic distinction between the absolute perspective of God and the relative perspective of humankind appears in clearly identifiable variations in Calvin's doctrines of creation and redemption. Before turning to a detailed description of these two variations, a comment on why I have selected creation and redemption as organizing principles of this study is in order.

As Gerrish has pointed out, Calvin operates with a three-fold structure of salvation-history in the *Institutes:* creation, fall/redemption, and consummation.[2] This structure is present not only in the *Institutes* but throughout his works. Though the stages do not always appear together or in the same order, the distinction among the three stages pervades Calvin's thought; for this reason it may be called a fundamental governing structure of his thought. That he has this distinction in mind at all times, even when he does not explicitly refer to it, is obvious from his comments in his sermons. He occasionally reminds his hearers that although their individual lives may be brief and insignificant, their tasks as Christians is an ennobling one: to contemplate all the works of the God who is active in history. God records his acts in history and the history of his acts in order that we may ponder his work from the creation of the world, through the time of the Fall and the coming of Jesus Christ, through our present existence as redeemed sinners, up to the end of time.[3]

Although Calvin does believe that the Fall is a discrete historical act, he does not treat it as a separate stage of salvation history. Instead, he pairs our fallen condition with our redemption in Jesus Christ and the Spirit. For this reason I have chosen to include the fallen condition as part of the second stage of salvation history rather than as a stage of its own. Also, while Calvin speaks from time to time about the third stage of consummation, it does not dominate his thought the way the first two stages do. For this reason I have chosen to focus on the distinction between the human and divine perspectives only as it appears in the first two stages, creation and fall/redemption.

My aim in the remainder of this study is to demonstrate that a basic distinction between the absolute perspective of God and the relative perspective of humankind, as it appears in its variations in the doctrines of creation and redemption, permeates Calvin's anthropology; and, that understanding the functioning of this dynamic perspectival structure aids in the interpretation of Calvin's doctrine of humankind. The claims I make are limited to his anthropology and do not, so far as I know, apply to his theology as a whole. An excellent argument for the fundamental structure of Calvin's entire theology has been made by E. A. Dowey in his *Knowledge of God in Calvin's Theology*.[4] Because of the similarity between Dowey's distinction, between the knowledge of God the creator and the knowledge of God the redeemer, and my distinction, between the perspective of God and the perspective of humankind, a few words about the differences between our distinctions are necessary.

First, Dowey persuasively argues that Calvin deliberately and intentionally structured his entire theology to accommodate the distinction between the knowledge of God the creator and redeemer, noting that in Calvin there is even a "conscious turning" from one to the other.[5] I make no similar claim, for I found no evidence suggesting that Calvin either consciously conceived of this structure or deliberately structured his anthropology in accordance with it. Second, Dowey's focus is an epistemological one, the knowledge of God. While, broadly speaking, I am concerned with the knowledge of ourselves in relation to God, more specifically I am interested in the complete portrait of humankind that emerges from the combination of varying perspectives. Third, Dowey's identification of the two-fold knowledge of God distinguishes between the knowledge of God made known to us in the revelation of the creator in nature and the scriptures, and the knowledge made known to us in the revelation of the redeemer in the scriptures and Jesus Christ. While I, too, employ a distinction between creation and redemption, it is not equivalent to Dowey's. I use this distinction only to refer to specific areas of theological inquiry that form different contexts for my fundamental distinction between the perspective of God and the perspective of humankind.

Finally, Dowey speaks of the dialectical relationship between the knowledge of God as creator and the knowledge of God as redeemer, explaining that the two orders of knowledge cannot be resolved in any logical unity but only in the final unity of the transcendent God.[6] The relationship between the two perspectives I identify in Calvin's anthropology are also discontinuous. The two, as I will show repeatedly, result in inconsistent and even contradictory statements about the self. I do not claim, however, that their final unity rests in a transcendent God. Though that may be so, I prefer to speak of their unity in terms of their interconnection in the complexly ordered whole of a dynamic perspectival structure that includes contradictory yet complementary truths about the self.

The Variation of the Distinction in the Doctrine of Creation

The variation of the distinction between the perspective of God and the perspective of humankind in the doctrine of creation results in two very different pictures of humankind. From the relative, human perspective, humankind appears as it does in Psalm 8— a little higher than the animals, a little lower than the angels. From the absolute perspective of God, however, it appears both as higher than all creatures because of its privileged participation in eternal life *and* equal to all creatures as an evanescent being wholly devoid of eternal life.

From the perspective of humankind, the vantage point within the universe, humankind appears to itself as higher than the animals because of its reasoning powers but lower than the angels because of its more fragile and infirm nature.[7] Though the evaluation from this perspective does not appear frequently, it is clearly a part of his anthropology, existing alongside the absolute evaluations of humankind from the perspective of God.[8] The two companion evaluations of humankind from this absolute perspective, one positive and one negative, however, clearly take precedence in his doctrine of creation.

From the absolute perspective of God, humankind appears not in comparison to the rest of mortal creatures, higher than some and lower than others, but in contradiction to all other mortal creatures *and* in contradiction to God the eternal creator along with all other mortal creatures. The first contradiction is based on Calvin's view of the privileged eschatological existence of human beings. From the very moment of their creation Calvin describes human beings as both temporal and eternal creatures.[9] He does not simply juxtapose these two estates or lives to one another, but presents them in a well-defined relationship: temporal life can only be fully and properly understood in terms of its two-dimensional orientation toward the future eternal life and the present reality of the eternal life. It is this eschatological orientation of human existence on earth, described as a *tendance à la vie celeste"* or a capacity to be *attirez plus haut,"* which differentiates human beings from animals.[10] In fact human beings were created with specific capacities such as reason and sense *in order that* they might be aware of this eschatological orientation of their life. They were constituted so as to know that they were called from a temporal life in the present to a second and better life and to realize that their present life is but a pilgrimage during which they must aspire to the eternal life which is ahead and above;[11] they were given ears so that they might be instructed that when "they have passed through this world there will be a heritage for them which is secured above."[12]

The horizontal vector of this eschatological orientation points to the radically historical character of human existence from its creation. Human beings are constituted by existence toward, knowledge of, and hope in a future eternal life. God did not create these creatures to keep them on the earth as animals, but to let them pass through this world so that they might finally be adopted into their true eternal heritage in the kingdom of God.[13] One specific theological consequence of this is that Adam and Eve in the Garden of Eden must be understood as unfulfilled beings, even though innocent. They too were on an historical journey toward a future fulfillment.[14] Even their life, unstained by sin, would have come to an end before the full revelation of God's goodness appeared and their intended destiny was fulfilled. The would not have met with a violent end, to be sure, but even if sin had never entered the drama, they would have passed through this life on their way to enduring life.[15] They were intended to be *homines viatores*, heirs of the heavenly kingdom living in the hope of full future citizenship.

The vertical vector of this eschatological orientation points to another aspect of their unique existence. Adam and Eve, beings chosen for a future life with the eternal God, were also chosen to enjoy the eternal reality of God during their pilgrimage, again, in a unique way. In other words, they were created not only as heirs who would someday inherit the eternal kingdom, but also as children who already eschatologically enjoyed the paternal solicitude of God while they awaited the fulfillment of that royal heritage.[16] As the horizontal eschatological orientation of their life taught them to aspire to the future life, so the vertical eschatological orientation of their life taught them to aspire to the life above the world. If they did so, they would know that God was their benevolent father and that they were called to respond to his loving gifts in the present world.[17] We were created, Calvin says,

> to this very end, and . . . maintained in this fragile life in order that we might know that it is God who cares for us here, and that we might sense his paternal goodness when he is pleased to so care for us and govern us. Thus our life must be precious to us for this reason.[18]

The response elicited by this knowledge about the participation in this eternal life through the present paternal benefits is active enjoyment of God's present goodness and sweetness while awaiting full revelation. Adam and Eve were called to a life of faithful delight in the presence of the eternal God as well as to a hope in the future eternal kingdom of God. Both this delight and hope are manifestations of the basic human response called forth by God: gratitude for the sweet and blessed life which was already theirs and gratitude for that blessed life which was promised to them.[19]

Both the vertical and horizontal dimensions of the eschatological orientation of human existence offer perspectives on temporal life which allow it be assessed with a high value; since it is both a foretaste of the second, better life and the actual place where God has chosen to reveal his benevolence to creatures, it has a very positive value, even as a pilgrimage. And further, because humankind alone is constituted so as to hope for the future benefits of that better life and enjoy the present benefits of God, it also is to be evaluated very positively. However, these two positive evaluations of human life in its temporal existence are not the whole of true knowledge of ourselves in the first salvation-historical stage. Both are made from a specific and limited perspective. That is, when looking at humankind from the perspective of God as father, it appears as the highest form of life since it alone carries the hope of a second life and experiences the benefits of God the father in a special way. Seen from this point of view, no other creature, not even an angel, is as favored. From this absolute perspective, therefore, humankind is to be praised as the creature with the highest value and dignity in the whole universe. Calvin uses this perspective repeatedly in his writings, as the analysis of his *imago dei* in chapter 2 shows. However, he also makes it clear that this positive evaluation of humankind from the absolute perspective yields only partial self-knowledge which must be supplemented if it is not to be misleading.

To complete and correct our self-knowledge of the created, nature of humankind a second evaluation from the absolute perspective of God appears. In order to prevent people from concluding that this special dignity and worth is theirs as an innate or autonomous power, Calvin draws a more negative and sobering conclusion, this time from the perspective of God as creator rather than God as father. Contrasting human beings, along with the rest of mortal beings, directly with the eternal life and majesty of the almighty creator, he judges humankind, as the rest of creation, to be "as nothing."[20] Before the permanent and enduring life of the eternal creator all else, regardless of its worth in other contexts, is evanescent, infirm, fragile, and shadowy; in short, "*une vie caduque.*"[21] Calvin introduces this second evaluation already in his discussion of Adam and Eve in the Garden of Eden to remind his readers that wherever there is any power of life whatsoever, it is to be understood first and always as a continuing gift of the God who alone is life.[22] It is clear in his writings that this particular harsh evaluation of human life by God as nothing but the life of a snail is not to be understood as a judgment of the righteous God on the sinfulness of humankind. Rather it is a judgment of the eternal creator on all creatures, which serves to warn men and women to persist in gratitude and avoid all impudence and pride. Before the Fall, the Tree of Life was placed in the center of the Garden of Eden precisely to remind Adam and Eve of this eternal judgment on their existence, just as the beauty and gifts of the garden were placed there to remind them of their dignity as beings especially favored by God now and in the future.[23]

With this we can see that already in the first salvation-historical stage various perspectives appear that result in widely divergent evaluations of human life. From the relative, human perspective, humankind appears as a somewhat indistinct image: a creature more than beasts yet less than angels. From the absolute, divine perspective, two different pictures emerge. Viewed in relation to God the father, humankind stands out clearly in all its splendor, shining with a dignity brighter than that of any other creature: the masterpiece of an artist. Yet viewed with all creation in contrast to God the almighty creator, it appears in all its lowliness and fragility: a snail on the face of the earth. The coexistence of these three distinct evaluations of humankind made from the two theological perspectives can be seen in Calvin's comments on the dignity of humankind.

Frequent, unannounced shifts in these perspectives in the discussion of the created nature of human beings allow for both a celebration and denigration of humankind. Occasionally Calvin accomplishes both in one stroke of his pen, as when he comments on I Peter 1:24, noting that it is as if Peter had said that we must know

> . . . in the first place, since God has honored us in making us his creatures, that we are already tied to him for this reason alone. When he preferred us to the brute beasts, he did so without finding anything of value in us, but of his pure goodness. . . .[24]

He also reminds his readers that "Granted that the flesh has some glory, in case that it should dazzle your eyes, know that the flower soon withers."[25] It is my understanding that these and other similar statements are best interpreted in light of the varying, shifting perspectives grounded in the distinction between the human and divine perspectives.

Calvin's denigration of human beings has been well-documented and widely accepted as his final evaluation of humankind, so we need mention only a few representative texts of this type before commenting upon them. He tells us that we should throw our lives into the hands of God "knowing that we are nothing at all."[26] Further, not content with the description of human beings as nothingness, he refers to men and women as "worms of the earth" and "vermin."[27] These epithets not being vivid enough, he proceeds to paint one image of humiliation after another upon the canvas holding his portrait of humankind: "You are nothing but a worm of the earth, nothing but dust, ashes, and rotting flesh."[28] There is no denying that this is a harsh, bleak picture of the human being. However, its true meaning becomes clear only when it is seen in its proper context and with its companion images. Such unrelentingly negative statements are made by Calvin only from the second, absolute perspective in which humankind is contrasted to the eternal God. This enables him to make the following statement:

> Here we see how great a difference there is between God and men; for men have no power in themselves but what God has

granted to them. If we were reasoning about the nature and excellence of man, we might bring forward the singular gifts which he has received from God; but when he is contrasted with God he must be reduced to nothing, for nothing can be ascribed to man without taking it from God.[29]

Since all these negative statements are made from only one perspective in Calvin's anthropology, they can be granted only limited significance.

Further, they must be interpreted in light of their intent. Calvin insists on contrasting men and women to God continually for very positive reasons: so that people will not claim for themselves more than is their due and God will be rightly honored. So he tells us that "God will never be duly honored by us unless we are reduced to nothing *(comme aneantis)* and confess that there is nothing in us but total poverty.[30] He puts the matter more starkly, almost mathematically, in a sermon on Job:

> . . . [M]en can never attribute to God the glory which is due him unless they strip themselves totally. Now when we claim to reserve for ourselves some portion of glory, however small it may be, the glory of God is diminished to that degree.[31]

Adam and Eve needed to be reminded of this lowliness and poverty *so that* they would not foolishly boast of their own excellence but "rightly glory in the liberality of [their] maker."[32] Thus Calvin consistently emphasizes the proper humility of the human creature as the only appropriate counterpart of God's glory. Such humility, and the constant reminders of our need for it, are necessary because we are ignorant of ourselves and boast of ourselves and our condition out of that ignorance. True knowledge of ourselves in contrast to the almighty eternal creator will enable us to respond to God properly. Thus, following Augustine, Calvin refers to humility as the sum of the heavenly philosophy, understanding that "the whole humility of man consists in the knowledge of himself."[33]

It is not enough to understand the context and intent of these denigrations of the self by Calvin. In order to interpret them correctly, we must also place them immediately alongside their companion evaluations from the absolute perspective of God, the positive evaluation and praise of the dignity of humankind. Using the absolute perspective of God as father to compare humankind with the rest of creation, Calvin is able to paint colorfully the dignity of the human creature, even without reference to Jesus Christ.

Though seldom quoted and rarely noted, his praises of the value and excellence of human nature are abundantly scattered throughout his works. He presents humankind as the "most illustrious ornament and glory of the earth,"[34] as those who have been "honored by God" in a special way,[35] as the "masterpiece of creation,"[36] "the brightest mirror in which we can behold His glory,"[37] as creatures with such a "noble and excellent nature" that even the heavens and the earth in all their splendor are not "elevated to such dignity."[38] Dignity is a constant element in his anthropology, in fact, and we must conclude therefore that true self-knowledge in the first stage of salvation-history includes a knowledge of human excellence as well as its nothingness.

Dignity and humility are companion evaluations and images in Calvin's portrait of the self and focusing on one without the other results in a false perception of the self. If the viewer dwells on the dignity without paying attention to the humility, she or he will see only a creature possessing an absolute, innate excellence and will not be moved to live a life of proper humility toward God or to honor or thank God. If the viewer focuses on the humility and neglects the dignity, she or he will fail to see the eschatological orientation of human existence, remain blind to the hope of the future life and the goodness of the present life, and consequently, fail to praise and thank God for the delicate artistry displayed in humankind and his paternal solicitude; fail to respect the dignity of other human beings and neglect one's duty to them; despair, for want of the knowledge that God will never forsake humankind since he recognizes his glory in it.[40] For a whole and true knowledge of humankind, even in the first stage of salvation history, the absolute perspectives of God as creator and God as father as well as the relative perspective of humankind must be taken into consideration. Already here Calvin's portrait of humankind appears complex. A similar conclusion must be reached for his view of humankind in the second stage of salvation history, fall and redemption.

The Variation of the Distinction in the Doctrine of Redemption

In the second stage of salvation history, fall and redemption, the distinction appears once again, leading to yet another set of divergent evaluations. This variation of the distinction, in the doctrine of soteriology, is clearly indebted to Luther's doctrine of the two kingdoms. Although Calvin rarely makes explicit reference to this peculiar Lutheran doctrine, there can be no doubt that it is an essential and pervasive thread in his anthropology.[41] His two clearest statements of the Lutheran distinction between the earthly kingdom and heavenly kingdom are found in the *Institutes*. The first passage in book 2 is easily recognizable as Augustinian-Lutheran.

> This, then, is the distinction; that there is one kind of understanding of earthly things, another of heavenly. I call "earthly things" those which do not pertain to God or to his kingdom, to true justice or to the blessedness of the future life; but which have significance with regard to the present life and are in a sense, confined within its bounds. I call "heavenly things" the pure knowledge of God, the nature of true righteousness, and the mysteries of the heavenly kingdom. The first class includes government, household management, and mechanical skills and the liberal arts. In the second are the knowledge of God and of his will, and the rule by which we conform our lives to it.[42]

The second passage, found in Book 4, uses slightly different terminology, substituting "temporal" or "political" for "earthly" and "worlds" for "governments," but the distinction it describes is also clearly indebted to Luther's doctrine.

> Therefore, in order that none of us may stumble on that stone, let us first consider that there is a twofold government in man: one aspect is spiritual, whereby the conscience is instructed in piety and in reverencing God; the second is political, whereby man is educated for the duties of humanity and citizenship that must be maintained among men. These are usually called the "spiritual" and "temporal" jurisdiction (not improper terms), by which is meant that the former sort of government pertains to the life of the soul, while the latter has to do with the concerns of the present life—not only with food and clothing but with laying down laws whereby a man may live his life among other men holily, honorably, and temperately. For the former resides in the inner mind, while the latter regulates only outward behavior. The one we may call the spiritual kingdom, the other, the political kingdom. Now these two, as we have divided them, must always be examined separately; and while one is being considered, we must call away and turn aside the mind from thinking about the other. *There are in man, so to speak, two worlds over which different kings and different laws have authority.*[43]

If these two passages from the *Institutes* were the only evidence supporting the claim that Calvin's use of the two kingdoms is as pervasive as Luther's, the argument would indeed be weak. However, almost all of Calvin's other writings, including his sermons, treatises, and commentaries, show that Calvin made frequent use of this theological distinction. While the language he uses to describe the separate perspectives varies throughout these works, the basic distinction remains constant in his soteriology.

Calvin often employs the royal and legal language so prevalent in Luther's works when he is describing the distinction between the two theological perspectives. It is common for him to point out the great dissimilarity between the way people judge and the way God judges. Human judgments are relative, while God's are absolute. Thus, if it is a question of standing before other human beings and submitting to their judgment, we will more than likely be able to find some justice in ourselves; but if we stand before God we are faced with a justice which is strange. If we would know the whole truth about ourselves and our justness, we "must go beyond the courts of human justice to a court of another justice" which we find in "the celestial seat."[44] At times Calvin describes this strange justice of God as not only different from human justice, but also in contradiction to it: "What the world judges right is often crooked and perverse in the judgment of God, who approves of no other manner of living than that which is framed according to the rule of his law."[45] Other times he contrasts them by reserving the term "judgment" for God's evaluation of women and men and referring to human evaluations as merely those "opinions which we can form about other people."[46] Though Calvin does rely heavily on this royal and legal language to define the two perspectives, this is by no means the only terminology which he uses.[47] For example, he occasionally refers to human judgment as a "sens charnel" or a "natural" judgment, employing the Thomistic distinction between the natural and supernatural.[48] More frequently, however, we find him using the language of two "worlds" or two "lives," taken from his doctrine of creation, to compare relative human judgments with the absolute judgment of God on sinful human beings.[49] Those who are judged good "according to the world," i.e., from the perspective of the temporal life alone, may not be justified in the eternal kingdom of God.[50] Each person may be said to carry both worlds within because of the eschatological constitution of human nature, thus being able to distinguish between temporal and eternal judgments, this life and the next.[51]

Calvin's use of these three different terminologies suggests that he had a firm grasp of Luther's fundamental distinction and that it was significant for his own thought. However, further evidence to support the claim that this distinction is a pervasive, fundamental structure in his anthropology is available. Calvin does not simply echo the basic theological distinction of Luther in his works; he develops his own way of applying it soteriologically in addition to applying it in his doctrine of creation. As noted above, Calvin occasionally presents human judgments as mere opinions when comparing them to the absolute judgments of God, stressing the uncertainty and confusion of these temporal judgments and the surety of the heavenly mysteries. This negative assessment of human judgments is intensified by Calvin's declarations that such judg-ments are also frivolous, deceitful, misleading, and condemned by God.[52] This appears to be yet another example of Calvin's harsh attitude toward human temporal life, and it seems to indicate that he sees the two perspectives only as contradictory. However, this nega-tive assessment is made only from the absolute point of view of God as redeemer and does not constitute the whole of Calvin's view. From the perspective of God the judge and redeemer, temporal judgments are worth nothing. If anyone should try to introduce them as evidence into the celestial court of justice, that person would be declared a murderer and dangerous criminal and the evidence would be rejected as false and inadmissible.[53] However, if such relative judgments are used properly, i.e., within their allotted realm of jurisdiction, they are then admitted as necessary, desirable, and good. Relative judgments within the temporal realm about greater and lesser goods, more or less virtuous actions, more or less persons, or even more or less sanctified persons, are necessary for the "police humaine."[54] In fact, there can be no good order in the temporal realm if the duty to praise and respect worldly excellence and punish worldly crimes is neglected.[55] Furthermore, Christians are required to concern themselves with the "bonne police entre les hommes" as well as with the heavenly kingdom of Jesus Christ.[56] Here it appears that human judgments are assessed more favorably when viewed from the perspective of the temporal world. They have their own integrity, though to a lesser degree, and are not direct contradictions of the judgments of God. It is only when they are

confused with the heavenly judgments that they must be condemned as contradictory of the judgments of God.[57]

Having established that Calvin consistently and carefully employs a type of distinction between the two kingdoms in his thought,
we now turn to a demonstration of how he applies this distinction in
his doctrine of redemption. As in the discussions of created human
nature, Calvin's statements about the lowliness and dignity of humankind could not be rightly interpreted without the distinction the
human and divine perspectives, so in his discussion of the fallen
condition and redemption of humankind, Calvin's statements about
the baseness and glory of humankind cannot be understood without
the same distinction.

The necessary earthly judgments we make about other human
beings are good within their limited realm and allow us to discover
some honesty, good reputations, understanding, spirit, reason, and
industry among fallen men and women. This knowledge of ourselves
is an essential part of our whole self-knowledge since we are temporal creatures living in a fallen world, and Calvin develops his view
of such judgments much more completely in this second stage.
However, by itself, this knowledge gained through earthly judgments is incomplete; it needs to be supplemented by two absolute
perspectives.[58] The first perspective of God is the judgment of the
righteous God against the sinner. While we may find "some honesty" in ourselves or see "what seems to be the most excellent in
human nature" when we judge ourselves according to this world,
when we come before God this partial righteousness only condemns
us.[59] In the pure light of that judgment seat, humankind shines with
no proper dignity, having been completely dulled by sin.[60] To the
righteous life of God humankind now appears as death itself.[61] Once
again Calvin proves himself a master at castigating the human race,
emphasizing that all are "totally vitiated" and have fallen into an
"abyss of total ruin."[62]

> . . . [E]ven though we may flourish, and even though before
> other people we have a certain beautiful luster, and even
> though it seems that we have something which gives us value,
> we are poor swine and there is nothing but rottenness and
> infection in us; God considers us abominable and we are
> damned and lost before him; the angels have contempt for us;
> all creatures detest and curse us and cry out for vengeance
> against us since we pollute them; because there is such corrup-

tion in human beings that the heavens and the earth are bound
to be infected by them until God changes them.[63]

Once again we hear a call to reduce ourselves to nothingness,
though this time Calvin has in mind a humility based on our
knowledge of our sinful condition.[64] This heavenly perspective
teaches us a new self-knowledge: that we are enemies of God and
not simply fragile mortals;[65] that there is nothing but brutality in us
and not one drop of goodness.[66] He paints one image of humiliation
next to the other on this part of the canvas also, calling humankind a
"poor worm of the earth, unhappy creature, miserable swine,"
"abyss of infection,"[67] and "dung."[68]

   But once again we find that this harsh judgment of humankind
is not the only knowledge of ourselves that we have from the
absolute heavenly perspective. Just as the absolute, eternal perspective applied to creation resulted in two companion evaluations of
humankind, humility from the perspectives of God as creator and
God as father, so the absolute heavenly perspective applied to
soteriology yields two companion evaluations, humility from the
perspective of God as judge and dignity from the perspective of God
in Jesus Christ. From the second heavenly perspective, Christians
are seen through the image of Jesus Christ to be heirs and children,
participating in the eternal life and glory of God the father. The
assessment here is positive: in Christ humankind is brought to its
"true grandeur" and full dignity.[69] Calvin proves himself eloquent in
his praise of humankind here, speaking of the royal dignity of those
who have entered the kingdom of Christ;[70] they are exalted above
the angels.[71] As with the two eternal perspectives, the two heavenly
perspectives are necessary complements to one another. If one
dwells on the dignity of Christ and the excellence of the new nature
given to Christians, one may be tempted to espouse perfectionism
or to despise non-Christians. However, if one dwells on the baseness
of the sinful creature, without paying attention to the images of
dignity that exist, one will detract from the glory of Jesus Christ or
fall into despair. Again, the knowledge of one's dignity in Jesus
Christ is used by Calvin to console believers. He tells them that
they are not to be afraid to be emptied of all glory themselves and to
humble themselves, because Jesus Christ will provide them with all
that is good.[72] He inverts the meaning of the image of the worm by
saying that those who feel that they are worms in the eyes of the

world should remember that the glorious Son of God was perceived by the world this way.[73] Both the image of baseness and the image of glory must be viewed as essential parts of the portrait of humankind; failure to see either one leads to an incomplete and false knowledge of humankind.

With the appearance of the distinction in the second stage of salvation history, then, several additional, distinct evaluations of human life appear. From the relative, earthly perspective of humankind, one can speak of humankind having some portion of dignity and excellence as well as some faults. From the first absolute, heavenly perspective of God as judge, however, humankind appears as totally debased, as a "five foot worm" or a grub crawling on the face of the earth, as lower than any beast.[74] But from the second absolute heavenly perspective of God in Christ, believers glow with the eternity and glory of Jesus Christ, shining brighter than the angels. The distinction between the human and divine perspectives, as it appears in soteriology, therefore, further complicates Calvin's portrait of humankind by adding several different complementary evaluations of humankind.

Divergences and Convergences of the Two Variations of the Distinction

As the foregoing discussion shows, the distinction between the relative perspective of humankind, with its comparative evaluation, and the absolute perspective of God, with its companion evaluations, pervades Calvin's anthropology, both in the doctrines of creation and redemption. The two variations of the one distinction are distinguishable but not separable from one another. Both include a relative perspective with a comparative evaluation and an absolute perspective with companion evaluations. Both assume that the relative perspective is accessible to all women and men and the absolute perspective only to those with the eyes of faith.[75] And, both of the variations contain much of the same imagery and terminology.[76] In spite of these broad similarities, however, the two variations are not to be conflated with one another. Though he uses the term "kingdom," for example, to describe the judgment of God in both applications, it is clear that he maintains a distinction between the eternal kingdom of God the father-creator-provider and the heavenly kingdom of God the judge-redeemer. Likewise, though he uses the one term "infirmity" to describe the human condition, he retains a distinction between the fragility of the mortal creature seen by the eternal creator and the corruption of the sinner condemned by the righteous judge.[77] As Calvin scholars have noted in other contexts, this is true of his use of the term "nature" as well.[78]

Though Calvin does use some of the same terms and images in his doctrines of creation and redemption, the two variations remain distinct from one another. To underline the distinctiveness of each variation and its anthropological evaluations, I have chosen to use a different set of terms when discussing them. For the doctrine of creation I will use the terms "temporal life" or "temporal perspective" for the perspective of humankind; the terms "eternal life," "eternal perspective," "God as creator," and "God as father" for the perspective of God; and the phrase "the distinction between the two lives" for the distinction itself. For the doctrine of redemption I will use the terms "earthly judgment" or "earthly perspective" for the perspective of humankind; the terms "heavenly judgment" or "heavenly perspective," "God as judge," "God in Christ," and "God as redeemer" for the perspective of God; and the phrase "the distinction between the two kingdoms" for the distinction itself.

While the two variations of the one distinction must be distinguished from one another, they should not be separated. The eternal judgments that result from the perspectives of God as creator and father and the heavenly judgments that result from the perspectives of God as judge and God in Christ, for example, are closely related to one another. This relationship appears in a number of areas. First, according to Calvin, sin results in part from a failure to maintain the distinction between the temporal and eternal perspectives. It may be defined as a misunderstanding and misuse of the distinction between the temporal and eternal, a misuse which introduces the contradiction between God and humankind and the need for the soteriological application of the distinction.[79] In failing to keep the eternal perspective in mind, Adam and Eve confused their temporal perspective with the final and ultimate truth about themselves. Not fixing their eyes on the infinite majesty of God or on their own lack of fulfillment, they grasped at a perfection that was not theirs yet and tried to rob the giver of every good gift. Second, even within the fallen condition of humankind, enough of the eschatological orientation which constituted the original human nature remains, both reminding human beings of their original destiny and rendering them unhappy and guilty.[80] Third, a proper understanding of the distinction between the two kingdoms leads to a proper understanding of the distinction between the two lives. True faith, salvific knowledge, renews the eschatological orientation of human existence by reintroducing the hope of a future life and the enjoyment of the present life. Because of this close connection between the doctrines of creation and redemption, the "kingdom of God and its mysteries" in Calvin's work can refer both to the narrower soteriological kingdom of Jesus Christ (or the heavenly court of the divine judge) and to the broader eternal kingdom of God the father, which existed before the Fall and will exist after glorification. This particular interconnection of the two applications in Calvin's anthropology requires closer examination if we are to uncover the basic anthropological configuration of Calvin in the second stage of salvation history.[81]

Before the Fall, Adam and Eve were children and heirs of the eternal kingdom of God the father. After the Fall, they were banished from that kingdom, thereby deprived of true knowledge of their eschatological orientation, their hope for a future life in that kingdom, and their present enjoyment of the benefits of that kingdom. Their temporal life, once a happy pilgrimage with a gentle end, became a miserable, misdirected, and truncated existence that ended violently. Because of original sin, all those who are not restored to their previous existence of knowledge of, enjoyment of, and hope in the eternal life of the kingdom of God are doomed to live equally horrible lives in this world. The only path to such restoration leads through the kingdom of Christ. This means that the eternal kingdom of God, as the true and proper inheritance of humankind, is now joined exclusively to the kingdom of Christ.[82] Only by entering Christ's kingdom of salvation can one see, enjoy, and finally enter the eternal kingdom of life promised at creation.

The interconnection of the variations in the doctrines of creation and redemption can be seen, then, in the knowledge of eternal life, the hope of a future eternal life, and the enjoyment and practice of the eternal life in the present existence of believers. While all human beings retain some knowledge of the future, eternal orientation of their life, it is through Christ alone that anyone gains true and full self-knowledge.[83] Knowledge of the mysteries of the heavenly kingdom includes knowledge of the original eschatological orientation of human life. It also restores the hope for a second, better life. Because of this, Calvin is able to describe the kingdom of God among men and women as

. . . nothing else than a restoration to the life of blessedness, true and eternal happiness; it is defined as the "newness of life by which God restores us to the hope of blessed immortality."[84]

When one enters the kingdom of Christ, one reenters the outer court of the temple, waiting once again to finally enter the Holy of Holies.[85]

The complex interrelation of creation and redemption in the second stage can also be seen in one final area: Calvin's view of the enjoyment and practice of the eternal life in the present life. As we saw earlier, entrance into the kingdom of Christ brings with it a knowledge of how to distinguish properly between the earthly and heavenly kingdoms. We must now add that it also brings a knowledge of how to distinguish properly between the temporal and eternal lives of human beings. It is this latter distinction that provides the gracious guideline that enables believers to live according to the will of God, since it contains the general rule for evaluating all aspects of temporal existence properly. Just as Adam and Eve contemplated eternal life in the Tree of Life so that they might live godly lives, so believers meditate on eternal life in the cross so that they might lead godly lives.[86] What was described earlier as a tendency "à la vie celeste" is now specified as a tendency "à nostre Seigneur Iesus Christ."[87]

It is told us that Jesus Christ is life and immortality because until such time as we are elevated by him and led to certain life, we become caught in this present life and wish to remain in the world, especially when something pulls us away from it. But when we consider that life which has been won for us by our Lord Jesus Christ, it will cost us nothing to leave all that holds us here below and aspire to the heavens above. . . . And mark well that when Saint Paul speaks of life and adds immortality, it is as if he had said that we have already entered into the kingdom of God by faith. Even though we are but strangers below and it seems as if there is nothing in us but death and malediction, even so the life and grace which are communicated to us by Christ will bear fruit. . . .[88]

True knowledge of the eschatological orientation of human life, restored in Christ, brings a fuller knowledge of the self which enables one to evaluate temporal existence properly, in all its aspects, in a way that the two kingdoms perspectives alone cannot do.

That is, with only the two kingdoms perspectives, believers would not be able to practice true Christian humility or true contempt for the present world, for they would not know the rule by which to make use of the gifts in the earthly kingdom.

It is the two lives distinction which brings the preeminent Christian virtue of humility into sharp focus. Only when one understands the temporality of one's existence vis à vis the eternal Creator can one fully and properly humble oneself before God. The humility that results from the knowledge of one's sinful condition before a righteous judge is a necessary but insufficient requirement for the Christian life. The humility that results from the knowledge of one's absolute dependence upon the eternal God is also necessary, just as necessary to the life of Christians as it was to the life of the innocent Adam and Eve. This is the reason why God laid down a rule for Adam and Eve in the garden and a law for Christians in the present stage of salvation history: to remind them of the distinction between their infirmity and God's eternity and call them to an existence of voluntary, grateful, and humble actions.[89] Because of the sluggishness of human beings, due to sin, however, knowledge of the distinction between the temporal and eternal and one's absolute dependence on God does not immediately and fully render Christians humble. Therefore, in addition to the law, God makes use of other goads to remind people of their fragility and temporality and elicit a response of proper humility: "One must know that the principal virtue of the faithful, when God punishes and afflicts them, is to become as nothing (comme aneantis)."[90] Even those who are made pure in Christ, therefore, in order to practice true Christian humility, must be reminded of the distinction between the two lives by afflictions from God and the words of theologians.

> For even if, properly speaking, faith mounts up from Christ to the Father, yet he means this: although faith rests in God, it will gradually disappear unless he who retains it in perfect firmness intercedes as Mediator. Otherwise, God's majesty is too lofty to be attained by mortal men, who are like grubs crawling upon the earth.[91]

This distinction not only supplements our knowledge of ourselves in relation to God by adding an eternal perspective to the heavenly perspective, thereby guiding our practice of true Christian humility; it also provides a framework for making temporal judgments, thereby guiding our practice of the true enjoyment and contempt of the present world. This distinction, therefore, is as essential to Christian ethics as the distinction between the two kingdoms. Without it, the *moral* lives of the regenerated would be guided only by natural law and the moral rules of the temporal life. The reintroduction of this distinction with Jesus Christ, however, enables regenerate women and men to develop a distinctive Christian ethic. While Christians do make use of natural and political law in their lives, it is the distinction between temporal and eternal which shows them to what degree they should have contempt for temporal matters and to what extent they should appreciate and enjoy them. When the temporal life with all its temptations is compared to the eternal life, one sees it in proper perspective and is able to remain detached from it and show contempt for it.[92] In fact, the knowledge that they are "born to a better life" enables Christians to break the power of their sinful appetites and lead better lives in the present.[93]

Even though contemplation of eternal life calls forth contempt for temporal life, however, it does not require condemnation of it. It is only from the absolute perspective of the heavenly kingdom of the righteous judge that the whole of temporal life is to be condemned as an evil contradiction to the life of God. From the perspective of the eternal kingdom of the benevolent father, the temporal world appears as imperfect, infirm, a lesser world.

> When he states that the rest shall be added, he means that the things which belong to this present life are in a way accessory, and so should take second place to the kingdom of God.[94]

That Calvin intends merely a comparison and not an outright contradiction between the eternal and temporal lives is evident. The temporal life, for all its miseries, has a positive value for two reasons. First, it is the scene of God's fatherly activity toward human beings and humankind's journey toward its final destiny. It is in the temporal life that we begin to "taste the sweetness of the divine generosity in order to whet our hope and desire to seek after the full revelation of this."[95] Second, the temporal world is not only the scene of our education in the enjoyment of and desire for God, but the place where we are called to reflect the glory of God by rendering service to him.[96] This knowledge of the positive yet limited value of the present world directs Christians to a true and grateful use and enjoyment of the temporal life.[97]

The theme of *contemptus mundi* which founds Calvin's Christian ethic cannot be fully understood, therefore, without interpreting it in light of the distinction between the two lives and its perspectives. From the absolute perspective of the eternal God, this world appears as a lesser world which deserves our contempt. On the other hand, from the perspective of God the eternal Father, temporal life appears as a theatre of gracious activity which is to be used and enjoyed.

We may conclude, then, that although the variations of the distinction between the human and divine perspectives in the doctrines of creation and redemption differ from one another, they are not finally separate from one another. In the second stage of salvation history, the distinction between the two lives is as essential as the distinction between the two kingdoms for a full understanding of his anthropology.

The Dynamic Perspectival Structure and Calvin's Portrait of Humankind

True and full self-knowledge for Calvin includes all the varied and divergent evaluations of humankind that we have uncovered in discussing his creation-eschatology and soteriology. With the changing variations of the distinction between the human and divine perspectives, there appears a portrait of humankind filled with a disturbing number of contrasting colors, conflicting angles, and asymmetrical lines. The result appears to be a tortuous mass of smaller images vying to be regarded as the focal point. Here one sees a masterpiece shining with the beauty of the eternal father, there a snail crawling before the eternal creator; here a royal heir of Jesus Christ, there a worm crawling before the eternal judge; here a Cato, there a Cassius. While such a portrait may appear odd and disturbing to us, Calvin was quite at home with it, as were others of his age.[98]

Calvin does not provide us with any indication of how these widely divergent and complementary evaluations of humankind cohere with one another. The only possible clues he gives about their relationship are found in his occasional assertions about the ability of believers to hold two or more of these evaluations simultaneously. For example, when discussing the notion of *simul iustus et peccator,* he assumes the coexistence of the perspectives of God as judge and God in Christ in the hearts of believers.

> The spirit of God shows us hidden things, the knowledge of which cannot reach our senses, Eternal life is promised to us, but it is promised to the dead; we are told of the resurrection of the blessed, but meantime we are involved in corruption. We are declared to be just and sin dwells within us; we hear that we are blessed but meantime we are overwhelmed by untold miseries; we are promised an abundance of all good things, but we are often hungry and thirsty; God proclaims that he will come to us immediately, but seems to be deaf to our cries. What should happen to us if we did not rely on hope, and if our minds did not emerge above the world, out of the midst of darkness through the shining word of God and by his Spirit?[99]

Similarly, when discussing Christian life and morals, he assumes that believers are able to hold the temporal perspective in their hearts along with the eternal perspectives of God as creator and God as judge, since both are just different "degrees" of understanding.[100]

Though Calvin simply assumes the coexistence of these contradictory yet complementary views of humankind without arguing for their coherence, we need not conclude that his final portrait of humankind lacks all unity. The complex, multi-dimensional, dynamic portrait of human being that appears does justice to our experience of the complex reality of the self, a being full of tensions and inconsistencies, yet nevertheless whole. As Pruyser notes,

> I take these various pairs of opposites to mean that man is a battlefield of forces, a unity with inner conflict. Calvin's portrayal of life is always sensitive to this inner state of turmoil, of which he registers all sorts of fluctuations. To put this in modern psychological terms, man is for Calvin a being in a state of tension, a dynamic system in an unstable equilibrium.[101]

The unity of Calvin's portrait of the self is no easy arrangement of balanced, symmetrical parts, no easily discernible ordering of consistent truths. Rather, it is a "unity with inner conflict," a unity incorporating inconsistent and contradictory truths about the self into a larger, ordered whole.

That Calvin's anthropology is such a complexly ordered whole is indicated by the pervasiveness of the distinction between the human and divine perspectives in its two variations in the doctrines of creation and redemption. Furthermore, this dynamic perspectival structure or order that unifies his many and divergent assessments of humankind is the distinctive feature of his Christian anthropology. If this is true, then failure to acknowledge this structure or order will make it difficult to interpret his anthropological statements accurately or fully. It is the goal of the remaining chapters to demonstrate how this peculiar perspectival structure operates in Calvin's doctrines of the *imago dei*, reason and revelation, providence and freedom, and immortality and resurrection, and how observation of this structure may lead to a more adequate interpretation of these difficult areas in his anthropology.

Notes

/1/   Hermann Bauke, *Die Probleme der Theologie Calvins*, p. 12.

/2/   Gerrish, *Reformers in Profile*, p. 155 ("Calvin's order of treatment is not existential, but quasi-historical; he presents his material as the story of the race.") Already here one might begin to suspect that we are dealing not with the anthropology of Calvin, but the anthropologies of Calvin, as Rudnick suggests in *From Created to Creator*, p. 52, n. 19. Her division of a prelapsarian human nature, an alienated human nature, and a totally transformed human nature, however, fails to take into account the continuity of salvation history in Calvin's thought and the close connection between creation and redemption.

/3/   See, for example, *CO* 33: 386–88 (s. 31 on Job 8): "Sachans que Dieu nous met comme sur un Theatre, et qu'il veut que nous discourions, non point seulement au temps de cent ans ou de plus, mais depuis la creation du monde."; and his comment that God is a God who "nous donne le moyen de nous enquerir du temps passe."

/4/   E. A. Dowey, Jr., *The Knowledge of God in Calvin's Theology*, 2nd ed. (New York: Columbia University Press, 1965). See also B. A. Gerrish's (and others') theological distinction between God the creator and God the redeemer, "Theology within the limits of Piety Alone: Schleiermacher and Calvin's Doctrine of God," in *Reformatio Perennis: Essays on Calvin and the Reformation in Honor of Ford Lewis Battles*, ed. B. A. Gerrish (Pittsburgh: Pickwick Press, 1981), pp. 67–80.

/5/   Dowey, *The Knowledge of God*, p. 49.

/6/   Ibid., p. 241. See also E. David Willis's argument in *Calvin's Catholic Christology: The Function of the So Called "Extra Calvinisticum" in Calvin's Theology* (Leiden: E. J. Brill, 1966, pp. 101–31) that the *extra Calvinisticum* functions to bind the two aspects of the knowledge of God closely together, emphasizing the unity of the act of knowing and the unity of God transcendent.

/7/   *CO* 33: 209, "Nous avons desia veu à quoy tend ce propos, c'est assavoir afin d'humilier les hommes, d'autant qu'ils sont bien loin de la perfection des Anges."

/8/ For this difference between the two perspectives, see *CO* 35: 260,
"Cest qu'en somme Dieu doit estre exalté par dessus toutes creatures:
tellement que les hommes ne presume pas de iuger de luy selon leur
naturel, et selon qu'ils voyent ici bas qu'on se gouverne; mais qu'ils cognois-
sent que c'est tout autre chose, et qu'il y a un telle diversité, que le jour
n'est pas si different d'avec la nuict"; *CO* 35: 432, " . . . et quand nous
ferons comparaison de Dieu avec les creatures, quelle proportion y a-il?"
/9/ For the statement of the "double estat" of Adam and Eve, see Richard
Stauffer's quotation of an unpublished sermon on Genesis in *Dieu, la
création et la providence dans la prédication de Calvin* (Berne: Peter Lang,
1978), p. 240, n. 204 [hereafter referred to as *Création et providence*]. For a
similar statement, see *CO* 33: 515. It is possible that Calvin adapted this
eschatological framework from the view of the temporal/eternal relation in
Budé. T. F. Torrance, in *Kingdom and Church: A Study in the Theology of
the Reformation* (London: Oliver & Boyd, 1956), maintains that Calvin's
entire eschatology was very much like Budé's, with only minor differences,
p. 89. It seems to me that their positions, though similar, are significantly
different. Calvin's understanding of the temporal/eternal relation is more
consistently historical than Budé's, for instance. His view does not display
as great a tendency toward spiritualization as Budé's. And, his view of the
highest good received is different from Budés. It is beyond the scope of this
dissertation to argue for influences and differences between Budé and
Calvin. However, even if it could be shown that Calvin uncritically borrowed Budé's eschatological structure, his combination of that structure
with the salvation-historical and the soteriological gives his thought an
originality and distinctiveness. Because this eschatological structure is essential to the creation of human beings (as I demonstrate in this chapter,
especially p. 20, n. 1 and chapter 5), whenever I speak of Calvin's doctrine of
creation I intend to include this eschatological orientation of human existence.
/10/ *CO* 35: 567, "We live in no other condition than to taste in part the
goodness of God, in order to be *attirez plus haut*, and even to be *tout ravis
à la vie celeste*"; *CO* 51: 469, "attirez iusque au Royaume des cieux"; *CO* 33:
158; *CO* 34: 467.
/11/ Both the term *"la haut"* and the term *"la vie future"* are used
constantly by Calvin when he is speaking of eternal life or the eternal
kingdom. See *CO* 29: 97; *CO* 34: 467; *CO* 35: 127.
/12/ *CO* 29: 32; also *CO* 25: 611.
/13/ *CO* 54: 392.
/14/ *CO* 33: 660; *CO* 23: 38–39. For the closest contemporary theological
anthropology which expresses this strong eschatological view of Calvin, see
Wolfhart Pannenberg's *What is Man?: Contemporary Anthropology in
Theological Perspective*, trans. Duane A. Priebe (Philadelphia: Fortress
Press, 1970). Pannenberg's anthropology is more future-oriented than Calvin's.
/15/ *CO* 23: 39; *CO* 33: 660; *CO* 33: 335; *CO* 35: 530.
/16/ *CO* 33: 389, "Car nous ne sommes point arrousez seulement pour
estre ici entretenus quelque espece de temps, mais pour parvenir à la vie
eternelle." This now/not yet character of Calvin's eschatology calls into

question those studies which stress an interpretation of eternal life as the future life in Calvin. Wallace, for example, understands the Meditation on the Future Life to be a meditation on the life ahead only and not on the life above as well, *Calvin's Doctrine of the Christian Life*, pp. 87–88. Torrance claims that "It is this tense relation between the present and the future that gives Calvin his characteristic nuance in eschatology: the eager straining of faith in hope, intent upon the future revelation of our life in Christ, *Kingdom and Church*, p. 110.

The now/not yet or above/ahead interpretation of humankind's participation in the eternal life in Calvin has led me to refer to this governing structure as eschatological rather than teleological. First, the term "eschatology" conveys more dynamic tension than the term "teleology"; second, the term "eschatology" connotes the historical understanding of human life in Calvin more than the ontological term "teleology" does; and third, the evaluative *judgments* which can made from within this structure call for the term "eschatological." By using this structure, Calvin does not intend to make general ontological statements but specific theological statements about the relationship between God and humankind. In other words, already in the first salvation-historical stage we are dealing with a state of grace, and not simply nature: "Nous croyons que l'homme, ayant esté creé pur et entier et conforme à l'image de Dieu, est par sa propre faute decheu de la grace qu'il avoit receu . . . ," *CO* 9: 743. This condition of grace means that humankind is subject to the special justice of God even before the fall, *CO* 26: 436, and this justice or judgment calls for the use of the term "eschatological."

/17/   For the closest contemporary theological anthropology which interprets this particular aspect of Calvin's anthropology, see H.R. Niebuhr's *The Responsible Self* (New York: Harper & Row, 1963).
/18/   *CO* 35: 85 [hereafter translations of all *CO* references are mine unless otherwise noted]. See also *CO* 33: 212, "il nous met en ce monde, voire pour se monstre Pere envers nous."
/19/   See Gerish's essay in *Reformers in Profile*, pp. 153–56.
/20/   *CO* 55: 230, " . . . one seems to be something until he comes to God, but that his whole brightness is as nothing [*comme aneanti*] in God's presence; to put it briefly, his glory is rooted in this world and has no place in the heavenly kingdom." See also *CO* 35: 86.
/21/   For fragility, see: *CO* 54: 79; *CO* 53: 100; *CO* 33: 584–85; *CO* 58: 160; *CO* 35: 20. For "une vie caduque," see: *CO* 34: 128, 229; *CO* 35: 305–6; *CO* 54: 168–69. For the infirmity and evanescence, see *CO* 53: 629, "Or regardons quelles distance il y a du ciel à la terre. Il semble donc que nous devons estre comme roseaux branlans, et qu'il n'y ait nulle fermeté. Or tant y a que Dieu veut que nous possedions son Royaume par espoir . . . "; and *CO* 29: 84–85, "Car nous sommes creatures mortelles quant à ce monde, nous ne faisons que passer, voire et bien viste. Or nous savons que la verité de Dieu est permanente: il faut donc qu'apres que nous serons decedez de ce monde, que la parole de Dieu demeure, et qu'elle soit cogneue, et que de main elle soit tousiours receue des hommes." That Calvin is not speaking of the difference between the righteous judge and the sinful creature but of the difference between the eternal creator and the mortal creature is clear

in the following two test cases. First, the judgment is made even upon Adam and Eve before the Fall: "Car devant qu' Adam eust este seduit pour trebuscher et pour nous mettre en la perdition à laquelle il nous a tous attirez, il estoit desia subjet a tentation, comme la chose l'a monstré. Car le diable ne l'eust peu seduire, s'il n'eust este subjet à tentation. Ainsi il avait desia en luy quelque infirmite, c'est à dire; il n'y avoit pas une vertu Divine, il estoit en degré et en mesure d'homme, tellement qu'il estoit muable, et l'a este par trop. . . . L'homme a este cree pur et net: voire, mais cependant si n'a-il pas laisse d'estre de sa nature subjet à tentation, encores qu'il n'y eust nul vice en luy," CO 46: 596. See Inst. 1.15.8 also. Second, this judgment is made not only of human beings, but also of angels: "Let us take the angels for a mirror of the uncorrupted state of our nature. They try to serve God; they are not tempted by evil desires as we are; there is no rebellion in them, nor sin; but even if their obedience to God is pure, according to our view, it is still imperfect if one compares it to the majesty of the infinite God," CO 34: 336–37. For further confirmation that this not a judgment on sin, see CO 50: 526.

/22/ CO 33: 72, 584–85. No nature, power, or life, however elevated it may be, can exist even for an instant without the power of God: "Nous ne pourrions donc consister une minute de temps, si nous n'estions conservez par la grace de Dieu," CO 33: 72.

/23/ CO 23: 36–39; CO 46: 596.

/24/ CO 55: 229–30.

/25/ CO 35: 240.

/26/ CO 35: 542. I have overstated the case here, since Calvin continues this passage by saying, "Sinon d'autant que nous subsistons en luy. . . ."

/27/ CO 34: 416; CO 33: 346.

/28/ CO 50: 526.

/29/ CO 36: 535–36.

/30/ CO 35: 391.

/31/ CO 35: 48. See also CO 31: 96–97, "God cannot bear seeing his glory appropriated by the creature in even the smallest degree, so intolerable to him is the sacrilegious arrogance of those who, by praising themselves, obscure his glory as much as they can"; and CO 35: 442, "Et ainsi nous avons à desirer, que Dieu nous face sentir sa gloire afin que nous entrions en cest examen de nostre povreté, et que nous puissions nous aneantir tellement, que nul ne se trompe plus en quelque folle phantasie."

/32/ Institutes of the Christian Religion, ed. J. T. McNeill, trans. Ford Lewis Battles, 2 vols. (Philadelphia: Westminster Press, 1960), 1: 184, Inst. 1.15.1 in OS 3: 174 [hereafter referred to as McNeill]: "Afterward, in the proper place, we shall see how far men are from the purity that was bestowed on Adam. And first, we must realize that when he was taken from earth and clay his pride was bridled. For nothing is more absurd than for those who not only 'dwell in this house of clay' (Job 4:19) but who are themselves part earth and dust to boast of their own excellence. But since God deigned to give not only life in earthen vessels, but also willed it to be the abode of an immortal spirit, Adam could rightly glory in the great liberality of his maker.

/33/ CO 31: 107. See also CO 33: 240–42, 621 and CO 35: 237. Calvin often pairs Christian humility or the call to deflate themselves (*aneantir*) with harsh words for the tendency of people to inflate themselves with lies (*cuyder*).

/34/   *CO* 31: 243–44.

/35/   *CO* 33: 508. See also *CO* 33: 212.

/36/   *CO* 33: 662.

/37/   *CO* 31: 88.

/38/   *CO* 35: 237.

/39/   I am convinced that even in the first salvation-historical stage true self-knowledge is two-fold for Calvin: to know one's lowliness and the heights to which one has been called now and in the future. Luchesius Smits, in *Saint Augustin dans l'oeuvre de Jean Calvin*, 2 vols. (Assen: Van Gorcum, 1958), relates that both Thomas à Kempis and Erasmus understood self-knowledge to mean knowledge of one's nothingness and that Budè understood it to mean knowledge of the eschatological tendency of human beings, 1:20–21. Calvin, following the Augustinian tradition, includes both humility and dignity in describing what is essential to true self-knowledge. And, this twofold knowledge of the self constitutes only one portion of Christian self-knowledge for Calvin, as we shall see in the next section.

/40/   *CO* 33: 481. It must be noted that in this passage on God's contemplation of himself in the creature and recognition of his grace in humankind, Calvin does add the qualifier "par maniere de dire." While it does prevent one from claiming too much for the passage, it must not be emphasized too strongly. See Torrance's *Calvin's Doctrine of Man*, p. 39.

/41/   Calvin's use of the general outline of Luther's two kingdoms doctrine is not an outright imitation, in part because he combines it with the salvation-historical and eschatological governing structures. That this particular soteriological structure is a pervasive and essential governing structure of his thought, in spite of his rare references to it in the *Institutes*, will be shown in the remainder of this section.

Calvin's use of Luther's two kingdoms doctrine has not gone entirely unnoticed in the Calvin literature. B. A. Gerrish suggests in *Grace and Reason: A Study in the Theology of Luther* (Oxford: Oxford University Press, 1962), p. 12, that Calvin's teaching on reason is a summing up of Luther's teaching, which relied heavily on the two kingdoms distinction. Torrance points out that in the 1536 edition of the *Institutes* Calvin used language very similar to Luther's language for the two kingdoms, and this terminology reappeared in the edition of 1559, *Kingdom and Church*, p. 155. Torrance briefly notes that Calvin's distinction differs from Luther's in that it unites both heaven and earth in the overarching kingdom of God's covenant (ibid., p. 156). It seems to me that the major difference lies in the fact that Calvin interconnects the two kingdoms distinction with the two lives distinction. Torrance mentions the two kingdoms in Calvin's anthropology in several other places (ibid., pp. 90–92, 125), but he does not analyze Calvin's use of this doctrine or stress its importance for understanding Calvin's theology on the whole. Thus, while not totally ignored, Calvin's use of the two kingdoms doctrine has certainly been overlooked as a key structural clue to his theology and anthropology. Part of what this study will attempt to prove is that one cannot accurately interpret any part of Calvin's anthropology if one does not see the pervasiveness and constancy of Calvin's use of the two kingdoms distinction. It must be singled out and analyzed as an essential feature of his thought if we are to understand him correctly.

/42/   McNeill 1: 272, *Inst.* 2.2.13 in *OS* 3: 256.

/43/   McNeill 1: 847, *Inst.* 3.19.15 in *OS* 4: 294. (Emphasis mine.) See *OS* 5: 471 (*Inst.* 4.20.1) for a brief mention of this earlier passage.

/44/   *CO* 34: 632; *CO* 35: 441–42; *CO* 33: 521; *CO* 34: 334, "la loy n'est pas une chose si parfaite n'exquise que ceste iustice infinie de Dieu"; *CO* 34: 632, "le Iuge celeste" to whom we must "rendre conte"; *CO* 50: 407, "Et puis c'est entrer au gouffre d'enfer, quand nous cuidons obtenir salut pour nos oeuvres: car nous renonçons à la mort et passion de nostre Seigneur Iesus Christ, là où il nous faloit cercher toute nostre iustice."

/45/   *CO* 32: 259–60.

/46/   *CO* 34: 632.

/47/   In light of this, Richard Stauffer's treatment of the two justices of God in *Création et providence*, p. 118ff., must be questioned on two points. First, he presents this language as existing *only* in Calvin's sermons and not in the *Institutes*, first implying and then concluding that Calvin had contradictory or incoherent views on the justice of God. Pierre Marcel has done an excellent job of showing how and why this conclusion is incorrect, "La Prédication de Calvin a propos du livre de M. Richard Stauffer," *La Revue Réformée* 29–30 (1978–79): 13–21. Second, Stauffer's interpretation of the two justices is a bit onesided. Though he claims that the second justice is a justice people can know, he does not dwell on this, choosing to focus instead on the fact that this justice is a justice *of God*, ibid., p. 118, for example. In my reading, this theocentric presentation of this second justice ignores the importance of the distinction between the two kingdoms and the positive nature of the temporal justice known and meted out by human beings on the basis of natural law. This second justice, in other words, the justice of the earthly kingdom, could just as easily be referred to as human justice.

/48/   *Co* 33: 510; *CO* 50, 651. Although he does use this terminology, it is by no means his favorite terminology. Torrance's *Calvin's Doctrine of Man* is a bit misleading, therefore, since it relies so heavily on this natural/supernatural language. See also *CO* 53: 629 ("La raison charnelle").

/49/   *OS* 4: 294–95 (*Inst.* 3. 19.15); *CO* 35: 170–71; *CO* 34: 503; *CO* 33: 431–32; *CO* 35: 23, 25; *CO* 50: 567–68; *CO* 12: 646; *CO* 53: 619, 623, 625, 631.

/50/   See note 49 above, esp. *CO* 12: 646 and *CO* 50: 567–68.

/51/   *OS* 4: 294 (*Inst.* 3.19.15); *CO* 33: 327; *CO* 35: 547; *CO* 46: 779.

/52/   *Co* 35: 211; *Co* 50: 621, 622; *Co* 26: 303; *CO* 51: 618.

/53/   *CO* 50: 651, "les hommes . . . sont moins que petits enfans quand il est question du royaume de Dieu" *CO* 50: 655, People such as this "nous coupent la gorge, non seulement pour nous priver de ceste vie caduque et transitoire, mais pour nous aliener du royaume des cieux" *Co* 51: 601.

/54/   *CO* 50: 658; *CO* 50: 567–68.

/55/   *CO* 12: 65 (Ep. 634 to Marguerite de Navarre). Calvin even calls it barbarous and inhuman to show contempt for the principalities and powers of the world below.

/56/   CO 26: 119.

/57/   CO 34: 503, "Or ici nous avons une bonne instruction et bien utile, c'est que l'esprit de l'homme pourra bien avoir quelque faculté d'entendre et de iuger quant aux choses basses, et qui concernent ceste vie caduque, mais quant à ce qui est celeste et qui appartient au royaume de Dieu, quant à ses iugemens, tout cela nous est caché"; CO 35: 23, "Or cependant il nous faut aussi faire ici comparaison de deux degrez, c'est à savoir, Que si c'est Dieu qui donne intelligence especiale aux hommes pour discerner des choses qui appartienent à ceste vie caduque: que sera-ce de la doctrine de l'Evangile, de la vraye religion et pure? Aurons-nous cela de nature?" CO 50: 567–68 contains a very lengthy and helpful discussion of this "police."

/58/   For a discussion of this partial knowledge given to human beings for "la bonne police du monde," see chapter 4.

/59/   CO 51: 617–18.

/60/   CO 50: 568; see also CO 51: 354 wherehe says our dignity is de-chiffree.

/61/   CO 51: 705.

/62/   CO 51: 351.

/63/   Ibid.

/64/   CO 35: 86, 95–96, 492; CO 33: 216.

/65/   CO 35: 210; see also CO 33: 223 where Calvin's call to "dive into oneself" is an invitation to contemplate the sinful condition of the human being.

/66/   CO 33: 729; CO 50: 599.

/67/   CO 35: 202. Many of the same terms he used to describe the mortal creature are used here, also. For example, "vermine" and "pourriture," CO 34: 416.

/68/   CO 49: 333; see also CO 49: 347 for a view of the worthlessness of human beings compared with the dignity of Jesus Christ.

/69/   CO 33: 215; CO 51: 468–69, 571; CO 50: 526.

/70/   CO 50: 557, 559, 560; CO 46: 112.

/71/   CO 50: 586, "les Anges de paradis sont exclus d'une telle dignité."

/72/   CO 35: 48. See also: OS 4: 148 (Inst. 3.6.3); CO 50: 601; CO 50: 557; CO 35: 206; and CO 40: 344–46.

/73/   CO 31: 224.

/74/   CO 33: 662; CO 35: 419; CO 34: 577, "nous sommes plus que brutaux" for rejecting God's gifts. Calvin often takes up the theme that because men and women are higher than any other creature, when they fall, they fall lower and suffer more.

/75/   CO 40: 422–25; CO 33: 725–26.

/76/   CO 55: 230, "A person seems to be something until he comes before God. But his entire brightness is as nothing in God's presence; to put it briefly, his glory is rooted in the world and has no place in the heavenly kingdom." CO 50: 526, "Tu n'est qu'un ver de terre, que poudre, cendre et pourriture. Davantage tu as un abysme de vices en toy et cependant que Dieu te vienne cercher, et quelle presomption serait-ce quand tu cuiderois estre de ses enfans?" The emphasis in the last quote is mine and is intended to point out that while the images are the same as those used to describe the mortal creature in the first sentence, the images in the second sentence refer to the sinful creature. While it is clear that Calvin does distinguish between the mortal and the sinful man or woman, it is not clear in the first sentence of this quotation whether he is using the terms "ver de terre, poudre, cendre, et pourriture" to refer to the mortal creature or to the sinful creature. It seems to me in this case that the word "davantage" indicates the former.

/77/   CO 46: 598, "Il nous faut donc distinguer entre l'infirmite de nature, laquelle a tousiours este en l'homme, et les infirmitez vicieuses qui sont survenues à cause du peche originel." This distinction is one of the reasons that Calvin will not accept the definition of sin as weakness and it is crucial to his anthropology.

/78/   For listings of Calvin's different definitions of this term, see McNeill 1:38, n. 7 and Torrance's *Calvin's Doctrine of Man*, pp. 90–92. Torrance gives copious references, but offers no clear discussion of the different definitions. I agree with these authors that Calvin's use of the term "nature" appears inconsistent if one does not recognize his varying definitions of the term according to the three stages of salvation history-creation-eschatology, fall/redemption, and final eschatology. At times he uses the term to refer to the created nature or original righteousness of humankind as untouched by sin, meaning that constitutive structure which God gave to Adam and Eve to distinguish them from the rest of creation, *OS* 4: 154 (*Inst.* 3.7.4). The fact that this "proper" human nature is not an absolute but subject to change or loss becomes clear when Calvin uses the same term to refer to the cor-rupted condition of humankind after the Fall. He believes that sin intro-duced such a radical change in human nature that one can correctly say that "by nature we are enemies of God," *CO* 51: 399, "de nature nous sommes ennemis de Dieu"; *CO* 51: 591; *OS* 3: 272 (*Inst.* 2.3.1). Original sin so altered human nature that one can speak of the corrupted nature as if it were a new nature from which sin flowed inevitably, *OS* 4: 212 (*Inst.* 3.12.5). Though Calvin frequently uses the term nature to refer to this corrupted condition, it is clear that he has two distinct definitions of the term which are not to be conflated and he reminds his readers of this occasionally.

> "Therefore we declare that man is corrupted through natural vitiation, but a vitiation that did not flow from nature. We deny that it has flowed from nature in order to indicate that it is an adventitious quality which comes upon man rather than a substantial property which has been implanted from the begin-ning. Yet we call it 'natural' in order that no man may think that anyone obtains it through bad conduct, since it holds all men fact by hereditary right," McNeill 1:254, *Inst.* 2.1.1 in *OS* 3: 240.

Part of the reason that Calvin can be so clear about the different definitions is that his highly developed exegetical skills allow him to uncover the different meanings in the scriptural texts. For another example of his clarity of distinction, see *CO* 7: 347. Even when he does not speak to the point explicitly, it is clear that by calling sinfulness "natural" he intends to point out the inevitability of our corrupted lives due to original sin rather than to suggest that we were originally created as corrupted, McNeill 1:289, *Inst.* 2.3.1 in *OS* 3: 271, "Whatever we have of nature, therefore, is flesh." The third definition of "nature" Calvin uses is that of the transformed nature of believers. When he refers to the new nature given in baptism and he intends to stress the fact that the power of sin has been broken and a new foundation for living has been established, *OS* 3: 279, 280–85, 315, 319 (*Inst.* 2.3.6, 2.3.7–9, 2.5.15, 2.5.19); *CO* 38:520, *CO* 51: 162. When Calvin thinks of the third stage of salvation-history, he has in mind yet another definition of "nature," i.e., the resurrected nature. Thus, he says of believers that they will be glorified in a way that iss not in their nature, but above their nature, *CO* 33: 349; *CO* 34: 491. Clearly he is using the term "nature" to indicate both the potentiality of human existence in the second stage and the newness of the resurrected life in discontinuity with life in that second stage.

/79/   *CO* 31: 510, to prefer this life to eternal life is sin; *CO* 53: 625, in a passage very reminiscent of Luther's definition of a theologian as one who knows how to distinguish rightly between the law and the gospel (*Luther's Works*, eds. Jaroslav Pelikan and Helmut T. Lehmann, 55 vols. planned [St. Louis Concordia Publishing House and Philadelphia: Fortress press, 1955—], 26: 115), Calvin says "D'autant donc que les hommes presument de leur sagesse propre, ils veulent mesler le ciel avec la terre, et confondent tout." Calvin's choice of the terms "ciel" and "terre" here is appropriate for his view of the two lives and the two kingdoms in their relation.

/80/   *CO* 33: 158, "What would we be if we did not know that we were created for a better life? It would be better for us if we were asses or cows: because the brute beasts enjoy the present life; they eat, they rest, they work without great apprehension. People don't eat one morsel of food without anxiety; in the midst of their desire, they are full of remorse. . . . If then, we have no hope of a second life, what will become of us? And, indeed, our Lord wanted this to remain imprinted on the hearts of all, as we see that it is in the hearts of the Pagans. Even though they became like brute beasts, they still retained some knowledge of the second life and the immortality of the soul. And on those who did not know it, God left some mark by which they are rendered inexcusable. . . ."

/81/   That the eschatological constitution of human nature is essential to Calvin's anthropology is clear. However, this is not often been noticed or understood correctly by Calvin scholars. Torrance takes note of Calvin's "eschatology of hope" in *Kingdom and Church*, pp. 90-164, but he neither develops this in relation to Calvin's anthropology nor analyzes the distinctive features of this eschatology as a governing theological structure. Also, his presentation relies too heavily on Calvin's *Psychopannychia* (ibid., p. 90), which does mention the future life, but which does not exhibit as developed a use of the two lives perspectives as Calvin's later works. Martin Schulze's *Meditatio futurae vitae: Ihr Begriff und ihre herrschende Stellung im System Calvins* (Leipzig: Dieterich, 1901) by no means ignores this feature of Calvin's thought either. However, his analysis of what Calvin means by this *meditatio* and how he uses it in his theology as a whole is not altogether accurate (see pp. 9 and 18). Although he recognizes that human-kind was created to this *meditatio* (ibid., p. 63), he does not discuss this in terms of the first salvation-historical stage or relate the structure associated with this to the two kingdoms structure. Bohatec's discussion of this in *Budé und Calvin*, p. 474 especially, is helpful but too cursory. Ronald Wallace's discussion of the meditation on the future life also fails to notice that the two lives perspective is an essential feature of Calvin's theology (*Christian Life*, pp. 87–88). He, like Torrance and the rest, focuses on the relation of this *meditatio* to Christ alone and ignores the role it plays in the doctrine of creation.

/82/   *CO* 48: 177.

/83/   *OS* 4: 2 (*Inst.* 3.1.2). See also *OS* 4: 170–71 (*Inst.* 3.9.1), where the emphasis is on the pilgrim character of the Christian life until death.

/84/   *CO* 45: 111.

/85/   *CO* 27: 466. This reentering is not to be understood as a simple return to a previous state of innocence or the restoration of a gift that was lost. Such a tidy balancing of the religious budget of humankind is not intended by Calvin. True to his strong salvation-historical sense and Irenaeus's understanding of the recapituulation in Jesus Christ, Calvin understands the restoration of knowledge and hope of eternal life to be continuous with the life of Adam and Eve in Paradise, yet beyond it. The adoption of believers as children of God and heirs in Jesus Christ which one finds in the second salvation-historical stage, surpasses the life of Adam and Eve as children and heirs. Adoption restores believers to innocence (at least from one perspective of the heavenly kingdom); but it also effects a qualita-tive change in their lives which moves them closer to the final fulfillment of the promise of eternal life than Adam and Eve ever were. Post-fall believers are sent out on the same pilgrimage as Adam and Eve with the same destination, but unlike their forbears, they are assured of reaching that destination. Their lives in Christ are not as fragile as they make their historical journey, since they cannot lose their inheritance. Though they, too, are infirm in their mortality and sinfulness, their life as a new founda-tion in Jesus Christ, a foundation which is firm.

> "Christ came endowed with the Holy Spirit in a special way; that is, to separate us from the world and to gather us into the hope of the eternal inheritance. Hence he is called the Spirit of Santification because he not only guides and arouses us by a generating power that is visible both in the human race and in the rest of living creatures, *but he is also the root and seed of eternal life in us*." (Emphasis mine). *CO* 35: 530. See also *CO* 54: 64.

Because this is so Calvin can compare the dignity given Adam and Eve at creation with the royal dignity given to believers in Christ and declare that the second is far above the first, even in the present life before glorification.

> "Or il est vrai, entant que nous sommes hommes, que desia nous sommes sa facture: *mais il y a plus*, c'est qu'il nous a

reformez a son image par la grace de nostre Seigneur Iesus
Christ," *CO* 33: 693.

"Il nous faut donc ici proceder par degrez: c'est de cognoistre
en premier lieu, puis que Dieu nous a honnorez en nous faisant
ses creatures, que desia nous sommes tenus à luy et n'y eust-il
autre raison. Mais quand il nous a preferez aux bestes brutes,
voire sans trouver dequoy en nous, qu'il l'a fait par sa pure
bonté: voila *encores en quoy* il s'est monstré plus amiable. . . .
Mais *outre tout cela*, i'ay esté baptisé au nom ne [sic] nostre
Seigneur Iesus Christ: et voici une second marque qui'il m'a
imprimee, pour me monstrer qu'il me vouloit tenir de son
troupeau," *CO* 35: 240.

Thus, in the second stage, in addition to the soteriological structure's
various perspectives, Calvin uses the perspectives of the salvation-historical
structure to evaluate human life. When comparing the life of believers with
that of Adam and Even before the Fall, from one of the absolute heavenly
perspectives, it is the believers' lives which appear better: they are guaranteed the royal dignity of Christ and full citizenship in the eternal kingdom.
When comparing the same two lives from the other absolute heavenly
perspective, however, the life of Adam and Eve is preferable; they had the
fragility of mortality alone and had not become subject to the infirmity of
sin, *CO* 33: 663. Because of this one might argue that the salvation-
historical stages provide another basic structure for Calvin's anthropology.
(See pp. 10–11 of this chapter for a related discussion.) The focus of this
study, however, is on the dynamic perspectival structure based on the
distinction between the temporal and eternal, earthly and heavenly perspectives.

/86/   *OS* 4:170–77 (*Inst.* 3.9).
/87/   *CO* 50: 595.
/88/   *CO* 54: 64.
/89/   *CO* 23: 38. With only the two kingdoms perspective, for instance, one cannot fully understand Calvin's third use of the law. See
chapter 4.
/90/   *CO* 35: 555, "la principale vertu des fideles, quand Dieu les
afflige et les punit, c'est d'estre comme aneantis."
/91/   McNeill 1:346, *Inst.* 2.6.4 in *OS* 3: 325.
/92/   *CO* 55: 416; *CO* 33: 657–58.
/93/   *CO* 45: 212.
/94/   *CO* 45: 212–13.
/95/   McNeill 1:715, *Inst.* 3.9.3 in *OS* 4: 173. See also *CO* 35: 85. For
Calvin's comments on those things of this life (wine, olives, music, etc.)
which are to be enjoyed and not endured or used out of necessity alone, see
CO 40: 549–52.
/96/   *CO* 34: 354.
/97/   *CO* 32: 222.
/98/   I am thinking here of Luther in particular, but of Erasmus, also.
In the *Enchiridion* (Rule 18) he says, "Man is a noble animal, for whose sake
alone God fashioned this wonderful machine of the world. He is likewise a

fellow citizen of the angels, a son of God, an heir of immortality, a member of Christ, a member of the Church. Our bodies are temples of the Holy Spirit, our minds at one and at the same time the likeness and shrine of divinity. Yet on the contrary sin is the foulest plague and pestilence of both body and mind," *Advocates of Reform*, ed. Matthew Spinka (Philadelphia: Westminister, 1953), pp. 368–69.

/99/   *CO* 55: 143. See also *CO* 7: 205, "Qui plus est, il [Paul] nous propose en sa personne, comme une image vive de l'estat des regenerez: disant que l'homme fidele est comme divisé en deux parties; c'est d'autant qu'il est reformé par la grace de Dieu, qu'il s'accorde au bien: mais entant qu'il a encor les reliques de sa nature, qu'il sent une contradiction. . . ."

/100/   *CO* 50: 567–68.

/101/   Paul Pruyser "Calvin's View of Man: A Psychological Commentary," *Theology Today* 26 (1969): 51–68, p. 53.

CHAPTER II

IMAGO DEI

> Accordingly, the integrity with which Adam was endowed is expressed by this word, when he had full possession of right understanding, when he had his affections kept within the bounds of reason, all his senses tempered in right order, and he truly referred his excellence to exceptional gifts bestowed on him by his maker. And although the primary seat of the divine image was in the mind or heart, or in the soul and its powers, yet there was no part of man in which some sparks did not glow.
>
> *Institutes* 1.15.3

The Controversies Over Calvin's Use of the "Imago Dei"

In his historical study *The Image of God in Man*, David Cairns touts Calvin as the theologian who has "given greater attention to the *imago dei* than any great theologian since Augustine, and whose contribution is even greater than Augustine's," adding that "little that is radically new and important on the subject has been said since Calvin."[1] The significance of the *imago dei* in Calvin's theology has been emphasized, notably by T. F. Torrance, who organized his study of Calvin's anthropology exclusively around this concept, and James Childress, who has argued for the importance of the *imago dei* for understanding the unity of Calvin's ethics.[2] While much has been written about this doctrine, there is no consensus about its interpretation. In fact, there is so little agreement that Richard Stauffer recently declared "the problem of the *imago dei*" to be "one of the most difficult problems in Calvin's theology."[3] Stauffer's point can easily be illustrated by identifying the controversies over Calvin's *imago dei* that have emerged in the last few decades. Six of these are: (1) whether the *imago dei* is found in all creation or uniquely in human beings; (2) whether the *imago dei* in human beings refers to the body as well as the soul; (3) whether the *imago dei* refers to natural as well as supernatural gifts; (4) whether the *imago dei* is a substantial endowment or a dynamic relation; (5) whether the *imago dei* is only deformed as a result of the fall, or totally lost; and (6) whether the restored *imago dei* in Jesus Christ takes precedence over the created *imago dei* in Adam and Eve. In each of these areas problems of interpretation remain; no definitive statement has yet appeared proving one of the two sides of each debate to be correct or the final coherence of both sides. On the contrary, some scholars, such as Stauffer, have recently emphasized the incoherence of Calvin's texts on the *imago dei*. Stauffer goes so far as to counsel that the contradictory nature of some of these statements be admitted and the temptation of scholars to systematize unilaterally Calvin's thought on the *imago dei* be resisted.[4] Stauffer's charge that scholars of the caliber of Wilhelm Niesel and T. F. Torrance force Calvin's statements on the *imago dei* into overly systematic patterns is correct. This does not imply, however, that there is no order whatsoever in Calvin's view of this doctrine. Calvin's doctrine of the *imago dei* is at once less tidy than Niesel and Torrance assume and more complexly ordered than Stauffer finds, for the distinction between the human and divine perspectives, in its two major variations, can be found throughout his statements on the *imago dei*. How the dynamic perspectival structure operates in each of the six controversial areas will be demonstrated by the following analyses.

Controversy No. 1: Whether the "Imago Dei" *Is Found in*
All Creation or Uniquely in Human Beings

There is no doubt that Calvin believes that the entire creation in some sense reflects the glory of God. He sees *imagines* of God's power, wisdom, and goodness in the world. The suggestion that he has in mind here the Irenaean distinction between *imagines* in creation and *imago* in humankind is not clearly supported by the texts; for Calvin insists that these *imagines* are not obscure hints, but such plain marks "engraved" in creation "that they can be known

also by touch to the blind."[5] Torrance quotes this and similar remarks in *Calvin's Doctrine of Man* to conclude that for Calvin
creation does not really or "properly" reflect God as an image. He
arrives at this conclusion via a long argument that must be summarized here. First he says that the wider sense of the image of God
refers to the "workmanship" of God in the universe.[6] But he adds
that,

> *Strictly speaking*, there can be no image where there is no
> beholding. And that is the point of Calvin's thought. Primarily,
> it is God Himself who beholds His own glory in the works of
> His hands, or rather who *images* Himself in these works.[7]

Further, according to Torrance's version of Calvin's *imago dei*, although the world is a mirror of God, it can reflect or image God only
if human beings see it "through the Word, which, properly speaking, is the image of God."[8] Therefore, he continues, if "selected
elements of nature" depend on a special relation to the word before
they can image God, "as he is familiarly exhibited to us in Christ the
Word," "how much more do the general elements of nature need
the Word before they can in a less familiar fashion image the glory of
God to men?"[9] His conclusion:

> All this means that *behind* Calvin's wider sense of the *imago dei*
> he thinks of the image as the reflection seen by the eye of the
> man who, *coming down from his knowledge of God*, reads it
> into nature, or who by means of the word *makes the mute
> creation speak* the glory of God. *Calvin's wide use of the* imago
> dei *is grounded upon the special relation of man to the Word of
> God, that is upon the narrow sense of the* imago dei.[10]

Torrance's distinction between the wider image in creation and
the narrower image in human being is helpful, and his argument for
the grounding of the wider image in the narrow one instructive. His
argument for the relation between the two, however, does not fully
comprehend the variety of Calvin's statements about the image in
creation. The difference between the wider and narrower image of
God is not only like that between a passive mute and an animated
speaker. The complexity of Calvin's view of the *imago dei* in creation
emerges when his perspectival approach is considered. From the
perspective of God as creator he views the entire creation in comparison with the eternal creator, claiming the title *imago dei* for

nature as well as humankind. From the perspective of humankind he focuses on the comparison between nature and humankind as the most excellent work of nature, claiming the title *imago dei* for both. But from the perspective of God as father he contrasts the whole of creation with humankind as the elect creature of God, reserving the title *imago dei* for the latter alone.

From the perspective of God as creator, then, all creation is declared to be the image of God. This is how we must understand such statements as that found in Calvin's introduction to Olivetan's translation of the New Testament.

> . . . [I]n all the parts of the world, in the heavens and the earth. God inscribed [*escrit/inscriptiones*], and, as it were, almost engraved [*quasi insculptas*] the glory of his power, goodness, wisdom, and eternity.[11]

The trinity of terms, "goodness, wisdom, and eternity," itself points to the fact that Calvin thinks of the world as the image of God, for these are the same terms he so often uses to describe the *imago dei* in humankind.[12] If one were to argue that he is using these terms here only to point to the mirror-like quality of creation and emphasize that only humankind can read the glory of God there, the following quotation would be strong counter evidence; for in this statement Calvin dignifies the creation by referring to it with an expression he usually reserves for Christ: "lively image."

> . . . [W]e [human beings] have both high and low so many signs of his presence and paternal care for us that if we are not exceedingly stupid and totally lacking in sense and reason, we *must* see it. Because the entire world is like a lively image in which God displays his power and eminence. . . . [13]

One could argue that this lively image of God in creation of which Calvin speaks here is only available to believers who make the world come alive through the Word, the true lively image. The quotation above indicates that this is an unwarranted narrowing of Calvin's use of the *imago dei*. For no one is so deprived of reason or the end for which human beings were created so as not to notice the image of God in the world in some way. Reason in human beings is never destroyed that completely.[14] Thus, it is not that the image of God is in creation *only* when believers perceive it. Rather, the image of God is always actually present in the world for all to see, though it is

seen with varying degrees of clarity and its presence has various
consequences.

> The world therefore is rightly called the mirror of divinity, not
> because there is enough clarity for men to know God by
> looking at the world, but because He makes Himself clear to
> unbelievers in such a way that they are without excuse for their
> ignorance. On the other hand, to believers he has given eyes to
> discern the sparks of his glory, as it were, shining out in every
> individual creature. The world was founded for this purpose,
> that it should be the sphere of divine glory.[15]

The image of God actually exists objectively in nature, not just
subjectively in the mind of the maker or in the mind of human
beings reflecting the mind of the maker.[16] This may be the thought
behind Calvin's admission in the *Institutes* that one can piously say
that "God is nature."[17] Whatever terms Calvin may use, "mirror,"
"imprinted marks," or "image," he intends to say from the perspective of God as creator that the image of God is in the whole of
creation, nature as well as humankind.[18]

When we shift our perspective to that of humankind, however,
clear comparisons among the many reflections or images of God in
creation appear.

> There is certainly nothing so obscure or contemptible, even in
> the smallest corners of the earth, in which some marks [*nota*] of
> the power and wisdom of God may not be seen; but as a more
> distinct image [*imago*] of Him is engraven in the heavens,
> David has particularly selected them for contemplation.[19]

Previously we heard him say that all nature is a theatre of God's
glory. Now he says distinctions must be made. The heavens are a
more distinct reflection of God than an ant, for instance. The tree in
the Garden of Eden was a brighter mirror than a speck of sand. Such
distinctions in the liveliness and clarity of the reflections of God can
be made after the Fall as well as before the Fall. After the Fall the
entire world remains an external aid by which believers are disci-
plined to a life of gratitude; but at the same time God sets certain
external signs above the rest as special images of his grace.[20] Thus
both before and after the Fall, from this perspective there are
brighter and dimmer mirrors, clear and blurry reflections of God.[21]
Though everything in creation reflects God, there is a definite

hierarchy of intensity and brilliance, ascending from inanimate matter through the heavens to humankind.

> There is presented to us in the whole order of nature the most abundant matter for showing forth the glory of God, but as we are unquestionably more powerfully affected with what we ourselves experience, David here, with great propriety, expressly celebrates the special favor which God manifests toward mankind; for this, of all the subjects which come under our contemplation, is the brightest mirror in which we can behold his glory.[22]

It is important to note here that Calvin does not deny that the entire creation reflects God, both as a mirror and an image. Contrary to Torrance's claim that the wider image in creation reflects God only when it is acknowledged by the narrower image in humankind, Calvin says that the entire world reflects this glory, whether or not it is acknowledged by human beings, for it is stamped with the indelible mark of the creator. He does not say that humankind speaks and nature is mute; humankind shines and nature does not. From both the perspectives of God as creator and humankind he affirms that the image of God is *in* creation.

Calvin does not, however, only assert that the whole of creation is the image of God and compare humankind and nature as brighter and duller images of God. He also reserves the title *imago dei* for humankind alone. From this perspective of God as father, humankind appears as the elect and privileged creature of God. Thus, it alone may rightly be called the image of God (*imago dei*); in contrast to it the rest of creation may only be called the marks, sparks, or lineaments of God (*nota, scintillae, lineamenta dei*)[23] It is in this sense that Torrance's claim that "properly speaking" only human beings deserve the title of the image of God must be understood. It is only one of a variety of views Calvin has of the *imago dei* in creation and must, therefore, be given limited significance in his anthropology.

Controversy No. 2: Whether the "Imago Dei" in Humankind Refers to the Body as well as to the Soul, Or to the Soul Alone

Calvin's view of the body and soul as *imago dei* is complex and difficult to interpret. On the one hand, he presents the body (as well as the soul) as a locus of the image of God.

And although the primary seat of the divine image [*imaginis*] was in the mind and heart, or in the soul and its powers, yet there was no part of man, not even the body itself, in which some sparks [*scintillae*] did not glow.[24]

On the other hand, he denies that the body is a locus of the image of God, reserving this lofty title for the soul alone.[25] In the *Psychopannychia* he says that

These expressions [after his image and likeness] cannot possibly be understood of [Adam's] body, in which, though the wonderful work of God appears more than in all other creatures, his image nowhere shines forth. God Himself, who is a Spirit, cannot be represented by any bodily shape. But as a bodily image which exhibits the external face ought to express to the life all the traits and features, that thus the statue or picture may give an idea of all that may be seen in the original, so this image of God must, by its likeness, implant some knowledge of God in our minds.[26]

He makes a similar statement years later in the *Commentary on Genesis;* and, comparing animal and human bodies, he elsewhere concludes that there is no difference at all since all were made out of the same earth; it is the human *soul* which differentiates human beings as the image of God.[27] We may interpret these contradictory statements by employing the distinction between the perspectives of humankind and God as father and affirming both sides.[28] From the perspective of God as father, both the body and soul, the whole person, are claimed to be a locus of the image of God. Both are created graciously by God and marked with goodness, wisdom, and justice. And, from the perspective of humankind, both body and soul may be called a locus of the image of God, for both are compared as duller and brighter mirrors, dead and lively images, blurred and clear marks. Because the soul shines more brightly than the body, however, it is more appropriately called the image of God.

The perspective of humankind is useful in interpreting Calvin's emphasis on the soul as the seat of the image of God. Calvin wants to avoid saying that the soul is itself the image of God (for reasons which will be made clear in the discussion of Controversy No. 4). He speaks of the soul as the selected locale in which God's glory shines the most clearly. Thus, he refers to it as the *seat* of the image. As the seat it is superior to the body as image, and for this reason is chosen as the synecdoche to speak of the whole person.

> [A]lthough the soul is not man, yet it is not absurd for man, in
> respect to his soul, to be called God's image [*imaginem*], even
> though I retain the principle I just now set forward that the
> likeness [*similitudinem*] of God extends to the whole excel-
> lence by which man's nature towers over all the kinds of living
> creatures. [29]

On the basis of his knowledge of Hebrew parallelism, both in the
Institutes and his *Commentary on Genesis*, Calvin rejects the distinction between the terms "image" and "likeness," as that between
substance and accidents, or nature and supernature. [30] Instead, he
uses the two terms to refer to the difference in clarity, brilliance, and
liveliness of the soul and body as images of God.

> If I say that one sees in the body of human beings such an
> excellence that already one can perceive the image of God, and
> if I go a bit further and speak of the soul, it is there that we find
> the lively image of God: it is there in the soul where we
> recognize what has been written, that God wanted to con-
> stitute humanity above all other creatures, and that he wanted
> to adorn him with a great nobility and dignity and power above
> all animals. [31]

He does not say that we cannot recognize the image of God anywhere else, including the human body, but only that we are more
likely to recognize it in its most vivid form, in the soul. From the
perspective of humankind, then, Calvin does not make an absolute
distinction between the soul as image of God and the body as non-
image. Rather, he compares the two as brighter and duller images
and emphasizes the soul as the brighter.

From the perspective of God as father, however, another emphasis is seen: the unity of the body and soul as manifestations of the
image of God which is given to the whole person. From this perspective the comprehensiveness of Calvin's definition of the image of
God stands out, for the image of God refers to *all* that distinguishes
human beings in their relation to God from the rest of the creaturely
world.

> For although God's glory shines forth in the outer man, yet
> there is no doubt that the proper seat of his image is in the soul.
> I do not deny, indeed, that the outward form, insofar as it
> distinguishes and separates us from brute animals, at the same
> time more closely joins us to God. And if anyone wishes to
> include under "image of God" the fact that, "while all other

living things being bent over to look earthward, man has been given a face uplifted, bidden to gaze heavenward and to raise his countenance to the stars," I shall not contend too strongly—*provided it be regarded as a settled principle that the image of God, which is seen or glows in these outward marks, is spiritual.*[32]

What Calvin seems to be saying here is that he is not opposed in principle to speaking of the body as a seat of the image of God, as long as the human perspective, with its elevation of the soul as the most appropriate term to refer to the uniquely human relationship to God, is not forgotten. When this perspective is kept in mind, the human body can properly be called a seat of the image of God. It, as well as the soul, when seen from the perspective of God as father is a mirror in which the glory of God shines forth in a unique way. If this were not so, Calvin's insistence in several of his works that the human body is distinct from that of animals would make little sense. In the sixth sermon on Genesis he mentions to his congregation that many people believe that the image of God has to do with the body and he tells them that he agrees, for "in truth is such an artifice in the nature of the human body that one can justly say that it *is* an image of God."[33] Similar comments are found in his *Commentary on Genesis* and the *Institutes*. He states that the "exquisite workmanship" of the human body shows God's care and enables men and women to find God in their bodies; for the body as a rare example of God's wisdom, power, and goodness, "contains enough miracles to occupy our minds, if we pay attention to them."[34] The sermons on Job, as well, contain many references to the human body as a work of art, the masterpiece of the artist-creator, suggesting that in a work so excellent people, even the unlettered, can see God's wisdom, power, and goodness.[35] The trinity of terms here once again suggest that Calvin is here elucidating the *imago dei* in terms of the human body.

When Calvin maintains in other places that the human body, created out of the same mud as the other animals' bodies, is no different, he departs from this language of the body as the *imago dei*. He usually does so to highlight the superiority of the soul over the body as the seat of the image of God. These two different presentations of the body as image of God are different emphases called for by particular polemical situations. When faced with spiritualizers, he brings into play the perspective of God as father, emphasizing the whole person and the body, therefore, too, as image of God. But when his opponents are anthropomorphizers, he employs the perspective of humankind, stressing the spiritual nature of the image and its primary seat, the soul. In Calvin's debate with Osiander it is also the second emphasis that is made. Since Osiander "*indiscriminately* [extended] God's image both to the body and to the soul" and mingled "heaven and earth" in so doing, Calvin had to set him straight by focusing on the soul as the image of God.[36] He does not say to Osiander that there is no sense in which the image of God can be applied to the body, but rather that the way in which Osiander has applied it is incorrect. Osiander spoke of the body as the image of God in such a way that he forgot the distinction made from the perspective of humankind between the soul as *the* seat of the image of God and the body as a duller reflection. Calvin's language here is very circumspect, however, for he wants to retain a proper reference of the image of God to both the soul and body.

His language is not always circumspect, however, and the result is that there are several passages on the body and soul as image of God which are extremely difficult to interpret. In the *Psychopannychia*, for example, Calvin had not yet developed his complex theological structure of shifting perspectives. There is one sentence in this treatise that denies the image to the body. Even if this sentence could not be interpreted in light of his perspectival approach, it could not be used to disqualify the countless others that support this interpretation.[37] There are several statements in Calvin's *Commentary on Genesis* which also present difficulties. Commenting on Genesis 1, Calvin writes:

> The Anthropormorphites were too gross in seeking this resemblance in the human body. Let that reverie therefore remain entombed.[38]

This sentence, however, can be interpreted in the same way Calvin's responses to Osiander were interpreted. Calvin is rejecting not all references to the body as image, but particular, gross references. He will not accept the crass view that the body is *the* image of God, but this does not mean that he refuses to consider the body as one of the mirrors in which the image of God shines. But what of the next sentence?

> Others proceed with a little more subtlety, who, though they do not imagine God to be corporeal, yet maintain that the

image of God is in the body of man, because his admirable workmanship there shines brightly; but this opinion, as we shall see, is by no means consonant with Scripture.[30]

This appears to contradict the previous interpretation of his statements. However, when this sentence is read in its context, it, too, fits with the rest of Calvin's *imago dei* statements on the soul and body. After rejecting the definition of the image of God as dominion over nature in the next sentence, Calvin quickly moves on to assert that "since the image of God has been destroyed in us by the Fall, we may judge from its restoration what it originally had been."[40] His purpose in this passage is to compare the image in fallen Adam with the restored image in Jesus Christ. In other words, he shifts to the perspectives of God as judge and God in Christ here in his discussion of the image of God in the body. From the first perspective we see that there is no image in the body. Sin has marred the beautiful crafting of our human bodies so that only "obscure lineaments" remain to be seen. But from the second, looking through the "perfection of our nature" in the lively image of Christ, we see that before the Fall Adam had "no part of him in which some scintillations of it did not shine forth," even though the chief seat was in the mind and heart.[41] Calvin returns to this theme later by noting that there was true immortal life in Adam and Eve's bodies as well as in their souls.[42] Shifting to the perspectives of God as judge and God in Christ he is able to maintain simultaneously that the image of God has been lost in the body in the Fall and that it is restored in Jesus Christ. This will be developed in the discussion of Controversy No. 5.

For Calvin, then, there are several different answers to the question of whether or not the *imago dei* can apply to the human body. From the absolute perspective of God as father, the whole of the self, including the body, is seen to bear the mark of God's power, wisdom, and goodness. From the relative perspective of humankind, however, the body is seen to be a less brilliant image than the soul and thus not the proper synecdochical term for the *imago dei*. And, from the perspectives of God as judge and God in Christ, the image in the body has been lost in the Fall but restored in believers. Each one of these perspectives with it peculiar assessment of the image in the body must be kept in mind if Calvin's statements are to be interpreted correctly. If they are, one can conclude that there is no controversy here, for Calvin maintains both sides of the debate.

Controversy No. 3: Whether the "Imago Dei" *Refers to Reason or Piety, Natural Gifts or Supernatural Gifts*

If one asks whether the *imago dei* refers to reason or piety, natural gifts or supernatural gifts, two diametrically opposed answers can be found in the literature on Calvin. Wilhelm Niesel take the position that the image is a supernatural gift consisting of true piety.

> The divine similitude consists not in the fact that man is endowed with reason and will, but in the fact that these faculties in original man were directed wholly toward knowledge of and obedience to God. Thus, Calvin can echo the expressions of the church fathers and say that body and soul are natural gifts which man has received, whereas, the similitude to God, on the contrary, is a supernatural gift. It is superadded to the psycho-physical constitution of man and is imparted from the outside. [43]

Battenhouse takes the opposite position, claiming that Calvin, unlike Aquinas, saw "right reason as a natural gift, bestowed on man in his first state to enable man to govern his life on earth and also 'to ascend even to God and eternal felicity.'"[44] Calvin's own statements warrant both conclusions. He often declares reason to be the feature which distinguishes human beings and animals.[45] On the other hand, he also says quite plainly "that it is the worship of God alone that renders men higher than the brutes and through it alone they aspire to immortality."[46] What can we make of such statements? Once again, distinguishing the perspectives from which these statements are made may be helpful.

Calvin's approach to the question of whether the image is to be defined as reason or worship is similar to his approach to the question of the body and soul as image. Just as the image could properly be spoken of as in the soul and body from one perspective *and* most appropriately in the soul from another perspective, so it can be defined as both worship and reason from one perspective *and* most appropriately as worship from the other perspective. From the absolute perspective of God as father, the image is seen as the right relationship of the *whole self* to God. This integrity of being, in which the whole self is rightly ordered to God, may be called true piety and is, as Torrance points out, a supernatural gift. Identifying the image as the gratuitous gift of true piety, the right ordering of the whole self to God, however, does not, as Torrance concludes, entail the rejection of reason as the image of God. On the contrary, when the image is defined as true piety, the right ordering of the whole self toward God, all parts of the self, including reason, are incorporated in the definition. From the divine perspective, the image of God is a comprehensive reality, as Calvin's masterful definition in the *Institutes* shows.

> Accordingly, the integrity with which Adam was endowed is expressed by this word, when he had full possession of right understanding, when he had his affections kept within the bounds of reason, all his senses tempered in right order, and he truly referred his excellence to exceptional gifts bestowed on him by his maker. And although the primary seat of the divine image was in the mind or heart, or in the soul and its powers, yet there was no part of man in which some sparks did not glow.[47]

Earlier we saw that the image shone in all parts of the human creature, including the body. Here we see that it includes all parts of the soul and specifically, reason. And, just as the body was intended to serve the soul in the unity of the self, so reason is intended to serve piety understood as the integrity of the self before God. Therefore, even when the image is defined as the supernatural gift of right relationship to God, as true piety, it includes reason. From this absolute perspective on the whole self, however, it is perhaps more appropriate to speak of the image as true piety than as reason.

When we shift perspectives and look at the image of God not from the perspective of God but from the perspective of humankind, it appears not as a supernatural gift of true piety but as a natural gift consisting of all those powers unique to human beings. This natural endowment of human beings, which incorporates all capacities that distinguish human beings from beasts, includes both reason and piety. From this perspective, however, piety is not the right ordering of the whole self toward God (true piety). Rather, it refers to the universal human practice of worship. All human beings, says Calvin, know that God is to be worshipped rather than feared, and all societies compose their own forms of worship.[48] And, from this perspective, reason is seen not primarily as an aid to true piety, but as a natural endowment that enables human beings *both* to understand nature and themselves, *and* to have "some knowledge of God" (*sensus divinitatis*).[49]

Thus, from the perspective of God the image is seen as a supernatural gift, from the perspective of humankind, a natural endowment. An expanded discussion of this difference follows in the next section. At this point I want to comment only on the image as reason and/or piety. Though from the perspective of God the image of God is most appropriately referred to as true piety, reason is not excluded from the definition of the image. It is included as one of the parts rightly ordered in the full integrity of the self. From the perspective of humankind the image is seen as both reason and piety (worship). Even though there are differences in the definitions of piety in both cases, the pairing of piety and reason in both perspectives is important to note. This close connection between reason and piety in Calvin's understanding of the image of God, no matter from which perspective, indicates the futility of trying to define the image of God as either reason alone or piety alone.[50]

Controversy No. 4: Whether the "Imago Dei" is a Substantial Endowment of the Human Creature or a Dynamic Relation Between God and the Human Creature

In Calvin's summary description of the *imago dei* in humankind the image is presented as both a natural endowment and an ordering of those endowments to that for which they were intended, namely, the glory of God. The *imago* is both a natural possession and a supernatural gift of a peculiar relationship to God; it is both a substantial endowment of the human creature and a dynamic relation between God and the human creature. This conclusion modifies Torrance's primary thesis in *Calvin's Doctrine of Man*. Throughout that study of Calvin's anthropology he returns again and again to one theme: the *imago dei* is only a gift and not a possession; it is an objective reality (that is, dependent totally on God) and not a subjective reality (that is, actually constitutive of the human subject); it is dynamic or relational and not substantial. Though Torrance's interpretation enjoys a wide acceptance among Calvin scholars, it does not provide a wholly accurate picture of Calvin's view on this point.[51] An analysis of Calvin's view of the dynamic and substantial quality of the *imago dei* both before and after the Fall will demonstrate how and where Torrance's thesis can be supplemented and modified.

Since the key to Torrance's thesis is his interpretation of Calvin's use of the term "mirror," it is necessary to include the following quotation before proceeding:

> There is no doubt that Calvin *always* thinks of the *imago* in terms of a *mirror*. Only while the mirror actually reflects an object does it have the image of that object. There is no such thing in Calvin's thought as an *imago* dissociated from the act of reflecting. He does use such expressions as *engrave* [sic] and *sculptured*, but only in a metaphorical sense and never dissociated from the idea of the mirror. Where the thought is of the mirroring of God, properly speaking the mirror is always the Word. . . . It is not often that Calvin uses the expression *imago dei* except in this intimate association with mirror and word. . . . This gives us, I believe, that key to Calvin's apparent confusion of thought.[52]

Torrance is correct to point out the importance of the term "mirror" for understanding Calvin's view of the *imago dei*. When Calvin asks himself in what the image of God in Adam consists, he answers: "A rectitude, justice, and integrity" so that, in sum, one could say that "man was like a mirror of this excellent glory which gleams fully in God."[53] He does not always use this term, however. Nor does he always think of the image in these terms. He is quite fond of describing the image with metaphors taken from the arts of coin-making, engraving, painting, and printing. He often speaks of the image, for instance, as having been imprinted *(imprimée)* in us at baptism *and* at creation;[54] and of its being engraved upon us or sealed upon us as the mark of a king upon an important document.[55] The frequent use Calvin makes of such images renders Torrance's distinction between "the *idea* of the mirror" and the "metaphorical sense" of all other terms questionable. Calvin clearly uses each and every one of these expressions as helpful metaphors to describe a complex reality. His habit of adding the metaphor-signals *"comme"* and *"quasi"* to the terms *"mirror"* and *"speculum"* alerts the reader not to interpret his use of the mirror image too literally.[56]

With his assertion that "the idea of the mirror" is the "key to Calvin's apparent confusion of thought," Torrance claims that the *imago dei* is exclusively a gift, an objective reality, and a relational or dynamic reality. This is already clear in the passage quoted above ("only while the mirror actually reflects . . .") A few pages later he draws the conclusion even more sharply:

> Strictly speaking, there can be no image where there is no one
> beholding. And that is the point of Calvin's thought. Primarily
> it is God Himself who beholds His own glory in the works of
> His hand, or rather who images Himself in these works.[57]

I believe it is Torrance's Barthian bias which has led him to this
narrow conclusion. He has selected one particular text from a sermon on Job to ground his interpretation.[58] Though this text is only
one of a variety of texts which Calvin uses, it does support Torrance's
own position of the priority of God the Subject over the human
creature. This Barthian fascination with the priority of God *the*
Subject prevents him from seeing both sides of Calvin's view. Thus,
when he speaks of the *imago dei* in humankind he points out *only*
that "it is not any natural property of the soul," but "a spiritual
reflection in holiness and righteousness."[59] The key point, however,
as he keeps reminding his readers, is that the *imago dei* in humankind "has to do fundamentally with God's beholding rather than with
man's" and he refers to this as "the objective basis for the image of
God in grace."[60] This narrow focus on God's beholding and the
neglect of what the image means *in and to* humankind reflect a
limited reading of Calvin on this point.

Torrance interprets the human side of the *imago dei* relation as
narrowly as he reads the entire God-human relation in Calvin's
doctrine of the *imago dei*, for he interprets it exclusively in a
dynamic and relational way. He rejects all terms of substance for the
image, declaring that Calvin does not think of the *imago dei* "in
terms of being, that is, in terms of being this or that in himself, but
in terms of a spiritual relation to the gracious will of God."[61] Torrance is so concerned to champion Barth's *analogia fidei* over Aquinas's *analogia entis* that he narrowly focuses on the *imago* as a
relational concept and ignores Calvin's understanding of the *imago*
as substantial.

Torrance's limited view of the *imago dei* in humankind is both
accurate and inaccurate. He is correct that for Calvin the *imago dei*
is a dynamic relation, a gift, and a spiritual communion with God.
He is incorrect in his conclusion that this is all the *imago dei* is for
Calvin. The full argument for this assessment of his conclusions will
be presented in the discussion of the remaining two controversies.
For the moment I will limit my remarks to Torrance's representation
of Calvin's mirror language as the key to his thought and his view of
the God-human relationship expressed in Calvin's *imago dei*.

Calvin does speak of men and women contemplating God in the mirrors of the world, their bodies, the scriptures, exemplary Christians, and Christ.[62] He does think of the *imago dei* as a dynamic relation and a response to the prior action of God. The *imago* is an "acknowledgment" in grateful confession of the giver of every good gift.[63] Or, as he sometimes say, "God put us in this world: *we are like witnesses of his power, justice, and wisdom*."[64] This latter quote in particular appears to support Torrance's thesis, for Calvin calls humankind witnesses rather than examples of God's wisdom, power, and justice. Calvin adds two qualifications to these statements about humankind's responsiveness, however, that Torrance neglects. First, his conception of human witnessing is much more active than Torrance's emphasis on reflection indicates; and second, he views the witnesses of and to God's power, wisdom, and justice, as also possessing in themselves the marks of God's power, wisdom, and justice.

Calvin's emphasis on the activity of the acknowledger can be seen in his use of the Renaissance image of the world as a theatre. In many instances he presents God as the primary actor and humankind as passive spectators who clap at appropriate times but are not otherwise involved in the drama on stage.[65] At other times, however, he presents human beings as actors as well as spectators, perhaps combining Juan Luis Vives's fable of the gods watching humankind perform spectacles for their amazement with Cicero's image of humankind as the privileged spectator of heaven and earth.[66] Whatever his influences may be, Calvin clearly perceives human beings as actors as well as spectators, and this should not be deleted from a discussion of the uniqueness of humankind as *imago dei*. This emphasis in his anthropology will be discussed in more detail in chapter 4. I mention it here to point out Torrance's one-sided view of the *imago* as mode of reflection.

Calvin's idea that the human subject possesses or contains certain gifts of God's wisdom, power, and justice as constitutive of itself can be seen in his use of the common Renaissance images drawn from the arts of coin-making, engraving, and printing. His frequent use of such images suggests to me that for Calvin the *imago dei* cannot be fully and accurately described as *only* a dynamic relation. If one does not describe the *imago also* in terms of actual qualities or endowments in human nature, that is, in terms of an inviolable constitution of human *being*, one misses the complexity of Calvin's view of the *imago dei* at this point. From the absolute perspective of God as *creator,* the *imago dei* appears as a dynamic relation with the Source of all being; it is nothing unless it receives the gift of being every moment in this relationship. But from the relative perspective of humankind, the *imago dei* appears as constitutive of human nature, as substantial being, and as natural endowment. It is a possession of all human beings insofar as they are human and not beasts. Both sides of his view must be presented or distortion will result. For example, one cannot understand Calvin's inclusion of the natural gifts in his definition of the *imago* unless one admits the *imago* as substantial as well as relational. And, one cannot comprehend Calvin's statements on the effects of sin on the *imago* unless one keeps both perspectives and their conclusions in mind.

Controversy No. 5: Whether the "Imago Dei" is only Deformed Or Totally Lost as a Result of the Fall

Does Calvin maintain that with the Fall the *imago dei* is actually effaced or only defaced? This, more than any other aspect of Calvin's doctrine of the *imago dei,* has lead to confusion. Stauffer suggests that at this point, as at others in Calvin's anthropology, we may be left only with "incoherence."[67] Niesel suggests that it is difficult to harmonize Calvin's "ruthless assertions" that the divine image is destroyed with his admissions that humankind retains its uniquely human gifts.[68] Torrance also notes the difficulty here, but offers an attempt to resolve the contradictions by using Calvin's distinction between the natural and supernatural gifts. He concludes that "there can be no doubt here that the remnant refers to the natural gifts, while spiritually the *imago dei* is wholly defaced."[69] Calvin does approve of the scholastic distinction, for he echoes it in the *Institutes,* saying that "The natural gifts in man were corrupted, but the supernatural taken away."[70] One must be careful not to jump too quickly to this distinction as a means to resolve the contradictions in his thought, however; for although he uses this language with approval, he interprets it to suit his own theological and anthropological vision.[71] Since he does not approve of all traditional understandings of this distinction to describe the effects of the Fall, he offers his own.[72] Specifically, using his various theological perspectives he reconstructs the scholastic distinction and speaks about the effects of the Fall on the *imago dei* in a complex though consistent way. These differing views of humankind, from the perspectives of God as creator, God as judge, God in Christ, and humankind, make it possible for Calvin to do justice to the scriptural confession that humankind is both totally corrupt and at the same time the most noble work of creation. Once all Calvin's statements on this aspect of the *imago dei* are seen in this light, they appear in a consistent pattern.

A review of Torrance's struggle with this problem in Calvin interpretation will serve as a prelude to the presentation of the textual evidence which supports this thesis. Torrance recognizes that simply pointing to the natural/supernatural distinction is not enough to solve the difficulties, conceding that

> it is difficult to see how there can be any ultimate reconciliation between Calvin's doctrine of total perversity and his doctrine of the remnant of the *imago dei*. . . . (Though the fact that he can give them in the same breath seems to indicate that he had no difficulty in reconciling them.) That there is an ultimate inconsistency seems demanded by Calvin's denial that there is any seed of election or any germ of righteousness in fallen man. In other words, both the doctrine of election as Calvin holds it and the doctrine of justification by faith alone seem to imply that there is no remnant of the *imago dei*.[73]

Because of his own theological assumptions Torrance does not linger long on Calvin's many statements about this remnant. Taking the doctrines of justification and election as normative, he treats the question of whether or not Calvin does speak positively about the retention of the image after the Fall as insignificant.

> If one is *forced* to speak of a remnant of the image of God, surely it can no longer image God's glory. There is no true righteousness or virtue here, and therefore nothing that *really* images the glory of God. That seems to be the sense in which Calvin holds to the doctrine of the remnant of the image of God.[74]

In addition to interpreting Calvin's statements about the remnant as insignificant anomalies or ways to point to the sinfulness of human beings, Torrance offers a third interpretation: these statements of the remnant of the image of God refer not to human beings at all, but rather to "the fact that God has not let go his original *intention* in regard to man."[75] According to this theory, the remnant consists in the fact that the objective basis of the *imago* in *God's intention* remains while the subjective possession of the *imago* is totally lost. This results in the strange conclusion that the *imago dei* as a remnant after the Fall remains *over* but not *in* humankind.[76] Though Torrance tries hard to squeeze Calvin's view into a Barthian framework, in the end his discussion of this aspect of Calvin's thought is confusing and inconclusive. He cannot decide whether Calvin is consistent ultimately or not and, if he is, how he should be interpreted. None of the arguments he presents is finally persuasive. And, all of them are finally incomplete presentations of Calvin's thought. Calvin does not use the concept of the remnant of the *imago only* to point to the sinfulness of humankind. Nor does he believe it consists in the "objective basis" of God's intention *alone*. He *also* uses it to celebrate the actual good remaining in human beings and to point to the obligations owed other human beings on the basis of their subjective possession of the image of God as a remnant. Since Calvin speaks of the remnant in both the positive and negative way, any presentation which mentions one and not the other will be a distortion of his view. Exactly how Calvin emphasizes both sides is the subject of the following analysis.[77]

Calvin explicitly says that sin destroys, extinguishes, erases, rubs out, and effaces the image in humankind.[78] He does mean by this that the image is totally, absolutely lost in the Fall. Though he occasionally qualifies these absolute terms by adding *"quasi"* or *"comme,"* he still intends them to refer to a total deletion and not a severe deformity of the image.[79] And, although he does say that the spiritual rectitude is lost while the natural gifts remain, these statements do not soften the effect of the absolute statements; for Calvin just as often remarks that all the natural gifts are totally lost as well.

> We are despoiled of the excellent gifts of the Holy Spirit, of the light of reason, or justice, and of rectitude and are prone to every evil. Now if anyone should object, that it is unjust for the innocent to bear the punishments of another's sins, I answer, whatever gifts God had conferred upon us in the person of Adam, he had the best right to take away when Adam wickedly fell.[80]

In other words, Calvin believes that the image of God was totally lost in the Fall; in no way does he soften this pronouncement. However, these statements are not the whole of Calvin's assessment of the image after the Fall. He complements this harsh view with a positive view of the retention of the image after the Fall. Once again both sides must be admitted as integral to his anthropology and once again the connection between the two is found in his use of shifting theological perspectives.

Calvin's absolute judgments of the obliteration of the image in the Fall are usually made from the perspective of God as judge His uncompromising view of the annihilation of the image underlines the total corruption of the self. This in turn serves his doctrine of soteriology, for insistence on the total corrupton of the self allows him to highlight simultaneously the insufficiency of all human merit and the sufficient, gratuitous character of God's redeeming grace. For example, when presenting the grace of Jesus Christ, Calvin usually contrasts the erasure of the image in sin with the restamping of the image in believers by Christ, the law, or baptism.[81] He deliberately underscores the discontinuity between Adam and Eve and redeemed Adam and Eve in order to assure a pious view of the prevenience of God's redeeming grace.

In general, then, when Calvin pronounces the image wholly lost, he is evaluating it from the absolute perspective of God as judge. Most of these statements, therefore, have a specific purpose; they are intended to point to the absolute judgment of God on all sinners and the absolute redemption of believers in Jesus Christ. Occasionally Calvin will even alert his audience that this is the context in which his comments on the obliteration of the image must be understood. While preaching an Ephesians 2:11–13, for example, he takes time out to inform the congregation that they "have seen this morning how God has destroyed [*aneanti*] all that humankind was, *in order that* there might be no foundation for salvation except the pure goodness of God."[82] The following two quotations offer further evidence that Calvin indeed understands the annihilation of the image to be an assessment made from the absolute perspective of God the judge and redeemer.

> Even though there is still some discretion between good and evil, *nevertheless* we say that what we have of clarity is converted into shadows *when it is a question of looking to God*, such that one cannot approach God at all by his reason or intelligence.[83]

Having commented that the image in Adam was obliterated by the Fall, he continues:

> It is alleged that there still remain in man such gifts of God as
> are not to be despoiled, and as distinguish him from all the
> other creatures. This is easily answered by remembering that
> however great these may be, they are corrupted by sin *and
> vanish away into nothingness*. It is only when applied with the
> knowledge of God that any of the endowments conferred upon
> us from above can be said to have a real excellency; apart from
> this, they are vitiated by that contagion of sin which has not left
> a vestige in man of his original integrity.[84]

It is in the context of such soteriological discussions that Calvin
refers to humankind as nothingness and the image as destroyed
completely. From the absolute perspective of God the righteous
judge all sinners appear as smooth coins. The image of God which
was stamped on them at creation has been erased. The effacement is
total; there is no remainder. Calvin does not leave Christians with
this bleak assessment, though. The companion to the pronouncement that all sinners have totally lost the image of God is the
message that all believers have been restored to the image of God
through Christ. From the perspective of God in Christ believers
appear as freshly minted coins. They bear the sharp and distinct
image of Jesus Christ which was stamped on them in baptism and is
continually renewed through the work of the Holy Spirit. Both
contrasting absolute judgments are made from the perspective of
God as redeemer. But these two assessments of the image of God in
humankind after the Fall, even when taken together, tell only half of
the story. The other half is presented from the perspective of humankind, emphasizing the retention of the image after the Fall. To
the displacement/replacement model Calvin adds a deformed/trans-
formed model for understanding the image after the Fall. While the
former emphasizes the discontinuity between salvation-historical
stages, the latter emphasizes the continuity. It is in the context of
this latter model that Calvin speaks of the remnants of the image.

Calvin uses many terms to speak of these remnants, traces,
vestiges, sparks, relics, and lineaments, but his primary message is
clear: the entire constitution of the self, including the supernatural
as well as the natural gifts, has been deformed rather than ex-
tinguished by sin. To express his view that humankind retains its
constitutive nature given at creation, he shifts from displacement/
replacement language to deformation/transformation language. It is
not annihilation and obliteration of which he speaks now, but rather
defacement, corruption, disorientation, repair, and restoration.[85]

Whereas from the perspective of God as judge total depravity meant that all of God's gifts are totally lost in the Fall, from the perspective of humankind total depravity means that the totality of the self is affected by sin. And from the perspective of humankind, total salvation means not that something wholly new is added to the self, but rather that the totality of the self is restored.

Calvin identifies some of these traces as: human dominion over creation, a "natural" sense of equity and subjection to laws, reason, and conscience.[86] It is understanding and will, the two parts of the soul (which is the chief seat of the image), that Calvin most often mentions as examples of such sparks. Reason and conscience remain after the Fall as particularly vivid witnesses to God in all human beings.[87] If Calvin identified only natural gifts as remnants, Torrance's resolution of Calvin's remnant doctrine might suffice to explain the difficulties. One could simply say that for Calvin the natural gifts are corrupted and the supernatural gifts are lost; the spiritual image is obliterated, while remnants remain in the natural gifts. This does not make sense, however, out of Calvin's varied statements on the *imago* after the Fall. We have already shown that Calvin believes all the natural gifts to be totally lost along with the spiritual gifts, since they count for nothing in the judgment of God the redeemer. Torrance's resolution of the difficulties in these statements of Calvin cannot include this absolute denial. Further, in direct contradiction to Torrance's view, Calvin is quite comfortable speaking of a remnant of the image as worship or piety. Though from the absolute perspective of God as judge there is no true (rightly ordered and saving) piety left in humankind; and though "religion is a virtue . . . which few men have,"[88] Calvin still identifies worship as a remnant of the *imago dei* after the Fall.[89] The *sensus divinitatis* for Calvin is engraved upon the human soul at creation and cannot be erased, though it can be defaced or distorted. It, like the conscience and intelligence, is an inviolable part of human nature. This view of the image from the perspective of humankind is added to Calvin's view of the image as wholly lost. From this relative perspective a retention of the eschatological orientation of Adam and Eve and the innate "aspiration" of all human beings for God after the Fall appear. From the perspective of God as judge, the *sensus divinitatis*, the aspiration to heavenly life, is completely gone; for when the issue is human sin and the need for redemption, all piety is to be counted as nothing. However, from the perspective of humankind, one can properly speak of a remnant of piety and worship in human beings after the Fall, at least as the *sensus divinitatis*, which can never be erased in human beings.[90]

Calvin speaks seriously of the whole image being both completely erased and only defaced. Though he speaks of obliteration more frequently than retention, we are not thereby justified in omitting the latter from his anthropology. Both sides must be recognized as integral to his doctrine of the *imago dei*. Also, since Calvin positively emphasizes the continuity of created human nature as well as its discontinuity, we are not justified in including the retention view in a negative way only. This is what the majority of Calvin scholars have done, observing that Calvin uses the remnant doctrine for one purpose: to render sinful human beings inexcusable before a righteous God.[91] There is a great deal of evidence to support this often repeated evaluation of the purpose of Calvin's remnant theory. Frequently Calvin locates the remnant in a particular gift only to remark on its inevitable corruption. Thus, the affections lead to inordinate desires, the conscience to misjudgment, reason to idle or even blasphemous speculation, and the *sensus divinitatis* to idolatry.[92] Here these remnants do function to condemn humankind as inexcusable ingrates before a God who lavishes such natural and supernatural gifts upon them. This is not the only use Calvin makes of the remnant theory, however, and to present it as if it were distorts his teaching.

In addition to using the remnant theory negatively, as one more way of underscoring the insufficiency of human merit to earn grace, Calvin employs the theory positively, to speak of the obligations each person has to other human beings and to God. He uses the existence of the remnant, for instance, as one of the building blocks for his basic principles of a Christian social ethic. He argues from the existence of the remnant of the image of God in all human beings after the Fall to the solidarity of the human race. "Above all, the image of God ought to be a bond of holy union among us. Therefore, here there can be no question of friend or enemy for no evil in man can destroy his nature."[99] He is clear that the image of God, as the distinguishing characteristic of the human race, binding all together in solidarity, remains engraved in all men and women after the Fall, whether they be Christians or not. When a murderer raises a hand against another person, therefore, God feels the injury and dishonor done to himself in his chosen image, a human being. Calvin has in mind here more than the intention of God for human beings. It is not simply God's intended purpose for humankind which men and women are to respect in others; it is the very image of God itself which is stamped as an indelible mark upon every created human being. In other words, at the basis of Calvin's social ethic lies his view that even after the Fall human beings retain the actual endowments of the image of God which others can recognize as the work of the hands of God.

When this evidence for a positive use of the remnant in Calvin's social ethic is combined with all the foregoing evidence— that metaphors of engraving are as central and frequent as the metaphor of the mirror; that the language of obliteration must be read in the context of the perspective of God as judge; that the remnant may be seen to actually exist in humankind after the Fall from the perspective of humankind—it is difficult to avoid the conclusion that Calvin consistently uses a perspectival approach in his doctrine of the *imago dei*. His use of shifting perspectives allows him to stress both the relational and the substantial aspects of the image of God and both the discontinuity and continuity of the image of God after the Fall. By focusing on only one side of each of these issues, scholars have missed the comprehensiveness and elegant complexity of Calvin's doctrine of the *imago dei*.[95] With this in mind it is easy to regard the entire Barth-Brunner controversy over the "point of contact" as a misplaced debate, for Calvin espouses both their positions.[96] I do not claim that the shifting perspectives thesis solves all the difficulties of interpreting Calvin's varied statements on the *imago dei*. Calvin is not always as cooperative as one would like, and one can find instances in which he mixes the natural/supernatural and defaced/effaced terminology in maddeningly confusing ways.[97] However, this interpretation does point to a consistent pattern in the texts themselves, so that there is no need to either impose an extraneous theological unity upon them or take refuge in a theory of inconsistency.

Controversy No. 6: Whether the Restored "Imago Dei" in Jesus Christ Takes Precedence Over the Created "Imago Dei" in Adam and Eve

Like the theory of the exclusively negative function of the remnant, the theory that the *imago dei* is to be interpreted exclusively through the restored image in Jesus Christ commonly appears in the Calvin literature. Both Niesel and Torrance, as well as

many others, underline this.[98] Once again I must argue that though
the general observation is correct, it represents only one side of his
complex, perspectival view. Calvin does say in the *Institutes* and
elsewhere that nowhere else can one recognize the excellent gifts of
the *imago dei* than in the restored image in Jesus Christ.[99] And he
does speak of Christ as *the* lively image and as the *proper "facture"*
of God, a work which is far superior to Adam.[100] However, Calvin's
confession of the excellence of Jesus Christ and his insistence on the
necessity of viewing the image of God through Jesus Christ do not
constitute his entire view of the image of Christ and Adam. Failing
to see this, scholars have concluded that Calvin's doctrine of the
imago dei is focused exclusively in Christ. But Calvin does not
advise his readers that the *imago dei* in humankind is known *only*
through Jesus Christ, or even that one must begin with Jesus Christ
to have any knowledge of the image. Rather, he points to the
centrality and decisiveness of Jesus Christ for a *full* understanding of
the image in humankind. The revelation of the image in Jesus Christ
displays more vividly and fully what humankind was created to be.
Thus, it completes, clarifies, and judges all other knowledge people
may glean about the image from the remnants. But this is not all
Calvin says. Knowledge of the fullness of the image in Jesus Christ
does not do away with the importance and necessity of knowledge of
the image through the remnants.[101] While the definition of the
imago dei as Jesus Christ, or as the mark of Christ on believers in
baptism, may be the primary meaning, it is not the *only* meaning.
And those who focus on this primary meaning to the exclusion of the
other meaning, therefore, distort Calvin's view. Specifically, their
emphasis on the exclusivity of the image in Christ leads them to
ignore or neglect Calvin's discussion of those endowments in human
nature which do remain after the Fall *for all to see*. While believers,
because of their knowledge of the image in Jesus Christ, may be
aware that these endowments are gifts from the giver of every good
gift and may respond with gratitude and praise, unbelievers possess
their own knowledge of the image of God in humankind. This
knowledge enables them to respond with genuine respect and justice to their companions. A fuller discussion of the general relationship between "natural knowledge" and "heavenly knowledge"
appears in the next chapter. For the moment I want to note only that
those studies which present Calvin's doctrine of the *imago dei* as
little more than an extension of or derivation from his Christology
are incomplete. Failing to attend to Calvin's positive use of the

remnant theory, they offer onesided impressions of this aspect of his doctrine of the *imago dei*.

Conclusion

The foregoing analysis of the six controversies over Calvin's doctrine of the *imago dei* demonstrates that the dynamic perspectival structure, consisting of the basic distinction between the human and divine perspectives and its variations in the doctrines of creation and redemption, not only is present in this part of Calvin's anthropology, but also assists us in interpreting this exceptionally difficult area of his thought. Calvin claims that the *imago dei* is both nature and humankind, both body and soul, both nature and supernature, both obscured and lost, both Adam and Christ, and does not argue, implicitly or explicitly, for the consistency of these two radically different sets of claims. The distinctive dynamic perspectival structure that pervades this area of his thought, however, provides his varied statements on the *imago dei* with a broad unity, a unity in which these necessarily contradictory yet complementary claims are interconnected as parts of a larger whole. Since Calvin's definition of the *imago dei* includes the notions of reason, the will, and the soul, his development of these anthropological issues may be expected to follow similar lines. That this is in fact the case will be demonstrated in chapters 3 through 5.

Notes

/1/ David Cairns, *The Image of God in Man*, 2nd ed., rev. (London: Collins, 1973), p. 150.

/2/ Torrance's *Calvin's Doctrine of Man*, with it exclusive focus on the model of the *imago dei* in Calvin's anthropology, is too systematic (in the pejorative sense) a presentation of Calvin's anthropology. It prevents Torrance from considering other aspects of Calvin's doctrine of humankind such as have been considered in chapters 1, 2, 4, and 5 of this study. Torrance's book would be more accurately entitled "Calvin's Doctrine of the *Imago Dei*." James Childress, in his unpublished study, "An Interpretation of Calvin's Ethics in Terms of the *Imago Dei*," (typewritten), p. 2, correctly uses the "idea of image heuristically" in order to interpret Calvin's ethics. The systematic importance of the image of God for Calvin's entire theology is concisely summarized by B. A. Gerrish in "The Mirror of God's Goodness: Man in the Theology of Calvin," *Concordia Theological Quarterly* 45 (1981): 213. While the *imago dei* is a central theme in Calvin's anthropology, it is not its exclusive focus. Further, if one seeks the distinctive feature of Calvin's anthropology, she or he will find it not in his selection of the traditional model of *imago dei* but in his perspectival approach, not only to this model, but to all anthropological issues. Further, Calvin does use other traditional models of humankind in developing his anthropology, such as *homo microcosmos* and *homo miracuclum* These are interpreted, however, through the dominant model of *homo imago dei*. See appendix 1 for a demonstration of this.

/3/ Stauffer, *Création et providence*, p. 201. Much indeed has been written on Calvin's view of the *imago dei*, including: ibid., pp. 201–5; Partee, *Calvin and Classical Philosophy*, pp. 50–54; Torrance, *Calvin's Doctrine of Man*; Cairns, *The Image of God in Man*, pp. 134–51; Dowey, *The Knowledge of God*, pp. 50–72; Nielsel, *Calvin*, pp. 67–70; and Gerrish, "The Mirror of God's Goodness." The limitations of these different presentations and analyses of Calvin's view of the *imago dei* will be presented in this chapter.

/4/ Stauffer, *Création et providence*, p. 201. Stauffer has in mind two tendencies in particular: the tendency to interpret the image as an attitude toward the creator rather than a quality conferred on the creature; and, the tendency to locate the discussion of the image in the doctrine of Christology rather than creation. Both these issues will be discussed in this chapter (See Controveries #2, #4, #5, and #6).

/5/ CO 48: 415 (Acts 17:27). My allusion here in speaking of the *imagines* and the *imago dei* is to the medieval distinction between the *vestigia* and the *imago dei*, the former referring only to creation and the latter only to humankind. See Cairns, *The Image of God in Man*, p. 86.

/6/ Torrance, *Calvin's Doctrine of Man*, p. 38. See the discussion of Torrance's work in appendix 1 of this study.

/7/ Ibid., p. 39. (Emphasis mine.)

/8/ Ibid., p. 40. (Emphasis in original).

/9/ Ibid., p. 41.

/10/ Ibid., pp. 41–42. (Emphasis mine.)

/11/ CO 9: 793, "C'est quand en toutes les parties du monde, au ciel, et en la terre, il a escrit et quasi engravé la gloire de sa puissance, bonté, sapience, et eternité." The same passage in Latin on col. 794 reads: "Sic adeo in singulis partibus istius universi sursum ac deorsum insculptas reliquit atque expressas gloriae, potentiae, bonitatis, sapientiae, aeternitatis significantissmas inscriptiones." The conclusion he draws from this is that all creatures can be "witnesses and messengers of God's glory to all men," CO 9: 795–96.

/12/ See quotations in this chapter, n. 11; n. 14; and n. 18.

/13/ CO 35: 535 (s. 1 on Ez.). (Emphasis mine.)

/14/ Ibid., "[E]t puis nous avons et haut et bas tant de signes de sa presence et du soin paternel qu'il ha de nous, que si nous ne sommes pas trop stupides et du tout despourveus d'intelligence et de raison, il faut que nous le voyons. *Car tout le monde est comme une image vive en laquelle Dieu desploye sa vertu et sa hautesse*, et puis, ce que nous sommes gouvernez sous sa main, *cela nous est encores un tesmoignage* plus familier de sa iustice, de sa grace et da sa misericorde." See pp. 54ff. of this chapter of the dissertation for an indepth discussion of whether the image is lost or only deformed in the Fall.

/15/   *CO* 55: 146 (Heb. 11:3).

/16/   For this reason Torrance's insistence that the image is not objectively present in nature, but only subjectively present in God's "beholding the works of His hands" (*Calvin's Doctrine of Man*, p. 35) or in humankind's acknowledgement of the "mute creation's" communication of the glory of God (ibid., pp. 40–42) is inaccurate.

/17/   McNeill 1:58, *Inst.* 1.5.5 in *OS* 3: 50.

/18/   See for example, *CO* 23: 686 (s. 1 on Justification), "Or regardons si ce n'est pas un beau *miroir* et excellent de la vertu infinie de Dieu, que ceste multitude infinie d'estoiles que nous voyons au ciel. . . ."; *CO* 51: 459, "Comme nous avons dit ce matin, que toutes les oeuvres de Dieu en general meritent bien que les ayons en reverence, d'autant que là il a *imprimé les marques* de sa bonté, et iustice, et vertu, et sagesse infinie"; *CO* 55: 145 (Heb. 11:3), "Continent porro haec verba optimam doctrinam: quod in hoc mundo conspicuam habeamus Dei *imaginem*." *OS* 3:45 (*Inst.* 1.5.1), "verum singulis operibus suis certas gloriae suae notas insculpsit, et quidem adeo claras et insignes ut sublata sit quamlibet rudibus et stupidis ignorantiae excusatio"; *OS* 3: 172 (*Inst.* 1.15.21) similarly; *OS* 3: 171 (*Inst.* 1.15.21).

/19/   *CO* 31: 194 (Ps. 19:1).

/20/   *OS* 5: 276–77 (Inst. 4.14.18); *CO* 31: 274 (Ps. 27:14). For Calvin this is the relationship of the sacraments, as special external signs, to the external signs of common grace in the whole of creation. Calvin also uses this distinction of the formerly clear but now obscure external signs of God's common grace and the currently clear image of God in Christ to show the historical difference between the law and the gospel, *CO* 55: 121 (Heb. 10:1).

/21/   *OS* 5: 276–77 (*Inst.* 4.14.18). Calvin adds here that God does this in order to awaken men and women out of the torpor and indifference which is common to them.

/22/   *CO* 31: 88 (Ps. 8:1). See also *OS* 3: 173 (*Inst.* 1.15.1).

/23/   *OS* 3: 178 (*Inst.* 1.15.3), "Certum est in singulis etiam mundi partibus fulgere lineamenta quaedam gloriae Dei: unde colligere licet, ubi in homine locatur eius imago, tacitam subesse antithesin quae hominem supra alias omnes creaturas extollat, et quasi separet a vulgo."

/24/   McNeill 1:88, *Inst.* 1.15.3 in *OS* 3: 178.

/25/   *CO* 7: 112 (*Contre les Anabaptistes*).

/26/   Calvin, *Psychopannychia* in *Tracts and Treatises*, 2 vols., ed. T. F. Torrance, trans. Henry Beveridge (Grand Rapids: Wm. B. Eerdmans, 1978), 2: 422–425.

/27/   *CO* 23: 26 (Gen. 1:26) where he says, "Nimis crassi fuerunt anthropomorphitae, qui eam in corpore humano quaerebant: itaque sepultum maneat illud delirium. Alii paulo subtilius, qui tametsi corporeum Deum non imaginantur, in corpore tamen hominis statuunt Dei imaginem: quia illic refulgeat tam admirabile artificium: sed haec opinio minime consentanea est scripturae, ut videbimus." For the comparison between animal and human bodies, see *CO* 44: 401–2 (Mal. 1:2).

/28/   Stauffer notes the difficulty in interpreting this aspect of Calvin's anthropology in his sermons: "le Réformateur n'a pas en face de ce problème une attitude bien determinée," Création et providence, p. 204.

/29/   McNeill 1: 188, *Inst.* 1.15.3 in *OS* 3: 178.

/30/   *OS* 3: 177 (*Inst.* 1.15.3); *CO* 23: 25–27 (Gen. 1:26). Cf. *CO* 9: 792 (1535 Preface to Olivetan's New Testament) in which he speaks of *similitudinem, imaginem,* and *notae* in the same sentence.

/31/   *CO* 32: 620 (s. 12 on Ps. 119).

/32/   *OS* 3: 176–177 (Inst. 1.15.3). (Emphasis mine.) For confirmation of this, see B. A. Gerrish's comment in *Reformers in Profile* that for Calvin the soul is not equivalent to the image, but is the seat of the image, which is properly defined as the mirror of God's goodness, p. 154.

/33/   "Il nous fault veoir où gist ceste image et ceste remambrance et similitude ou conformité de Dieu, si c'est au corps ou en l'ame . . . Il y en a beaucoup qui rapportent cecy au corps; et à la vérité il y a ung tel artifice en la nature du corps humain qu'on peult bien dire que cest ung image de Dieu. Car si sa majesté apparoist en toutes les parties du monde, par plus forte raison en ce qui est beaucoup plus exquis. Mays tant y a qu'on ne trouvera point là une telle perfection comme emporte ceste image et conformité dont parle Moyse; il s'en fault beaucoup." Quoted from unpublished sermons by Stauffer, *Création et providence*, p. 204.

/34/   *CO* 23: 25 (Gen. 1:26). See also *OS* 3: 46–47 (Inst. 1.5.3).

/35/   *CO* 33: 481 (s. on Job 10); *CO* 33: 487.

/36/   McNeill 1:187, *Inst.* 1.15.3 in *OS* 3: 177. See also his response to Osiander on the same topic in *OS* 3: 445 (*Inst.* 2.12.7) and *CO* 33: 481 and *OS* 3: 47 (*Inst.* 1.5.3), where he speaks of the infant suckling the mother's breast as a sign of the praise due to God.

/37/   *Psychopannychia* in *Tracts and Treatises*, 2: 423.

/38/   *CO* 23: 26 (Gen. 1:26).

/39/   Ibid.

/40/   Ibid.

/41/   *CO* 23: 26–27 (Gen. 1:26).

/42/   *CO* 23: 45 (Gen. 2:16).

/43/   Niesel, *The Theology of Calvin*, p. 68. Niesel goes on to say here that "it should not be asserted that the similitude to God is an addition to the creaturely status of man, that the former might even be absent. There is no neutral psychological-physical constitution of man. The fact that man was originally created in the image of God means rather that his whole psychological-physical existence was thereby moulded. . . ."

/44/   Roy W. Battenhouse, "The Doctrine of Man in Calvin and Renaissance Platonism," *Journal of the History of Ideas* 9 (1948): 447–71.

/45/   *CO* 54: 315 (s. 26 on 2 Tim. 4:2–5); *CO* 48: 417 (Acts 17:28); *CO* 34: 577 (s. 107 on Job 29); *OS* 3: 174–76 (Inst. 1.15.2); *CO* 7: 247 (*Contre la secte des Libertins*) [hereafter referred to as *Des Libertins*].

/46/   McNeill 1: 147, *Inst.* 1.3.3 in *OS* 3: 40. See also *OS* 3: 37–38 (Inst. 1.3.1); *CO* 44: 410 (Mal. 1:2). See *A Reformation Debate: Sadoleto's Letter to the Genevans and Calvin's Reply,* ed. John C. Olin, trans. Henry Beveridge (New York: Harper & Row, 1966; reprint ed., Grand Rapids: Baker Book House, 1976), p. 59 [hereafter referred to as *Reply to Sadoleto*], p. 59.

/47/   McNeill 1:188, *Inst.* 1.15.3 in *OS* 3: 178. Similar summary and comprehensive definitions of the *imago dei* may be found in: *CO* 23: 26–27 (Gen. 1:26); *CO* 33: 660; and *OS* 4: 211–12 (*Inst.* 3.12.4–3). Gerrish is correct in stating that "It is apparent that what Calvin seeks in his definition is comprehensiveness. The image is anything and everything that sets man apart from the rest of God's creation; or again, by argument back from the restoration of the image in Christ, it is anything and everything that we receive by redemption," "The Mirror of God's Goodness," p. 214. The only definition of the *imago dei* that Calvin consistently rejects as an exclusive definition is that of dominion, *CO* 23:27; *OS* 3: 47–48 (*Inst.* 1.5.4); *CO* 33: 449; *Psychopannychia* in *Tracts and Treatises*, 2:423. But even this definition is finally included in his comprehensive of the *imago* as integrity of the self.

/48/ *OS* 3: 34 (*Inst.* 1.2.1); *OS* 3: 38–39 (*Inst.* 1.3.2).

/49/ *OS* 3:37 (*Inst.* 1.3.1). For an excellent discussion of the *sensus divinitatis* in Calvin, see Dowey, *The Knowledge of God*, pp. 50–56, 72–75.

/50/ For the pairing of these two terms in Calvin's thought, see: *CO* 33: 509 (s. 41 on Job 10); *CO* 33: 157 (s. 12 on Job 3); *CO* 33: 146 (s. 11 on Job 3); *CO* 33: 759 (s. 61 on Job 18); *CO* 33: 153–54 (s. 12 on Job 3); *CO* 34: 521 (s. 103 on Job 28); *CO* 48: 415–16 (Acts 17:27); *CO* 49: 23 (Rom. 1:19); *OS* 3: 182–83 (*Inst.* 1.15.6); *OS* 3: 228–29 (*Inst.* 2.1.1).

/51/ Torrance's view, outlined in this section, has been widely accepted by both Barthian and non-Barthian Calvin scholars alike. Gerrish, for instance, says that "we can *properly* speak of man as being the divine image only when we truly refer his excellence to the exceptional gifts bestowed upon him by his maker," *Reformers in Profile*, p. 154; though he has clarified his position and stated Calvin's view more accurately in his recent article, "The Mirror of God's Goodness"; "To sum up: In Calvin's view, the image of God in man denotes not an endowment only but also a relationship," p. 215. Niesel is much less circumspect than either Torrance or Gerrish, declaring that "The divine similitude consists not in the fact that man is endowed with reason and will, but in the fact that these faculties in original man were directed wholly towards knowledge of and obedience to God," *Calvin*, p. 68. Even Cairns, in his otherwise careful study of Calvin's view of the *imago*, follows Torrance too closely in presenting Calvin's view as exclusively dynamic: " . . . the image of God in man consists in the acknowledgement of God's goodness and greatness," *The Image of God in Man*, p. 136. "Thence it may be said that man is in God's image insofar as he reflects back God's glory to him in gratitude. As Torrance has pointed out, the picture of the mirror is the governing one in Calvin's mind, though he occasionally uses the figure of an engraving," Cairns, *The Image of God*, p. 137. Recently, Stauffer has called attention to the prevalence of this one-sided interpretation of Calvin's *imago*, noting that Torrance and Niesel have over-systematized Calvin's view by saying that it is not so much "a quality conferred on man by the creator as an attitude of man toward his creator," *Création et providence*, p. 201. Stauffer attempts to correct this misinterpretation by showing that Calvin considered the *imago dei* "as a reality in each human creature" (p. 204) that remains even after the Fall. The evidence he adduces for this from Calvin's sermons and the point itself served as a valuable starting point for the expanded discussion here.

/52/ Torrance, *Calvin's Doctrine of Man*, pp. 36–37. (Emphasis mine.)

/53/   *CO* 33: 660 (s. 53 on Job 14).

/54/   *CO* 33: 145 (s. 11 on Job 3); *CO* 32: 594 (s. 10 on Ps. 119); *CO* 32: 717–18 (s. 20 on Ps. 119); *CO* 51: 599 (s. 28 on Eph.); *CO* 33: 145–46 (s. 11 on Job 3, baptism).

/55/   *CO* 33: 153–54, 482; *CO* 35: 47–48; *CO* 34: 643; *CO* 27: 8; *CO* 45: 365 (Mt. 13:21); *CO* 47: 382 (Jn. 17:11); *OS* 5: 313 (*Inst.* 4.16.9). These and the other metaphors he uses show that the mirror metaphor is only one among many and not the controlling metaphor in Calvin's thought on the *imago*.

/56/   Calvin himself uses the same "qualifying language" with the mirror metaphor that Torrance says he uses only for the engraving metaphors. For example, in *CO* 8: 102 he says that in the land of Canaan "sainct Paul donc nous represente, *comme en un miroir,* que Dieu. . . ." (Emphasis mine.)

/57/   Torrance, *Calvin's Doctrine of Man,* p. 39. See also his conclusion to this chapter on p. 51: "That is man's true rectitude: to be created in the image of God is to be opposite to or to respond to Him in such a way that God may be able to behold Himself in man as in a mirror."

/58/   Ibid., p. 39. The quotation is taken from the sermon on Job 10:7 (*CO* 33: 481): "Because he is not cruel, it is certain that the acknowledges His own work. God, in a manner of speaking, mirrors Himself and contemplates Himself in men. The original reads: "Car il n'est point cruel, il est certain qu'il recognoist son ouvrage. Dieu par maniere de dire, se mire et se contemple aus hommes. . . ."

/59/   Ibid., p. 52. See also, p. 61: "*Imago dei* is thus man's destiny in God's gracious intention. It is the original truth of his being which is also future."

/60/   Ibid., p. 47. He also says on p. 77 that "If in Calvin's thought the *imago dei* has thus to do first of all with God's gracious beholding of man as His child, which is the objective basis of the *imago,* and then with man's response to that declaration of God's grace in coming to Him as a Father and yielding to Him the gratitude and honor which are due in such a filial relation, which is the subjective basis for the *imago,* it is implied throughout that God has created man just for this relation with God and in that relationship has already given the *imago dei* its being in the sphere of man's understanding." See also his claim on p. 62 that the image is therefore dynamic and not substantive.

/61/   Ibid., p. 80.

/62/   *CO* 37: 21 (Is. 40:21), "God has exhibited this world as a mirror to men, that by beholding it they may acknowledge his majesty, so that it is a lively image of invisible things. . . ."; *CO* 9:823 (Preface des Anciennes Bibles Genevois, 1446): Scripture is "un miroir auquel nous contemplons la face de Dieu, pour estre transfigurez en sa gloire"; *CO* 35: 535 (s. on Ez.): Scripture is "le vray miroir"; *CO* 12: 645 (Letter #982 to Budé family): lives of other Christians can be mirrors.

/63/   *CO* 33: 759 (Job 15); *CO* 47: 5 (Jn. 1:4).

/64/   *CO* 33: 476 (s. 38 on Job 10). See also *CO* 35: 568 (s. 4 on Ez.).

/65/   *CO* 33: 539 (s. 43 on Job 11); *CO* 48: 414–15 (Acts 17:26); *CO* 23: 33 (Gen. 2:3).

/66/   *CO* 33: 197–98 (s. 15 on Job 4). For Juan Luis Vives's "A Fable About Man," see *The Renaissance Philosophy of Man,* ed. Ernst Cassirer (Chicago: University of Chicago Press, 1948), pp. 387–93. For Cicero's comment, see *On the Nature of the Gods* 2: 56.

/67/ Stauffer, *Création et providence*, p. 201.

/68/ Niesel, *Theology of Calvin*, p. 81.

/69/ Torrance, *Calvin's Doctrine of Man*, p. 95. See also p. 83. On p. 88 Torrance points out that Calvin's doctrine of total depravity can only be seen in relation to his doctrine of justification, but he does not relate this insight to his discussion of the erasure/effacement of the image. Thus he concludes: "There is no doubt that the student of Calvin is faced with a difficult problem here, for *in spite of* taking this total view of man's corruption, Calvin can still admit that *something remains* in fallen man." (Emphasis mine.) In other words, Torrance himself is not persuaded that his theory of the supernatural/natural distinction solves the problem of the fallen image in Calvin.

/70/ NcNeill 1:260, *Inst.* 2.2.4 in *OS* 3: 245.

/71/ See *OS* 3: 254–56 (*Inst.* 2.2.12); *CO* 23: 100 (Gen. 4:20).

/72/ *OS* 3: 244–47 (*Inst.* 2.2.4).

/73/ Torrance, *Calvin's Doctrine of Man*, p. 93. On p. 101, however, Torrance says that Calvin is consistent and clear in his views of reason after the Fall, arguing that it functions only to condemn and to lead to perversion.

/74/ Ibid., pp. 93–94.

/75/ Ibid., p. 97.

/76/ Ibid., p. 99. He also says here that the purpose of this remnant is for humankind to merit God's wrath. His statement that the image remains over but not in seems to be in contradiction to his earlier statement on p. 97 that "all creatures reflect God's image" in the sense that they are the work of God as natural creatures.

/77/ Cairns *suggests* such an interpretation, saying that "When Calvin talks of what God gives in the image, then he says it is not wholly lost, but when he speaks of what we contribute, then he must talk of it as obliterated in the natural man since the Fall," *The Image of God in Man*, p. 140. Gerrish also suggests it in "The Mirror of God's Goodness," pp. 219–20.

/78/ *CO* 40: 456 (Lec. on Ez. 18, *deleta*); *CO* 31: 93 (Ps. 8:6, *deleta*); *CO* 23: 52 (Gen. 3:1, *deleta*); *OS* 4: 22 (Inst. 3.2.12, *deleri*); *CO* 27: 8 (s. 69 on Dt., *aneantis*); *CO* 31: 101 (Ps. 9:11); *CO* 33: 482 (s. 39 on Job 10); *CO* 51: 350 (Eph. 2:1, *exstinguitur*); *CO* 49: 95 (Rom. 5:12, *depravavit, abdicatus*); *CO* 47: 57 (Jn. 3:6), "Quare non tam unusquisque nostrum a parentibus suis vitium et corruptionem contrahit, quam omnes pariter in uno Adam corrupti sumus, quia statim post eius defectionem Deus, quod naturae humanae dederat, abstulit"; *CO* 23: 62 (Gen. 3:6, *spoliati, perditi*); *CO.* 50: 568 (s. 23 on Gal., *effacé*); *CO* 33: 482 (s. 39 on Job 10, *effacé*); *CO* 33: 512–13 (*effacé*).

/79/ For example in *CO* 33: 694 (s. 56 on Job) and *CO* 50: 598 (s. 26 on Gal.) where he prefaces the deletion or loss with "*comme.*"

/80/ *CO* 23: 62 (Gen. 3:6). See also *CO* 51: 386 (s. 12 on Eph. 2: 11–13), "Car nous avons veu ce matin comme il a aneanti tout ce qui estoit des hommes, à fin qui'il n'y ait qu'un seul fondement de salut, c'est à scavoir, la pure bonté de Dieu"; *CO* 31: 92–93 (Ps. 8:6), where having just defined the image as consisting in hope for immortality, reason, conscience, will, and religion (making no distinction between the supernatural and natural gifts), he concludes that they are all destroyed. Also, his use of the term "denuded" implies that the loss is not reserved to the supernatural gifts alone but is total, *CO* 9: 792, 794. Or see *CO* 33: 660 (s. 53 on Job 14) where he also makes no distinction between the supernatural and natural gifts: "Car ceste image de Dieu qu'emporte-elle? Une droiture, une iustice et intregrité, que Dieu avoit là deployé ses grans thresors, tellement qu'en somme l'homme estoit comme un miroir de ceste gloire excellente qui reluit pleinement en Dieu or par le peché nous sommes alienez de *toutes ces graces* nous sommes bannis du royaume de Dieu." And see *CO* 51: 596–97 (s. 28 on Eph. 4:17): "Car quand les philosophes ont parlé de l'excellence et de la dignité qui est en la nature humaine, ils ont toujours mis la raison comme un principauté. Et puis ils ont mis la discretion d'entre le bien and le mal, quand les hommes disputent en eux et qu'ils cherchent, qu'ils font leurs revolutions: voilà comme un bureau qu'ils ont dressé, à fin de constituer l'homme iuge du bien et du mal. Il sembleroit donc que saint Paul aneantist ici par trop les hommes, quand il dit que la raison n'a en soy que vanité, mensonge et tromperie." He continues by confirming Saint Paul, noting that all other opinions of the reason of conscience of humankind are but *cuider*. *CO* 23: 62 (Gen 3:6) states that we have lost all our gifts, not only the holy spirit, but also reason and justice.

/81/   *CO* 51: 621 (Eph. 4:23–26); *CO* 40: 456 (Lec. on Ez. 18); *CO* 51: 459 (s. 18 on Eph.); *CO* 47: 388 (Jn. 17:22); *CO* 48: 418 (Acts 17:28); *CO* 49: 106–7 (Rom. 6:5); *CO* 27: 204 (s. 84 on Dt. 12); *CO* 27: 8 (s. 49 on Dt. 10). It is only in this context that Cairns's statement that there is a break between the natural person and the redeemed person which does not involve any gradual transition is correct, *The Image of God in Man*, p. 110.

/82/   *CO* 51: 386. In a later sermon on Ephesians he complains that the philosophers have left too much dignity to human nature and that such a view must be contradicted since it leaves a foothold for humankind on the ladder of grace. He supplies the contradiction by emphasizing that humankind is nothing, neither rational nor just nor discerning, without redemption in the spirit and Christ, *CO* 5: 596.

/83/   *CO* 9: 743 (*Confession de foi des eglises de France*).

/84/   *CO* 31: 589 (Ps. 62:10), "*evanescere in nihilum.*"

/85/   *CO* 35: 47–48 (s. 122 on Job 33); *CO* 7: 347 (Letter to Cordelier); *CO* 51: 562 (s. on Eph 4:20); *CO* 33: 694 (s. 56 on Job 15); *CO* 51: 379 (s. 11 on Eph. 2:8–10).

/86/   For dominion, see: *CO* 23: 143 (Gen. 9:2, *reliquiae*); *CO* 33: 277 (s. 22 on Job 5). See *CO* 31: 95 (Ps. 8) for his listing of the *reliquias* of reason, conscience, religion, and community.

/87/   For reason see: *OS* 3: 255 (*Inst.* 2.2.12); *OS* 3: 259 (*Inst.* 2.2.17), "in universo genere humano perspici naturae nostrae propriam esse rationem"; *OS* 3: 257 (*Inst.* 2.2.14); *CO* 58: 200 (*Response à certaines calomnies*); *CO* 7: 202; *CO* 51: 592 (s. 28 on Eph. 4:17–19). See also pp. 80ff. of chapter 3. For conscience, see: *CO* 35: 239 (s. 137 on Job), "il nous laisse quelque discretion de bien et de mal imprimee en nos coeurs"; *CO* 7: 183; *CO* 23: 65 (Gen. 3:8), "Insculptam est omnium cordibus boni et mali discrimen. . . ." For a fuller discussion of this, see chapter 4, pp. 132ff. The large number of texts that express this remnant of conscience in Calvin's works, both treatises and sermons, indicates that Stauffer's claim that "Cette conception est fort rare dans la prédication. Elle n'apparait que dans quelques textes, en particulier dans le trent-neuvieme sermon sur le livre de Job," *Création et providence*, p. 205, is incorrect. Calvin does say also that the conscience is wholly lost, *CO* 51: 605 (s. 29 on Eph. 4:20–24), but this does not nullify his many statements that the conscience is not lost. The two evaluations must stand side by side in his thought as the assessments made from his shifting perspectives.

/88/   *CO* 48: 30 (Acts 2:12).

/89/   *CO* 33: 157; *CO* 49: 24; *OS* 3: 182–83 (*Inst.* 1.15.6).

/90/   As he remarks in his Commentary on Romans 1:20: "But we are not so blind that we can plead ignorance without being convicted of perversity. We form a conception of divinity, and then we conclude that we are under the necessity of worshipping such a Being, whatever his character may be. Our judgment, however, fails here before it discovers the nature or character of God. Hence the apostle in Heb. 11:13 ascribes to faith the light by which man can gain real knowledge from the work of creation," *CO* 49: 25. See *CO* 55: 71–72 (Heb. 6:4) "respondeo solos quidem electos Dei spiritu regenerationis dignari: et in hoc discerni a reprobis quis reformantur ad illius imaginem, et arrham spiritus accipiunt in spem futurae haereditatis, et eodem spiritu obsignatur in eorum cordibus evangelium. Sed hoc obstare nego quominus reprobos etiam gustu gratiae suae aspergat, irradiet eorum mentes aliquibus lucis suae scintillis, afficiat eos bonitatis suae sensu, verbumque suum utcunque eorum animis insculpat"; *OS* 3: 37 (*Inst.* 1.3.1); *OS* 3: 39 (*Inst.* 1.3.3), "Insculptum mentibus humanis esse divinitatis sensum, qui deleri numquam potest"; *CO* 47: 57 (Jn. 3:6); *CO;* 47: 6 (Jn. 1:5), "Nam omnibus ingenitum est aliquod religionis semen: deinde insculptum est eorum conscientiis boni et mali discrimen." Yet in *CO* 47: 117 (Jn. 5:25) he contradicts this by saying that although we may have remnants of understanding, and discernment, no part of humankind aspires to the heavenly life after the Fall. He means by this latter denial of a remnant of the knowledge of supernatural things that humankind is dead as far as the kingdom of God is concerned. Thus, the two evaluations are not diametrical opposites but represent two assessments from two different contexts and perspectives. From the perspective of justification, there is no seed of religion left. From the perspective of sanctification, however, there is a seed left.

/91/   Niesel, *The Theology of Calvin*, p. 102; Torrance, *Calvin's Doctrine of Man*, pp. 104–5, 112; Dowey, *The Knowledge of God*, pp. 83, 135. Partee, *Calvin and Classical Philosophy*, p. 123, simply reports Dowey's and Parker's evaluation of natural knowledge.

/92/   *CO* 7: 202 (*Des Libertins*); *CO* 51: (s. 28 on Eph. 4:17–19); *CO* 7: 193 (*Des Libertins*); *CO* 33: 212 (s. 17 on Job).

/93/   *CO* 50: 251 (Gal. 5:14).

/94/   *CO* 23: 147 (Gen. 9:6); *CO* 43: 227 (Jn. 1:13); *CO* 33: 512–13 (s. 41 on Job 10); *CO* 26: 227 (s. 29 on Dt. 4); *CO* 34: 655 (s. 113 on Job 31); *CO* 7: 204 (s. 54 on Dt. 12). See Stauffer's citations from the unpublished sermons on Genesis (*Création et providence*, p. 203) also.

/95/   For this reason Gerrish's statement that "Man is fallen man, who can possess the divine image (in the unique human sense) only as it is restored to him through Christ," *Reformers in Profile*, p. 154, is incomplete, showing only one half of Calvin's view. Likewise, Stauffer's emphasis on the image as "une realité crée en l'homme, realité qui n'est pas lié au fait que Dieu peut se réflechir ou non dans la créature humane," *Création et providence*, p. .204, is incomplete because it shows only the other half of Calvin's view. Calvin's dipolar view of the image of God presents it as both a substantial and a relational reality, a fact which Gerrish claims in his more recent work, "The Mirror of God's Goodness," p. 214. Cairns simply says that his definition of image as gratitude is not exhaustive, *The Image of God in Man*, p. 139.

/96/   See Dowey's discussion of the texts in "The Barth-Brunner Controversy on Calvin," appendix 3 of *The Knowledge of God*, pp. 247–49. Dowey attributes the misunderstandings to their failure to keep the distinction between the natural and revealed knowledge of God in mind.

/97/   *CO* 9: 743, "Nous croyons que l'homme, ayant estré crée pur et entier et conforme à l'image de Dieu, est par sa propre faute decheu de la grace qu'il avoit receue: et ainsi s'est aliené de Dieu qui est la fontaine de iustice et de tous biens: en sorte que sa nature est de tout corrumpue. Et estant aveuglé en son esprit et depravé en son coeur, a perdu toute integrité sans avoir rien de residu. Et combien qu'il ait encores quelque discretion du bien et du mal, toutes fois nous disons que ce qu'il ha de clarté se convertit en tenebres, quand il est question de chercher Dieu, tellement qu'il n'en peut nullement approcher par son intelligence et raison. Et combien qu'il ait volunté par laquelle il est incité à faire cecy ou cela, toutesfois qu'elle est du tout captive sous peché, tellement qu'il n'ha nulle liberté sinon celle que Dieu luy donne."

/98/   Niesel, *Theology of Calvin*, p. 70, "There is no theological anthropology which can exist apart from Christology. . . ."; Torrance, *Calvin's Doctrine of Man*, pp. 36, 52, 80; see also Cairns, *The Image of God in Man*, p. 137, "Calvin followed Luther in his equation of the image with man's original righteousness and restoration in Christ. He has, therefore, chosen the New Testament image as fundamental and he is thus faced with the problem of relating it to the Old Testament image, which is common to all mankind." It is my view that Calvin solves this problem of the Old and New Testament images with his use of the two perspectives. Also see Stauffer, *Création et providence*, p. 201.

/99/   *OS* 3: 179 (*Inst.* 1.15.4). See also *CO* 49: 95 (Rom. 5:12).

/100/   *CO* 53: 628 (s. 52 on 1 Tim.); *CO* 47: 19 (Jn. 1:18); *CO* 49: 559 (1 Cor. 15:47); *CO* 33: 694 (s. 56 on Job 14); *OS* 4: 1 (*Inst.* 3.2.1); *OS* 4: 30 (*Inst.* 3.2.20); *CO* 33: 690 (s. 55 on Job 14).

/101/   *CO* 51: 191 (Eph. 4:24); *OS* 3: 398–99 (*Inst.* 2.9.1); *CO* 9: 815–16. *OS* 1: 37–38 (1536 edition of the Institutes) shows this relationship very clearly).

CHAPTER III

HEAVENLY WISDOM AND EARTHLY WISDOM

> As truth is most precious, so all confess it to be so. And yet, since God alone is the source of all good, you must not doubt that whatever truth you anywhere meet with proceeds from him, unless you would be doubly ungrateful to him; it is in this way you have received the word descended from heaven.
>
> Letter to Bucer, 1549

Heavenly Wisdom and Earthly Wisdom in Relation

The issue of the use of reason in Christian theology is traditionally spoken of as Reason and Revelation or Faith and Reason. Although in this chapter we will examine topics related to this issue, I have assigned a somewhat different title to the discussion. Calvin does indeed use the terms "reason" *(ratio, raison)* and "faith" *(fides, foi)* quite often.[1] He also uses the terms "knowledge" *(cognitio, cognoissance)* and "understanding" *(entendement)* frequently.[2] His most characteristic term, however, is "wisdom" *(sapientia, sagesse)*, and in his use this one term includes both faith and reason. His revision of the first sentence of the *Institutes* in the second edition indicates his concern to find a comprehensive term for his religious epistemology. The 1536 edition reads: "Almost the whole of sacred doctrine [*sacra doctrina*] consists of two parts: knowledge of God and of ourselves"; while the 1539 edition reads "Almost the whole of our wisdom [*sapientia nostra*] . . . ."[3] Most of Calvin's terms and discussions related to this issue are better understood in reference to the general category of wisdom.[4] Also, Calvin himself, both in the *Institutes* and his commentaries, more frequently uses the term "wisdom" than "knowledge," "reason," or "understanding." I have chosen the title "Heavenly Wisdom and Earthly Wisdom" for this chapter both because of its appropriateness to the discussion and its frequent use by Calvin.

One of the major questions to be addressed in this chapter is whether or not Calvin's view of the relation between earthly and heavenly wisdom fits a particular type for understanding reason and revelation. As a first step toward answering this question, I will examine his use of the comprehensive term wisdom. Does his view of the relation between earthly wisdom and heavenly wisdom fit one of the classic types in Christian theology for understanding reason and revelation; (1) Reason and Revelation in Mutual Harmony, (2) Reason and Revelation Mutually Opposed, (3) Revelation Dominant, (4) Reason Dominant, or (5) Reason as Preparation for Revelation?[5] The answer to this question shows, once again, his complex and consistently used perspectival approach. Understanding this is crucial to understanding correctly his individual statements on "faith and reason" as well as his position on the use of philosophy.

Controversies Over Calvin's Type of Reason and Revelation Relation

The question of which Reason and Revelation type fits Calvin best has received diverse answers. Some claim that Calvin clearly exemplifies the Reason and Revelation in Mutual Harmony type; others the Reason and Revelation Mutually Opposed type. Still others, noting the difficulties in interpreting Calvin's divergent statements on this issue, conclude that, though he was inconsistent or ambivalent, the core of his position falls within one of these two types or the Revelation Dominant type.[6] When Calvin's view is analyzed in detail, each of these conclusions appears both correct and incorrect. They are correct because each points to a definite part of Calvin's position. They are incorrect because they are incomplete; they either present a part of his position as the whole or assert the final inconsistency of his position.

Those who argue that Calvin best fits the Reason and Revelation Mutually Opposed type have no trouble finding textual evidence to support their conclusion. Few readers of Calvin have missed his mocking of reason and his panegyrics on faith. Calvin's negative remarks on reason cannot be denied. However, they must be interpreted properly. His devaluations of temporal and earthly wisdom fall into two basic groups: assessments made from the perspectives of God as creator and God as judge.

When seen from the vantage point of the one, eternal creator, all temporal wisdom appears frail, uncertain, even impotent. *Strictly speaking*, God alone is truth and heavenly wisdom alone is wisdom. What is temporal wisdom in comparison with the eternal wisdom of God? Calvin's answer is extreme.

> [T]here is no wisdom [*sagesse*] or human doctrine which deserves to be compared to that which we learn in the school of God. It is true that one can study human doctrines and acquire a certain judgment from them; we know that letters serve to polish the good natural sense of a man. But what is the upshot of all this, when we have achieved the most perfect knowledge known to man in all things, that is, in all that we can be instructed by men? This is nothing but the ABCs! because all this knowledge pertains to the present life and does not bring us up to the heavens. Just as our life is fragile and nothing, so we must confess that all the knowledge [*science*] we learn from men is nothing but smoke; it's a transitory thing which evaporates. And, just as there is nothing other than the kingdom of the eternal God, so there is nothing but his unique truth, which is a permanent wisdom [*sagesse*], a certain foundation, and a truth which is lasting. Here, then, is what David wanted to show us: that we can indeed be instructed by men, but this is only an ABC until we enter the school of God.[7]

From this perspective, in contrast to the eternal wisdom of God, all human knowledge, however good and valuable in itself, appears as nothing but childish babbling. It is in this context that Calvin speaks of the eternal wisdom as "mysterious," "hidden," so far above and beyond temporal wisdom that it cannot be penetrated by it.[8] It is in this context, also, that Calvin contrasts the uncertainty of all temporal wisdom with the "degree of uncertainty which is beyond the capacity of the human mind" but which is given with faith.[9] All that is not the truth of heavenly wisdom is opinion, says Calvin, in a clear allusion to Plato's distinction between *epistemē* and *doxa*. For this reason all human knowledge, whether it results from the study of letters, philosophy, or custom, cannot ground self-knowledge; it is too uncertain to deliver the absolute truth on which eternal life depends. The two types of wisdom, then, lead to two types of trust and uncertainty.

> Hence we learn from this passage what manner of trust we are
> to have in the gospel. It is a trust which does not depend on
> human authority, but rests on the known and certain truth of
> God, and is lifted above the world. In a word, it is as far
> removed from conjecture as heaven is from earth.[10]

Here Calvin is clearly stating his preference for and approval of the
absolute wisdom given in faith.[11] However, it is important to note
that by using the comparison between heaven and earth as his
analogy here Calvin is drawing our attention to the *contrast* rather
than the *contradiction* between eternal and temporal wisdom. Like
some of his presentations of temporal life that we analyzed in chapter 1, temporal wisdom here is presented as fragile and empty *only
in contrast* to the solid and full wisdom of God's truth. Seen on its
own, it is certainly necessary and valuable for the journey toward
eternal life. Seen from the perspective of God as creator, however, it
is nothing. From this perspective Adam and Eve's wisdom about the
garden, even before they fell, was smoke compared to the word God
addressed to them and the wisdom they would have in their eternal
life. These particular negative judgments on temporal wisdom,
then, must be interpreted from the perspective of God as creator.
They do not, therefore, suggest that Calvin intended a wholesale
rejection of the value of reason for Christian faith.

Calvin's attacks on reason are at times far harsher, however,
than these contrasts between temporal and eternal wisdom. In
addition to contrasting uncertain temporal wisdom with absolute
eternal wisdom, he opposes the blindness of earthly wisdom to the
full light of revelation. He intends by such remarks to say that there
is absolutely no wisdom, "not even a spark," without God.[12] Without the spirit of God's wisdom enlightening them, people have no
conscience, no taste of the future life, no knowledge of God, and
even no reason or intelligence at all.[13] We are all blind by birth,
living in a darkness which only Jesus Christ can illumine.[14] When
elaborating on this blindness Calvin offers an even more extreme
judgment upon earthly wisdom.

> We are indeed all born blind, but yet amid the darkness of
> corruption and vitiation in nature some sparks still shine, so
> that men are different from the brute beasts. Now if any man is
> puffed up by proud confidence in his own reason and refuses to
> submit to God, he may seem, apart from Christ, to be wise,
> but Christ's brightness will make him foolish. For the vanity of

the human mind only begins to appear when heavenly wisdom
is brought into view.[15]

When Calvin speaks here of heavenly wisdom, he has something
different in mind from a truth surpassing the capacity of the human
mind in the way literary eloquence surpasses the ABCs. When he
refers to the heavenly wisdom *of Christ* he usually means the
judgment of God on the corruption of the human mind. The heavenly wisdom of Christ is in contradiction to all earthly wisdom and
vice versa. From this perspective of God as judge, all earthly
wisdom appears not just as fragile and fleeting and crude, but as
falsehood, pure folly, and "the mother of all errors.[16] It can only lead
us astray, deceive us.

> Our reason is so overwhelmed by so many forms of deception,
> is subject to so many errors, dashes against so many obstacles,
> is caught in so many difficulties, that it is far from directing us
> aright. . . . [O]ur diligence, insight, understanding, and care-
> fulness [are] so completely corrupted that we can devise or
> prepare nothing right in God's eyes. No wonder that it seems
> too hard for us who grudgingly suffer ourselves to be deprived
> of the gifts of reason, which we count the most precious gift of
> all! But to the Holy Spirit, who "knows that all the thought of
> the wise are futile" and who clearly declares that "every imag-
> ination of the human heart is solely evil," it seems most fitting.
> If whatever our nature conceives, instigates, understands, and
> attempts is always evil, how can that which is pleasing to God,
> to whom holiness and righteousness alone are acceptable, ever
> enter our minds? Thus we see that the reason of our mind,
> wherever it may turn, is miserably subject to vanity.[17]

Because it is so deceitful, earthly wisdom is looked down upon as
carnal by those who are enlightened by the spirit of God.[18]

These devaluations of earthly wisdom as contradictions to
heavenly wisdom are absolute. All wisdom apart from the spirit of
God, whether found in the Persians, the Greeks, or the church, is
prone to falsehood and deceit. Everything that is apart from Christ
and the Holy Spirit is "fleshly wisdom."[19] These statements about
our total blindness, the obliteration of our capacity to reason, and
the absolute contradiction between carnal wisdom and the wisdom
of Christ are extreme. He clearly states that all wisdom is lost in the
Fall, insisting that we are all utterly blind and asking, "Can we be
wise without the wisdom of God."[20]

Yet, once again, we find that these are not the only or final evaluations Calvin makes. He also speaks of the glimmers of wisdom that all persons have after the Fall and even praises the earthly wisdom of unbelievers. He claims that all the works of God, including human beings, deserve to be revered because they bear "the marks of God's goodness, justice, power, and infinite wisdom."[21] After the Fall women and men are not totally deprived of all wisdom or reason. If they did not retain some wisdom they would be no different from asses and dogs.[22] And, this wisdom which is retained includes not only "natural reason" but a knowledge of the future life, immortality of the soul, and the existence of God.[23] Once again, then, we are faced with apparently contradictory statements. And once again, an argument will be made that he consistently uses his shifting theological perspectives to build a complex position, in this case a position which acknowledges both the absolute lack of value in earthly wisdom for salvation and the positive value of earthly wisdom for temporal life. In fact, Calvin's treatment of wisdom closely parallels his understanding of the *imago dei*. From the absolute perspective of God as judge the *imago* and earthly wisdom are totally lost; from the perspective of humankind, however, the *imago* and earthly wisdom are retained, though severely deformed. The sparks of glimmers of wisdom which remain after the Fall may be understood in the same way that the remnants of the *imago dei* are. This close parallel is suggested by Calvin's inclusion of wisdom (understood as both reason and worship) in his comprehensive definition of the *imago dei*; it will be demonstrated by the following discussion.

Two arguments must be made: first, that Calvin's negative evalutions of earthly wisdom occur within a limited theological context and cannot, therefore, be lifted out as sufficient evidence for his position on the issue of faith and reason; and second, that Calvin evaluates earthly wisdom positively. Calvin does say that the wisdom remaining in human beings after the Fall is not efficacious for salvation. It is too weak in matters of heavenly wisdom to give true and certain guidance; or, as he says, the common light of nature is "a far lowlier thing than faith."[24] The remnant of wisdom can only conceive that there is a God (*quod sit Deus*), while only heavenly wisdom can grasp "what befits us and is proper to his glory, in fine, what is to our advantage to know of him" (*qualis sit Deus*).[25] Since this latter knowledge is given only in faith, one cannot say, *properly speaking,* that God is known at all where there is no true religion.[26] His point here is simply that human wisdom is inefficacious for salvation and therefore, in that sense, said to be nonexistent. However, he goes further to suggest that it is the improper *use* of wisdom which deserves to be judged most harshly and not human wisdom itself. Often Calvin makes this clear by adding qualifying phrases to his more extreme statements. For example, he writes that "The wisdom of the world is useless and valueless *when it lifts itself up against God*"[27] or, "natural ability counts for nothing *in the kingdom of God*";[28] or, he counsels that we should despise and spit in the faces of the most subtle and wisest ones of the world, *if they "rail against God*";[29] or, finally, he warns that *when carnal reason is not properly bridled by humble obedience to God and aimed at the service of God,* it is dangerous.[30]

In several extended passages Calvin makes the soteriological context of his argument against earthly wisdom quite clear. In commenting upon Paul's statement that God had made foolish the wisdom of the world he distinguishes two forms of pride in the use of earthly wisdom: taking earthly wisdom for the whole of wisdom and not grounding it in heavenly wisdom; and attempting to penetrate heavenly wisdom by means of earthly wisdom.

> Paul here means whatever man can comprehend, not only by his own natural mental ability, but also by the help of experience, scholarship, and knowledge of the arts. For he contrasts the wisdom of the world with the wisdom of the Spirit. It follows that whatever knowledge a man may come by, apart from the enlightening of the Holy Spirit, is included in the wisdom of this world. He says that God has made all that ridiculous, or condemned it as foolish. You must think of that as done in two ways. For whatever knowledge and understanding a man has *counts for nothing* unless it rests upon true wisdom; and it is of no more value for grasping spiritual teaching than the eye of a blind man for distinguising colors. Both of these must be carefully attended to, that (1) knowledge of all the sciences is so much smoke apart from the heavenly science of Christ; and (2) that man with all his shrewdness is as stupid about understanding by himself the mysteries of God as an ass is incapable of understanding musical harmony. For, in this way, Paul gives the lie to the consuming pride of those who exult in the wisdom of this world, so that they despise Christ and the whole teaching of salvation, thinking that they are happy if they cling to the things of this world. He also checks

> the arrogance of those who, trusting in their own capacity, seek
> to penetrate into heaven.[31]

I have quoted this passage at length because it shows so clearly that
it is particular uses of reason or earthly wisdom and not earthly
wisdom itself that Calvin condemns. Also, it specifies two uses
which are improper. It is not only those who use earthly wisdom to
storm the kingdom of God who are foolish and sinful. The more
passive response of valuing earthly wisdom as an ultimate good
rather than as a relative good is also foolish and sinful. This second
form of rebellion demonstrates the unity of Calvin's view of the
created eschatological structure of humankind, the *imago dei*, and
earthly wisdom. To deny the superior value of heavenly wisdom by
clinging to the wisdom of the present life is to refuse the purpose for
which human beings were created: to enjoy God now and in the
future life. Taking earthly wisdom as the ultimate and sufficient
wisdom denies the eschatological structure, the *imago dei* and the
knowledge of God implanted in all. It is thus a form of rebellion
against God to refuse to use the gift of earthly wisdom for the
purpose for which it was intended. It is condemned from the perspective of God as judge.

These two forms of sin involving the use of earthly wisdom
suggests that there is proper and positive use of earthly wisdom.
This is, in fact, the case, as the following lengthly passage makes
clear.

> At the same time an answer is given to the question, how it
> comes about that Paul throws to the ground, in this way, every
> kind of knowledge which exists apart from Christ, and, as it
> were, tramples under his feet what is well known to be the
> chief gift of God in this world. For what is more noble than the
> reason of man, by which he stands out far above all other
> animals? How greatly deserving of honour are the liberal sci-
> ences, which refine man in such a way as to make him truly
> human! Besides, what a great number of rare products they
> yield! Who would not use the highest praise to extol states-
> manship, by which states, empires, and kingdoms are main-
> tained?—to say nothing of other things! I maintain that the
> answer to this question is obvious from the fact that Paul does
> not utterly condemn, either the natural insight of men, or
> wisdom gained by practice and experience, or education of the
> mind through learning; but what he affirms is that all those
> things are useless for obtaining spiritual wisdom. And it is
> certainly madness for any one to presume to ascend to heaven,

relying on his own acumen, or the help of learning; in other words, to investigate the secret mysteries of the kingdom of God, or force his way through to a knowledge of them, for they are hidden from human perception. Let us therefore take note that we ought to confine to the circumstances of the present case what Paul teaches here about the futility of the wisdom of this world, viz. that is remains on the level of this world but does not reach to heaven at all. It is also true, in other ways, that apart from Christ every branch of human knowledge is futile, and the man who is well grounded in every aspect of learning but is yet ignorant of God, has nothing: quickness of mind, shrewd judgement, liberal sciences, knowledge of languages, all are in some way spoiled, whenever they fall into the hands of ungodly men.[32]

This passage indicates that Calvin sees a use for the remnants of wisdom in human beings other than to insure the guilt of all sinners. This positive use will be discussed in a moment. This passage also makes it clear that Calvin's harsh judgment of all earthly wisdom as utter blindness and foolishness is made within a specific context, that is, from the perspective of God as redeemer. When the issue is salvation, human merit and God's grace, then the only thing that one can say is that we are "absolutely destitute of all wisdom and righteousness."[33] Because the "gospel *deprives us of all credit for wisdom*, virtue, and righteousness, and leaves us with nothing but the utmost ignominy," we must confess that we are stripped of all wisdom.[34] When the question is salvation, one cannot speak of sharing wisdom with God; this would be to make a "pact" similar to the pact of cooperation the Romans make between the will of human beings and the will of God.[35] Since there is no partial wisdom from the perspective of God as redeemer we must be "emptied of our own understanding" if we wish to reach saving knowledge.[36] Christians, then, in this view, are opposed to the proud and wise because of their humility and foolish ignorance. They alone are truly wise, however, for the beginning of their piety is the knowledge that God alone is wise and they are ignorant. True self-knowledge requires such learned ignorance, the confession of how little one knows, just as much as it requires a confession of one's lack of dignity and the loss of the *imago dei* in sin.[37] Further, true wisdom attaches this humble confession to humble obedience to God, for the beginning of piety is "the willingness to be taught when we have renounced our own judgment and follow wherever God calls."[38] Its rule is "Listen and obey."[39] True wisdom, therefore, recognizes the limits

of its understanding within God's will and submits to God's ac-
comodations; it does not try to ascend to God, but waits for God to
descend to it.[40] For this reason, true wisdom belongs only to the
disciples of Christ, for Christ alone is wisdom, the light of all
truth.[41] Believers "attain full perfection of wisdom in him."[42] This is
the only ascent possible he claims, through the pure wisdom of
Jesus Christ, which raises one far above all earthly wisdom.[43] This
perfect wisdom of believers in Christ, however, appears foolish and
ignorant to the world. Calvin at times glories in the contradiction
between the apparent foolishness of heavenly wisdom and the supposed achievements of earthly wisdom. In doing so he underlines
the equality of the students in the school of Christ and eschews
intellectual as well as spiritual elitism. He reasons that

> God preferred to call the poor and foolish and the obscure of
> birth, before the great and wise and highborn. Had God
> treated all on equal terms, that would never have sufficed for
> the breaking of human arrogance. So he pushes aside those
> who appeared to be superior, so that He might really reduce
> them in standing. [This does not mean that the wise and the
> great are not saved, for] . . . in putting the strong and wise and
> great to shame, God does not exalt the weak and uneducated
> and worthless, but brings them all down to one common
> level.[44]

The common level of all women and men is their status as ignorant
and sinful creatures before God. All need to be students in the
school of Christ, therefore, since all are totally lacking in wisdom.

From the perspectives of God as creator and God as judge,
then, Calvin sees an infinite contrast between temporal and eternal
wisdom and an absolute contradiction between earthly and heavenly
wisdom. In both instances earthly wisdom is presented in predominantly negative terms. However, this is not the whole of his view. As
we suggested earlier, Calvin also envisions a positive use of human
wisdom in terms of the remnant theory of the *imago dei*. Just as the
entire *imago dei* functions two ways after sin, both negatively and
positively, so the remnants of wisdom function in two ways. The
first, negative function of earthly wisdom is rarely missed by Calvin
scholars. Just as many asserted that the only function of the remnants of the *imago dei* was to render all inexcusable before God, so
many conclude that the sparks of intelligence or natural knowledge
that remain after sin function only to condemn human beings.[45]

This conclusion, like that about the *imago dei* as a whole, is only partially correct. Calvin does indeed say often that while some sparks of intelligence remain, they do not enable persons to see the way, and so they "shine in the darkness to render men without excuse."[46] "The right order of things," according to Calvin, was surely that persons "contemplating the wisdom of God in His works by the aid of the innate light of [their] own natural ability" might come to knowledge of God. But this order was perverted by sin and persons do not acknowledge God in his works, even though they remain bound to do so because of the remains of wisdom which exist in them.[47] God continues to attract sweetly persons to the knowledge of himself, but since they follow their own order, they arrive only at error and vanity instead of true and saving knowledge.[48] This factory of idols which results from the remnants of wisdom after the Fall is the way in which Calvin interprets Plato's myth of the cave.[49]

> For when the Gospel is removed like the extinguishing of a light, the fallacious and feeble wisdom of the flesh shines in the darkness and gains control, and indeed a spurious sanctity spreads its proud wings everywhere. But as soon as the only Sun of Righteousness, Christ, bursts on the scene with the brightness of this gospel, those things which were previously filling its place of supreme honor not only vanish, but are looked upon as filth. Naturally that gives rise to those tears! This is the fatal stumbling block to which Paul refers elsewhere, that "seeking to establish their own righteousness, they did not subject themselves to the righteousness of God" (Romans 10:3).[50]

It is pride and not corporeality which keeps people from the truth and lures them with false images according to Calvin. The shadows of earthly wisdom are exposed only when the sun, the heavenly wisdom of Christ, appears. Heavenly wisdom, then judges all earthly wisdom as idolatry (filth) and all who lack Christ as ignorant and sinful. All are held responsible for their faulty sight, however, because enough sparks of light remain to light the way to truth.[51]

There is no doubt that Calvin views the remnants of wisdom as accusing witnesses against the self as sinner from the perspective of God as judge. These remnants can also be viewed, however, from the perspective of humankind; when they are, their positive role in human life comes into focus. Its major positive function is to preserve order in the creation, as Calvin suggests in his famous distinction between earthly and heavenly knowledge in the *Institutes*.

> This, then, is the distinction: that there is one kind of under-
> standing [*intelligentia*] of earthly things; another of heavenly. I
> call "earthly things" those which do not pertain to God or his
> kingdom, to true justice or to the blessedness of the future life;
> but which have their significance and relationship with regard
> to the present life and are, in a sense, confined within its
> bounds. I call "heavenly things" the pure knowledge of God,
> the nature of true righteousness, and the mysteries of the
> heavenly kingdom. The first class includes government, house-
> hold management, all mechanical skills, and the liberal arts. In
> the second are the knowledge of God and his will, and the rule
> by which we conform our life to it.[52]

We are clever enough, Calvin seems to be saying, when it comes to
matters of our present life. Although we do not have perfect knowledge of "earthly things" and we often sin by proudly overrating our
abilities in these areas, this wisdom is nonetheless a positive thing.[53]
It maintains order in the world (government, domestic economy,
ecclesiastical authority) and it can even help to render persons more
humane (liberal arts). These remnants of earthly wisdom, then,
preserve God's good creation for the benefit of all.

These remnants existing in women and men also serve another
function; they elicit praise from believers for the benevolent God
who shows special grace even in common nature. The keenness, wit,
and judgment one witnesses in unbelievers as well as believers must
be acknowledged as gifts of a bountiful God. Furthermore, since
God is the sole author of all the wisdom with which persons are
endowed, this wisdom is to be counted a good and even praiseworthy thing.[54] Flowing from the source of all wisdom, earthly
wisdom is to be cherished and used for the convenience and ease of
the present life. These gifts, then, "are by no means to be despised,"
for they represent a capacity "worthy of commendation."[55] Since
these rays of divine light shine on unbelievers and believers for the
benefit of all in the present life, Christians have a duty to praise
earthly wisdom wherever they find it. If they do not, they are
ungrateful to God. They are not to confuse such sparks of wisdom
with the true and full heavenly wisdom; they are not to use earthly
wisdom for the wrong purposes; but they neglect earthly wisdom to
their own peril.

This positive understanding of earthly wisdom applies to philosophy and knowledge of the future life as well as to government
and the mechanical arts. Calvin speaks of the remnants of wisdom
that enable one to taste something of the things above and to desire

to search out the truth. These remnants do condemn everyone as guilty before God, but they also, like government, preserve order among human beings and elicit the praise of believers. Calvin's careful praise and complex understanding of the positive and negative value of philosophy will be discussed in detail in the next section of the chapter. For now I will only illustrate the point with a lengthy quotation from a letter Calvin wrote to Bucer in 1549.

> As truth is most precious, so all men confess it to be so. And yet, since God alone is the source of all good, you must not doubt, that whatever truth you anywhere meet with, proceeds from him, unless you would be doubly ungrateful to him; it is in this way you have received the word descended from heaven. For it is sinful to treat God's gifts with contempt; and to ascribe to man what is peculiarly God's is a still greater impiety. Philosophy is, consequently, the noble gift of God, and those learned men who have striven hard after it in all ages have been incited thereto by God himself, that they might enlighten the world in the knowledge of the truth. But there is a wide difference between the writings of these men and those truths which God, of his own pleasure, delivered to guilty men for their santification. In the former, you may fall in with a small particle of truth, of which you can get only a taste, sufficient to make you feel how pleasant and sweet it is; but in the latter, you may obtain in rich abundance that which can refresh the soul to the full. In the one, a shadow and an image is placed before the eyes which can only excite in you a love of the object, without admitting you to familiar intercourse with it; in the other, the solid substance stands before you, with which you may not only become intimately acquainted, but may also, in some measure, handle it. In that, the seed is in a manner choked; in this, you may possess the fruit in its very maturity. There in short, only a few small sparks break forth, which so point out the path that they fail in the middle of the journey,— or rather, which fail in indicating the path at all,—and can only restrain the traveller from going farther astray; but here, the Spirit of God, like a most brilliant torch, or rather like the sun itself, shines in full splendor, not only to guide the course of your life, even to its final goal, but also to conduct you to a blessed immortality. Draw then from this source, wherever you may wander, and as soon as he finds you a settled abode, you ought to make that your place of rest. . . .[56]

Calvin has an equally complex view of the use of earthly wisdom in Christian theology. Sound reason, good judgment, and even the liberal arts and philosophy as we shall see, are to be used in the communication of the truth of heavenly wisdom. However, such earthly wisdom must serve the end of praising God and be grounded in the heavenly wisdom of Christ. It is the heavenly wisdom which completes, clarifies, and corrects all other wisdom.[57] In fact, the remnants of earthly wisdom find their place and interpretation only in the context of the gospel. Only if the positive though relative value of earthly wisdom is kept in mind can it be used properly in Christian theology; but is must be used since it is a singular gift of God. The remnants of earthly wisdom then, seen from the perspective of humankind, have a positive value and function for unbelievers and believers.

If we review Calvin's varied assessments of earthly wisdom, does one of the basic types of understanding Faith and Reason or Reason and Revelation emerge as dominant? Is it adequate to describe his complex perspectival view of wisdom as predominantly a view of Reason and Revelation in Mutual Opposition or Reason and Revelation in Harmony or Revelation Dominant? From the perspective of God as creator all temporal wisdom, sin aside, appears as valueless, so much smoke in the eyes of God. From the perspective of God as judge all earthly wisdom appears as futile and damning; for it leads only to falsehood in its attempts to deny its relativity by taking itself for its end or storming the gates of heaven. In fact, in this view all earthly wisdom must be confessed as lost in the Fall; heavenly wisdom alone is worthy of the name.[58] If one focused only on these two assessments of the power of earthly wisdom, one might conclude that Calvin is greatly indebted to the Occamist tradition, for clearly they show his stress on the absolute distinction between faith and reason. Such statements have led some interpreters to place his view of earthly and heavenly wisdom under the Reason and Revelation in Mutual Opposition type.[59] This type cannot adequately describe his position, however, since Calvin makes positive assessments of earthly wisdom and the relationship between earthly and heavenly wisdom as well. From the perspective of humankind, the shadowy remnants of human wisdom are seen as a boon to the temporal life, for they preserve the order of God's creation and they point to the indiscriminate kindness of God. Also from this perspective, earthly wisdom is seen as a necessary and valuable tool for Christian theology. If, on the other hand, one focuses on these positive assessments of earthly wisdom, one might conclude that Calvin belongs without doubt under the Augustinian-Thomistic type of Revelation Dominant; for they show clearly that Calvin

understands earthly wisdom as a "handmaiden" to Christian theology.[60] This is Leroy Nixon's provisional thesis in *John Calvin's
Teachings on Human Reason*. Locating Luther under the Reason
and Revelation Mutually Opposed type and Augustine and Thomas
under the Revelation Dominant type, he claims that "Calvin's teachings on human reason were in certain important respects nearer to
Aquinas than to Luther."[61]

Both the claim that Calvin's view of earthly and heavenly
wisdom fits the Augustinian-Thomist type and that it fits the
Occamist-Lutheran type are incomplete. Given the complex, perspectival view of the negative and positive value of earthly wisdom
in relation to heavenly wisdom, each of these conclusions over-
simplifies Calvin's view. To locate Calvin accurately in a typology of
Reason and Faith we would have to place him with equal appropriateness under both of these types. Taking a cue from the Renaissance critique of scholastic theology's excesses in harmonizing faith
and reason, Calvin stresses the distinction between the two. He
uses this perspective when faced with Roman scholastics or other
"philosophizing" Christians who impiously blur the distinction and
threaten the correct understanding of the prevenience of grace. But,
taking a cue from Augustine and perhaps even Aquinas, Calvin
emphasizes the unity of the two types of wisdom and the dominance
of faith. He uses this perspective when faced with "fanatics" such as
the Anabaptists and spiritualists who so far separated reason and
faith that reason was removed altogether from the realm of faith and
theology. Both emphases are crucial to his view of faith and reason.
He may have drawn from the Occamist-Lutheran tradition for the
one emphasis and the Augustinian-Thomist tradition for the other.
The fact is that he thought it necessary to find a way to put both
together. Reinhold Niebuhr accurately notes this in saying that
"Calvin's attitude toward reason stands between the Catholic [not
corrupt enough] and the Lutheran [too corrupt] viewpoint."[62] As far
as Neibuhr is concerned, Calvin's mediating position is inconsistent,
but in the end more adequate to the facts of our experience.[63]
Niebuhr is essentially correct, for Calvin's view of temporal and
eternal, earthly and heavenly wisdom is a creative answer to the
problem of faith and reason in a time when the Thomistic synthesis
was being called into quesiton. Calvin's view, though similar to
Luther's view of grace and reason,[64] is a distinctive mediating position between an easy synthesis and diastasis. This middle ground

can be detected in his view of the relationship between theology and philosophy as well. Here, too, he employs his distinctive perspectival approach to construct a complex view.

Heavenly Philosophy and Earthly Philosophy[65]

Many of Calvin's general statements about "philosophy" or "the philosophers" are indeed negative. For example, he speaks of the philosophers in his sermons as men who dispute with great subtlety but who are ignorant of the truth of God.[66] He often uses the word "philosophy" pejoratively to refer to an impious mixture of human reason and the gospel. Those who do not receive the truth of God through the Scriptures alone, but try to dress it up with other ideas are guilty of turning the gospel into "worldly" or "profane Philosophy."

> I said that prudence must be shown [by ministers], because we must always have regard to what is beneficial, provided that there is no cunning, in which many take an excessive pride, when they alter the Word of God to suit their own methods, and devise for us some vague philosophy or other, which is a mixture of the Gospel, and their own fancies; because, of course, this concoction is more pleasing. From this we have free will, from that the merit of works, from that the denial of God's providence and God's gracious election. But, . . . the counsel of God . . . is included in His word, and must not be sought anywhere else. For many things are hidden from us in this life, the full manifestation of which is deferred until that day in which, with new eyes, we shall see God as he is, face to face. Therefore, the men who make known the will of God are those who expound Scripture faithfully and from it establish a people in faith, in the fear of the Lord, and in all godly practices. But, as I have just said that this sentence condemns those who, by their philosophical arguments corrupt the purity of Scripture with their own leavening influences, in order not to teach anything out of step with the common understanding of men; and that is offensive, so Paul thunders violently against those who, out of fear of the cross and persecutions, speak only enigmatically.[67]

This passage seems to indicate that Calvin believed that all philosophy was of no value; it is a dangerous, corrupting influence on theology and therefore must be kept far outside the theologian's province as interpreter of Scripture. He is so passionate here that he is not above poisoning the wells, insinuating that those who use philosophy in their theology do so out of a cowardly fear of the consequences of confessing the straight truth of the gospel! He seems to be saying that the use of philosophy in theology results from bad motives and leads only to dire consequences such as the introduction of profane notions like freedom of the will and merit. In many other places Calvin harps on the theme that philosophy is nothing but vain and frigid speculation.[68] Having nothing better to do, philosophers exercise their reason by engaging in disputes and sophistries.[69] Even his beloved Augustine is guilty of this criticism of philosophy as idle chatter not grounded in the word of God; Calvin accuses him of being "philosophical" in his ingenious and speculative interpretation of a passage of scripture.[70] In still other places, Calvin's criticism is harsher still, for he describes the work of philosophers as the work of blind men.[71]

To this negative assessment of all philosophers Calvin adds an even harsher judgment contrasting all temporal philosophy with the eternal of "hidden" philosophy as he calls it. The scriptural teaching, he claims, ought to be enough to "banish popular delusions [and] to refute the subtleties of secular philosophy."[72] All temporal philosophy, in contrast to the *docta* of eternal philosophy is mere opinion and so to be scorned and avoided in theology. Eternal philosophy is not speculative but practical. It does not deal in sophistries but helps one understand how to live a life of salvation and be restored to full humanity.[73] As such, this secret and hidden philosophy (or Christian philosophy or the philosophy of Christ) is as far above temporal philosophy as the creator is above the creature.

Calvin does not limit himself to absolute contrasts between temporal and eternal philosophy from the perspective of God as creator. He also points out the absolute contradiction between the two from the perspective of God as redeemer.

> For in Christ he offers all happiness in place of our misery, all wealth in place of our neediness; in him he opens to us the heavenly treasures that our whole faith may contemplate his beloved son, our whole expectation depend on him and our whole hope cleave to and rest in him. This, indeed, is that *secret and hidden philosophy* which cannot be wrested from syllogisms. But they whose eyes God has opened surely learnt by heart, that in his light they may see the light.[74]

Outside the "perfect doctrine" taught by Christ "there is nothing worth knowing" and one must decide with Paul, therefore, to "know nothing precious . . . except Jesus Christ and him crucified."[75]

> This is very true, because *it is not lawful to go beyond the simplicity of the gospel*. And the prophetic dignity in Jesus Christ leads us to know that in the sum of doctrine as he has given it to us all parts of perfect wisdom are contained.[76]

The heavenly philosophy *is* the simplicity of the gospel and this stands in contradiction to all earthly philosophy. The error of some of the "papist" philosophies becomes clear in this light. They substituted subtlety of speculation for the pure simplicity of the gospel and even made this a condition of belief.

> [W]hom, then, do the papists call uneducated whose ignorance allows them to be taught by images alone? Those indeed, whom the Lord recognizes as his disciples, whom he honors by the revelation of his heavenly philosophy, whom he wills to be instructed in the saving mysteries of his kingdom.[77]

All one needs to know is already contained in the hidden, heavenly philosophy of Christ. Christian philosophy, therefore, bids reason and all earthly philosophy give way and submit.[78] The contradiction is absolute; true wisdom lies in the heavenly philosophy alone and all earthly philosophy is ignorance.

This absolute contradiction between earthly ignorance and heavenly philosophy, between that which can be known by natural reason alone and that which is revealed only in Christ, cannot be denied. The question, however, is whether or not this unrelentingly negative judgment upon earthly philosophy is the whole of Calvin's position on philosophy. The answer is no. When Calvin draws the absolute contradiction between the blindness and worthlessness of all philosophy and the heavenly philosophy of Christ, he has in mind only a perverted use of earthly philosophy. When earthly philosophers, of whatever school or belief, attempt to storm the gates of heaven with their philosophical reasoning, they are to be castigated. When they confuse the simplicity of the gospel by adding to it philosophical ideas (which make it more palatable to them), they are to be denounced. It is because earthly philosophy has been put to such perverted uses against the humble philosophy of Christ that Calvin believes it necessary to emphasize the absolute contradiction between the two. When the issue is justification, earthly and heavenly philosophy must be shown to be as far removed from one another as heaven and earth. Calvin's view here is similar to Luther's and Melanchthon's, both of whom insisted that the scriptures and philosophy had different views of law, sin, and grace. Because the philosophical views of law, sin, and grace posed such a dangerous threat to believers' salvation, Calvin saw it as his pastoral responsibility to make it clear that earthly philosophy had no place whatsoever in heavenly philosophy. This emphasis on the distinction between the two types of philosophy, however, is made only from the perspective of God the redeemer. From the perspective of humankind the relation between earthly and heavenly philosophy appears quite different.

From the perspective of humankind earthly and heavenly philosophy do not appear as contradictory or mutually exclusive. Rather, they appear in a much more positive relation of completion, clarification, and correction. From this perspective one can say that earthly philosophy definitely knows something worthwhile, though not as much as heavenly philosophy. Earthly philosophy is seen to have a relative though positive value. It contributes to our understanding of temporal things, but is of no use for understanding eternal things. It may understand the "reasons of things which can be seen now," but not those of anything beyond the present.[79] It can know, for example, something about the sun, but not anything about the creation of the world.[80] Or, it can know many ethical concepts, but it cannot know the true nature and end of virtue.

> This is the main difference between the gospel and philosophy. Although the philosophers speak on the subject of morals splendidly and with praiseworthy ability, yet all the embellishments which shine forth in their precepts is nothing more than a beautiful superstructure without a foundation, for by omitting principles, they propound a mutilated doctrine, like a body without a head. The manner of teaching among the Roman Catholics is much the same. Although they speak incidentally of faith in Christ and the grace of the Holy Spirit, it is quite clear that they are nearer to the pagan philosophers than to Christ. . . .[81]

Calvin's point here is that heavenly philosophy is a necessary supplement or foundation which completes, clarifies, and corrects earthly philosophy. Earthly philosophy's partial knowledge of the truth, while a relative good, can only function properly if it is grounded in the full knowledge of the heavenly philosophy. For example, although the pagans knew that persons were inconstant and that it was difficult to follow virtue, they did not know that there is not one drop of good in anyone without grace.[82] And, because they do not know the full truth about the relationship between God and human beings, they usually leave out the main point in their fine discussions of ethics and politics; that is, all their fine precepts cannot contain or bestow righteousness on anyone.[83] Without knowledge of the radical nature of sin, they concluded that earthly philosophy was enough to live a moral life. Calvin's assessment of their partial knowledge, then, is both positive and negative. It is splendid and praiseworthy. Yet, since it is not grounded in and directed toward the heavenly philosophy, it profits them nothing.[84]

This assessment, although somewhat negative, is significantly different from the previous one. Here Calvin, although criticizing earthly philosophy as partial knowledge, does recognize that it is genuine knowledge that has positive value, both for believers and unbelievers. He does urge that the distinction between heavenly and earthly philosophy be kept in mind, even when he compares them as partial and full knowledge. But the distinction between partial and full knowledge is a relative distinction which is not equivalent to the distinction he makes between earthly and heavenly philosophy in which he emphasizes their mutual exclusion. Earthly philosophy, from this perspective, offers general glimpses of the truth about temporal things and thus functions to great advantage among unbelievers by compelling them to see just enough of the truth to preserve the good order of the creation. As such, even when it is not completed, corrected, and clarified by the heavenly philosophy, it functions as a relative good. Believers, furthermore, may make positive use of these glimpses of the truth in earthly philosophy in their own theological witnesses to the heavenly philosophy, as long as they are sure to complete, clarify, and correct this information so that it does not lead people astray.

This more positive assessment of the partial knowledge of earthly philosophy and its use for both believers and unbelievers applies to eternal things as well as to temporal things. Calvin is even willing to admit that earthly philosophy can have partial knowledge of God, as long as it is clear that such knowledge is impotent with regard to salvation. So, for example, he admits that earthly philosophers can know that "all the parts of the world are quickened by God's secret inspiration"; but he denies that they can know that this divine providence consists in the fatherly favor of God's special care for us.[85] Or, they can know that God exists, but not that God is one.[86] Or, as we saw with heavenly and earthly reason, earthly philosophers can know that God exists, but not what God's essence is.[87] Or, they can know that God is eternal, but not how God wishes to be worshipped with true religion;[88] or, that religion is first among all things, but not in what true religion consists;[89] or, that all excellence comes from God, but not what it means to show proper gratitude to God.[90] This partial knowledge must not be confused with the full knowledge of heavenly philosophy, but it is not to be despised as absolute ignorance.

Thus, the perspectival structure emerges once again. From the perspective of God as creator, all temporal philosophy stands in stark contrast to the eternal philosophy. From the perspective of God as redeemer, all earthly philosophy stands in absolute contradiction to the philosophy of Christ. From the perspective of humankind, however, philosophy appears as partial knowledge which must be completed, clarified, and corrected by theology, but which functions positively for both believers and unbelievers. The emphasis here is on philosophy as a guarantor of God's truth in a sinful world and the servant of theology. With these two perspectives, Calvin is able to judge each philosopher's works with great care. With pastoral diligence he shows how each philosopher is a fool when contrasted to Christ. But, with careful discrimination he also points out which statements are true and which untrue in each philosophy, comparing them to the heavenly philosophy's full knowledge.[91] Calvin's treatment of specific philosophies provides detailed examples of these two assessments.

Calvin's statements about specific philosophical schools, thinkers, and ideas display a complex pattern based on the distinction between the human and divine perspectives. According to the perspective of God, all philosophical schools, thinkers, and ideas, without qualification, are worthless to the theologian. According to the perspective of humankind, however, individual schools, philosophers, and ideas can be evaluated and ranked for their usefulness and appropriateness for heavenly philosophy. On the one hand, all philosophy is ignorance. On the other hand, distinctions can be made among the various philosophical schools. Although Calvin does not provide a master list of his ranking of the schools, one can be reconstructed from his works. At the very lowest level is Materialist philosophy (represented most often by the Epicureans),

for this school fails to perceive even a glimpse of the truth on almost
every issue. I was unable to find any instances of Calvin praising the
Epicureans. He usually mentions them only to point out their errors
(in the doctrines of creation, immortality, providence, and the liberal arts), "so that the truth may stand in a clearer light through their
contradiction."[92] In other words, with this school of philosophy
there can be only a negative pedagogical use in Christian theology.

The case is somewhat different with the next school of philosophy in Calvin's ranking, Aristotelian philosophy. Calvin recognizes
that Aristotle was a man of genius and learning.[93] He occasionally
has high praise for Aristotle's politics, noting, for instance, that
Aristotle shares the heavenly philosophy's position on monogamy.[94]
However, while he may be helpful in understanding certain temporal matters, his philosophy is wholly false in its understanding of
eternal matters.[95] He was the head of those mischievous thinkers
who devoted their "talents to obscure and conceal the providence of
God."[96] Because he used his powers of reasoning to "extinguish all
light" on eternal issues, Aristotle is one of the most dangerous
philosophers. In this assessment of earthly philosophy Calvin includes those medieval Aristotelian philosophers and theologians
who used Aristotle's works to deny the scriptural doctrine of grace.[97]

Only slightly higher than Aristotle on Calvin's list of earthly
philosophy is the Stoic school. Unlike Aristotle, the Stoics admitted
God's providence of the world. But they distorted this truth by
interpreting it according to their own fantasies instead of the heavenly philosophy. They also correctly located the highest good in
virtue; but they failed to see what true virtue is. Finally, their
anthropology was false and arrogant; they allotted a great deal of
power to human reason and left the Holy Spirit powerless.[98]

Plato is ranked highest on Calvin's list and Calvin's careful
assessment of his work illustrates his complex view of the relationship between earthly and heavenly philosophy.[99] On the one
hand, Plato's philosophy appears along with all the other earthly
philosophies as absolutely false and ignorant in contrast to the
heavenly philosophy. From the perspective of God as redeemer, the
whole of Plato's work is thrown out of theology. But, from the
perspective of humankind, Plato's work appears quite different.
From this perspective Calvin can discriminate among the ideas of
Plato's philosophy, accepting some, completing and clarifying
others, and correcting still others. Plato's sagacity enabled him to
perceive much truth in the area of virtue and government, for

instance.[100] Regardless of whether or not Plato attributed these things to God's special gift or nature's teaching, there is much in these areas of Plato's thought that can be followed.[101] So far Plato does not appear much better than Aristotle, though Calvin cites Plato more positively more frequently. Plato's top ranking on Calvin's list is based on his glimpses of eternal as well as temporal truths. Plato, according to Calvin, knew the proper distinction between holiness as worship of God and righteousness as conduct toward persons.[102] Plato also correctly identified the highest good of the soul as its likeness to God, a teaching which is in no way contradictory to the heavenly philosophy.

> Besides, if all men are born and live to the end that they may know God, and yet if knowledge of God is unstable and fleeting unless it makes progress to this degree, it is clear that all those who do not direct every thought and action in their lives to this goal degenerate from the law of their creation. This was not unknown to the philosophers. Plato meant nothing but this when he often taught that the highest good of the soul is likeness to God, where, when the soul has grasped the knowledge of God, it is wholly transformed into his likeness.[103]

Calvin does not indicate that anything must be added or clarified at this point. He is content to use this glimpse of truth in Plato about eternal things as a supporting argument in his theology. Calvin follows a similar procedure in his discussion of the mass. He tentatively cites Plato in his favor against the Roman mass, noting of a passage in the *Republic* that it "positively seems to be referring to the practice of expiation in the mass as it exists today in the world."[104]

Calvin handles Plato's view of the future life a bit differently in his theology. Calvin expresses a preference for Plato's view over others', since it recognizes both the immortality of the soul and the chief end of humankind as the enjoyment of God. Calvin is also very critical of Plato's view as insufficient and misleading, in need of clarification.

> For Plato, says, with equal truth and wisdom, that a good hope is the nutriment of old age; and therefore old men who have a guilty conscience are miserably tormented, and are inwardly racked as by a perpetual torture. But to this we must add, what Plato knew not, that it is godliness which causes a good old age

to attend us even to the grave, because faith is the preserver of
a tranquil mind.[105]

Because Plato had been enabled by God to perceive glimpses of the
truth, there are many ideas in his philosophy which confirm the
heavenly philosophy and which need only to be completed and
clarified to be properly used in Christian theology.

There are other ideas in Plato's philosophy, however, that must
be mentioned in theology only to be corrected or condemned.
Plato's view of providence is one example. Calvin praises Plato for
teaching that there is one God and that all things subsist in him,
suggesting that it was the will of God to use this philosopher to
awaken others to this knowledge.[106] However, while Plato's view of
providence is far superior to those of all other philosophers, it is
nonetheless false and in need of correction. Calvin uses the doctrine
of providence as his touchstone in evaluating the relative truth of
philosophies from the perspective of humankind. This touchstone
reveals the same ascending rank from the Epicureans, to the Aristotelians, to the Stoics, to Plato. But he is clear that although Plato is
ranked highest, he, "the most religious of all and most circumspect,
also vanishes in his round globe."[107] Plato, with less excuse than the
others, stumbles in his doctrine of providence and must be corrected in the heavenly philosophy so that his view will not lead
persons astray.

For his touchstone for ranking different schools and different
ideas within schools, Calvin uses not only the doctrine of providence
but the soteriological doctrines of law, sin, and grace, also. This
principle of evaluation is operative in his treatment of Plato's view of
sin, *anamnesis*, and demons. In each of these cases Calvin does not
merely correct Plato's view; he rejects it outright. He regularly
points out the falsity of Plato's view of sin as ignorance, which
suggests that he considered this an especially dangerous doctrine.
This view, which denied the radicality and pervasiveness of sin,
stood in direct contradiction to the heavenly philosophy.[108] The
same is true of the Platonic doctrine of *anamnesis*.[109] Calvin rejects
this for several reasons, the most important being that it arrogantly
attributes the spirit or intellect to the human substance rather than
to God. As he did with the *imago dei*, Calvin wants to make clear
here that the intellect is wholly a gift of God. If one speaks of a
substantial view of the intellect only and does not supplement it

with a relational view (see chapter 2), the doctrine of grace is endangered. The same is true of Plato's view of demons, which is to be rejected because it threatens the doctrine of prevenient grace, since it challenges the sole sufficiency of the redeemer by introducing spiritual intermediaries.[110] Thus, even though Plato fares much better than most other philosophers, these three ideas of his are to be completely rejected as antithetical to the heavenly philosophy.

Calvin's use and evaluation of Plato's philosophy in particular and philosophy in general is complex. From the perspective of God as creator, there is an absolute contrast between temporal and eternal philosophy so that the former appears as so much smoke and ignorance. From the perspective of God as redeemer there is an absolute contradiction between earthly philosophy and heavenly philosophy so that the former appears as utter blindness and falsehood. In this light one uses earthly philosophy in theology only negatively, that is, to highlight the glory of the heavenly philosophy. From the perspective of humankind, however, distinctions appear between and within philosophical schools, so that earthly philosophy appears as both true and false. In this light one uses philosophy in theology positively, both to witness to the fact that God has spread the gift of intellect among philosophers to preserve a modicum of truth in a sinful world, and to confirm, illustrate, and elucidate the truth of the heavenly philosophy.

It is my contention that the complexity of Calvin's view of temporal and eternal philosophy, earthly and heavenly philosophy, is more adequately understood when his perspectival approach is taken into consideration. The distinction between the perspectives of God and humankind in its two applications makes it possible to discern an order or pattern among his various statements on philosophy and theology. From the perspectives of God as creator and God as redeemer, eternal or heavenly philosophy and temporal or earthly philosophy appear as mutually exclusive; they stand in absolute contrast or contradiction to one another. And, from these perspectives the proper use of philosophy in Christian theology can only be a theological use; that is, temporal or earthly philosophy is used to highlight the clear, transcendent, and superior truth of the eternal or heavenly philosophy. From the perspective of humankind, however, eternal or heavenly philosophy and temporal or earthly philosophy appear to be in greater harmony with one another, though with the former clearly dominant. And from this perspective two further uses of philosophy in Christian theology emerge, a civil use and a pedagogical use. Earthly philosophy is used by God among unbelievers to restrain wild fantasies and false imaginations. It is also used among believers to confirm and illustrate the truth of heavenly philosophy.

Calvin's three-fold evaluation and use of earthly philosophy, as I have outlined it here, parallels his well-known view of the three uses of the law. Even though there is no exact correspondence between the law and earthly philosophy, the basic pattern for their relation is similar. The same is true of the three uses of earthly philosophy and the three uses of the law. From the perspective of God as redeemer, the heavenly and earthly philosophy are seen to be mutually exclusive, just as the gospel and law are. From this perspective, therefore, there can only be a negative use of earthly philosophy and the law. Just as the law, in its theological use, drives a person to the sweet grace cradled in the gospel by convicting one of one's absolute lack of merit, so a presentation of the subtle speculations of earthly philosophy drives one to the practical simplicity of the heavenly philosophy by convicting one of the utter worthlessness of one's own knowledge for salvation. And, just as the law is impotent to bestow righteousness, so earthly philosophy is impotent to bestow truth.

The parallel can be seen in the second and third uses as well. From the perspective of humankind both the law and earthly philosophy are seen as means to preserve God's good creation. In other words, earthly philosophy, like the law, has a civil as well as a theological use. It contributes much good to the world by preventing persons from degenerating into total falsehood. The glimpses of truth which God grants to individuals like Plato keep God's truth alive in a world oriented toward falsehood. The third, pedagogical or didactic, use of the law in Calvin is paralleled by a third, more positive use of earthly philosophy. Just as the Christian is called to use the law or order social and political life on earth, so she or he is to use philosophy to order intellectual life. Though Calvin does not neatly identify the pedagogically useful philosophical principles as he does the regulative legal principles for the Christian life, there is a parallel between the two. This can be seen in part in his reasoning for his introduction of the third use. Just as the covenant of a gracious God preceded the giving of the law, thus uniting law and gospel, so the truth of God preceded both the heavenly and earthly philosophies, thus uniting them. In both cases an appeal to the will of God is made to introduce a third, positive use of that which has *also* been acknowledged as being in contradiction to the gospel. My point here is simply this: Calvin's third, positive use of earthly philosophy should not be overlooked any more than his third use of the law. Just as Christians use the decalogue and meditation on the life of Christ to shape their zeal into a life of sanctification, so Christian theologians are called to use earthly philosophy to help teach the truth of the Christian philosophy. Clearly there is no exact correspondence here, for Calvin does not equate the law of the Christian life with the positive use of earthly philosophy, but the parallel should by now be clear. Overall, the parallel between the three uses of the law and the three uses of earthly philosophy points to the broad coherence of Calvin's collection of contradictory yet complementary views of philosophy.

Since Calvin's view of the relation between theology and philosophy incorporates both an absolute contradiction and a relative comparison between the two, it is misleading to use his statements on philosophy to support claims that he fits one traditional type for understanding reason and faith. Yet this is what many scholars do; though there is little agreement among scholars on Calvin's use of philosophy. Niesel ignores the entire issue in his lengthy discussion of the knowledge of God in Calvin's theology.[111] Dowey, addressing this topic, correctly point to the precedence of the revealed word of God in Calvin's theology. However, he interprets this to mean only that "Calvin, contrary to the scholastic tradition, and with an excellent appreciation of Old Testament ways of thinking, *eschews all philosophy in connection with the revelation of the name of God. . . .*"[112] It has been the fashion for Neo-Orthodox interpreters of Calvin, who wish to emphasize his rejection of philosophy, to identify him as a *biblical theologian*.[113] This title has also been used by those interpreters who recognize Calvin's debt to and use of philosophy, but who wish to emphasize that philosophy did not determine the content of his theology in any way.[114]

Quite a number of scholars have noted Calvin's debt to and use of philosophy. The conclusions so far, however, have been general and limited, emphasizing Calvin's use and not his rejection of philosophy. Grislis and Wendel note that Calvin borrowed from philosophy with discrimination, repudiating some ideas and accepting others.[115] Joseph C. McClelland repeats Boisset's judgment that

Calvin was a critical student of Plato.[116] Charles Partee, at the end of *Calvin and Classical Philosophy*, arrives at the following conclusion:

> This study has undertaken to demonstrate that John Calvin belongs to that part of the Christian tradition which affirms philosophical achievements (Part One); that the way in which Calvin uses philosophical insights is instructive (Part Two); and that while Calvin sees distinctions among the classical philosophers, he is not an uncritical admirer of those whom he prefers (Part Three). Without doubt Calvin's knowledge of classical philosophy influences his thinking. It would be a mistake, therefore, to dismiss Calvin's references to philosophy as an inconsequential residue of his early humanistic training. It would be no less a mistake to think that Calvin provides a definitive synthesis of classical and Christian philosophy.
>
> Calvin does, however, offer a model for dealing with philosophy. Calvin's remarks on Cicero and Seneca are certainly and his comments on Plato and Aristotle are almost certainly, derived from a first-hand acquaintance with their writings. But it is more important to recognize that Calvin's use of philosophy is *historical* rather than *systematic*. Thus Calvin looks to philosophy for illustration of the truth rather than as a guide to it. By implication, Calvin answers the question, "What has Athens to do with Jerusalem?" by suggesting that Athens is valuable for the purpose of "in-Sight-seeing." Calvin may be less enthusiastic about philosophy than Erasmus, Zwingli, and Melanchthon, but he is also less hostile than Luther and Colet. Calvin is convinced that "None will ever be a good minister of the word of God except that he be a first-rate scholar." As a first-rate scholar, Calvin refers to philosophic insights when it occurs to him to do so. Calvin does not attempt to deal with all the concerns of philosophy but rather with those which he thinks will illuminate his discussion of the Christian faith.
>
> It has been said that Reformed theology consists of "the Bible, the whole Bible, and nothing but the Bible." Of course, Calvin affirms the centrality of the Scripture, but, by his example, he suggests that one who knows only the Bible does not even know the Bible. Calvin has a sound respect for the values of the theological tradition. Moreover, he states that it is ungrateful to ignore the philosophers entirely or to despise the insights which God has granted to them.[117]

I have quoted Partee's conclusion in full because it illustrates why many studies of Calvin's view of philosophy, though correct, may be incomplete assessments. Several problems arise in this interpretation of Calvin's use of philosophy. First, though he comments on the mutual contradiction between earthly philosophy and the heavenly philosophy and on the negative, theological use of the former, Partee's emphasis is on Calvin's positive, third use of earthly philosophy. Calvin does indeed appreciate and use earthly philosophy positively in his theology; but, as the foregoing analysis has shown, this is only one aspect of his complex, three-fold view of philosophy. Partee's conclusion, therefore, though welcome for its illumination of Calvin's favorable use of philosophy, is just as limited as Dowey's emphasis on Calvin's rejection of philosophy. Second, the overly general nature of Partee's concluding statements (Calvin is "not an uncritical admirer of those whom he prefers."; Calvin looked to philosophy for illustration of the truth rather than as a guide to it.) needs to be supplemented by the more specific conclusions reached in this analysis about the three-fold use of philosophy and the detailed evaluations of specific philosophies. For example, Calvin did not use philosophy only to illustrate the heavenly philosophy (pedagogical use). He also uses it negatively to highlight the superiority of the heavenly philosophy (theological use). And, he sees an important use for it among unbelievers as a guide (though an uncertain one) to the truth (civil use).

Furthermore, because Partee understands "systematic" as that which pertains to whole systems of philosophy or sustained philosophical argumentation, he concludes that Calvin is not systematic in his use of philosophical concepts.[118] Calvin does indeed use philosophy eclectically; but this does not mean that there is no order at all in his use of it. Here as elsewhere the constant presence of the distinction between the perspective of God and the perspective of humankind in its two variations lends a broad coherence to all his varied statements. Partee is correct that Calvin does not offer us a new definitive synthesis of classical philosophy and Christianity (in the manner of Augustine or Aquinas). The dynamic perspectival structure operating throughout his discussion of the relationship between philosophy and theology, however, offers a distinctive approach to this issue. Because of this, Calvin's view of philosophy and theology, like his view of earthly and heavenly wisdom, does not fit neatly into any one pattern of understanding.[119]

Christian Philosophy and Self-Knowledge

One final bit of evidence supporting this interpretation of Calvin's complex and creative solution to the problem of earthly and heavenly philosophy must be examined. Partee maintains that Calvin is not doing philosophy. Joseph McClelland concurs, contending that Calvin, because he uses philosopical data critically, is not a Christian philosopher. He adds that Calvin's style is too dynamic and his speech too broken for his theology to be philosophy of any sort. He also distinguishes between philosophy as a serious preparation for death and theology as a guide for new life, identifying Calvin with the latter task. [120] Once again, these comments are misleading, for Calvin, by his own admission, is a Christian philosopher. The question is, what did he mean by this?

Calvin speaks of his theology as an exposition of the "Christian philosophy," as Partee and others have noted. [121] In the Argument to the *Institutes* he presents this exposition as his duty as a reformer called by God.

> Perhaps the duty of those who have received from God fuller light than others is to help simple folk at this point, and as it were, to lend them a hand in order to guide them and help them to find the sum of what God meant to teach us in his word. Now, that cannot be better done through the scriptures than to treat the chief and weightiest matters comprised in the *Christian philosophy.* For he who knows these things will be prepared to profit more in God's school in one day than another in three months, particularly as he knows fairly well to what he must refer each sentence, and has this rule to embrace all that is presented to him. [122]

This is not the only term Calvin uses. Just a page before this citation he refers to his purpose as preparing candidates in "sacred theology." [123] There is no evidence that he meant to distinguish sharply between the two terms. While he uses these two interchangeably, neither one is Calvin's key term for the task of theology. He also speaks of its as "heavenly doctrine" [124] and "sacred doctrine." [125] More often than either of these, though, he uses the term "hidden philosophy" or "heavenly philosophy" for Christian theology. The latter formulation is used frequently in the *Institutes* and the *Treatise on Scandals.* [126] But how did Calvin understand this term and why did he choose to use it rather than any of the others?

Clearly Calvin did not intend to associate himself with the Libertines by his use of the term "Christian philosophy" for to them the term meant a speculative set of spiritualistic ideas. [127] There is a question, however, whether Calvin's use of the terms "Christian philosophy" and "heavenly philosophy" aligns him with the

Brethren of the Common Life and Erasmus against the scholastics. Erasmus used the terms "Christian philosophy" and "philosophy of Christ" to refer to a way of life, a path of devotion and piety, rather than a set of doctrines. Though he built this view on the medieval definition of Christian philosophy as the monastic way of life, he believed this "lived wisdom" applied to all Christians and not monks alone.[128] There is also a question whether Calvin's use of the term indicates the influence of Guillaume Budé, for whom Christian philosophy meant, not simply moral teachings, but a body of certain and true knowledge about God and humankind.[129]

We can only answer these questions by exploring in greater detail Calvin's understanding of the purpose and content of the heavenly philosophy. It is not enough to say that ther term "Christian philosophy" was commonly used by Christian humanists and that therefore Calvin quite naturally used this term to designate Christian theology. Nor is it sufficient to define Christian philosophy so generally that it refers to a "theological program" of reform based "not only on a reformation of the understanding of Scripture and a recovery of Patristic thought," but also includes "an appreciation of the insights of classical philosophy."[130] This broad net catches too many Christian humanists. It does not aid us in distinguishing Calvin's Christian humanism from that of Erasmus, Budé, the Libertines, or the Florentines. Nor does it enable us to differentiate between Calvin's heavenly philosophy and the Christian philosophy of Erasmus, Budé, Ficino, and Pico. Only a careful analysis of Calvin's heavenly philosophy will do this.

There are three points at which Calvin's heavenly philosophy resembles Budé's Christian philosophy more than Erasmus's. First, for Calvin the heavenly philosophy contained knowledge about doctrines as well as morals. Since the close relation between these two will be developed in chapter 4, it need not detain us here. Second, as we saw earlier, Calvin sees a great discontinuity between heavenly philosophy and earthly philosophy.[131] For this reason, like Budé, he speaks of heavenly philosophy as a *rival system to all other philosophies*. Once known, heavenly philosophy supplants all classical philosophies. This contrast, while not the whole of Calvin's view of earthly philosophy, is not emphasized by Erasmus. Both Budé and Calvin considered Christian philosophy or heavenly philosophy to be a body of true knowledge which was more comprehensive and more certain than any other body of knowledge. It was not just a set of moral teachings or a guide to a new way of life, but a rival system of interpreting reality, *a rival philosophy*. Budé presents this view in *De Transitu Hellenismi ad Christianum*, a book which influenced Calvin greatly when it appeared in 1535.[132] Calvin adopts this view as well, as we shall see in the following paragraphs. For this reason it is difficult to accept without qualification Neisel's definition of Calvin's Christian philosophy as "a synthesis of the contents of Scripture."[133] Partee, declaring Neisel's definition to be "essentially correct," repeats that Calvin's Christian philosophy is "basically a key to correct understanding of Scripture."[134] He adds only that this definition does not exclude the "appreciation of insights of classical philosophy."[135] But Calvin's heavenly philosophy cannot be adequately defined as an exposition or synthesis of scripture or the sum of Christian doctrine, for following Budé, Calvin presents heavenly philosophy as a rival body of certain knowledge. Furthermore, Calvin understands this certain knowledge to consist of two parts, knowledge of God and knowledge of ourselves. This is the third point at which he resembles Budé.

From Augustine through the Medieval theologians, Christian Socratism was thought to be essential to Christian theology.[136] Calvin stands in a long line of Christian theologians when he defines the heavenly philosophy as the knowledge of God *and* self. Two of the more immediate historical influences on Calvin at this point are Bucer and Budé.[137] More important than the question of the origin of this idea in Calvin, however, is the question of how he understood and used it.

When we raise the issue of heavenly philosophy and self-knowledge, we raise the question of how the knowledge of self given in heavenly philosophy is related to the knowledge of self given in earthly philosophy. It is simply the question of the relation of earthly and heavenly philosophy in a new key. It is not surprising, therefore, that the answer should be similar. Calvin distinguishes three uses of earthly philosophy in self-knowledge. He emphasizes the absolute contradiction between the self-knowledge given in both philosophies, setting up the heavenly philosophy as a rival to all classical philosophies. The limits and falsities of earthly philosophy's knowledge of the self are pointed out to highlight the certainty and truth of the heavenly philosophical view of the self. He also points out the proper value and use of self-knowledge gained through earthly philosophy in the temporal kingdom. And, thirdly, he envisions a critical and pedagogical use of certain earthly philosophical truths about the self in the heavenly philosophy's anthropology.

Calvin insists that all letters, including earthly philosophy, avail naught for the knowledge of the self. According to him, there is "none but God who knows us and who can pronounce the truth about us."[138] He opposes the two types of knowledge about the self, therefore, as false and true.

> With good reason the ancient proverb strongly recommended the knowledge of the self to man. For if it is considered disgraceful for us not to know all that pertains to the business of human life, even more detestable is our ignorance of ourselves, by which, when making decisions in necessary matters, we miserably deceive and even blind ourselves!
>
> But, since this precept is so valuable, we ought more diligently to avoid applying it perversely. This, we observe, has happened to certain philosophers, who, while urging man to know himself, propose the goal of recognizing his own worth and excellence. And they would have him contemplate in himself nothing but what swells him with empathy and assurance and puff him up with pride. But knowledge of ourselves lies first in considering what we are given at creation and how generously God continues in his favor toward us, in order to know how great our natural excellence would be if only it had remained unblemished; yet at the same time to bear in mind that there is in us nothing of our own, but that we hold on sufference whatever God has bestowed upon us. Hence we are ever dependent upon him. Secondly, to call to mind our miserable condition after Adam's fall; the awareness of which, when all our boasting and self-assurance are laid low, should truly humble us and overwhelm us with shame.[139]

Elsewhere Calvin adds a third part to the heavenly philosophy's self-knowledge which stands in contradiction to the knowledge of earthly philosophy: the knowledge that Christ's benefits have been imparted to believers so that they are one with him, his righteousness overwhelming their sin and his salvation wiping out their condemnation.[140] In each of these three areas of self-knowledge, created excellence, sinful condition, and salvation for a future life, earthly philosophers are wholly ignorant and wrong. In each case they lack the light of the heavenly philosophy which would illumine the depths and heights of the self. Thus, they are totally ignorant of humankind's origin and created nature[141] and its present sinful condition;[142] and, they have absolutely no knowledge of the true destiny of humankind, its *summum bonum*, the celestial life.[143] All this knowledge is given only to believers in Jesus Christ, who have perfect self-knowledge in contemplating his image in themselves.[144]

This absolute denial of any self-knowledge in earthly philosophy is made within the context of soteriology. Only if one asks
whether or not the self-knowledge to be had in earthly philosophy
can save one before the eternal judge, must one conclude that all
self-knowledge outside of Jesus Christ is ignorance and falsehood.
From the perspective of humankind, it is equally clear that philosophy does have some knowledge of the created nature, fallen condition, and true destiny of humankind, as we shall show in a moment. But, this self-knowledge is impotent to bestow grace on
humankind. Calvin is quite comfortable with both assertions:
earthly philosophy has no self-knowledge; it has some self-knowledge. It is from the perspective of God as redeemer that the first
judgment is made.

> The philosophers who had great and excellent minds never
> knew what the celestial life is. It is true that God made them
> speak of it to render witness to the world, in order to remove
> any excuse of ignorance. And they pronounced the beautiful
> words that men were not created to only live here a short
> while. . . . *But what of this? This was not a certain knowledge*
> [*cognoissance*]. . . .[145]

The absolute contradiction between true and false knowledge of the
self is closely connected with Calvin's view of the certainty of the
heavenly philosophy over against its earthly rivals. This is what lies
behind Calvin's absolute contradiction between earthly and heavenly philosophy and his presentation of the heavenly philosophy as a
rival interpretation of reality. This is where the issue ends for Calvin:
either one lives by the "eternal and unchangeable truth of God" or
one dies by the opinions of mortals.[146] There is no inbetween; the
two are, almost literally, worlds apart.

> Why then does it please men to grasp at the chance of stagger-
> ing and tottering in the changeable breezes of the world when
> God makes us firm on the eternal foundation of his Word? Why
> do they prefer to be tossed about in the midst of storms of
> opinions rather than lie quietly in the safe harbor of certain
> truth, where God invites us?[147]

This is the ultimate question for Calvin. He is preoccupied with the
notion of certainty in his presentation of the Gospel, heavenly
philosophy, and self-knowledge. He is convinced that the God who

has accommodated to humankind so unostentatiously in the scriptures

> has spoken clearly and without ambiguity, but declares the
> certainty and steadfastness of his word; as if he had said that he
> does not promise largely with an intention to deceive, or amuse
> hungry men by words, but actually performs what he has
> promised. This demonstrates the ingratitude of those who,
> when they are called, do not answer; since God has no other
> design than to make us partakers of all blessings of which we
> are otherwise empty and destitute.[148]

One of the reasons that Calvin denounces theological speculation and cavilling is that they lead one away from the certainty of salvation in that "invisible certitude in the truth of God."[149] Faith alone is grounded in the absolute certainty of the word of God. But to enjoy this certainty, one must be raised above all human faculties and opinions, including the best of earthly philosophy; if not, one "will never be moved to tend toward this happy life reserved for us in heaven."[150]

The certitude of faith cannot be achieved by non-Christian philosophy. If we want to certify for ourselves that God indeed loves us, we must be raised above our natural powers.[151] Dowey sums this up nicely: "The certainty of faith is knowledge but a suprarational knowledge in which the mind, being raised above itself, achieves a suprarational certainty of personal salvation."[152] Just so the certainty of heavenly philosophy is raised above and stands in contradiction to the certainty of all earthly philosophy.[153] And the only way to receive it is by listening to the word of God in the scriptures:

> [T]he only way in which we differ from the pagans and infidels,
> is that we have a religion which is assured and founded in the
> infallible truth of God instead of all the others which are led
> about by doubtful opinions or hardened with perverse obstinancy, yet without certitude. . . .[154]

The word of God alone offers certainty because it comes from God and thus could not and "did not originate in the minds of men."[155] Calvin's doctrine of the spirit in connection with the word is set against the background of this preoccupation with certainty. As he explains,

Since all that God says is utterly certain, he wants us to receive it into our minds with a firm and unwavering assent. Secondly, we should note that, since this degree of certainty is beyond the capacity of the human mind, it is the office of the Holy Spirit to confirm within us what God promises in his words.[156]

It is the spirit which guarantees the absolute certainty unique to the heavenly philosophy.[157]

From the perspective of God as creator, therefore, there is an absolute contrast between the absolute certainty of the eternal philosophy and the doubtfulness of all temporal philosophy. This certainty is guaranteed by the word and the spirit of God. There is no need, then, in Christian theology for other rational or philosophical arguments.[158] This is indeed Calvin's viewpoint. However, it is not his only viewpoint. From the perspective of humankind, other philosophical arguments (based on reason, nature, experience, etc.) appear as helpful confirmations of the certain truth of the heavenly philosophy. These two perspectives help to explain Calvin's odd argument about the truth of God in scripture in the *Institutes*. He first tells his readers that the scripture is in no need of proof; he then immediately proceeds to offer a full set of proofs.[159] From the one perspective there is only a contradiction between the certainty of the scriptures and the uncertainty of earthly philosophy. From the other perspective there is a relative distinction between the two, which enables the theologian to make use of earthly philosophy in the service of the heavenly philosophy.

When Calvin concentrates on the absolute contrast between the certainty of the eternal philosophy and the uncertainty of temporal philosophy and the absolute contradiction between heavenly and earthly philosophy, he introduces the first use of that self-knowledge possessed by earthly philosophers: the theological use. The self-knowledge they may have, partial and impotent as it is, functions to condemn them if they are not believers in Jesus Christ. Everyone retains enough knowledge about the created nature, the fallen condition, and the final destiny of humankind to stand condemned and responsible.[160] This self-knowledge, from the perspective of God, leaves them without excuse, just as all remnants of the *imago dei* do. All this self-knowledge, then, no matter how noble and advance, is but doubt and falsehood in the eternal or heavenly kingdom. Thus, it stands in absolute contradiction to the certain and true knowledge of the self given in the heavenly philosophy. As

such, the self-knowledge of earthly philosophy only condemns and
drives one on to the truth of Christianity.

> For surely it is the height of folly in any man for a mere
> momentary happiness—a very dream—to abdicate the crown
> of heaven, and renounce his hopes for eternity. Here it must be
> apparent . . . that the doctrine of this psalm is very different
> from that taught by the philosophers. I grant that they may
> have ridiculed worldly ambition with elegance and eloquence,
> exposed the other vices, and insisted upon the topics of our
> frailty and mortality, but they uniformly omitted to state the
> most important truth of all, that God governs the world by his
> providence, and that we may expect a happy issue out of our
> calamities, by coming to that everlasting inheritance which
> awaits us in heaven.[161]

Earthly and heavenly philosophy are rival interpretations of life and
the self, therefore, and the former has a negative use in the exposition of the latter.

Once again, however, we find that this is not the only evaluation and use of earthly philosophy's self-knowledge in Calvin's view;
there is also a civil use. The remnants of self-knowledge about
human nature, its sinful condition, and final destiny preserve order
among men and women. They prevent persons from degenerating
into beasts by setting limits to their capacity for sin. Philosophers'
discussions of human dignity, covetousness, and the fragility of the
present life, for instance, all hold the sinfulness of unbelievers in
check and restrain evil in the world. The self-knowledge of non-
Christian philosophy, as partial as it may be, does serve a positive
function, therefore. This civil use of philosophy's self-knowledge
significantly qualifies Torrance's conclusion that it is possible to know
the self *only* in relation to God's grace.[162] From the perspective of
God as redeemer, this is true. But from the perspective of humankind, this is false. All persons, unbelievers included, have actual
self-knowledge which enables them to order their individual and
communal lives. Biéler's remarks on this point are more circumspect, for he admits that unbelievers can know some things about
the self, though "nothing essential," he adds; only God's word
provides essential knowledge about humankind's original condition,
actual sinfulness, and final destiny.[163] If by "essential" Biéler means
"saving" knowledge, then he is correct. To say that only the heavenly
philosophy provides saving and certain self-knowledge is not to deny

that earthly philosophy provides limited self-knowledge for use in the earthly kingdom.

Calvin's view does not stop here, for there is a third use, a pedagogical use, of the self-knowledge attainable by non-Christian philosophy in addition to the theological and civil uses. The bits of self-knowledge present in other philosophies can also be used by Christian theologians in their elucidation of the heavenly philosophy. Christian theologians can complete what is partial, redirect what goes askew, and correct all errors which contradict the heavenly truth about the self. This use makes it clear that the heavenly philosophy is distinct from, though by no means separated from, earthly philosophy. It is not simply a rival philosophy, as seen from the perspective of God as redeemer. It is also the crown of all philosophy, when seen from the perspective of humankind. As the pinnacle of philosophical development it does not simply "appreciate" the insights of classical philosophy, as Partee states; it approves, supplements, alters, criticizes, and rejects earthly philosophy's self-knowledge in its exposition of the self-knowledge of the heavenly philosophy.

As Calvin understood the heavenly philosophy, therefore, it is both a rival to all temporal and earthly philosophy and the crown of all non-Christian philosophy. As rival it stands in contrast and contradiction to other philosophies. As crown, it critically incorporates all other philosophies. Both of these viewpoints appear in his presentation of the self-knowledge of the heavenly philosophy. For Calvin true self-knowledge includes the created nature, the sinful condition, and the final destiny of humankind. His view of the first two was covered in chapters 1 and 2. One of the goals of the heavenly philosophy, insofar as it concerns self-knowledge, is to present the truth about human dignity. Another is to uncover the depths of human sin. Though he often speaks of true self-knowledge in terms of depravity, this is only one of the emphases of the heavenly philosophy's presentation of self-knowledge, as we saw in the first two chapters.[164] The third goal is to faithfully present the celestial heritage of humankind. This goal for the self-knowledge of heavenly philosophy was also discussed in chapter 1. It is reconsidered here for the light it sheds upon Calvin's understanding of heavenly philosophy as knowledge of the self and its relation to earthly philosophy.

The goal of faithfully presenting the celestial heritage of humankind has two distinct tasks: to provide persons with the right attitude toward death and to provide them with the right attitude toward life. The first task was commonly recognized as the goal of philosophy by Platonists. Philosophy was understood as a preparation for death, a *meditatio mortis*. Calvin was definitely aware of this interpretation of the goal of philosophy. In fact, he was critical of this interpretation for two reasons: earthly philosophy is impotent to calm human anxiety about death; and earthly philosophy is useless for counseling persons about the proper attitude toward the present life. Each of these criticisms must be examined.

Everyone is naturally afraid of death and no one desires to die, observes Calvin. This is a favorite theme of his in exegeting scripture.

> Saint Paul says that we do not desire death at all, and that it is even impossible for a person to become accustomed to it and desire to die. We flee from it as much as possible. And why? Because God etched this sense in us that death is a malediction, a corruption of nature, and a change of the order of God from what it was before the Fall. Thus we must run from death, since it is contrary to our flesh and its frightfulness shocks us through the knowledge that God has given us.[165]

Death is frightening; yet persons in their stubbornness insist on treating the present life as if it were immortal. They try to avoid the fear of death, which is natural to them, by losing themselves in the world. But, their avoidance does not succeed, for God continually confronts them with death to vividly remind them that their life on earth is fragile and vanishing.[166] God even uses the remnants of self-knowledge concerning the celestial life as such reminders. And God even uses those philosophers to whom he has granted special intelligence to remind persons that the present life is not immortal. Plato's keen insights into the immortality of the soul, for example, functioned to keep the fear of death alive in persons and condemn them in their stubborn refusal to live and die for God. His insights into immortality also functioned positively; they restrained hedonism in some persons. Though Plato's views of immortality, therefore, were valuable self-knowledge, having both a theological and a civil use, they could not make one willing to die any more than natural feeling or avoidance techniques could. God alone works the true readiness for death in one's heart.[167] Granted there are differences between Platonists and Epicureans at the moment of death, still it is true that

> where there is no promise of any eternal inheritance *im-
> planted in our hearts*, we shall never be torn away from this
> world. We are naturally desirous of existence, and that feeling
> cannot be eradicated, unless faith overcome it. . . .[168]

Earthly philosophers may have an inkling of the future life because of the remnants of self-knowledge which they retain, and they may rightly counsel persons to avoid the fear of death; but it is the heavenly philosophy alone, with its true knowledge of the eschatological structure of human existence, that is able to bestow the hope of the future life upon believers. Here is where it differs from all other philosophies; it alone knows that death is but "the hope of our life."[169] With the confident and certain hope of their celestial heritage in Jesus Christ, believers are able to fulfill the will of God to live and die to him. Thus, they are able to "face death with a joyous courage and not with clenched teeth, as unbelievers do."[170] Death for them is but a symbol of their immortality. If they did not know this, they would die in fear. Death, therefore, humbles those who prefer the temporal to the eternal life and exalts those who are joined to eternal life in Christ.[171] This understanding of death distinguishes Calvin's heavenly philosophy from all other philosophies, for it reconceives the task of philosophy as *meditatio futurae vitae* rather than continuing it as *meditatio mortis*.

It is not only the attitude toward death which distinguishes Calvin's heavenly philosophy as *meditatio futurae vitae* from the earthly philosophies' view of *meditatio mortis*. As the phrase implies, the heavenly philosophy concentrates on the future life and the proper way to understand death in relation to it. But, it also concentrates on the eternal life in the present, and the proper way to understand temporal life in relation to it. Calvin's heavenly philosophy, as *meditatio futurae vitae*, not only helps one overcome the fear of death but also provides a guide for the present life. In this it goes beyond all non-Christian philosophies.[172] It surpasses all philosophies by offering preparation for both life and death. When Calvin speaks of the hope of the future life he does not simply dwell on the right attitude toward death that this entails. He focuses on the implications for the Christian life.[173] The heavenly philosophy, then, as true self-knowledge, is a practical philosophy of life. "The Christian philosophy bids reason give way to, submit to and subject itself to the Holy Spirit, so that man himself may no longer live but exhibit Christ living within him."[174] Christian philosophy involves both doctrine and a way of life. In its comprehensiveness it is both rival to and crown of all earthly philosophy.

Just as unbelievers knew something of the future life and its relation to death, so they can know something of the judgment of eternal life upon the temporal life. The proper understanding of the present life also appears as a remnant of self-knowledge. Thus, in addition to preparing themselves in some way for death, unbelievers may make a genuine effort to live well in the present world. They may see, for instance that all worldly ambition is to be ridiculed in the light of immortality; Calvin notes that the earthly philosophers have taught well concerning this.[175] But, here too they do not and cannot have full and true saving knowledge of how to live a joyful, active, grateful, and responsive life in the temporal world. Their insights may restrain evil, but they cannot provide the rule for living well in the sight of God.

For two reasons, then, unbelievers face a truncated and hopeless existence, in spite of the insights about self-knowledge offered by earthly philosophers. They have no true hope of a future life and thus live in fear of death, in spite of all their attempts to avoid it. And, they have no true knowledge of the temporal life, and thus are deluded by the false promises of happiness of temporal goods and joys.[176] Since in comparison with those who believe in the heavenly philosophy, these persons do not know how to die or how to live, they are "wholly destitute of wisdom."[177] They lack true self-knowledge because they do not know these three things: how to be governed by God; what the end of human creation is (i.e., that we were placed in this world only to pass through it); and the celestial heritage where we have our eternal life.[178] It is the heavenly philosophy alone, that hidden philosophy of Christ revealed by God in word and spirit, that can provide the full and true wisdom about the self which is necessary if one is to live and die to God.

For this reason it seems to me that Calvin offers his exposition of the heavenly philosophy as a rival interpretation of reality. Like all good philosophy, it has been divided into two parts, the knowledge of God and the knowledge of ourselves. He goes a step further by dividing self-knowledge into the knowledge of living and the knowledge of dying. His Christian philosophy included both doctrine and a guide for living. Partee claims that, although Calvin believes theology is superior to philosophy, he did not want to substitute his theology for it or "seek to displace philosophy in a higher synthesis in which all of philosophy's legitimate concerns are resolved."[179] It is true that Calvin's heavenly philosophy cannot be considered an "exhaustive philosophical program."[180] Calvin considered many philosophical problems of no importance, even silly. His view, however, of the absolute contradiction between the heavenly philosophy and earthly philosophy as well as his emphasis on the comprehensiveness of the heavenly philosophy and its superiority lead me to conclude that Calvin perceived a spiritual battle between philosophy and theology. They are rivals for the truth and the hearts and souls of human beings. In this context, seen from the perspective of God, there can be one winner, eternal or heavenly philosophy. However, when it is clear that this certain truth of the gospel is above all earthly philosophy, then he is free to show how the heavenly philosophy incorporates the best teaching of non-Christian philosophy. From the perspective of humankind, then, the heavenly philosophy does not appear so much as a rival as the crown of all philosophy. From the perspective of God, it appears that the choice is between philosophy and theology. From the perspective of humankind, it appears that the choice is for both philosophy and theology. Calvin's understanding of the heavenly philosophy, then, is no less complex than his view of other anthropological concerns, for here, too, he uses his distinctive perspectival approach.

Conclusion

Calvin's understanding of the relationship between faith and reason and philosophy and theology is distinctive. A complex, dynamic perspectival structure operates throughout his discussions of this issue, illuminating several different relationships between the two terms. From the perspectives of God as creator and God as redeemer, the two stand in absolute contrast and contradiction to one another, being mutually exclusive; earthly wisdom and philosophy are to be rejected in favor of heavenly wisdom or the Christian philosophy. But from the perspective of humankind, earthly wisdom and philosophy are retrieved as necessary and valuable supplements to the heavenly wisdom and Christian philosophy since they are complementary. Because both relationships are essential to Calvin's view, theories which locate him in only one traditional Reason and Revelation type are insufficient. Calvin's view of faith and reason is best interpreted as a combination of the Reason and Revelation in Mutual Opposition type and the Revelation Dominant type. He emphasizes the former to incorporate the insights of Occam and Luther; the latter to incorporate the contributions of Augustine and Aquinas. He employs the former against the "papists" and humanists, both of whom jeopardized the truth of God's grace by not rightly distinguishing it from philosophy; and he uses the latter against the radical reformers, who jeopardized the truth of God's grace by not properly relating it to human wisdom.

Notes

/1/   *CO* 35: 237–38 (s. 137 on Job 35); *CO* 45: 207 (on Mt. 22:23).

/2/   *OS* 3: 31 (*Inst*. 1.1.1); *OS* 3: 256 (*Inst*. 2.2.13).

/3/   T. H. L. Parker notes this change in terminology in *Calvin's Doctrine of the Knowledge of God* (Grand Rapids: Wm: B. Eerdmans, 1959), pp. 15–16, but for a different reason.

/4/   Although the index to the *Corpus Reformatorum* lists very few references to *sapientia* and many for *cognitio* and *notitia*, this reflects the indexer's bias more than Calvin's actual use of the terms. Calvin's treatise *De Scandalis* (*OS* 2: 262–340), for instance, consistently uses this term more than any other. Calvin speaks there of wisdom in general (*OS* 2: 169, 177; *Concerning Scandals* [hereafter referred to as *Scandals*], trans. John W. Fraser [Grand Rapids: Wm. B. Eerdmans, 1978], pp. 12, 25), the wisdom of the flesh (*OS* 2: 176; *Scandals*, p. 24), human wisdom (*OS* 2: 175–77, 214; *Scandals*, pp. 22–24, 80), heavenly wisdom (*OS* 2: 170, 172, 207; *Scandals*, pp. 16, 18, 70), Christ's wisdom (*OS* 2: 167; *Scandals*, p. 11), the eternal and infinite wisdom of God (*OS* 2: 177, 233; *Scandals*, pp. 25, 109), and true wisdom (*OS* 2: 173; *Scandals*, p. 19), in each case choosing the term *sapientia*. The same term is found frequently in his *Commentary on I Corinthians* and also in the *Institutes* (e.g., see 1.1.1 in *OS* 3: 31; 1.52 in *OS* 3: 46; 3.20.48 in *OS* 5: 137; 4.10.29 in *OS* 5: 187; 4.17.24 in *OS* 5: 376).

/5/   This particular typology is adapted from Leroy Nixon's in *John Calvin's Teachings on Human Reason* (New York: Exposition Press, 1963), pp. 185–203. To the four he outlines (as indicated above), I have added a fifth: Reason as Preparation for Revelation.

/6/   The proponents of these various judgments will be identified in the course of the discussion.

/7/   *CO* 32: 633 (s. 13 on Ps. 100). See also: *CO* 33: 576 (s. 46 on Job 12); *CO* 49: 359 (*sapientia*) (I Corinthians 3:19).

/8/   *OS* 5: 375 (*Inst*. 4.17.24); *OS* 4: 370 (*Inst*. 3.21.1); *CO* 49: 337 (I Corinthians 2:7); *CO* 51: 462 (s. on Eph. 3:9–12); *CO* 40: 584–85 (Lect. 8 on Dan. 2:28); *CO* 35: 9 (s. 119 on Job 32); *CO* 31: 88 (Ps. 8:1); *CO* 33: 532 (s. 43 on Job 3); *OS* 2: 177 (*Scandals*, p. 25).

/9/   *CO* 50: 24 (II Corinthians 1:21).

/10/   *CO* 52: 151 (I Thess. 2:13). See also his preface to the *Institutes* (*OS* 2: 22).

/11/   Cf. William Bouwsma's conclusion in "Calvin and the Crisis of Knowledge in the Renaissance," *Calvin Theological Journal* 17 (November, 1982):

190–211. He argues that Calvin's choice is in favor of the Renaissance retreat from the absolute truth assumed in medieval theology. This conclusion, however, does not allow him to do justice to many of Calvin's statements praising the absolute certainty of faith. He ignores many of these comments. Those he does treat, he interprets on the basis of the scant biographical data available on Calvin's own faith and doubt struggle and in terms of Calvin's hermeneutic for the scriptures. This information leads him to conclude that Calvin's statements on the absolute certainty of heavenly wisdom are mere vestiges or signs of a lingering ambivalence about the retreat from absolute truth. The structure I have used to interpret Calvin's remarks on absolute certainty allows for a more orderly interpretation than this psychological and hermeneutical approach. This complex structure shows that Calvin is not a Renaissance man with lapses of longing for the security of the Middle Ages. Rather, Calvin is a fully Renaissance man who is attempting to join together the Thomist-Augustinian tradition of faith and reason and the Lutheran corrective to that tradition. With his complex structure he attempts to affirm both the Renaissance suspicion of the absolute and the Medieval celebration of the absolute.

/12/   CO 36: 334 (Is. 19:11). See also CO 55: 246 (Eph. 2:15); CO 37: 170 (Is. 47:13); and CO 55: 412–13 (James 3:15).

/13/   CO 23: 779 (s. 3 on Gen. 22); CO 54: 329 (s. 27 on II Tim.); CO 49: 326 (I Cor. 1:21); CO 50: 561 (s. 23 on Gal. 3); CO 35: 211 (s. 135 on Job 34); CO 7: 165 (*Des Libertins*).

/14/   CO 31: 363 (Ps. 36:9); CO 49: 338 (I Cor. 2:8); CO 47: 19 (Jn. 1:18).

/15/   CO 47: 231 (Jn. 9:34).

/16/   CO 9: 312–13 (*De Occulta Providentia Dei*). See also CO 47: 6 (Jn. 1:5) and CO 33: 346 (s. 28 on Job 7).

/17/   McNeill 1: 284–85, *Inst.* 2.2.25 in OS 3: 267–68. See also: CO 37: 170; CO 47: 13; CO 33: 576–78; CO 47: 6; CO 35: 244; OS 2: 174 (*Scandals*, p. 20).

/18/   OS 4: 378 (*Inst.* 4.17.25); CO 54: 627–30 (s. 52 on I. Tim. 6:15–16).

/19/   CO 7: 169 (*Des Libertins*); CO 50: 17 (II Cor. 1:12); OS 5: 146 (*Inst.* 4.8.13).

/20/   CO 47: 125.

/21/   CO 51: 459 (s. 18 on Eph. 3:9–12).

/22/   CO 34: 523 (s. 103 on Job 28). See also OS 3: 260 (*Inst.* 2.2.17).

/23/   CO 47: 9 (Jn. 1:9); CO 33: 158 (s. 12 on Job 3).

/24/   CO 47: 9 (Jn. 1:9).

/25/   McNeill 1:39, *Inst.* 1.2.1 in OS 3: 34.

/26/Because he fails to note the different kinds of knowledge in Calvin and the true difference between faith and reason, Battenhouse is incorrect in saying that ". . . faith and knowledge are closely identified in Calvin's thought. Hence, unbelief, the failure of the hearth or of choice, is closely associated with a departure from 'right reason'; and the critic may see here, I think, an affinity with the Stoic view that this is what gives rise to the passions. Calvin teaches us that from unbelief, as from a root, sprang first a loss of reason and judgment leading to mad ambition, then pride and obstinacy, so that now man has become 'of himself nothing else but concupiscence,'" "The Doctrine of Man in Calvin," p. 456.

/27/   *CO* 49: 324–25 (I. Cor. 1:20).

/28/   Ibid.

/29/   *CO* 33: 586 (s. 57 on Job 12).

/30/   *CO* 35: 244 (s. 138 on Job 35). See also *CO* 53: 42 (s. 4 on I Tim. 1: 5–7).

/31/   Commentary on I Corinthians 1:20 in *Calvin's New Testament Comentaries*, ed. David W. Torrance and Thomas F. Torrance, vol. 9: *The First Epistle of Paul to the Corinthians*, trans. John W. Fraser (Grand Rapids: Wm. B. Eerdmans, 1960), 9: 38 (*CO* 49: 324–25). See also *OS* 4: 414 (*Inst.* 3.24.4); *OS* 3: 157 (*Inst.* 1.14.4); *CO* 33: 576–78 (s. 46 on Job 12); *CO* 55: James 3:13); *CO* 36: 337–38 (Is. 19:13); *CO* 53: 625 (I Tim. 6:15); *CO* 49: 324–25 (I Cor. 1:20).

/32/   Commentary on I Cor. 1:18–20, Fraser 9: 38–39 (*CO* 49: 324–25).

/33/   *Scandals*, p. 22 (*OS* 2: 175).

/34/   *Scandals*, pp. 12–13 (*OS* 2: 169).

/35/   *OS* 2: 175 (*Scandals*, p. 22).

/36/   *CO* 49: 326–27 (I Cor. 1:21).

/37/   *OS* 4: 30 (*Inst.* 3.2.20); *CO* 35: 345 (s. 146 on Job 37). *CO* 33: 569 (s. 46 on Job 12); *CO* 49: 328 (I Cor. 1:25); *OS* 4: 371 (*Inst.* 3.21.2); *CO* 35: 347 (s. 146 on Job 37); *CO* 35: 363 and 364 (s. 148 on Job 38).

/38/   *CO* 36: 117–118 (Is. 5:21). See also *CO* 34: 258 (s. 82 on Job 21).

/39/   *CO* 33: 535 (s. 43 on Job 11).

/40/   *CO* 33: 57 (s. 4 on Job 1); *CO* 53: 625 (s. 52 on I Tim. 6:15); *CO* 35: 347 (s. 146 on Job 37); *CO* 35: 69 (s. 124 on Job 33); *CO* 49: 23 (Rom. 1:19).

/41/   *CO* 52: 100 (Col. 2:3); *CO* 55: 71 (Heb. 6:4); *CO* 44: 490 (Mal. 14:2).

/42/   *CO* 49: 331–32 (I Cor. 1:30).

/43/   *CO* 47: 62 (Jn. 3:13); *CO* 55: 143 (Heb. 11:1); *CO* 33: 528 (s. on Job 11); *CO* 54: 58 (s. 5 on II Tim. 1).

/44/   Commentary on I Cor. 1:26–27, Fraser 9: 43–44 (*CO* 49: 329–30).

/45/   Dowey, *The Knowledge of God in Calvin's Theology*, p. 72; Niesel, *The Theology of Calvin*, p. 49; Torrance, *Calvin's Doctrine of Man*, p. 101.

/46/   *CO* 40: 226 (Ez. 11:1–2). See also *CO* 47: 6 (Jn. 1:5); *OS* 3: 45 (*Inst.* 1.5.1); *CO* 35: 207–8 (s. 143 on Job 36).

/47/   *CO* 49: 326 (I Cor. 1:21); *CO* 47: 9 (Jn. 1:9); *CO* 35: 4 (s. 119 on Job 32).

/48/   *OS* 3: 59 (*Inst.* 1.5.14). See also *OS* 3: 64 (*Inst.* 1.6.4) and *CO* 31: 136 (Ps. 14).

/49/   *CO* 48: 497 (I Cor. 12).

/50/   *Scandals*, p. 24 (*OS* 2: 176).

/51/   *OS* 3: 264–65 (*Inst.* 2.2.22).

/52/   McNeill 1:272, *Inst.* 2.2.13 in *OS* 3: 256–57. See also *CO* 33: 574 (s. 46 on Job 12) and *OS* 3: 264–65 (*Inst.* 2.2.22).

/53/   *CO* 34: 510–11 (s. 102 on Job 28); *CO* 37: 118 (Is. 44:19); *CO* 35: 343 (s. 146 on Job 37).

/54/   *CO* 40: 585 (Lec. 8 on Dan. 28); *OS* 3: 34 (*Inst.* 1.2.1); *CO* 33: 252 (s. 20 on Job 5); *CO* 40: 579 (Lec. 7 on Dan. 2); *CO* 40: 579–80 (Lec. 7 on Dan. 2); *CO* 35: 22 (s. 120 on Job 32).

/55/   *CO* 23: 100 (Gen. 4:20).

/56/   *Letters of John Calvin*, ed. John Bonnet, trans. David Constable

(Edinburgh: n.p., 1857), 4 vols., 2: 212–13 [hereafter referred to as *Letters*] (*CO* 9:50). This passage alone would be sufficient to refute Bouwsma's claim that Calvin was not concerned with absolute truth and that he relied more on audial than visual mataphors.

/57/   *CO* 48: 507 (Acts 23:6); *OS* 3: 259 (*Inst.* 2.2.16). This means that while the scriptures complete, correct, and clarify reason, reason can also be used to confirm the truth of scripture. J. T. McNeill denies this, however, with his odd comment in his edition of the *Institutes*, 1:54, n. 25. He comments that while there is evidence that Calvin is arguing on the basis of human reason for the presence of God in the creation, "such biblical allusions as he makes are comparative and confirmatory, not constitutive of his argument." True, his biblical allusions in this argument are not fully constitutive of his argument. They are not used as simple comparisons, however, for the scriptures complete, correct and clarify reason's gleanings and sanctified reason can confirm what has otherwise been established as the certain truth of God. This idea of "complete, correct, and clarify," I borrowed from Reinhold Niebuhr's view of the relationship between faith and reason in *The Nature and Destiny of Man* (New York: Chas. Scribner's Sons, 1941), 1:123–49.

/58/   Torrance misses this absolute rejection of human reason in Calvin, noting only that reason becomes perverted, *Calvin's Doctrine of Man*, p. 117. His conclusion is odd in light of the fact that he insists that the *imago dei* has been totally lost in the Fall. As we have suggested in this chapter, Calvin's view of the *imago dei* and his view of reason are closely related to one another. Torrance fails to make this connection and speaks only of the image as wholly lost and reason as perverted.

/59/   Hiram Haydn, *The Counter-Renaissance* (New York: Harcourt, Brace & World, 1950), p. 98.

/60/   Dowey, *The Knowledge of God*, p. 134.

/61/   Nixon, *John Calvin's Teachings*, p. 191.

/62/   Neibuhr, *Nature and Destiny of Man*, 1: 284, n. 4.

/63/   Ibid. He writes, "It is hardly logical to claim that something which is only 'partially vitiated' exhibits 'nothing but deformity and ruin.' But there is at least an approach in this inconsistency to the fact that reason is both a servant of sinful self-love and an organ of judgment upon it."

/64/   See B. A. Gerrish, *Grace and Reason*. There is a great need in Calvin studies for a parallel work to be written on Calvin's view of reason.

/65/   Once again I must stress the limited goal of this inquiry. Just as this is not a treatise on Calvin's epistemology, so this is not a study of Calvin's view of philosophy. I am interested in how Calvin's view and use of philosophy help to clarify his view of reason; and I am interested in his view of reason only insofar as it has a bearing on the larger anthropological question. For more indepth studies of Calvin and philosophy, See Partee, *Calvin and Classical Philosophy* and Babelotzky, *Platonische Bilder*.

/66/   *CO* 3: 367 (s. 148 on Job 38). See also *CO* 35: 433 (s. 153 on Job 39).

/67/   *CO* 48: 466–67 (Acts 20:26–27). See also *CO* 54: 319 (s. 26 on II Tim. 4:2–5); *CO* 53: 651 (s. 54 on I Tim. 6:20–21).

/68/   *CO* 55: 574 (Pet. 3:5–8).

/69/   *CO* 48: 404 (Acts 17:16); *CO* 48: 408; *CO* 28: 23.

/70/   *CO* 31: 594 (Ps. 63:3).

/71/   *OS* 3: 57 (*Inst.* 1.5.12).

/72/   McNeill 1: 120–21, *Inst.* 1.13.1 in *OS* 3: 108.

/73/   *OS* 4: 149 (*Inst.* 3.6.4). See also *OS* 4: 34 (*Inst.* 3.2.24).

/74/   McNeill 2: 850, *Inst.* 3.20.1 in *OS* 4: 297. (Emphasis mine.)

/75/   McNeill 1: 496, *Inst.* 2.15.2 in *OS* 3: 474.

/76/   Ibid. (Emphasis mine.)

/77/   McNeill 1: 107, *Inst.* 1.11.7 in *OS* 3: 95–96.

/78/   *OS* 4: 152 (*Inst.* 3.7.1).

/79/   *CO* 34: 512 (s. 102 on Job 28).

/80/   Ibid. See also *CO* 47: 4 (Jn. 1:3); *CO* 38: 75 (Lec. on Jer. 10:12–13); *CO* 35: 367 (s. 148 on Job 38); *CO* 35: 303 (s. 143 on Job 36).

/81/   Commentary on Romans 12 in *Calvin's New Testament Commentaries*, eds. David W. Torrance and T. F. Torrance, trans. Ross Mackenzie, 12 vols. (Grand Rapids: Wm. B. Eerdmans, 1976), 8: 262, Rom. 12:1 in *CO* 49: 233.

/82/   *CO* 33: 729 (s. 58 on Job 15).

/83/   *CO* 37: 265 (Is. 53:11); *CO* 32: 321–24 (Ps. 127:1–2).

/84/   *CO* 54: 268 (s. 22 on II Tim. 3:10–13); *CO* 35: 668 (s. on Is. 53).

/85/   McNeill 1:198, *Inst.* 1.16.1 in *OS* 3: 188; *CO* 39: 588 (Lec. on Lam. 3)

/86/   *CO* 44: 374 (Zach. 14:9); *CO* 39: 459 (Lec. on Jer. 51:19).

/87/   *CO* 40: 620–1 (Lec. 13 on Dan. 3:3–7).

/88/   *CO* 40: 620 (Lec. 13 on Dan. 3:3–7).

/89/   *OS* 5: 479 (*Inst.* 4.20.9).

/90/   *CO* 40: 709 (Lec. 25 on Dan. 5:13–16).

/91/   *CO* 36: 337–38 (Is. 19:13); *CO* 47: 217–18 (Jn. 9:-1).

/92/   *CO* 48: 403 (Acts 17:16). See also *OS* 3: 47–48 (*Inst.* 1.5.4) and *OS* 3: 56–57 (*Inst.* 1.5.12).

/93/   *CO* 32: 145 (Ps. 107:43).

/94/   *CO* 23: 46 (Gen. 2:18), "Platonem et alios philosophos saniores."

/95/   *OS* 3: 266 (*Inst.* 2.2.23); *OS* 3: 185 (*Inst.* 1.15.7).

/96/   *CO* 32: 145 (Ps. 107:43).

/97/   Ibid.

/98/   *CO* 48: 403 (Acts 17:16). See also *CO* 23: 47 (Gen. 2:18). For a fuller discussion of Calvin's view of the Stoics, see Partee, *Calvin and Classical Philosophy*, p. 122ff. and Egil Grislis, "Calvin's Use of Cicero in the *Institutes* 1:1–5: A Case Study in Theological Method," *Archiv für Reformationsgeschichte* 62 (1971): 5–37.

/99/   *OS* 3: 265 (*Inst.* 2.2.22); *OS* 3: 267 (*Inst.* 2.2.25); *OS* 3: 433 (*Inst.* 3.25.2); *OS* 5: 130–31 (*Inst.* 4.18.15); *OS* 5: 486 (*Inst.* 4.20.14). For a fuller discussion of Calvin's view of Plato, see Partee, *Calvin and Classical Philosophy*, pp. 105ff. and Babelotzky, *Platonische Bilder*.

/100/   *CO* 31: 452 (Ps. 45:7); *OS* 5: 486 (*Inst.* 4.20.14); *CO* 36: 82 (Is. 3:4); *CO* 23: 201 (Gen. 14:18); *CO* 34: 165–66 (s. 74 on Job 20).

/101/   *CO* 23: 46 (Gen. 2:18).

/102/   *CO* 51: 204 (Eph. 4:17).

/103/   McNeill 1: 46–47, *Inst.* 1.3.3 in *OS* 3: 40.

/104/   McNeill 2: 1443, *Inst.* 4.18.15 in *OS* 5: 430–41.

/105/   *CO* 23: 345 (Gen. 25:8); *CO* 23: 219 (Gen. 15:15).

/106/ *CO* 32: 95 (Ps. 104:29).
/107/ McNeill 1: 64, *Inst.* 1.5.11 in *OS* 3: 55.
/108/ *CO* 55: 221 (I Pet. 1:14); *OS* 3: 265 (*Inst.* 2.2.22); *OS* 3: 267 (*Inst.* 2.2.25); *OS* 4: 376 (*Inst.* 3.23.2).
/109/ *CO* 33: 542 (s. 43 on Job 11); *OS* 3: 257 (*Inst.* 2.2.14).
/110/ *CO* 40: 569 (Lec. 6 on Dan. 2:11); *CO* 32: 434 (Ps. 148:5).
/111/ Niesel, *The Theology of Calvin*, pp. 22–53.
/112/ Dowey, *The Knowledge of God*, p. 10. See also p. 13 where he remarks that "Here, *as everywhere in Calvin's theology, the only successful medium* of intercourse between God and fallen man is the Word." (Emphasis mine.)
/113/ See B. B. Warfield's discussion of Calvin's doctrine of the doctrine of God in *Calvin and Augustine* (Philadelphia: Presbyterian & Reformed Publishing Co., 1952), pp. 162–63.
/114/ See Partee, *Calvin and Classical Philosophy*, pp. 146, 14.
/115/ See Grislis, "Calvin's Use of Cicero," pp. 5–37 and François Wendel, *Calvin et l'humanisme* (Paris: Presses Universitaires de France, 1976), pp. 63–98.
/116/ Joseph C. McClelland, "Calvin and Philosophy," *Canadian Journal of Theology* 11 (January 1965): 45.
/117/ Partee, *Calvin and Classical Philosophy*, p. 146. See also his Introduction to the study.
/118/ Ibid., p. 95.
/119/ A close parallel to this view may be found in Luther's view and use of philosophy, especially as it is so clearly analyzed and presented by B. A. Gerrish in *Grace and Reason*.
/120/ McClelland, "Calvin and Philosophy," pp. 48, 53.
/121/ Partee, *Calvin and Classical Philosophy*, chapt. 2, esp. p. 12. It is odd, however, that Partee, throughout this chapter, entitled "Calvin's Description of Christian Philosophy," notes only four instances of the term "Christian philosophy" in Calvin's work (*Inst.* 1.11.7; 1.12.1; 3.6.4; and 3.7.1). This is hardly sufficient evidence on which to base his claim that this is the term that Calvin chose to describe his theological work (p. 12). I have found many more instances of this term in Calvin's work and will identify them in the course of this section of the chapter.
/122/ McNeill 1: 67, *OS* 3: 7. (Emphasis mine.)
/123/ *OS* 3: 6 (Letter to the Reader).
/124/ *CO* 47: 52 (Jn. 3:1).
/125/ *OS* 1: 37 (1536 edition of *Inst.*).
/126/ *OS* 2: 170, 173 (*Scandals*, pp. 15, 20); *OS* 4: 152 (*Inst.* 3.7.1).
/127/ Jean LeClerq, "Pour l'histoire de l'expression 'Philosophie chrétienne,'" *Mélanges de Science Religieuse* 9 (1952): 225.
/128/ Ibid., p. 221.
/129/ For the reference to Budé, see Bohatec, *Budé and Calvin*, pp. 30–31.
/130/ Partee, *Calvin and Classical Philosophy*, Preface. See also, p. 12.
/131/ Calvin, Erasmus, and Budé all see philosophy as a preparation for Christian faith, but Calvin emphasizes also the absolute contradiction between the two. At times he even interprets the preparation of philosophy for

faith in terms of the contradiction: "The voice of the prophet cries 'Prepare the way of the Lord,' (Is. 40:3) and what reason is there for preparing it, except when men are driven to acknowledge the need, and to begin to have a longing for Christ, at whom they used to scoff in the days when they pleased themselves. In the same way let us also prepare the way for ourselves to Christ, and indeed that pious longing will be like horses and ships to us, enabling us to pass by all obstacles. For just as you need a cultivated and well-prepared mind to engage in the study of the higher disciplines, so you require a trained mind for the heavenly philosophy. For what taste is there for it when there is disgust? How can an entrance be effected when a total iron hardness has enclosed and barred the heart?" *Scandals*, p. 20 (*OS* 2: 173). Calvin is substituting the preparation of humility and longing for the preparation of philosophical studies.

/132/ This is the judgment of Ford Lewis Battles and André Malan Hugo, editors and translators of Calvin's *Commentary on Seneca's "De Clementia"* (Leiden: E. J. Brill, 1969), pp. 114–15.

/133/ Niesel, *The Theology of Calvin*, p. 23.

/134/ Partee, *Calvin and Classical Philosophy*, p. 14.

/135/ Ibid.

/136/ See Étienne Gilson, *The Spirit of Medieval Philosophy*, trans. Alfred Howard Campbell Downes, The Gifford Lectures for 1931 (New York: n.p., 1940), chapt. 2.

/137/ Bohatec, *Budé und Calvin*, p. 31, n. 47 and pp. 241ff. Babelotzky agrees with Bohatec's claim that Calvin was influenced by Budé in this, adding only, that the influence of Plato is present here, also, *Platonische Bilder*, p. 90. Ford Lewis Battles, editor and translator of a different version of *Institutes of the Christian Religion* (Atlanta: John Knox, 1969), p. 327, claims, however, that this correlation of the knowledge of God and ourselves shows a clear parallel with the work of Bucer. Luchesius Smits points out the parallel understandings of the relation of self-knowledge and God-knowledge in Thomas à Kempis, Erasmus, Budé, and Calvin in *Saint Augustin dans l'oeuvre de Calvin*, 1: 20ff.

/138/ *CO* 33: 542 (s. 43 on Job 11). See also *CO* 33: 539.

/139/ McNeill 1: 241–42, *Inst.* 2.1.1 in *OS* 3: 228.

/140/ *OS* 4: 34 (*Inst.* 3.2.24).

/141/ *CO* 48: 418 (Acts 17:28).

/142/ *CO* 23: 139 (Gen. 8:21); *CO* 36: 545 (Is. 32:5–6); *CO* 51: 206 (Eph. 4:19).

/143/ *CO* 55: 48 (Heb. 4:10); *CO* 55: 446–47 (II Pet. 1:4); *CO* 33: 654 (s. 53 on Job 14); *CO* 34: 156 (s. 74 on Job 22); *CO* 34: 503–4 (s. 101 on Job 28); *CO* 48: 462–63 (Acts 20:21); *CO* 51: 205–6 (Eph. 4: 18–19).

/144/ *CO* 35: 84–85 (s. 125 on Job 33); *CO* 54: 47 (s. 4 on II Tim. 1:8–9); *CO* 8: 396–97 (Four Sermons).

/145/ *CO* 53: 623 (s. 52 on I Tim. 6:15–16). Emphasis mine.)

/146/ *Scandals*, p. 62 (*OS* 2: 202).

/147/ *Scandals*, p. 110 (*OS* 2: 234).

/148/ *CO* 37: 429–30 (Is. 45:19).

/149/ *CO* 35: 3 (s. 119 on Job 32); *CO* 46: 780.

/150/ *CO* 8: 625.

/151/   *CO* 50: 591.
/152/   Dowey, *The Knowledge of God*, p. 185.
/153/   *CO* 53: 625 (s. 52 on I. Tim.).
/154/   *CO* 9: 823-24.
/155/   *CO* 48: 570 (Acts 28:25).
/156/   *CO* 50: 24 (II Cor. 1:21): *OS* 2: 202 (*Scandals*, p. 62).
/157/   *CO* 51: 153; *CO* 50: 522 (s. 20 on Ga. 3:15–18). Dowey notes that
Calvin uses this in his formal definition of faith, but he interprets it only in
terms of objective and subjective knowledge, not in terms of certainty, *The
Knowledge of God*, pp. 176–77.
/158/   *CO* 51: 574 (s. 26 on Eph.).
/159/   *OS* 3: 68–70 (*Inst.* 1.7.4) and *OS* 3: 71–74 (*Inst.* 1.8).
/160/   *CO* 49: 326–27 (I Cor. 1:21); *CO* 33: 509 (s. 41 on Job); *CO* 35: 425 (s.
152 on Job); *CO* 54: 315 (s. 26 on II Tim.).
/161/   *CO* 31: 487 (Ps. 49:13). See also *CO* 53: 635 (s. 53 on I Tim. 6:17–19);
CO 33: 158 (s. 12 on Job 3); *CO* 53: 96 (s. 8 on I Tim. 1:17–19).
/162/   Torrance, *Calvin's Doctrine of Man*, pp. 14–15.
/163/   André Biéler, *The Social Humanism of Calvin*, trans. Paul T.
Fuhrmann (Richmond, Virginia: John Knox Press, 1964), p. 13.
/164/   *OS* 3: 252–53 (*Inst.* 2.2.10) and *OS* 4: 163 (*Inst.* 3.8.3)
/165/   *CO* 34: 468 (s. 98 on Job 27).
/166/   *CO* 34: 464 (s. 98 on Job 27).
/167/   *CO* 50: 62 (II Cor. 5:5)
/168/   *CO* 40: 631 (Lec. 15 on Dan. 3:16–18). (Emphasis mine.)
/169/   *CO* 35: 96 (s. 126 on Job 33).
/170/   *CO* 35: 513 (s. 159 on Job 42).
/171/   *CO* 31: 486 (Ps. 49:11).
/172/   *CO* 50: 64 (II Cor. 5:8).
/173/   *CO* 54: 392 (s. 2 on Tit. 1:1–4).
/174/   McNeill 1: 690, *Inst.* 3.7.1 in *OS* 3: 152. See also *CO* 35: 49–50 (s.
122 on Job).
/175/   *CO* 31: 180 (Ps. 49:2).
/176/   *CO* 31: 399 (Ps. 39:5); *OS* 3: 172 (*Inst.* 3.9.2); *CO* 31: 486 (Ps. 49:11).
/177/   *CO* 31: 487 (Ps. 49:13).
/178/   See chapter 1, pp. 18–22.
/179/   Partee, *Calvin and Classical Philosophy*, p. 21.
/180/   Ibid.

CHAPTER IV

DIVINE PROVIDENCE AND HUMAN FREEDOM

> Now in the schools three kinds of freedom are distinguished: first from necessity, second from sin, third from misery. The first of these so inheres in man by nature that it cannot possibly be taken away, but the two others have been lost through sin. I willingly accept this distinction, except in so far as necessity is falsely confused with compulsion.
>
> John Calvin

Introduction

Scholars have yet to agree on Calvin's view of the will and human freedom. It is a commonplace, as Allen Verhey notes, to speak of Calvin as a determinist.[1] Many scholars, Kristeller among them, state flatly, as if it were self-evident, that Calvin denied all freedom to the human will.[2] Others argue that Calvin was a voluntarist, placing the will over reason in the self and the power of God over the love of God in theology proper.[3] Battenhouse claims that "Calvin challenges men to activism no less than Pico challenges him to dynamic creativity," even though they may differ on the extent of the will's freedom.[4] Still others, noting that Calvin offers both a strict doctrine of predestination and a strict moral code, conclude that Calvin is neither a determinist nor a defender of human freedom; rather, he exhibits a fundamental contradiction in his thought at this point.[5] More recently, John Leith has asserted that Calvin's doctrine of the will is not contradictory but rather a profound analysis of Christian experience that is preeminently doxological.[6]

In order to help clarify Calvin's doctrine of the will and human freedom I will analyze his view of human will and freedom in relation to the various forms of creative and redemptive providence, highlighting the distinctive character of his perspectival approach.[7] Before proceeding to the detailed analysis of Calvin's view I will briefly sketch the main contours of his contribution.

Calvin develops his doctrine of the will and human freedom in conjunction with his doctrine of the *imago dei*, and, once again, the perspectival structure appears. As one of the two fundamental faculties of the soul, the seat of the *imago dei*, the will *(voluntas)* is both defaced and erased by sin. From the relative perspective of humankind, the will *(voluntas)* is an inviolable gift of the creator that remains after the Fall. From the absolute perspective of God as redeemer, however, free choice *(liberum arbitrium)* is wholly lost after the Fall. As the following discussion will show, his careful distinctions between *voluntas* and *liberum arbitrium* and the distinction between the divine and human perspectives enable him to affirm freedom of the will as constitutive of human beings and deny freedom of choice as destructive of God's free grace.

In Book 1 of the *Institutes*, immediately before discussing the providence of God, Calvin identifies will as one of the two fundamental faculties of the soul.

> Thus let us, therefore, hold . . . that the human soul consists of two faculties, understanding [*intellectum*] and will [*voluntatem*]. Let the office, moreover, of understanding be to distinguish between objects, as each seems worthy of approval or disapproval; while that of the will, to choose [*eligere*] and follow what the understanding pronounces good, but to reject and flee what it disapproves.[8]

He explains this theologically in the next section.

> Therefore God provided man's soul with a mind, by which to distinguish good from evil, right from wrong; and with the light of reason as guide, to distinguish what should be followed from what should be avoided. For this reason, the philosophers called this directing part *to hēgemonikon*. To this he joined the will [*voluntatem*], under whose control is choice [*electio*]. Man in his first condition excelled in these preeminent endowments, so that his reason, understanding, prudence, and judgment not only sufficed for the direction of his earthly life, but by them men mounted up even to God in eternal bliss. Then was choice [*electio*] added to direct the appetites and control all the organic motions, and thus make

the will [*voluntas*] completely amenable to the guidance of the reason.

In this integrity man by free will [*libero arbitrio*] had the power, if he so willed [*vellet*] to attain eternal life. Here it would be out of place to raise the question of God's secret predestination because our present subject is not what can happen or not, but what man's nature was like. Therefore Adam could have stood if he wished [*vellet*], seeing that he fell solely by his own free will [*propria voluntate*]. But it was because his will [*voluntas*] was capable of being bent to one side or the other, and was not given the constancy to persevere, that he fell so easily. Yet his choice of good and evil was free [*libera tamen fuit electio boni et mali*], and not that alone, but the highest rectitude was in his mind and will [*voluntate*], and all the organic parts were rightly composed to obedience, until in destroying himself he corrupted his own blessings.

Hence the great obscurity faced by the philosophers, for they were seeking in a ruin for a building, and in scattered fragments for a well-knit structure. They held this principle, that man would not be a rational animal unless he possessed free choice of good and evil [*libera boni et mali electio*]. . . . Well reasoned so far—if there had been no change in man. But since this was hidden from them, it is no wonder they mix up heaven and earth! They, as professed disciples of Christ, are obviously playing the fool when, by compromising between the opinions of the philosophers and heavenly doctrine, so that these touch neither heaven nor earth, in man—who is lost and sunk down into spiritual destruction—they still seek after free choice [*liberum arbitrium*].[9]

I have quoted this crucial passage of the Institutes in full because it sets the terms of the following analysis. At creation humankind, as *imago dei*, was given the gift of will *(voluntas)*, which included the capacity of choice *(electio)*. It was also given the gift of freedom: freedom from necessity, freedom from sin, and freedom from misery. At the Fall, only the latter two were lost; the former was retained.

Now in the schools three kinds of freedom are distinguished: first from necessity, second from sin, third from misery. The first of these so inheres in man by nature that it cannot possibly be taken away, but the two others have been lost through sin. I willingly accept this distinction, except in so far as necessity is falsely confused with compulsion.[10]

Calvin makes use of this threefold distinction throughout his discussion of will and freedom, although he redefines the first freedom as freedom from compulsion rather than necessity. When he discusses creative and redemptive providence the perspective of humankind appears, emphasizing that the will (*voluntas*) is constitutive of human existence and retains its freedom from compulsion. When he discusses the redemptive providence of election and justification the perspective of God as judge appears, emphasizing that the power of choice (*electio*), originally included in the gift of will (*voluntas*), has been lost, and along with it the freedom from sin, or the free choice (*liberum arbitrium*) between good and evil.[11] Both emphases must be uncovered if we are to have a full understanding of his view of the will and human freedom.

Creative Providence: Universal and Particular Providence and the Affirmation of Will [voluntas] and Freedom from Compulsion

Calvin develops his view of the retention of the will (*voluntas*) after the Fall and his affirmation of continuing human freedom from compulsion in his doctrine of universal and particular providence. In this doctrine he argues for a specific type of divine determinism that does not deny this inviolable human freedom from compulsion or coercion.

Universal providence, one type of creative providence, involves God's government of the universe according to the laws or order of nature.[12] Another way of stating this is to say that God is the principal cause of all things, even though they may have other, secondary causes.[13] For example, although it may appear that it is solely by the operation of natural causes that infants are born and nourished by their mothers, one must acknowledge that it is in and through these secondary causes that the providence of God, preserving the order of creation as the principal cause of all, shines forth. This providential government is to be understood not as a goddess of inevitability but in terms of the continuously active will of a just and good God. Without God as the principal cause to maintain them, all creatures would perish immediately.[14] God is continuously active in the order of nature sustaining it.[15] For this reason, one could say that the whole of nature is a series of miracles of God. Because we have grown so accustomed to the workings of nature, such as the birth and nourishment of infants, we do not perceive these ordinary occurrences as the miracles of God that they are.[16] It is because the order of nature is a series of miracles that Calvin can speak of this "universal providence of God as special."[17] By this he means that God takes special care at each moment of the workings of nature to move each thing as the principal cause. Everything, then, is a miracle.[18]

Calvin emphasizes this interpretation of his doctrine of universal providence for the express purpose of evoking the proper gratitude due to the creator. In interpreting universal providence in this active and continual way he explicitly rejects all pantheistic views and all views that dwell on natural causation to the exclusion of God. His emphasis on the order of nature as "God's book" and a constant stream of divine miracles calls forth gratitude to the creator.[19] The proper human response to this is the correct use of the secondary causes and the correct gratitude toward the principal cause. It is in the latter that many, especially Aristotelians, have failed.

> Philosophers think that they have reasoned skillfully enough about inferior causes when they separate God very far from his works: it is a diabolical science, however, which fixes our contemplation on the works of nature *and* turns them away from God.[20]

As much as Calvin rails against those who honor inferior causes over the principal cause, he finds those who attribute all events to fortune, fate, or chance even more reprehensible.

> [T]hose philosophers who assign the supreme authority to nature are much sounder than others who place fortune in the highest rank. If Fortune rules there is total chaos and neither nature nor God has a place and Epicureanism reigns.[21]

Those who attribute everything to fortune instead of to the providence of an active and purposeful God entangle God in a web, weaving natural causes together into a veil that shields our eyes from seeing God's care for the world.[22] Both Aristotelians and those who believe in blind fortune, therefore, fail to distinguish properly between secondary causes and the principal cause, God. Because this was such a common error in Calvin's day, he is quite circumspect when speaking of the coextensiveness of God's universal providence and the order of nature.

> I confess of course that it can be said reverently, provided that it proceeds from a reverent mind, that nature is God; but because it is a harsh and improper saying, since nature is rather the order prescribed by God, it is harmful in such weighty

> matters, in which special devotion is due, to involve God
> *confusedly* in the inferior course of his works.[23]

His aim in discussing universal creative providence is to underline
God's constant and active relation with the world. In doing so,
however, he never loses sight of the distinction that remains between God and the creation, between the principal cause and inferior causes.

While Calvin presents universal providence as active, total,
immediate and purposive, thereby distinguishing it from Aristo-
telianism and Stoicism, it is in his view of particular providence that
these four traits are highlighted. Particular creative providence refers to God's capacity to work against and without the order of
nature.[24] It is Calvin's discussion of particular providence that highlights the theological point he attempted to make in his discussion of
universal providence: that gratitude is due the creator for the miracle of every instant of life. In other words, even when the discussion
shifts to God's acts against and without the order of nature, Calvin's
focus is on God's acts *with* the order of nature in universal providence. It is because of the sluggish and sinful nature of humankind
that God acts in particular providence to govern the world. Because
we do not see the miracles of God in ordinary events such as
childbirth, God causes miracles that operate without or against the
ordinary course of events to stimulate our gratitude.[25] His point,
then, in treating particular providence, is not to affirm the nomi-
nalist doctrine of the power of God over nature, but to underline
pedagogically the need for continual gratitude to the creator for the
continuous care of the creation.

Calvin's treatment of particular creative providence serves another purpose: to distinguish the Christian view of providence from
popular indeterminisms more clearly. Against those who put their
faith in chance or blind fortune, Calvin emphasizes that God is the
cause of *all* events, both the ordinary political order and the dramatic reversals of political fortune sometimes experienced by
princes.[26] God's providence is total, encompassing life and death, all
creatures, and all of human affairs, whether any of these be "natural"
or "unnatural." This is the first argument against those who believe
in chance. The second concerns the purposiveness of God's providence. Adopting the image of the wheel of fortune, Calvin acknowledges that the world is full of sudden changes. He adapts this
popular image, however, to make his own theological point. The

image of the wheel does not connote fortune, blind chance, or accident, but the purposiveness of a God who controls all ordinary and extraordinary events toward what he perceives needs to be done.[27] He alters the image of the wheel of fortune then according to the image of the wheels of the chariot of God in the book of Ezekiel. The wheels do not roll willy-nilly, but according to the direction given them by God through the agency of the angels. And, he sometimes adds, the wheels are not blind but "full of eyes."[28] All things, then, no matter how odd or extraordinary, are directed by the hidden energy and will of God. It is only because of our own blindness that we do not see the structure of God's will in all events but only endless revolutions.[29] Without proper knowledge of the totality and purposiveness of God's universal and particular providence, persons invent "a blind chance to match their blindness."[30]

Particular creative providence also served to distinguish Calvin's position from that of the Epicureans. Against the Epicureans Calvin emphasizes the activity of God's providence. To counter their impious view of God sitting idly on a chaise lounge in heaven watching the world go by, Calvin stresses that the "providence we describe belongs not only to his eyes but to his hands."[31] Though God's throne is in heaven, God keeps a constant hand in the affairs of the earth.[32] God does not sleep in heaven, relinquishing the reins to chance or fortune, but uses an active and immediate power over all things.[33] Since it is particular providence that highlights this, this is the type of providence that Calvin refers to most often in his polemic against the Epicureans.

He also emphasizes the activity and immediacy of God's providence, as seen most clearly in particular providence, against the common medieval and Renaissance distinction between divine command and divine foreknowledge or permission. Theologians such as Valla had tried to harmonize divine government and human freedom by distinguishing between foreknowledge and willing, arguing that

> [b]ecause God foreknows the action of a man does not mean
> that his action is necessitated, because he performs it quite
> willingly—and what is willing cannot be necessitated.[34]

Calvin rejects this commonly accepted distinction between divine decree and divine foreknowledge as a way of salvaging human freedom.[35] He insists that it falsifies both divine freedom and human freedom. According to his view, God's foreknowledge and power to

effect must never be separated.[36] Foreordination and foreknowledge, then, are to be understood as the same thing, namely, that "by
which God rules and regulates all."[37] The false distinction between
the two falls into the same error as Epicureans did: robbing God of
the active and immediate care over the world. To define divine
providence as foreknowledge alone is to turn God from the caring
parent that he is into a cold and idle Apollo.[38] Or, it robs God of all
control of the world, giving all the credit to Plato and his celestial
mysteries.[39] Thus, Calvin allows a distinction between foreknowledge and foreordination on his terms only.

> And although the foreknowledge of God is former in order
> (because God first foresees what he will determine, before he
> actually determines it), yet he [Peter] puts the foreknowledge
> of God after the counsel and decree of God, to the end that we
> may know that God wills nothing and appoints nothing except
> for that which he longs before directed to its ends. For men do
> often decree many things rashly, because they decree them
> suddenly. Therefore, so that Peter may teach that the counsel
> of God is not without reason, he adds "with his foreknowl-
> edge."[40]

When Calvin speaks of foreknowledge, therefore, he means "previously appointed,"[41] and when he speaks of providence, he means
"active caring";[42] but the two can never be separated without dis-
honoring God. It is the particular providence of God that highlights
God's immediate and active care over the entire creation.

Calvin's thorough delineation of the totality, activity, purposiveness, and immediacy of God's universal and particular providence constructs a divine determinism that seems to leave little
room for human freedom. His rejection of the distinction between
foreknowledge and foreordination especially seems to support a
denial of all freedom. One of the reasons why Calvin rejected this
distinction was that its proponents believed in a "confused government" in which God gave creatures the liberty to follow their own
natures and choose freely between good and evil.[43] His objection to
this parceling out of freedom is that it leaves God idle. Clearly the
divine determinism of his doctrine of creative providence rules out
an understanding of freedom of the will as the free choice between
good and evil *(liberum arbitrium)*. It is not clear, however, that this
divine determinism rules out the understanding of the will as natural human inclination or desire *(voluntas)* and freedom as freedom
from coercion. In fact, Calvin argues that it does not in responding

to two absurd conclusions his opponents drew from his view that God decrees all particular actions: (1) God is evil, and (2) evildoers are not free, and therefore, not responsible for their actions.[44]

Calvin indirectly defends the will *(voluntas)* and freedom from coercion in his divine determinism in his argument against the determinisms of the Stoics, the Sorbonnists, and the Libertines, and in his response to the objections of Pighius. He distinguishes his view from the determinism of the Stoics by emphasizing God's fatherly and purposeful care in both universal and particular providence. Though the Stoics may talk of providence, they teach only a cruel necessity to which God is bound as well as human beings.

> Although the Stoics said that the world is under the providence of God, yet they later spoiled that principle of their teaching with an absurd fiction or fantasy. For they did not say that God rules the world by his purpose, justice, and power, but they constructed a labyrinth out of a complicated system of causes so that God himself was bound by the necessity of fate, and was violently swept along with the heavenly machine just as the poets bind Jupiter with golder fetters, because the fates govern, while he is doing something else.[45]

While Calvin points to God's "purpose, justice, and power" as the key to the distinction between Stoic fate and Christian providence, he explicitly argues for a specific interpretation of the relation between divine justice and power in his battle with the Sorbonnists.

Calvin appears to be quite sensitive to the charge that his view of particular providence aligned him with the view of God as an arbitrary and absolute power held by many theologians at the Sorbonne. He was extremely critical of the Sorbonnist view of God as *ex lex,* charging that it was unscriptural since it presented God as a tyrant.[46] He argued further against these "papists" that

> to make God beyond the law is to rob him of the greatest part of his glory, for it destroys his rectitude and his righteousness. Not that God is subject to law, except insofar as He Himself is law. For such is the consent and agreement between his power and his righteousness that nothing proceeds from him that is not considered, legitimate, and regular.[47]

His constant refrain is that God's power and justice, or power and love, power and wisdom, and power and goodness, can never be separated from one another.[48] There is no naked power in God,

arbitrary and absolute as the power of a cruel tyrant. God's providence, therefore, is best understood not as power but as righteousness.[49] And the human response is best understood, then, not as
fear but as security, trust, gratitude, and joy.[50]

Calvin repeats this argument against the Libertines, who had
adopted a pantheistic version of determinism. In Calvin's view their
theology destroyed the distinction between God and the devil,
making God equally responsible for all events.[51] To counter this
impious view he once again insists that God's power and goodness
cannot be separated, adding only that God's freedom is demonstrated in his constancy and faithfulness to his purposes, promises,
and commitments. In other words, God's freedom and power are not
limited by anything external to himself, even human freedom, but
only by his own goodness, wisdom, justice, and love. Or as Allen
Verhey so aptly puts it, "It is more accurate to say, then, that for
Calvin God's freedom is not so much limited by his goodness as
constituted by (and genuinely known in) his goodness."[52] Verhey is
also correct in concluding that

> Calvin's alternative to the arbitrary omnipotence of the divine
> spirit of the Libertines is not "chance" or "fortune" or a radical
> indeterminism. The alternative is rather the constant care of
> God's fatherly hand, or providence.[53]

Thus Calvin opposes his divine determinism, the doctrine of
providence understood as righteousness rather than power, to the
Stoic, Sorbonnist, and Libertine forms of determinism. The implication is that his view leaves room for the inherent faculty of the will
(voluntas) and human freedom because the necessity of fatherly care
is not equivalent to the coercion of a disinterested power. His
argument here is weak and very sketchy. More often than not he
asserts that God is a father and not a cruel tyrant. And, most of his
argument rests on a claim that itself is only weakly supported,
namely, that God's power and justice can never be separated. Calvin
himself admits that the way in which these two are related remains
hidden to us, urging that the best we can do is to insist on their
inseparability. He supplements this rather weak argument, however, with a stronger and more direct one for the inviolability of the
will (voluntas) and freedom from coercion.

While to the Libertines the will and freedom were but fig-
ments of the imagination (cuider), to Calvin they were indelible
marks of the imago dei imprinted on the soul as a substance.[54] To

deny them, therefore, was to deny the gifts of the creator who remains faithful to the creation. In other words, Calvin's argument that divine providence does not destroy but sustains the created human constitution gifted with will and freedom is based on his view of the *imago dei* as effaced but not erased by sin.[55]

> As for man, the Scripture clearly teaches us that from the time he turned away from God his soul has been full of ignorance and vanity, full of perversity and rebellion against God, given over to evil, oppressed and vanquished by weakness. *Nevertheless* it continues to call him a creature of God, possessing in himself those natural conditions which God placed in him, *unless all of it is corrupted and depraved by sin.*
>
> Consequently, according to Scripture, man's soul is a spiritual substance endowed with sense and reason, in order to understand and pass judgments, and endowed also with will [*volunté*], in order to choose and desire those things that his life wants.
>
> True, the Scripture immediately admonishes us that our intelligence is perverted because of sin—so much that we are blind and our will [*volunté*], is corrupt, even to such an extent that only iniquity flows out of it. Nevertheless the soul continues to exist in its essence and to retain the inseparable qualities of its nature, according to the order that God has established.
>
> Consequently, to reduce the soul to imagination is an impudent act of resisting the truth, beyond the fact that by doing so the Libertines cause man to misunderstand himself to the end that he no longer cares about his soul, which our Lord hoped we would prefer above all the world (Matt. 16:26).[56]

Sin does not destroy the freedom from coercion that constitutes human beings. Calvin develops this same argument in his *Defensio Sanae et Orthodoxae de Servitute et Liberatione Humani Arbitrii Adversus Calumnias Pighii Campensis.*

In responding to Pighius's third argument, that if divine providence rules all things by necessity there is no need for human laws and discipline, Calvin explains that he is not a Stoic, believing in a fate that drags human beings along in its course against their wills. Rather, divine providence governs the world by bending *(flectere)* wills *(voluntates)* to its decision *(arbitrio)*. The necessity by which God governs by his stable and eternal plan *(consilium)* does not exclude intermediate causes, which God destined to be used in submission to his will.[57] The use of intermediate causes implies that human beings have the capacity to deliberate. This is exactly what

Calvin says in the *Institutes:* "[W]ith respect to future events . . . one can easily bring human deliberations [*deliberationes*] into agreement with God's providence."⁵⁸ In fact, God has given human beings the gift of "taking counsel and caution" so that they "may comply with his providence in the preservation of life."⁵⁹

What Calvin is arguing is that the necessity of divine providence is not the necessity of fate that drags human beings kicking and screaming against their wills. It is not coercion, which violates the very humanity of men and women by denying their *capacity to will* or their ability to deliberate. The necessity of divine providence, from the perspective of humankind, does not destroy *this* freedom of the will [*libera voluntate*].⁶⁰ So far we have seen Calvin develop this argument by maintaining the continuity of the *imago dei* after the Fall and the complementarity of the first cause and intermediate causes. His third major argument for the retention of the will (as the *faculty* [*voluntas*] in the soul) and freedom from coercion concerns the responsibility of the wicked for their actions. This argument will be presented under the heading of General Redemptive Providence.

Redemptive Providence I: General Redemptive Providence and the Affirmation of Will and Freedom from Coercion

I refer to Calvin's understanding of God's purposeful and benevolent activity in preserving and directing the world to the end of salvation as general redemptive providence. I use the adjective "general" to connote Calvin's view that this providence of God affects all events and all persons, regardless of whether or not they are believers; for God directs the actions of the wicked as well as those of the redeemed to the end that he perceives to be necessary. Or, as Calvin puts it, the wicked cannot even get out of bed in the morning if it is against the ordinance of God.⁶¹ Once again the totality, immediacy, and activity of divine providence are evident. And, in this case of general redemptive providence, they raise the difficult question of whether God is the author of evil. This is precisely the conclusion the Libertines had come to, thereby absolving human beings of all responsibility for sin and of the duty to live a moral life. Predictably, Calvin finds this conclusion abhorrent, insisting that human freedom is necessary for a proper understanding of sin. He constructs an argument affirming human freedom in relation to general redemptive providence in the following way.

Calvin adduces quite an array of arguments to absolve God of the responsibility of sin and evil and secure enough freedom for human beings to charge them legitimately with this responsibility. There are two major arguments: (1) God is the principal cause though not the immediate author of all actions; and (2) human freedom from coercion is not obliterated by sin. The first represents Calvin's adaptation of the medieval distinction between supreme, remote, mediate, and proximate causes. In any act of sin, God is the supreme cause, the devil the mediate cause, and the person the proximate cause.[62] This distinction allows Calvin to admit that God is the cause of evil without conceding that God is the author of evil.[63] A different way of saying this, without the technical medieval terminology, is that God, the devil, and human beings all operate in the same event in different ways toward different ends.[64] Therefore, wicked persons are not excused when God uses their actions for his own good ends, for the work is "qualified by the intention of the one who does it."[65] Calvin illustrates this distinction between God as the principal cause and human beings as the authors of all actions with his own version of Plato's myth of the charioteer. In his version it is not the soul that drives the horses of intellect and desire, but God who drives the chariots of both the wicked and the righteous souls. It is God who holds the reins of the wild, sinful horses, directing them ultimately to his own chosen destination; yet it is the horses who run. In this way God may be said to be the principal cause of the acts of the wicked, in that he keeps a bridle on them and guides them toward his own ends, but it is the horses who are responsible for each step.[66] This ultimate control of the wicked's actions displays the redemptive providence of God.[67] But such a work of bridling the wicked must be recognized as an alien work of God rather than the proper work, which is to save, and love, and care for his own.[68]

Calvin's second argument affirming human freedom is closely related to the first. If God is not the author but only the first cause of evil, then human beings remain free from compulsion. Calvin returns again and again to the positive claim that God does not use persons to effect his will as if they were inanimate creatures.

> One need not imagine that God uses evil people as stones or blocks of wood; but he uses them as reasonable creatures according to the quality of the nature which he has given them. When, therefore, we say that God works through wicked peo-

ple, that does not preclude the wicked operating in their own way [endroit]. The Scriptures give us many examples of this.[69]

By "reasonable creature" Calvin means a creature endowed with a substance called the soul, upon which the imago dei is imprinted. Since neither the soul nor the imago dei is wholly lost in the Fall, human beings do not cease to be free from coercion because of sin.[70] Therefore, for God to run roughshod over the inviolable gift of freedom to humankind by the creator would be an absurd contradiction of himself. Human freedom from coercion is not destroyed, therefore, by the Fall.

> We do not make the minds of men to be impelled by forces external to them, so that they rage furiously, nor do we transfer to God the cause of hardening, in such a way that they did not voluntarily and by their own wickedness and hardness of heart spur themselves on to obstinacy. What we say is that men act perversely not without God's ordination that it be done, as Scripture teaches.[71]

Calvin adds another argument in favor of his divine determinism and the retention of human freedom from coercion: an argument for the retention of the will after the Fall. Echoing Augustine he maintains that the will, understood as the faculty voluntas, has not been wholly lost or effaced by sin. Rather, it has been corrupted or defaced.[72] We retain the formal capacity to choose (electio), but we are no longer free to choose between good and evil (liberum arbitrium). Due to our enslavement to sin our wills are able to choose only sin.[73]

In responding to Pighius's question of why evildoers are punished by law if they act by necessity Calvin appeals to his own understanding of the government of divine providence and its relation to human freedom. He explains that to say that the wicked sin by necessity does not mean that they do not sin by their own voluntary (voluntaria) and deliberate (deliberata) wickedness. Necessity means only that God accomplishes his work, which is fixed and stable, through the work of the wicked. Nevertheless, the will (voluntas) and intention (propositum) to do evil reside in the evildoers, which makes them guilty for their actions.[74] Though sinners have lost the ability to choose freely between good and evil (liberum arbitrium), they have not lost the faculty voluntas; for they choose evil. In other words, from the perspective of humankind we can say that sin corrupts the faculty *volu.itas*, but does not destroy it.[75] This Augustinian argument is also found in his treatise against the Libertines.

> However, we must also note that capacity for election [*election*] and will [*volunté*] we have by nature. For the rest we know that both have been depraved by sin and that our Lord reforms them changing them from evil into good. *Thus, that we are able to discern, to will, or to do ourselves is a natural gift;* that we are able to elect, desire, and do only evil results from the corruption of sin; that we desire to do good and have the power to execute it results from the supernatural grace of the spirit, who regenerates us into a divine life.[76]

Though one may argue that such a view of the retention of the faculty of *voluntas* after the Fall, as the formal capacity to choose, is a rather weak interpretation of human will, one cannot deny that Calvin teaches that the will, as the faculty *voluntas*, is not destroyed by sin but remains as an inviolable gift of the creator.

Calvin's arguments for the retention of the faculty *voluntas* and the freedom from coercion after the Fall, made from the perspective of humankind, enable him to distinguish the divine determinism of his doctrine of providence from all indeterminisms *and* all other types of determinism. These arguments, essential as they are to his anthropology, constitute only one half of his doctrine of the will and human freedom, however. The other half he develops in his doctrine of the special redemptive providence of election and justification.

Redemptive Providence II: The Special Redemptive Providence of Election and Justification[77] and the Denial of Free Choice [liberum arbitrium] and Freedom from Sin

While Calvin's affirmation of the will as *voluntas* and human freedom as freedom from coercion served him well in his arguments against the Libertines and other such antinomians, it does not serve him well in the fight with "papists" and other "philosophical" theologians. It does not precisely because these theologians confuse *voluntas*, the natural faculty that is formally retained after the Fall, and freedom from coercion with freedom of choice *(liberum arbitrium)*, the capacity to choose freely between good and evil. Valla is only the most recent in a long line of Christian theologians who have made this error because they adopted the Greek rather than the scriptural understanding of will and freedom.[78] It is because of this common confusion of the two understandings of will and freedom that Calvin insists on developing an unmistakable denial of free choice and freedom from sin alongside his clear affirmation of the faculty of the will and freedom from coercion. Given his understanding of the retention of the faculty *voluntas* and freedom from coercion after the Fall, Calvin himself would technically be able to speak of free will, in the sense of *libera voluntas*. This is exactly what he admits in his response to Pighius and in the *Institutes*.[79] However, he explains that he chooses *not* to use this terminology because *libera voluntas* is commonly understood by theologians to be the equivalent of *liberum arbitrium*.[80] Since Calvin denies the existence of *liberum arbitrium* in his doctrines of election and justification, and, since most other theologians confuse the concept and term *liberum arbitrium* with the concept and term *libera voluntas*, he refuses to use the term *libera voluntas*. Even though, from the perspective of humankind, he defends the concept of *libera voluntas* as a human faculty retained after the Fall, he makes a rhetorical decision not to refer to this concept with the confusing term *libera voluntas*. It is important that this rhetorical decision not be interpreted as a rejection of the concept of the human will. The point is that however limited his terminology may be by the debate over *liberum arbitrum*, he does affirm the will as *libera voluntas* and human freedom from coercion. This affirmation is an essential part of his doctrine of the will and human freedom and must be set alongside his denial of free choice from the perspective of God as redeemer if we are to understand his view accurately.

Calvin develops his denial of *liberum arbitrium* in the context of the perspective of God as judge in the doctrines of election and justification. While from the relative perspective of humankind he could argue that a certain type of will and freedom were retained after the Fall, from the absolute perspective of God as judge he must argue that the will, as part of the *imago dei*, and freedom are *wholly* lost. "Whatever is of our own will is effaced."[81] Therefore, whenever the "papists" or other sophists try to distribute will and freedom between God and human beings, Calvin reminds them that "in all things the will of man is opposed to the will of God. For we differ from God as depravity differs from rectitude."[82] To underscore his point, he adds: "Scripture . . . is much more profound in its philosophy, for it sees that *nothing but perversity* has remained in the heart of man since Adam was deprived of the image of God."[83] Without this absolute and mutually exclusive perspective of God as judge, the philosophers and "papists" are unable to understand the totality of sin.

Likewise, without the absolute perspective of God as redeemer, these same men are unable to understand the totality of regeneration. It is this misunderstanding that is the theme of many of Calvin's sermons.[84] The "papists," by making themselves partly responsible for their regeneration because of their contribution of free will, claim themselves as creators of their second birth and thus render God a mere "demi-creator."[85] Calvin responds by emphasizing that *creatio ex nihilo* must be taken as seriously at the second creation of humankind in regeneration as it is at the first. For, he repeats, free choice is not at all like the Samaritan left half-dead on the road, waiting only to be revived by God.[86] Free choice is wholly dead in humankind and God alone can be said to have free choice of the will.[87] In believers, therefore, it is created wholly anew, *ex nihilo*, through their union with the perfect freedom of Jesus Christ.[88]

Faced with such a misunderstanding of the will and freedom, Calvin emphasizes that our free choice *(liberum arbitrium)* is lost and that we are not free from sin. To be able not to sin *(posse non peccare)* is not a possibility after the Fall. The bondage of the will to sin, into which humankind freely entered and still freely chooses, means that the only possibility is not to be able not to sin *(non posse non peccare)*.[89] Because this is so, there is "nothing in [us] that can be agreeable to God," according to him.[90] Since we are "unworthy in ourselves,"[91] the highest wisdom concerning the self is that of humility or self-denial. This is how Calvin crowns his discussion of the Christian life according to the life of Christ in the *Institutes:*

> We are not our own; let not our reason nor our will, therefore, sway our plans and deeds. We are not our own; let us not therefore set it as our goal to seek what is expedient for us according to the flesh. We are not our own; in so far as we can, let us therefore forget ourselves and all that is ours.[92]

Absolute self-negation, however, is the corollary of the praise and honor of God. He completes the eloquent passage on self-negation in the *Institutes*, therefore, this way:

> Conversely, we are God's. Let us therefore live for him and die for him. We are God's. Let his wisdom and will therefore rule

> all our actions. We are God's; let all the parts of our life
> accordingly strive toward him as the only lawful goal.[93]

His point is that there is no concurrence between God and humanity, no cooperation or parceling out of responsibility.[94] Humankind
has and is nothing while God is everything. There is only mutual
exclusion or contradiction between the human will, understood as
the freedom to choose between good and evil, and the divine will.
From the perspective of God as judge, then, free choice (liberum
arbitrium) and freedom from sin are wholly lost.

Calvin's Doctrine of the Will and Human Freedom Reconsidered

In the previous sections we have examined both Calvin's affirmations and denials of freedom and will. The fact that both the
positive and the negative evaluations are essential to his position on
the relationship between divine government and human freedom
implies that many of the interpretations of Calvin on this issue are
incorrect; they are misleading because they present only one of
these two sides as the whole of Calvin's position. For example,
Hiram Haydn presents Calvin's position as only the denial of freedom and the belief in the "irrelevance of the moral life to salvation."[95] Likewise, Reinhold Niebuhr claims that Calvin's Reformation view of freedom is totally contradictory to the Renaissance view;
that is, he believes that Calvin denied freedom.[96] Focusing on
another aspect of this doctrine, Niesel argues that Calvin speaks of
divine grace rather than human freedom. Attempting to refute the
Weberian thesis that for Calvin good works prove one's faith, Niesel
explains Calvin's affirmations of good works as "concessions made to
the Romans" and asserts that his real point was justification by faith
alone and not by good works.[97] While each of these conclusions can
be supported by Calvin's work, each is a one-sided presentation of
Calvin's doctrine of the will and human freedom. Selecting only
those statements made from the absolute perspective of God as
redeemer as significant or essential, they either ignore or misin-
terpret those statements made from the perspective of humankind.[98]

While these views of Calvin's doctrine of the will and human
freedom from the perspective of God as redeemer are still prevalent

in Calvin research today, recently presentations of his doctrine from the perspective of humankind have been offered. While the former emphasize the contradiction between the divine and human wills and the loss of human freedom, the latter emphasize the harmony between the two wills and the retention of human freedom. Battenhouse, for example, stresses Calvin's affirmations of human freedom and moral progress.[99] Allen Verhey's recent introduction to his translation of excerpts of Calvin's "Treatise Against the Libertines" argues that Calvin rejected determinism and allowed for human freedom and that he did not teach that the will was totally lost at the Fall.[100]

Neither of these emphases is wholly inaccurate. But neither is wholly accurate either, for each presents only one side of Calvin's perspectival doctrine of the will and human freedom. Not all scholars have stressed only one side or the other in their presentations of Calvin's anthropology. In fact, many have called attention to the existence of both the affirmations and negations in his thought. They have disagreed, however, over the proper interpretation of this very double-sidedness they all agree upon. Some conclude that Calvin is, in the end, contradictory. Henri Bois, for example, examining Calvin's doctrine of predestination, determines that Calvin oscillates between supra- and infralapsarianism depending on his audience. He attributes Calvin's supralapsarianism to his metaphysical determinism and his infralapsarianism to his Pelagian psychology and morality. He concludes that, though the metaphysical standpoint is stronger in Calvin's works, there is no doubt that the two stand in unresolved contradiction.[101] Georgia Harkness argues similarly, noting that Calvin's critics

> have frequently pointed out an irreconcilable conflict between his doctrine of God's absolute sovereignty and man's responsibility. The author believes this criticism to be just. Man must be free in order to be responsible. If one cannot justly be blamed for what we cannot help, the predestination doctrine leaves little ground for their sins more sharply than does any other form of theological belief. There is a conflict here which Calvin does not reconcile,[102]

Observing Calvin's two views that the new order is both an abrogation and a fulfillment of the old, natural order, David Little concludes not that Calvin's view is contradictory but that it is "ambiguous."[103] Bohatec and Dowey both refrain from offering explanations and merely assert that Calvin is concerned with both good works and justification.[104]

Two other explanations are often given for the double-sidedness of Calvin's view of divine government and human freedom: paradox and the distinction between supernatural and natural. In his discussion of predestination and responsibility in Calvin, Paul Jacobs speaks of the "tension" between these two. He adds, however, that this tension is overcome in the mystical union of the believer with Christ and in Calvin's doctrine of the unity of the trinity.[105] Recently, Allen Verhey also points to the presence of the two sides in Calvin's view. He denies that the relation between God and human freedom is one of contradiction. Rather,

> The contradiction is located here where the freedom God gives is both affirmed, because it is an act of freedom, and denied, because it denies the source of freedom and enslaves to sin. The contradiction is signed by the notion of voluntary bondage.[106]

His main point is that God's freedom is the constant source rather than the contradiction of human freedom and in arguing for this he suggests that Calvin's affirmations and denials of human freedom exist in paradox with one another. A larger number of scholars has attempted to explain the double-sidedness of Calvin's view of divine government and human freedom by distinguishing between the natural and supernatural. They argue that Calvin affirms human freedom in natural activity, but denies it in supernatural activity. Scholars as varied as John Leith, Charles Trinkaus, Paul Pruyser, and Charles Partee support this view.[107] Leith sums the position up neatly.

> While Calvin speaks of the loss of freedom of will in the sense of contrary choice, a close reading indicates that he only denies freedom of the will as the power of choice in certain particular situations in which the self is deeply involved and in particular in the self's relationship to God. The freedom of the self resided both in the understanding and the will and some measure of this freedom of choice remains to fallen man. Calvin is even enthusiastic about the accomplishments of fallen man in physics, dialectic, mathematics, and other like disciplines. He is also open to the accomplishments of fallen men in the political and social ordering of life. The one point on which Calvin is adamant is that fallen man does not have the freedom of contrary choice in the relationship to God. Having rejected

God and turned away from him, man by his own efforts, cannot turn back to God. . . . *This particular point was of such primary importance to Calvin that his writings sometimes gave the impression that fallen man in no area of his existence has the freedom which is the power of contrary choice.*[108]

It is my conclusion that none of these explanations for the co-existence of Calvin's affirmations and denials of the will and human freedom is adequate. As a faithful interpreter of scripture and an astute theologian he was capable of looking at one issue from different points of view. He recognized that different scriptural contexts, such as those in which *James* and *Romans* were written, required a variety of ground to be covered.[109] He also recognized that different theological contexts called for a variety of responses, such as the arguments with the "papists" and the Libertines. Nor is it sufficient to point to a paradox between divine government and human freedom to explain his view of the will. While Calvin does speak of the paradox of divine government and human freedom, at times all too quickly evading the arguments of his opponents by invoking this "mystery," this is too general a characterization of his complex position to be of much help in interpreting it.[110] Calvin's recognition that different theological issues require different approaches makes the explanation of paradox appear inadequate. He points out in a commentary that it is the focus of the doctrine of soteriology in one passage that calls for the absolute denial of will understood as free choice. Other foci, such as responsibility, require other conclusions.[111] He understood the complexity of the Christian experience and the need for a balanced theology to witness to this. He chides Luther, for example, for his inappropriate and unrelenting use of hyperbole in his discussions on the freedom of the will, implying that his predecessor's theology did not bear sufficient witness to the complexity of the Christian life.[112] The explanation based on the natural/supernatural distinction is also not sufficient for understanding Calvin's view of the will. Calvin himself indicates that this distinction may be of some help in understanding this doctrine,[113] but our analysis of Calvin's various affirmations and denials of the will and human freedom suggests that this distinction falters at points. From the perspective of God as redeemer operative in the doctrine of justification and redemption, for example, it appears that *all* human freedom is lost and free choice is obliterated.[114] These absolute statements do not leave room for a retention of the will or freedom as a "supernatural" gift. It is from the perspective of humankind operative in his doctrine of creation and general redemptive providence that human beings appear to retain the faculty of will *(voluntas)* and freedom from coercion.

It is my conclusion that the thesis concerning Calvin's shifting theological perspectives helps to interpret Calvin's double-sided view of the will and human freedom.[115] Rightly distinguishing between free choice *(liberum arbitrium)* and free will *(libera voluntas)*, freedom from sin and freedom from coercion, Calvin is able both to deny the will and human freedom in relation to divine government and to affirm the will and human freedom in relation to divine government. The distinction between the perspective of God and the perspective of humankind helps to illuminate this careful distinction of key theological terms in the debate over the freedom of the will. It is from the perspective of God as judge, which appears in Calvin's discussions of election and justification, that the absolute denial of the will, understood as free choice *(liberum arbitrium)* or the ability to choose freely between good and evil, and the denial of freedom from sin are seen. It is from the perspective of humankind, which appears in Calvin's discussions of creative and redemptive providence, that the affirmation of the will as free will *(libera voluntas)*, the constitutive human faculty remaining after the Fall, and the affirmation of freedom from coercion are seen. The thesis of perspectivalism, then, helps us to understand Calvin's often perplexing statements on the will and his careful contribution to the issue of human freedom and divine government.[116]

Notes

/1/   Allen Verhey, "Calvin's Treatise 'Against the Libertines,'" introduction by Allen Verhey, trans. Allen Verhey and Robert G. Wilkie, *Calvin Theological Journal* 15 (1980): 198.
/2/   Paul Oskar Kristeller, *Renaissance Thought II: Papers on Humanism and the Arts* (New York: Harper & Row, 1965), p. 59.
/3/   E.g., Georgia Harkness, *John Calvin: The Man and His Ethic* (New York: Abingdon, 1958), p. 74; Rudnick, *From Created to Creator*, p. 51; Langdon Gilkey, *Reaping the Whirlwind* (New York: Seabury Press, 1976), p. 175ff.
/4/   Battenhouse, "The Doctrine of Man," p. 467.
/5/   Henri Bois, "La Prédestination d'apres Calvin," *Revue du Metaphysique et de Morale* 18 (1968): 678.
/6/   John H. Leith, "The Doctrine of the Will in the *Institutes of the Christian Religion*," in *Reformation Perennis: Essays on Calvin and the Reformation in Honor of Ford Lewis Battles*, ed. B. A. Gerrish (Pittsburgh:

Pickwick Press, 1981), pp. 49, 57, 62. Leith also expresses the voluntarist interpretation of Calvin, by remarking that "Calvin's understanding of the human will stands very close to the center of his theology both in popular appraisal and in fact," ibid., p. 49.

/7/ For an explanation of why I have chosen the title, "Divine Providence and Human Freedom" for this chapter rather than the more traditional "Grace and Free Will," see appendix 3.

/8/   McNeill 1: 194, *Inst.* 1.15.7 in *OS* 3: 184–85.

/9/   McNeill 1: 195–96, *Inst.* 1.15.8 in *OS* 3: 185–86.

/10/   McNeill 1: 262, *Inst.* 2.2.5 in *OS* 3: 247. Though he attributes it to the schoolmen, Calvin is actually indebted to Bernard of Clairvaux for this distinction of the three freedoms. See Jill Raitt, "Calvin's Use of Bernard of Clairvaux," *Archiv für Reformationsgeschichte* 72 (1981): 98–121 (esp. pp. 102–11).

/11/   An essential part of Calvin's doctrine of the Christian moral life is his insistence of the Christian's restored freedom from misery through salvation by Jesus Christ. An analysis of this view, while related to the thesis here, is beyond the limits of the investigation.

/12/   *CO* 35: 334 (s. 145 on Job 37).

/13/   *CO* 7: 186.

/14/   *CO* 33: 584–85 (s. 47 on Job 12).

/15/   *CO* 40: 51–52 (Ez. 1:24).

/16/   *CO* 31: 226 (Ps. 22).

/17/   *CO* 43: 62 (Amos 4); *CO* 36: 222 (Is. 10:15).

/18/   This is also the conclusion Friedrich Schlieiermacher comes to in his *Speeches on Religion: Speeches to its Cultured Despisers*, trans. John Oman (New York: Harper & Row, 1968), p. 114.

/19/   *CO* 33: 426 (s. 34 on Job 9).

/20/   *CO* 31: 289 (Ps. 29:5). (Emphasis mine.)

/21/   *CO* 40: 577 (Lec. 7 on Dan. 2:21); *CO* 31: 680 (Ps. 73:11)

/22/   *CO* 23: 529 (Gen. 42:1).

/23/   McNeill 1:58, *Inst.* 1.5.5. in *OS* 3: 50. (Emphasis mine.)

/24/   *CO* 8: 351–52 (*De praedestinatione*, 10.6)

/25/   *CO* 33: 593 (s. 48 on Job 12). See also *CO* 33: 595 (s. 48 on Job 12).

/26/   *CO* 33: 593 (s. 48 on Job 12); *CO* 33: 599 (s. 48 on Job 12).

/27/   *CO* 33: 593 (s. 48 on Job 12).

/28/   *CO* 40: 214 (Ez. 10:10); *CO* 40: 33 (Ez. 1:4).

/29/   *CO* 40: 33 (Ez. 1:4).

/30/   *CO* 31: 331 (Ps. 33).

/31/   *CO* 8: 347 (*De praedestinatione*, ch. 10).

/32/   *CO* 31: 123–24 (Ps. 11); *CO* 41: 678 (s. 33 on Dan. 10:11).

/33/   *CO* 32: 359 (Ps. 135:6–7); *CO* 8: 347 (*De praedestinatione* 10.1); *CO* 40: 221 (Ez. 10:17); *CO* 31: 331 (Ps. 33).

/34/   Lorenzo Valla, "On Free Will," in *Renaissance Philosophy*, compiled by Arturo B. Fallico, ed. and trans. Arturo B. Fallico and Herman Shapiro (New York: Random House, 1967–   ), 1: 47. See also 1: 53 and 57. For a different solution to the problem, see Pietro Pompanazzi's "On God's Foreknowledge and Human Freedom," ibid., 1: 231–80. For a discussion of Pompanazzi's contribution to this problem, see Ernst Cassirer, *The Individ-*

ual and the Cosmos in Renaissance Philosophy, trans. Mario Domandi (New York: Harper & Row, 1963), pp. 80–83.

/35/   *CO* 49: 143 (Rom. 8:7); *CO* 30: 26 (s. 46 on Sam.); *CO* 9: 195–99 (*Calumniae nebulonis de occulta providentia Dei cum responsione*, art. 3) [hereafter referred to as *De providentia*]; *CO* 23: 318 (Gen. 22: 14); *CO* 8: 359 (*De praedestinatione* 10.11).

/36/   *CO* 9: 294 (*De providentia*); *CO* 48: 415 (Acts 17:26).

/37/   *CO* 48: 39 (Acts 2:23).

/38/   *CO* 40: 575 (Dan 2:20, lec. 7).

/39/   *CO* 23: 322 (Gen. 41:17).

/40/   *CO* 48: 39 (Acts 2:23).

/41/   *CO* 48: 415 (Acts 17:26).

/42/   *CO* 23: 318 (Gen. 22:14).

/43/   *CO* 48: 39 (Acts 2:23).

/44/   Ibid.

/45/   *CO* 48: 405 (Acts 17:18); *CO* 58: 202 (*Response à certaines calomnies*); *CO* 8: 353 (*De praedestinatione* 10.7); *CO* 9: 287 (*De providentia*).

/46/   *CO* 33: 540 (s. 43 on Job 11).

/47/   *CO* 8: 361 (*De praedestinatione* 10.13).

/48/   *CO* 33: 475 (s. 38 on Job 10); *CO* 33: 371 (s. 30 on Job 8); *CO* 33: 589 (s. 47 on Job 12).

/49/   *OS* 3: 205 (*Inst.* 1.17.2).

/50/   *OS* 4: 159–60 (*Inst.* 3.7.9).

/51/   *CO* 7: 192–94 (*Des Libertins*, ch. 15).

/52/   See Verhey's excellent discussion of this in his introduction to his translation of Calvin's treatise, "Against the Libertines," *Calvin Theological Journal* 15 (1980):. 190–205.

/53/   Ibid., p. 200.

/54/   *CO* 7: 183 (*Des Libertins*, ch. 12); *CO* 7: 193 (*Des Libertins*, ch. 15).

/55/   See chapter 2, pp. 54–61.

/56/   *CO* 7: 183 (*Des Libertins*, ch. 12). The translation here is taken from Benjamin Wirt Farley, *John Calvin: Treatises Against the Anabaptists and Against the Libertines* (Grand Rapids, Mich.: Baker Book House, 1982), pp. 236–37. See also the discussion of the soul as a substance in chapter 5, pp. 152–61.

/57/   *CO* 6: 257. See also *CO* 6: 266.

/58/   McNeill 1: 215–16, *Inst.* 1.17.4 in *OS* 3: 207.

/59/   Ibid.

/60/   *CO* 6: 266.

/61/   Quoted by Stauffer, *Création et providence*, p. 276.

/62/   *CO* 9: 307 (*De providentia*).

/63/   *CO* 8: 353–54 (*De praedestinatione*, 10.7).

/64/   *OS* 3: 292 (*Inst.* 2.4.2); *CO* 48: 40 (Acts 2:23); *CO* 32: 184 (Ps. 115:2); *CO* 33: 584–89 (s. 47 on Job 12); *CO* 7: 191 (*Des Libertins*, ch. 14); *CO* 7: 188 (*Des Libertins*, ch. 14).

/65/   *CO* 7: 189–90 (*Des Libertins*, ch. 14).

/66/   *CO* 23: 553 (Gen. 45:8); *CO* 47: 258 (Jn. 11:9); *CO* 8: 353 (*De praedestinatione*, 10.9).

/67/   *CO* 36: 215 (Is. 10:5); *CO* 8: 357–58 (*De praedestinatione*, 10.10); *CO*

27: 691 (s. 121 on Dt. 21).

/68/ *CO* 55: 297–98 (Jn. 12:40).

/69/ *CO* 7: 188–89 (*Des Libertins*, ch. 14).

/70/ *CO* 7: 191 (*Des Libertins*, ch. 14); *CO* 33: 617 (s. 49 on Job 13); *CO* 49: 711 (s. 11 on I Cor. 11); *OS* 2: 206 (*Scandals*, p. 68); *OS* 3: 255 (*Inst.* 2.1.12); *OS* 3: 260 (*Inst.* 2.2.17). This may be the reason that Calvin declares in the *Inst.* 2.2.7 (*OS* 3: 251) that there is some free decision in humankind after the Fall, but that it is unwise to call it *liberum arbitrium* since this has been understood only as the free choice between good and evil.

/71/ *CO* 8: 357–58 (*De praedestinatione*, 10.10). For this reason Stauffer's presentation of Calvin's view of providence is not quite accurate on this point. He says that for Calvin, "Dieu, dans sa Providence, *permettent* l'action des méchants . . ." *Création et providence*, p. 277. (Emphasis mine.) Calvin, even though he is not always careful with his own terminology, definitely wishes to distinguish between God permitting and ordaining the actions of the wicked.

/72/ The model of salvation that is implied by such a view is a continuous rather than a discontinuous one.

/73/ *OS* 3: 250 (*Inst.* 2.2.8).

/74/ *CO* 6: 256.

/75/ *CO* 6: 267. See also *CO* 7: 183.

/76/ *CO* 7: 191. (Emphasis mine.)

/77/ For an explanation of how I understand the relationship in Calvin's theology between special redemptive providence, general redemptive providence, and creative providence on the one hand and between election and justification on the other, see appendix 4.

/78/ *CO* 6: 350.

/79/ *CO* 6: 279–80.

/80/ *CO* 6: 279.

/81/ McNeill 1: 297, *Inst.* 2.3.6 in *OS* 3: 279–80; *CO* 49: 130 (Rom. 7:15); *CO* 8: 108; *OS* 4: 221 (*Inst.* 3.14.1).

/82/ *CO* 49: 142 (Rom. 8:7).

/83/ *CO* 49: 130 (Rom. 7:15). See also *OS* 3: 246 (*Inst.* 2.2.4).

/84/ This is the major polemical strain in Calvin's sermons, for he considers the doctrine of grace to be essential to the salvation of souls.

/85/ *CO* 51: 380–81 (s. 11 on Eph. 2:8–10).

/86/ *CO* 47: 117 (Jn. 5:25); *CO* 50: 642 (s. 29 on Gal.).

/87/ *CO* 8: 353 (*De praedestinatione* 10.7).

/88/ *CO* 52: 178 (I Thess. 5:23); *CO* 51: 598 (s. 28 on Eph. 4:17–19); *CO* 51: 469 (s. on Eph.). Actually Calvin claims on the basis of the discontinuous model of salvation that humankind, when saved by Christ, not only receives back its free will, but a persevering free will which even Adam and Eve did not have, *OS* 3: 289 (*Inst.* 2.3.13).

/89/ *CO* 6: 355. Calvin is indebted to Augustine for this classic distinction. See Augustine's "On Rebuke and Grace", chapter 33 in *Nicene and Post-Nicene Fathers*, volume 5, ed. Philip Schaff (Grand Rapids, MI: Eerdmans, 1971), p. 485; and "On Man's Perfection in Righteousness," chapter 9 (Ibid., p. 161)

/90/ *CO* 8: 109 (*De praedestinatione*).

/91/   *CO* 8: 95. See also *OS* 3: 273 (*Inst.* 2.3.2).
/92/   McNiell 1: 690, *Inst.* 3.7.1 in *OS* 4: 151. See also *OS* 3: 284 (*Inst.* 2.3.9).
/93/   Ibid. See also *OS* 3: 253 (*Inst.* 2.2.10).
/94/   *CO* 8: 103.
/95/   Haydn, *The Counter-Renaissance*, p. 103.
/96/   Niebuhr, *Nature and Destiny of Man*, 2: 153, 204, 210–11.
/97/   Niesel, *Theology of Calvin*, pp. 176–78.
/98/   See for example Arthur C. Cochrane's conclusion against Bohatec and Brunner that Calvin left no remnant of natural law, "Natural Law in the Teachings of John Calvin," in *Church-State Relations in Ecumenical Perspective*, ed. Elwyn A. Smith (Pittsburgh: Duquesne University Press, 1966), p. 200.
/99/   Battenhouse, "The Doctrine of Man," pp. 455, 458.
/100/ Verhey, "Against the Libertines," p. 198. See also Steven Ozment's recent related question of whether Calvin was really a Protestant on the issue of justification and works. He responds by saying that Calvin ended up "'re-Catholicizing'. . . Protestant theology at its most sensitive point, the doctrine of justification by faith," *The Age of Reform, 1250–1550: An Intellectual and Religious History of Late Medieval and Reformation Europe* (New Haven and London: Yale University Press, 1980), p. 374. Though Ozment distinguishes Calvin's position from the humanist view that doctrine was subject to moral critique, he concludes that Calvin's more complex understanding of good works as attestations of grace or presumptive evidence of favor muddied Luther's distinctive Protestant teaching on justification by grace through faith alone, ibid., p. 379. His argument on this and the next page is quite loose. He does say by way of generalization, however, that "A further difference between humanists and Protestants stemming from the persistence of scholasticism within Protestantism is the Protestant disinclination to subject their teaching to moral critique. The reformers did not permit ethics to sit in judgment on the truth of their doctrine. It became the hallmark of the Anabaptists, Spiritualists, and rational critics of the Reformation, almost all of whom were deeply influenced by Erasmus, to make moral results the test of doctrinal truth and to criticize the followers of Luther, Calvin, and Zwingli for failing to improve the moral quality of life," p. 315.
/101/ Bois, "La Prédestination d'apres Calvin," p. 671.
102/   Harkness, *John Calvin*, p. 74. At a later point she describes this not as a contradiction but as a paradox: "The moral effect of the calvinist theology was to give rise to a set of paradoxes. Intense practical activity was joined with mystical self-forgetfulness; shrewd concern for success in this life with absorption in the next; zealous service to neighbor with equally zealous persecution for doctrinal aberrations; man's abasement with his exaltation; autocracy with democracy; conservatism with progress. These paradoxes root in a fundamental inconsistency—the attempt to deny, and at the same time to affirm, human freedom," pp. 88–89.
/103/ Little, "Natural Law," p. 175.
/104/ Bohatec, *Budé und Calvin*, p. 355, speaks of the paradox between a "psychological formal freedom" and an "actual material freedom." See

Dowey, *Knowledge of God in Calvin's Theology,* p. 228, also
/105/   Paul Jacobs, *Prädestination und Verantwortlichkeit bei Calvin*
(Darmstadt: Wissenschaftliche Buchgesellschaft, reprint ed., 1968), pp.
133–34.
/106/   Verhey, "Against the Libertines," p. 203.
/107/   Leith, "The Doctrine of the Will," pp. 53, 61–62 (emphasis mine);
Trinkaus, "Renaissance Problems," p. 74; Pruyser, "Calvin's View of Man,"
p. 60; Partee, *Calvin and Classical Philosophy,* pp. 73–74.
/108/   Leith, "The Doctrine of the Will," p. 53.
/109/   In his preface to his commentary on James he comments that there is
no reason to reject this epistle since the whole scripture is full of various
testimony and one cannot expect each book to cover the same ground (*CO*
55: 381). And in his commentary on Galatians 3:12 he makes the following
astute comments: "The law clearly does not conflict with faith; otherwise
God would be unlike Himself. But we must always remember that Paul's
language is adapted to these particular circumstances. The contradiction
between the law and the gospel lies in the cause of justification," *CO* 50:
209.
/110/   *CO* 33: 587–88, 594, 604 (s. 47 on Job 12). Calvin himself offers
other, equally inadequate solutions. For example, he often reaches a point
where he refuses to defend his position any longer, retreating into mystery,
CO 23: 553 (Gen. 45:8).
/111/   See the quotation from the commentary on Galatians in n. 109
above.
/112/   *CO* 6: 244.
/113/   *OS* 3: 313–16 (*Inst.* 2.5.14–16).
/114/   Leith's comment, that Calvin only "gives the impression" of denial in
both the natural and supernatural realms is inaccurate, therefore, "The
Doctrine of the Will," p. 59.
/115/   Childress's excellent work on Calvin's ethics uses the tension of the
metaphor of image of God to draw out an "ambiguity and ambivalence
within a general framework of unity" in Calvin's thought, unpublished
paper, p. 2. His work was concentrated on Calvin's ethics alone, however,
and does not develop the two theological perspectives he mentions other
than in terms of the image metaphor.
/116/   One of the major problems that results from this perspectival view of
human freedom is seen in Calvin's treatment of the issue of slavery. From
the perspective of God, he proclaims both denial of free choice *and* the
freedom of all believers through Christ. But from the perspective of humankind, he insists that the bondage of slaves to human masters is not inconsistent with a Christian life. He sees no "transformation" of the socio-political
realm at all at this point. See *CO* 49: 416 (I Cor. 7:22); *CO* 33: 161 (s. 12 on
Job 3); *CO* 23: 643 (s. 1 on Melch.); *CO* 34: 655 (s. 133 on Job 31).

CHAPTER V

IMMORTALITY AND RESURRECTION

> [Humankind consists of] two substances. Yet neither is so mingled with the other as not to retain its own distinctive nature. For the soul is not the body, and the body is not the soul. Therefore, some things are said exclusively of the soul that can in no wise apply to the body; and of the body, again that in no way fit the soul; of the whole person, that cannot refer—except inappropriately—to either the soul or body separately. Finally, the characteristics of the mind are (sometimes) transferred to the body and those of the body to the soul. Yet the one who consists of these parts is one person, not many. Such expressions signify that there is one person in human beings composed of two elements joined together, and that there are two diverse underlying natures that make up this person.
>
> *Institutes* 2.14.1

Introduction

While many scholars have noted Calvin's frequent use of the two terms "immortality" and "resurrection," few agree on how these terms and their relation are to be understood. Quistorp, for instance, asserts that Calvin's use of the concept of immortality is an inconsistency in his thought, a vestigial Platonism which operates as a contradiction to his Christian theology.[1] Partee and Babelotzky, while not concurring with this extreme judgment, are at pains to explain how Calvin could have used the concept of the immortality of the soul without falling prey to the philosophy of Plato.[2] Neither of these positions provides an adequate interpretation of Calvin's view of the immortality of the soul. The present study attempts to provide such an interpretation through an analysis of Calvin's view of immortality, resurrection, and their theological relation that highlights his perspectival approach.

Since the question of immortality and resurrection is inseparable from the question of the soul's relation to the body, this analysis will also attempt to offer a more adequate interpretation of this "psychological" aspect of Calvin's anthropology. Here, too, there has been much confusion among Calvin scholars. Calvin has been accused of relying on the Platonic view of the soul to such an extent that he may be called a spiritualist[3] or even a dualist.[4] Quistorp raises the charge of contradiction once again, arguing that Calvin tries to combine two diametrically opposed concepts, the Platonic view of the soul and the Hebraic notion of bodily existence.[5]

This chapter, therefore, will cover three areas: the immortality of the soul, the relation of the soul to the body, the relation of immortality to resurrection. Many of the primary materials used here are the same as those used in previous chapters. However, I have chosen to make use of Calvin's treatise *Psychopannychia* as well. Calvin's first theological work (following the Commentary on Seneca's *De Clementia* by only two years and predating the 1536 edition of the *Institutes*), this treatise is probably the most controversial of all of Calvin's works. Some have argued that *Psychopannychia* represents only the "early, more humanistic Calvin" before his radical turn to the reforming principles of Luther and, therefore, that it should not be used to support Calvin's mature theological position on the immortality of the soul.[6] I have determined, however, that this treatise is fundamentally consistent with Calvin's later, "Reformed" statements about the immortality of the soul. The differences which do exist can be accounted for by Calvin's use of this complex theological shifting perspectives. For this reason I have chosen to cite this text with the same authority as Calvin's later works dealing with the immortality of the soul. An extended argument for this assessment of *Psychopannychia* may be found in appendix 5.

The Soul and Immortality in Calvin

Calvin's view of the immortality of the soul is complex, for he both denies and affirms immortality, according to the context in which he is speaking. All of his arguments, however, are grounded both exegetically and theologically. In fact, one of the most striking things about Calvin's view of the soul, the flexibility of his definition and use of the term, depends on exegesis. He provides several lists of the various meanings that the term "soul" carries in the scriptures: life, will or desire, the entire person, respiration or breath, the vital motion of the body, the affections of the spirit, an immortal essence.[7] The particular definition he chooses for the soul, then, depends on the scriptural context in which it occurs and the theological context in which he is using it. He does, however, interpret the use of the word "soul" in the scriptures and in his own theological reflections as "whole person" or "life itself" more often than in the more restricted definition of "immortal essence."[8] The reason for this particular narrowing of the scriptures' wide variety of meanings of the term "soul" may be his attempt to distinguish his position from that of some philosophers. He rejects the common philosophical definition of the soul as "the vital force of the body" or "the form of matter" because these diverge from the scripture's witness to the soul in terms of the special relationship between human beings and God. Calvin wants to reserve the term "soul" for human beings alone, and therefore he does not apply the term to all living things as the philosophers commonly did.

Though Calvin's preferred definition of the soul is "whole person," he accepts the definition of the human soul as an immortal essence.[9] The affirmation of the human soul as an immortal essence is necessary for a number of different theological reasons. First, if the soul were not an immortal essence, humankind could not be the image of God, for there would be no spiritual essence for this image to be imprinted upon. In other words, the definition of the soul as immortal essence supports the view of the uniqueness of the human creature, which Calvin argues for mainly on the basis of the *imago dei*.[10] Second, without the concept of the soul as an immortal essence, the scriptural witness to the future, eternal life for which humankind was created, is lost. Thus, a second major anthropological focus of Calvin, the eschatological structure of human existence, is linked to the immortality of the soul.[11] Third, the concept of the soul as immortal essence is a sign of the unboundedness of the grace of God's providence. Calvin adduces this argument against the Anabaptists who taught the sleep of the soul, maintaining that their view is unscriptural and that it denies God's providence, which extends to believers when they are dead as well as when they are alive.[12] These three basic theological principles, plus the principle of accurate and faithful exegesis, form the cornerstones to Calvin's view of the soul as an immortal essence. He appeals to different principles depending on his opponents. For example, when arguing with the Anabaptists, he appeals to the principles of *imago dei*, accurate exegesis, God's providential grace, and the future life. Confronted with humanists, he appeals only to the principles of *imago dei* and the future life. In other arguments, furthermore, he changes the emphasis of his position as well as his theological evidence. Against the Libertines, for example, Calvin qualifies the view of the soul as an immortal substance, stressing its created nature; but against the Anabaptists, he stresses that the soul is an immortal essence.

When he is up against the humanists and Libertines, Calvin's argument concerning the immortality of the soul has two foci: the distinctiveness of the human soul among all the creatures of nature; and the distinctiveness of the human soul over against God. In an argument closely paralleling his doctrine of the *imago dei*, Calvin presents the immortality of the human soul as a sign of both its privileged relationship to God and its absolute difference from God.[13] He emphasizes the first against those humanists who questioned whether the human soul was an immortal essence and adopted the general philosophical definition of the soul as "the vital force of the body." To take such a view was to deny humankind as the *imago dei* and the eschatological structure of human existence, two essential elements of Christian anthropology according to Calvin. Therefore, they must be exposed and condemned.

> It is common knowledge that Agrippa, Villanovus, and their like have always proudly rejected the gospel, as if they were so many Cyclops. They have finally lapsed so far into folly and madness that not only did they spread execrable blasphemies against the son of God, but also in regard to the question of the life of the soul, they held that they themselves were no different from dogs and pigs. Others, like Rabelais, Deperius, and Goveanus, having sampled the gospel, have been struck with the same blindness. And what is the reason for that except that they had previously profaned that sacred pledge of eternal life by making a mockery and a laughing stock of it, with the impudence of the impious.[14]

While these humanists denied the distinctiveness of the human soul by denying that any soul was immortal, the Libertines were more prone to deny the distinctiveness of the human soul by claiming that all souls were as immortal as the Godhead itself, that is, eternal, having no beginning or end. Calvin accuses the Libertines of aligning themselves with those "ancient philosophers who hold that only one spirit extends everywhere and all have" a portion in it, proceed from it, and return to it.[15] It is not that the Libertines, like the humanists he was fighting, denied the immortality of the soul. On the contrary they claimed too much for the immortality of the soul when they confused it with the eternity of God. Their leveling of God and all souls called for his careful interpretation of the immortality of the soul. He does this by developing his notion of the soul as a *created*, immortal essence, a position dependent on the traditional scholastic distinction between the immortality and the eternity of the soul. Anxious to deny that the soul is eternal, that is has no beginning or end, and eager to maintain that though it has a beginning it does not die, he uses the circumspect phrase "created, immortal essence." With this in mind he marshals evidence against the Libertines that highlights the absolute difference between God, who alone is eternal and immortal, and created immortal souls. In *Contre la secte des Libertins* he lists five major signs that support this absolute distinction: (1) the human soul is subject to ignorance, (2) to passions, (3) to inconstancy and variety, (4) to fragility and error, and (5) to sin.[16] He argues that, *properly speaking*, human souls are not immortal; that is, they are not immortal by nature. They are immortal only in the sense that they participate by grace in the existence of God, who alone is truly immortal. Like one of his definitions of the *imago dei*, this view of the immortality of the human soul is relational rather than substantial.[17] The immortality of the human soul is a gift of grace just as our justification is; it is but a "borrowed good."[18]

> It seems that our souls have this power in themselves to vivify the body and give it vigor. Now this is quite true in part: but we must know beyond this our souls are not immortal by their own power, that their life is not enclosed in them as if that were its root. Where is their life then? In God. Therefore, since God put some little drop and spark of life in the soul of men, there is its vigor and nowhere else.[19]

Or, as he explains elsewhere, the spirit of God is not in us according to its essence; rather, God's power is spread in such a way that we live off it like plants from the life of the sun.[20] While it may be true that human souls are immortal, the full truth is that God alone by nature is immortal and eternal. The Libertines have corrupted the doctrine of the immortality of the soul, then, by confusing immortality and eternity, a derived life with the source of all life, the created with the creator.

To bolster his argument that the soul is not immortal according to its essence, that is, eternal, but derives its life from God alone, Calvin teaches the creation *ex nihilo* of the human soul. He contrasts this view with the common philosophical theory of traducianism, which holds that human souls are passed on to children by their parents in the process of generation. He also contrasts it to the view that each soul passes out of God *(ex dei traduce)* directly, without the mediation of the parents, as light from light, or fire from fire. He counts the latter view, which holds that human souls share the same substance with God, as dangerous both because of its Manichean tendencies and because of its denial of the distinction between the human soul and God.[21] He believes the former view is dangerous because it obscures the fact that the human soul is distinct from God. To counter them both he develops a view that admits that human bodies are created by generation from the bodies of their parents and denies that human souls are generated by those of their parents. Each human soul, according to Calvin, is created by God *ex nihilo*[22] at the very moment a child is conceived in the belly of the mother.[23] What he is trying to emphasize by means of this view of human generation is that the human soul is distinct from God, since it is a "truly created substance" which is immortal only by the special favor bestowed upon it by God, not by its own substance or essence.[24] The view of the creation *ex nihilo* of the soul, then, plays a role in Calvin's theology as part of his argument against the Libertine view of the substantial immorality of all souls.

Calvin's development of a relational rather than substantial immortality of the soul to distinguish immortality and eternity stretches to cover not only the origin of the soul in the human body, but also the entire existence of the human soul and all souls. To make his point he notes that even the angels have a relational rather than a substantial immortality. And the little sparks of immortality that human souls have by creation and participation in God would be quickly blotted out by shadows, if God did not maintain and preserve them each minute of their lives.[25] The immortality of the human soul, as a created essence, is a gift both at the time of its creation in the womb and at every moment of its preserved life.

Calvin finds it necessary to stress that human immortality is relational at every moment of the soul's life because some philosophers,
while admitting that God created and formed humankind, conclude
that once God has set humankind on its way, each soul conducts and
governs itself.[26] According to Calvin, this obscures the goodness of
God's providence and the true nature of the immortality of the
human soul.

While against the Libertines Calvin spends his time denying
the substantial immortality or eternity of the soul, focusing on it as a
created being, against the Anabaptists, as against his humanist foes,
he emphasizes the immortality of the soul. He bases this side of his
view of the immortality of the human soul on scriptural evidence
and on two essential anthropological theses: the *imago dei* and the
eschatological structure of human existence. While against the Libertines he lists five signs that deny the substantial immortality or
eternity of the human soul, against the Anabaptists he lists five signs
that affirm the immortality of the human soul. Each of the three
positive lists of the signs of the immortality of the human soul that
Calvin provides is connected with the *imago dei*.

In each of the three lists connecting the *imago dei* and affirming the human soul as an immortal essence we find four common
signs: wide-ranging knowledge of the environment (#1), historical
knowledge (#2), sleep and presentiments of the future (#4), and
conscience (#5). The fifth sign (#3 in each list) varies; in the first list
it is identified as creativity, in the second knowledge of God and the
angels, and in the third the ability to confer with events and people
of the past. The two lists he provides in the *Institutes* as part of his
discussion of the *imago dei* merit quotation in full.

> Yet the powers of the soul are far from being confined to
> functions that serve the body. Of what concern is it to the
> body that you measure the heavens, gather the number of
> the stars, determine the magnitude of each, know what
> space lies between them, with what swiftness or slowness
> they complete their courses, how many degrees this way or
> that they decline? I confess, indeed, that astronomy has
> some use; but I am only showing that in this deepest in-
> vestigation of heavenly things there is no organic symmetry,
> but here is an activity of the soul distinct from the body
> [#1]. I have put forth one example, from which it will be
> easy for my readers to derive the rest. Manifold indeed is
> the nimbleness of the soul with which it surveys heaven and
> earth [#1], joins past to future [#2], retains in memory

something heard long before, nay pictures to itself whatever it pleases [#2]. Manifold also is the skill with which it devises things incredible, and which is the mother of so many marvelous devices [#3]. These are unfailing signs of divinity in man. Why is it that the soul not only vaguely roves about but conceives many useful things [#3], ponders concerning many, even divines the future—all while man sleeps [#4]? What ought we to say here except that *the signs of immortality* which have been implanted in man cannot be effaced? Now what reason would therefore be to believe that man is divine and not to recognize his Creator? Shall we, indeed, distinguish between right and wrong by that judgment which has been imparted to us, yet will there be no judge in heaven [#5]? Shall we think ourselves the inventors of so many arts and useful thing [#3] that God may be defrauded of his praise even though experience sufficiently teaches that what we have has been unequally distributed among us from another source?[27]

Furthermore, that man consists of a soul and a body ought to be beyond controversy. Now I understand by the term "soul" an immortal yet created essence, which is his nobler part. Sometimes it is called "spirit." For even when these terms are joined together, they differ from one another in meaning; yet when the word "spirit" is used by itself, it means the same thing as soul; as when Solomon speaking of death, says that then "the spirit returns to God who gave it" (Eccl. 12:7). And when Christ commended his spirit to the Father (Luke 23:46) and Stephen his to Christ (Acts 7:59) they meant only that when the soul is freed from the prison house of the body, God is its perpetual guardian. Some imagine the soul to be called "spirit" for the reason that it is breath, or a force divinely infused into bodies, but that it nevertheless is without essence; both the thing itself and all Scripture show them to be stupidly blundering in this opinion. It is of course true that while men are tied to earth more than they should be they grow dull; indeed, because they have been estranged from the Father of Lights (James 1:17), they become blinded by darkness, so that they remain untouched by a sense of their own immortality. Surely the conscience, which, discerning between good and evil, responds to God's judgment, is an undoubted *sign* of the immortal spirit [#5]. For how could a motion without essence penetrate to God's judgment seat, and inflict itself with dread at its own guilt? For the body is not affected by the fear of spiritual punishment, which falls upon the soul only. From this it follows that the soul is endowed with essence. Now the very knowledge of God sufficiently proves that souls, which transcend the world, are immortal, for no transient energy could penetrate to the fountain of life [#3].

In short, the many pre-eminent gifts with which the human mind is endowed proclaim that something divine has been engraved upon it; all these are testimonies of an immortal essence. For the sense perception inhering in brute animals does not go beyond the body, or at least extends no farther than to material things presented to it. But the nimbleness of the human mind in searching out heaven and earth and the secrets of nature [#1], and when all ages have been compassed by its understanding and memory; in arranging each thing in its proper order, and in inferring future events from the past [#2], clearly shows that there lies hidden in man something separate from the body. With our intelligence we can conceive the invisible God and the angels, something the body can by no means do [#3]. We grasp things that are right, just, and honorable, which are hidden to the bodily senses [#5]. There-fore, the spirit must be the seat of this intelligence. Indeed, sleep itself, which benumbs man, seeming even to deprive him of life, is no obscure witness of immortality, since it suggests not only thoughts of things that have never happened, but also presentiments of the future [#4]. I have briefly touched upon those things which secular writers grandly extol and depict in more brilliant language; but among godly readers this simple reminder will be enough.[28]

In the thirty-ninth sermon on Job 10, again speaking of the *imago dei*, he offers the following list: (1) We can evaluate things we have never seen, (2) We have memory, (3) We can confer with people and events of the past, (4) We can inquire into the future, and (5) We can judge what we read and what we and others say.[29]

Calvin's linking of his argument for the soul as an immortal essence with the doctrine of the *imago dei* plays a crucial role in his argument against the Anabaptists. It enables him to conclude that when the Anabaptists teach the sleep of the soul between its death and resurrection they deny that the soul is an immortal essence, and thereby deny the distinctive role of humankind in creation as the image of God. This is clearly unscriptural, according to Calvin. To this argument for the immortality of the human soul based on the doctrine of the *imago dei* Calvin adds another based on the es-chatological structure of human existence. Often in his sermons he refers to the immortality of the soul as the end of our creation, calling his congregation to strive after heavenly immortality, in order that each member may have the hope of eternal life after death.[30] In teaching the sleep of the soul, therefore, the Anabaptists are also denying the end for which God created humankind, heavenly im-mortality.

Unlike his argument against the Libertines, which emphasized the created nature of the soul, Calvin's argument against the
Anabaptists stresses the soul as an immortal essence. The two
arguments are similar in that they share a common end: to praise
and glorify God the giver of every good gift. Calvin accuses the
Libertines of confusing the immortality of the soul with the eternity
of God, thus depriving the source of that immortality, God, of his
due praise and gratitude. He accuses the Anabaptists, who deny
that the soul is an immortal essence, of ignoring God's privileged,
grace-filled, and providential relationship with the *imago dei*, humankind, thereby depriving God of due gratitude and praise. Both
the Libertine confusion or conflation and the Anabaptist denial
come down to the same thing: ingratitude to God the giver of every
good gift.

In addition to sharing the same end of impiety, the two arguments fit well together. Arguing the created nature against the
Libertines and the immortal essence against the Anabaptists, Calvin
develops his own version of the scholastic definition of the soul as
immortal though not eternal: a created, immortal essence. In his
case it is his shifting theological perspectives that enable him to
emphasize one or the other half of this same doctrine. When he
wants to emphasize the created nature, the perspective of God as
creator comes into play. When he wants to stress the soul as an
immortal essence, the perspective of humankind appears.

Calvin is not always careful, however, to hold together both
sides of this circumspect doctrine of the soul as a created, immortal
essence. Occasionally he goes so far as to deny the immortality of
the soul altogether, rather than simply circumscribe the meaning of
its immortality by distinguishing it from eternity. For example,
when the doctrine of grace is challenged by the Libertines, who
parceled out the credit for salvation between God and humankind,
Calvin insists on the absolute discontinuity between God and creatures. Using the absolute perspective of God as redeemer he sometimes speaks as if the soul is not immortal, for he says that sin
destroys all the signs of immortality and all our knowledge of immortality.[31] Only believers can be said to have immortal souls, since
they alone have regained the immortality they lost in sin through
faith in Jesus Christ.[32]

While these denials do not occur frequently, they do indicate
that his doctrine of the soul as a created, immortal essence is not

altogether neat.[33] These denials directly contradict his insistence on the immortality of the soul against the Anabaptists. When the doctrine of creation is called into question by these theologians, Calvin states in no uncertain terms that the soul is an immortal essence. From the relative perspective of humankind, it appears that all persons retain immortality of the soul after sin and knowledge of it through the various signs that God left stamped upon it.[34] If one looked only at the passages against the Libertines that seem to deny the immortality of the soul because of the doctrine or sin, she or he might conclude that Calvin was a biblical theologian who eschewed the philosophical doctrine of the immortality of the soul in favor of the biblical doctrine of the resurrection of the body. On the other hand, if one looked only at his argument for the soul as an immortal essence against the Anabaptists, he or she might conclude that he remained a Platonic dualist giving lip service to the biblical doctrine of resurrection. Neither conclusion is true, for Calvin claims both that the soul is immortal and that it is not immortal. His shifting perspectives help to make sense out of this view of the soul, which is almost as complex as his view of the *imago dei*. While his dominant view of the soul is that of a created, immortal essence, a position that does not deny but carefully interprets the notion of immortality, he complicates this by introducing a denial of immortality from the perspectives of God as judge and redeemer. It is his perspectival approach that allows him both to emphasize the different sides of the doctrine of the soul as a created, immortal essence at different times *and* to complicate that doctrine by introducing a denial of immortality.

Psychology: Relation of the Soul and Body

Before turning to discuss Calvin's view of the relation between immortality and resurrection, a brief analysis of his view of the relation of the soul and body may be helfpul. Scholars are almost as divergent in their assessments of Calvin's psychology as they are in their conclusions about the view of the *imago dei*. Battenhouse calls him outright a philosophical dualist.[35] Schulze and Quistorp shy away from calling him a dualist, but both accuse him of retaining a spiritualizing tendency that elevates the soul and denigrates the body.[36] Partee tries to avoid both charges by arguing that Calvin uses the Platonic distinction of soul and body, but subordinates it to his basically biblical anthropology of the whole person. He explains it this way:

> Calvin's view of man is perhaps more indebted to the insight of the philosophers than any other area of his thought. Many of the philosophers' insights concerning man in the state of nature had long been accepted in Christian theology. It is not surprising that Calvin, like almost every other Christian thinker adopts the soul/body dualism and that he exalts the soul's relation to God. However, to think that Calvin's anthropology is basically philosophical ignores or dismisses his criticism of the philosophers and the totality of the position he occupies.[37]

Partee does not go on to elaborate Calvin's criticism of the specific views of the soul and body and their relation. He simply asserts that the differences between Calvin and the philosophers are as striking as the similarities, mentioning as examples Calvin's sharp distinction between the natural and redeemed man and his addition of the resurrection of the body to the immortality of the soul.[38] Willem Balke, in his recent study *Calvin and the Anabaptist Radicals,* merely repeats the conclusion of Partee by speaking of the "formal Platonism" one finds in Calvin's *Psychopannychia.*[39] Rather than accepting or avoiding the charges of dualism and spiritualization, Doumergue rejects them both. Against Schulze, he argues that Calvin's view of the soul and body is contradictory rather than similar to Plato's and is clearly apostolic and evangelical.[40] And, Doumergue notes, along the way to his conclusion that Calvin's view of the body is apostolic, that Calvin both exalts and denigrates the body. Margaret Miles argues that Calvin's view of the body shows a "curious ambivalence" and that his esteem for the body is not without qualification.[41] Though a bit more cautious than Doumergue, she, too, concludes that Calvin wished to present the whole life of the person.[42]

Once again we are faced with a variety of disparate interpretations. And once again the texts seem to support almost all of the views. Those who argue that Calvin is a dualist can quote from Book 4 of the *Institutes:* "But whoever knows how to distinguish between body and soul, between this present fleeting life and that future, eternal life, will without difficulty know that Christ's spiritual kingdom and the civil jurisdiction are things completely distinct."[43] And those who charge Calvin with spiritualizing can quote sermon 144 on Job 37, that "our souls are more precious to [God] than our bodies."[44] And for those who claim that he affirms the body as part of the whole person, the discussion of the resurrection in the *Institutes* can be quoted:

> For it would be utterly absurd that the bodies which God has dedicated to himself as temples should fall away into filth without hope of resurrection! What of the fact that they are also members of Christ? Or that God commands all their parts to be sanctified to him? Or that it is his will that his name be praised with men's tongues, that pure hands be lifted to himself, that sacrifices be offered? What madness is it for that part of man, deemed by the Heavenly Judge worthy of such shining honor, to be by mortal man reduced to dust beyond hope of restoration? Similarly, Paul, when he exhorts us to obey the Lord both in body and in soul, for both are of God, surely does not allow that what he has, so to speak, claimed as sacred to God should be condemned to eternal corruption![45]

These passages, and others like them, are best understood when read in the context of Calvin's shifting theological perspectives, as the following analysis will demonstrate.

Again the distinction between the human and divine perspectives and its two variations allows Calvin to make at least three judgments on the soul and body and their relation. First, from the absolute perspective of God as creator he stresses the similarity of the body and soul and their unity. From this perspective both appear together as nothing, fleeting shadows with no life of their own.[46] They also from this perspective both appear as wholly good and worthy of the providential care bestowed on them by God.[47] Second, from the perspective of God as redeemer the soul and body appear in absolute contradiction to one another; the soul is exalted and the body condemned. And third, when the relative perspective of humankind is introduced, the soul and body appear not as two equals, but as a superordinate and a subordinate. From this perspective neither the unity and similarity nor the contradiction between the two is stressed; rather, there is a clean hierarchical distinction in which the soul is preferred to the body.[48] Each of these views is essential to Calvin's view of psychology and each must be considered. The first presents no real difficulties, since Calvin's positive and negative judgments on the creation from the perspective of God as creator are by now familiar. The third also presents no difficult obstacles, for it is consistent with Calvin's other hierarchical rankings within the order of creation. It is the second judgment that requires more detailed investigations, since it is this view of the relation between the soul and body that has so often been used as evidence of Calvin's Platonic dualism.

The first judgment Calvin makes about the soul and body emphasizes the unity of the person by stressing the similarity of the soul and body in their distinction from God. The soul is like the body in that in comparison with the power of the spirit of God it is nothing.[49] Calvin's argument against the substantial immortality of the soul and in favor of the soul as a created, immortal essence stresses this similiarity, also. From the perspective of God as creator Calvin also stresses the similarity and unity of the soul and body as privileged creatures of a benevolent and gracious God. God is a God to human bodies as well as to human souls[50] and his glory shines forth in human bodies[51] as providential grace. That human bodies as well as souls are the recipients of God's providential grace is a common theme in Calvin's theology, especially his sermons: "For it seems that eating and drinking are not worthy of being regarded by God; but he wishes to preside over them in order that we may know the fatherly solicitude that he has toward us, not only toward our souls, but also toward our bodies, even though they are frail and corruptible."[52] Because God's grace in providence extends to the body and the soul, the human response must involve the body and soul. The body is subject to God no less than the soul, and thus should render God glory and service.

> Since God created our bodies as well as our souls, and nour-
> ishes and maintains them, this is good enough reason why he
> should be served and honored with our bodies. And further-
> more, we know that the Lord honors us by calling not only our
> souls his temples, but also our bodies. . . .[53]

From the absolute perspective of God as creator, then, the soul and body appear as two created entities seen in unity before their creator.

Calvin also stresses the similiarity of the soul and body as judged and redeemed creatures from the perspective of God as redeemer. He continually reminds his readers that the soul is like the body in that it, too, is but a worm, nothing but a mass of iniquity.[54] Though Calvin stresses the similarity of the soul and body as creatures full of sin from this perspective, he occasionally interrupts the flow of his argument to remind his readers that if one is going to compare the soul and body in terms of sinfulness, it is the soul that would deserve the worse penalty. He describes sin as despoiling women and men of "that part of us in which the divine especially shines, and in which there are such clear tokens of immortality that the condition of the body is better and more excellent than that of the soul."[55] Calvin stresses the similarity and unity of the soul and body as recipients of God's redeeming grace as well as of his judgments on sin. He insists that God regenerates the whole person, body as well as soul.

> Since the "animal nature" which we have first of all, is the image of Adam, so we will conform to Christ in his heavenly nature; and when that happens our restoration will be complete. For we now begin to bear the image of Christ, and we are daily being transformed into it more and more; but that image depends upon gradual regeneration. But then it will be restored to fullness in our body as well as our soul.

Calvin must include the body in the restoration of the *imago dei*, since his original definition of the *imago* included the body as well as the soul.[57] And he does:

> For how is the whole man entire, except when his thoughts are pure and holy, his affections are honorable and well-arranged, and when too his body itself devotes its energies and service to good works alone? The philosophers hold that the faculty of understanding is like a mistress, while the affections are the means of exercising command, and the body renders obedience. We now see how well everything corresponds. Only if a man harbor nothing in his mind, has no ambition in his heart, and does nothing with his body that is not approved by God, is he pure and entire.[58]

Likewise his view of the final destiny of the human being emphasizes the unity of the soul and body, for the body as well as the soul will be part of the new heaven and earth in the final restoration of all creation.[59]

While Calvin emphasizes the unity of the soul and body in creation and providence over against the Anabaptists, he stresses the unity and similarity of the soul and body in sin and redemption when he is faced with philosophers or theologians who imperil the doctrine of the gratuitous grace of God in Christ. When the "papists" or the Libertines split the self into parts, so as to reserve a portion of purity or initiative for humankind, Calvin responds by highlighting the view of the whole sinful self seen from the perspective of God as judge and redeemer. We have just seen this in his view of the soul and body in the doctrine of sin and redemption. It is also evident in his version of the faculties of the soul. Calvin stresses not only the unity of the body and soul but also the unity of the parts of the soul from the perspective of God as redeemer.

Unlike medieval anthropologies, in which the discussion of the faculties of the soul played a major role, Calvin's Renaissance anthropology displays little direct interest in this question.[60] In fact, in his introduction to his discussion of the soul's faculties in the *Institutes* he notes that he considers the issue trivial and useless, much better suited to the subtle minds of the philosophers than Christian theologians.[61] The question was simply not crucial to him, as the immortality of the soul was, since its resolution was not necessary to faith and had little practical import. Characteristically, however, Calvin does not refrain from giving his opinions on the matter, reasoning that a discussion of the faculties of the soul can be profitable and therefore it is not forbidden, as long as one is not led astray by it in the doctrine of sin.[63] After outlining a more detailed and a more summary version of Aristotelian faculty psychology, both of which he admits are true and to which he has no serious objection, Calvin offers his own simple and straightforward faculty psychology as an alternative that can be used effectively in the heavenly philosophy. In this abbreviated view the soul consists of two faculties: understanding, which distinguishes between objects, approving or disapproving of them; and will, which chooses and follows what the understanding approves and rejects and flees what the understanding disapproves.[64] Throughout his works he refers to these two faculties of the soul and the two chief parts of the soul that God claims for himself.[65]

In the *Institutes* Calvin claims that his two-fold division of the soul is only probable, that it might lead to obscurity, that it could be passed over, and that he would not strongly oppose anyone who divides the soul another way.[66] His modesty here, however, belies his theological concern with this issue, a concern that the soul be taken in its entirety and not overly divided. His neat division of the soul into understanding and will precludes the more complicated views of the soul advocated by the "papist" defenders of free will and some Libertine defenders of the powers of reason. Calvin clearly

rejected all more complex divisions of the soul which distinguished a
higher part of the soul from the lower parts because they compro-
mised the radical doctrine of grace. For example, in his lectures on
Ezekiel he mentions that in one interpretation of Ezekiel's vision the
four animals are said to refer to passion, lust, reason, and the
conscience *(synteresis)*. This he rejects as puerile.[67] Knowing that
the *synteresis* had been used by medieval theologians to claim a role
for the soul in the reception of grace, he omitted it from his simple
division of the faculties of the soul. Also, his view precludes the
Platonic division of the soul into a rational and irrational part. Such a
division would endanger the doctrine of sin, since it envisions sin
arising out of the juncture of the rational and irrational parts of the
soul. Realizing this, Calvin self-consciously opposes his interpretation of the divisions of the soul to this philosophical division.

> [Paul] applies the word *mind*, not to the rational part of the soul
> honored by philosophers, but to that part which is illumined by
> the Spirit of God, so that it may understand and will aright.
> Paul not only mentions understanding, but also connects with
> it the earnest desire of the heart.[68]

And, Calvin's division precluded the "papist" division of the soul
into the spirit, or *mens*, and the soul, or understanding, which held
that the *mens*, as "the superior part of the soul," was not prone to
sin.[69] He goes on to explain that the word spirit is not a synonym for
the *mens*, "which the advocates of free will call the superior part of
the soul, but the gift of heaven. [Paul] explains that it is those whom
God governs by his spirit who are spiritual, and not those who obey
reason on their own impulse."[70] Because of this misunderstanding,
so detrimental to the doctrine of gratuitous grace, Calvin sorts out
the terms spirit and soul according to his own simple alternative of
the divisions of the soul. He frequently notes that the terms soul and
spirit are, generally speaking, used as synonyms and that they are to
be understood that way unless otherwise indicated.[71] However,
when the two terms are used together, the soul is to be understood
as the will and the spirit as the understanding.[72] This simple alternative does away with the distortion which understands soul as the
vital impulse and spirit as "that part of man which has been renewed."[73] It is clear, then, that for Calvin the "probable" and simple
alternative of dividing the soul into understanding and will alone
plays a crucial role in his argument against misunderstandings of the

gratuitous grace of God. His brief theological division enables him
to claim that the entire soul, with all of its parts, is subject to sin and
to the gracious influence of God. "Whenever the Lord accosts us by
His Word, he is dealing seriously with us to affect all our inner
senses. There is therefore, no part of our soul which should not be
influenced."[74] Far from a trivial diversion of the mind, his division
of the faculties of the soul is a weapon in his arsenal used to defend
the true doctrine of grace. And, in Calvin's view of the faculties of
the soul and his use of the simple division into understanding and
will, the primary emphasis is on the unity of the soul. His arguments stress the fact that the soul is better understood theologically
as a whole rather than in parts. Thus, his view of the faculties of the
soul supports his view of the relation between the body and soul
outlined above; both highlight the whole self, as seen from the
perspective of God as redeemer.

While in the context of certain arguments Calvin stresses the
similarity and unity of the soul and body, focusing on the whole self
from the perspectives of God as creator and redeemer, at other times
he stresses the inequality of the body and soul, focusing on the self
as soul alone from the perspective of humankind. When arguing
with Osiander, whom Calvin charges with confusing the soul and
the body, Calvin underlines the distinctive character of each.[75] In
order to interpret correctly Calvin's view of the relation of the soul
and body, it is essential to understand exactly how he makes this
distinction. He believes that if Adam had not sinned, there would
not be as great a distinction between the soul and body as currently
exists. For if Adam had not sinned, there would be no violent or
harsh separation of the soul from the body, but only a gentle translation into a new state of being.[76] The radical distinction between soul
and body, therefore, is limited to the second stage of salvation
history, sin and redemption in the present life.[77] However, within
this stage, scriptures teach us to distinguish sharply between the
soul and the body[78] and to refer the nobler part of the self or the
principal part of the soul.[79] And this is exactly what Calvin does; he
distinguishes the body and soul by elevating the soul over the body.
It is "the principal part of men,"[80] "a thing more excellent in us
than the body,"[81] the noblest part of humankind.[82] For this reason,
it can be said that God, who is a God to our bodies as well as our
souls, is a God "especially to [our] souls."[83] It is also for this reason
that the image of God finds its seat in the soul rather than in the
body,[84] for it is the soul which directs and rules the body and not

vice versa.[85] Therefore, if "[t]yrants torture, maim, burn, scourge, and hang," one must remember that "it is only the body."[86]

Often in the context of making this distinction between the noble soul and the base-born body Calvin employs the scriptural metaphor of tabernacle for the body. "Each of our bodies is called a tabernacle because the soul dwells in it."[87] He uses this particular metaphor to point to the beauty and dignity of this dwelling place of the soul as a creation of God. But, when he alters the metaphor slightly, a much different point is made. He frequently speaks of the body as "the house in which [we] dwell."[88] He interprets the terrestial tabernacle to mean a frail lodging *(loge caduque)*,[89] a house of mud *(maison de fange)*,[90] or a poor hut.[91] And his point is that since we inhabit such an infirm and corruptible house we cannot glorify ourselves.[92] One drop of rain and our house of mud and dust is gone.[93] Our hopes, therefore, should be placed on the glorious tabernacle of the incorruptible body we will inherit at the resurrection, not on the present *"sepulchre."*[94]

This metaphor of the body as the dwelling place of the soul is evidence that Calvin retains a spiritualizing tendency. Even when he stresses the unity and similarity of the body and soul from the perspectives of God as creator and redeemer, he retains a view of the superiority of the soul. This does not mean, however, that he is a dualist. While Calvin does elevate the soul over the body and show a clear preference for the soul throughout his work (spiritualism), he does not denigrate, reject, or finally separate the soul from the body in his work (dualism). As he explains in his thirty-ninth sermon on Job, this particular distinction between the two substances of the soul and body is a comparison between what is lesser and what is greater, not a contradiction between what is evil and what is good.

> There must be a guest lodged in our bodies. And who is this guest? The soul. Thus we see that the principal part of men is the spirit which God placed in them. Our bodies show such great and excellent workmanship that we become confused by them; for what does it mean for that which surmounts them, which goes even higher, and which has more dignity? Here are the degrees that we must reach.[95]

From this perspective, then, the body has a positive, though limited, value.[96] It is much less than the soul, but not evil. It is important to remember that it is only when the body is compared to the soul, a created immortal essence and the seat of the *imago dei*, from the perspective of humankind that it appears to be a house of mud and dust. Seen from the perspective of God as redeemer, on the other hand, the body appears similar to and in unity with the soul as worthy of God's creating, preserving, and restoring grace.

This complex assessment of the body as similar to and in union with the soul when seen from the perspectives of God as creator and redeemer and less than the soul when seen from the perspective of humankind parallels Calvin's view of the temporal life as it was presented in chapter 1. In fact, Calvin's judgment of the temporal life can aid us in understanding his view of the body, for he uses the body as a synecdoche for the temporal life.

> Why then does he mention souls only, when the glory of the resurrection is promised also to our bodies? As the soul is immortal, salvation is properly ascribed to it, as Paul is sometimes accustomed to say—"That the soul may be saved in the day of the Lord" (I Cor. 5:5). It is the same as though he had said "Eternal Salvation." There is an implied comparison with the mortal, fading life which belongs to the body. At the same time, the body is not excluded from participation in glory, so far as it is connected to the soul.[97]

In his commentary on Romans 12:1 he explicitly identifies the body as a synecdoche denoting all the parts of the whole person, "for the members of the body are the instruments by which we perform our actions."[98] And, in this context, painting the comparison or distinction between the soul and the body as the greater to the lesser from the relative perspective, he uses the body as a synecdoche for the impermanence of the temporal life. When he wishes to compare the eternal and temporal life, he often uses the shorthand of the two synecdoches, soul and body.[99] Sometimes he chooses to use "the inner person" and "the outer person" as the synecdoches for the spiritual and temporal lives.[100] In both cases his assessments parallel those we found in his presentation of the temporal. Seen from the absolute perspectives of God as creator and redeemer, the body is similar to and in unity with the soul as a recipient of God's grace, just as the temporal life is similar to the eternal life as a gift of God. But seen from the relative perspective of humankind, the body appears far lower than the soul, just as the temporal life appears far less valuable than the future life. Both judgments of the soul's relation to the body represent Calvin's view, just as both views of the temporal life represent his position. By means of his shifting theological perspectives, he is able to stress the unity and similarity of the body and soul against some opponents and the superiority and distinctiveness of the soul against other opponents.

If this were all Calvin said about the relation of the soul to the body, it would not be too difficult to refute the interpretations of him as a dualist. However, Calvin adds another view of the relation of the body to the soul that complicates matters. In addition to viewing the body and soul as similar and in unity before God and the soul as superior in comparison with the body, Calvin sees the soul in contradiction to the body.

> Here, I say, is the reason why we must long and seek and desire death: because when we are cleansed of this body, which is like a house full of stench and infection, we will be fully reformed to the image of God, and that image will reign in us and all that is corrupt in our nature will be annihilated.[101]

Such statements are not difficult to find in Calvin. But since Calvin's use of the Platonic metaphor of the body as the prison house of the soul is so often used to support the claim that Calvin is a dualist, we will examine his contradiction of the soul and body by means of his use of this metaphor. It is argued that Calvin's use of this Platonic imagery indicates his approval of the Platonic dualistic anthropology and that this acceptance of a philosophical anthropology corrupts his otherwise biblical anthropology. But Calvin's use of this common Platonic metaphor for the body does not necessarily mean that he is an anthropological dualist. He uses the image with a number of different meanings, none of which he takes directly from Plato. The first meaning of the image of the body as the prison house of the soul is this: the soul is subject to evil and death as long as it is in the body. While this may seem to be an approval of Plato's view of the body as a source of evil and a hindrance of the soul, Calvin actually has something quite different in mind. This meaning of the image of the body as the prison house of the soul has to do not with the evils of matter but the servitude of sin. In many places Calvin joins these two ideas together, the prison house of the soul and the servitude of sin.[102] He is clear that the word body can be used as a synecdoche for the sinful condition of humankind. This is indeed how he at times uses and explains it.

> By the body of death he [Paul] means the mass of sin, or the constituent parts from which the whole man is formed, except

that in his case alone the remnants of sin were left, which held him captive. . . . Paul wanted to teach us that the eyes of God's children are opened so that they discern with prudence from the law of God the corruption of their nature and the death which proceeds from it. The word body means the same as outward man and members, because Paul notes that the origin of sin is that man becomes carnal and earthly. Although he still surpasses the brutes, his true excellence has been taken from him, and what remains is filled with innumerable corruptions, so that, insofar as his soul is degenerate, it may rightly be said to have changed into his body.[103]

Here and elsewhere Calvin uses the term body as a synecdoche for sinful existence and soul as a synecdoche for redeemed existence.[104] In this meaning of the word body in connection with the image of the prison house, then, Calvin is not referring to matter as the source of evil or the opponent of spirit but to the opposition of sin.

The word body . . . is not to be taken in the sense of flesh, skin, and bones, but for the whole body of man's existence. We may quite certainly infer this from the present passage, for the other clause, which we will shortly add concerning the parts of the body, extends also to the soul. Paul thus refers disparagingly to earthly man, for the corruption of our nature prevents our aspiring to anything worthy of our origin. . . .

The objection that there is a difference in the case of the soul is easily answered by the assertion that in our present degenerate state our souls are fixed to the earth and so enslaved to our bodies that they have fallen from their proper excellence. In a word, the nature of man is termed corporeal because he has been deprived of heavenly grace, and is only a kind of deceptive shadow or image. There is the additional fact that this body is contemtuously referred to by Paul as *mortal* for the purpose of teaching us that the whole of human nature is liable to death and destruction. He now gives the name of sin to that original depravity which dwells in our hearts, and which impels us to sin and from which properly all our evil deeds and wickedness flow.[105]

If there be any doubt left that Calvin uses the word body as a synecdoche for human sinful existence, his commentary on Romans 6:6 should remove it: "The body of sin, which he mentions a little later, does not mean flesh and bones, but the whole mass of sin, for man, when left to his own nature, is a mass of sin."[106] Furthermore, Calvin's careful exegesis of the scriptural opposition of spirit and flesh supports this interpretation of the image of the body as a prison house of the soul as a synecdoche for sinful existence. When Calvin uses the term "flesh" he usually notes explicitly that he is referring to "human nature as subject to death" or "the corruption of sinful nature" and not to skin and bones.[107] He defines the opposition this way:

> "Flesh" is the designation applied to men at birth and for as long as they retain their natural character, because they are corrupt, and have no reputation for anything, nor do they desire anything but what is gross and earthly. The spirit on the other hand, is called the renewing of corrupt nature, while God reforms us after his own image.[108]

In these contexts, then, the contradiction between the soul and the body which is expressed in the image of the body as the prison house of the soul actually refers to the contradiction between the spirit and the flesh.[109] Thus, Calvin offers another view of the relation between the soul and body. Seen from the absolute perspectives of God as judge and redeemer, the soul (as a synecdoche for the redeemed life) and the body (as a synecdoche for sinful existence) appear in absolute contradiction to each other. When it is understood that he uses these terms here as synecdoches for spiritual and fleshly existence and that he sees the contradiction between the soul and body as only one of three different relationships between the soul and body, it is difficult to charge him with Platonic anthropological dualism. This point may be underscored by a brief glance at Calvin's other meaning for the image of the body as the prison house of the soul.

Calvin uses the image of the body as the prison house of the soul to convey not only the contradiction between spiritual and carnal existence but also the comparison between the eternal and temporal lives. In his commentary on John 1:14 he makes it clear that the term "flesh" can be used in both ways.

> When Scripture speaks of man derogatorily it calls him "flesh." How great is the distance between the spiritual glory of the Word of God and the stinking filth of our flesh. Yet the Son of God stooped so low as to take to Himself that flesh addicted to so much wretchedness. "Flesh" here is not used for corrupt nature (as in Paul) but for mortal man. It denotes derogatorily his frail and almost transient nature: "All flesh is as grass" (Is. 40: 6). . . . But we must notice at the same time that this is the rhetorical synecdoche—the lower part embraces the whole

> man. Apollinaris was therefore foolish to imagine that Christ
> was clothed with a human body without a soul. . . . Nor when
> Scripture calls men flesh does it thereby make them soul-
> less.[110]

And, just as the term "flesh" can be used to denote sinfulness and
transience, so the image of the body as the prison house can denote
both sinfulness and frailty. Occasionally when Calvin uses this image, therefore, he refers to the frailty and transience of the temporal
life as compared with the firmness and surety of the eternal life.[111]
While each of Calvin's uses of the image of the body as the prison
house of the soul cannot be exactly interpreted, we can say on the
basis of the textual evidence that he uses the image in two distinct
ways: to refer to the sinful condition of humankind after the Fall, the
servitude of sin; and to refer to the transience of the temporal life
which all mortals share, the exile from the kingdom of God.

Calvin's complex perspectival view of the relation between the
body and soul makes it impossible to classify him neatly as a dualist.
Battenhouse's and Partee's charges of dualism are incorrect for several reasons. First, Calvin used the Platonic image of the body as the
prison house of the soul to denote the contradiction between the
flesh and the spirit.[112] Because he uses the terms "body" and "soul"
in this context rhetorically and not literally, he does not conflate
Paul's teaching with Plato's at this point, as the following quotation
demonstrates.

> The word body signifies the more solid mass as yet unpurified
> by the spirit of God from earthly defilements, which delights
> only in what is gross. It would be absurd otherwise to ascribe to
> the body the blame for sin. Again, the soul is so far from being
> life, that it does not even of itself have life.[113]

In other words, his self-conscious use of the imagery to refer to the
battle of forces within sinners being redeemed rather than to a
contradiction of substances helps to clear him of the charge of
dualism. Second, Calvin's contradiction between the body and soul
from the perspectives of God as judge and redeemer is offset by his
view of the similarity and unity of the soul and body from the
perspectives of God as creator and redeemer.

Quistorp's and Schulze's charge that Calvin retains a spiritualizing tendency is essentially correct but incomplete. Calvin's
comparison between the soul and body and his view of the superi-

ority of the soul, emphasized from the perspective of humankind, but present also in the perspectives of God as creator and redeemer, is supplemented by his insistence on the unity and similarity of the two from the perspective of God as creator. It is also complicated by his contradiction of the two from the perspective of God as redeemer. By focusing on only the first of these views of Calvin's complex doctrine of the relation of the soul to the body this charge inadequately represents Calvin's position.

Finally, Partee's and Balke's conclusion that Calvin exhibits only a "formal Platonism," and Miles's and Quistorp's conclusion that Calvin is inconsistent in his remarks on the body do not adequately interpret the texts.[114] Calvin's views of the relation of the soul to the body can be more adequately understood in light of his shifting theological perspectives. From the perspective of God as creator, the body and soul appear together in their similarity and unity as recipients of God's grace in creation and providence. From the perspectives of God as judge and redeemer, the soul and body also appear together in their similarity and unity as recipients of God's judgment and regeneration. From this same perspective the soul and body appear in absolute contradiction to each other as synecdoches for grace and sin. Finally, from the perspective of humankind, the soul appears on a higher level than the body, as more favored by God as the seat of the *imago dei*. Each view is essential to Calvin's psychology as he develops it in response to various opponents. To ignore one of these views is to offer an incomplete interpretation of his theology at this point, the complexity of which may be found in the *Institutes* 2.15.1. While explaining the mystery of Jesus Christ as two natures in one person, he takes as his analogy the mystery of the human creature as two substances in one person. Humankind, he says, consists of

> two substances. Yet neither is so mingled with the other as not to retain its own distinctive nature. For the soul is not the body, and the body is not the soul. Therefore, some things are said exclusively of the soul that can in no wise apply to the body; and of the body, again that in no way fit the soul; of the whole man, that cannot refer—except inappropriately—to either the soul or body separately. Finally, the characteristics of the mind are (sometimes) transferred to the body and those of the body to the soul. Yet he who consists of these parts is one man, not many. Such expressions signify that there is one person in man composed of two elements joined together, and that there are two diverse underlying natures that make up this person.[215]

The complex mystery of the self as body and soul can only be adequately presented if different shifting perspectives allow one to take different views of the self at different times. Perhaps the only non-misleading summary of Calvin's view of the soul and body, then, is the traditional shorthand used for the complex mystery of the two natures of Jesus Christ in one person, *distinctae non divisae*.

Immortality and Resurrection

Calvin had a number of possibilities open to him for relating immortality and resurrection. He could have rejected the immortality of the soul as a philosophical doctrine incompatible with the gospel.[116] He could have simply conflated the philosophical doctrine of the immortality of the soul with the biblical witness to the resurrection of the body. Or he could have adopted the position of Pompanazzi, arguing on the basis of the theory of double truth that the philosophical doctrine of immortality and the theological doctrine of resurrection were both true in their own spheres. He did none of these. Instead, he developed a complex view of the distinction between and the unity of immortality and resurrection. His view of immortality and resurrection does not, therefore, support the claim that he was an anthropological dualist. Those who argue that immortality was a foreign intrusion in his otherwise biblical theology are as misguided as those who argue that resurrection was an intrusion in his otherwise philosophical, dualistic anthropology. Rather, Calvin's view of immortality and resurrection supports the view of the relation between the soul and body presented above: two distinct yet related substances in one person.

The resurrection of the body is not a foreign intrusion in Calvin's otherwise dualist anthropology, but an essential and constant theme. He refers to baptism as "a seal of our future resurrection,"[117] and declares the resurrection to be "a fundamental principle of faith."[118] These statements are not merely the empty verbal protests of a dualist who wishes to establish his Christian orthodoxy by simple assertion. The resurrection of the body is an essential element in Calvin's understanding of the eschatological structure of human existence. Far from being introduced at the last moment to insure Calvin's orthodoxy, the resurrection of the body is a constant theme of Calvin's anthropology. As we saw in chapter 1, Calvin interprets the life of Adam and Eve in the garden of Eden as a full

life, body and soul. And they were intended to pass over into the
future life, which was also a full life for body and soul, without a
violent rupture between the body and soul. They were to pass from
the weak temporal life into the firm future life without losing their
wholeness. Both body and soul were in need of a less corruptible
quality to enjoy the future life, and they were to take on this quality
in their journey through the temporal life.[119] But with sin came
death. Sin caused the body to be subjected to physical death, the
violent separation of the soul from the body. It also caused the soul
to be subject to spiritual death, the violent alienation of the soul
from God.[120] Each person now experiences both kinds of death.
Believers, however, have the threat of physical death removed in this
life through faith, the hope of the immortality of the soul between
the death of the body and its final resurrection, and the assurance
that they will reach the final consummation of their salvation in body
and soul. Each of these is an essential stage in the progression of the
believer from the life of finitude and sin to the incorruptible life for
which all men and women were created. Meditation on the future
life gives one the confidence to face death without fear. Proper
knowledge of the immortality of the soul and God's providential care
for it after the death of the body gives one hope. And knowledge of
the resurrection of the body gives one assurance that the happiness
that the immortal soul enjoys with God after the death of the body
will be brought to fullness and completion.[121] The resurrection of
the body, then, for Calvin is a completion of the process of being
restored to the incorruptible life for which mankind was created.[122]
This process begins during the life of the believer, is continued after
her or his death, and is consummated with the final resurrection. It
is because of this view of the gradual process of restoration in the
image of God that Calvin is able to speak of "the blessed immortality" of the body as well as the soul.[123] He does not find it odd to
say that "both our souls and our bodies were destined for heavenly
incorruption and an unfading crown."[124] Seen as two stages of one
process of restoration to the full image of God, immortality and
resurrection, though distinct from one another, are not separated
from one another. From the perspective of humankind, immortality
and resurrection are but stages of growth along the journey toward
maturity.[125] And, from this perspective immortality of the soul and
resurrection can both, as legitimate parts, be used as synecdoches
for the whole future life. This is indeed how Calvin often uses the
two terms. Although he sometimes pairs the two,[126] he often uses

the two interchangeably. This is especially true when he is speaking of Jesus as the pledge of the inheritance of the future life for all believers. In his discussion of the resurrection in the *Institutes*, for instance, he comments that "in the nature which [Christ] took from us he so completed the course of mortal life that now, having obtained immortality, he is the pledge of our coming resurrection."[127] Throughout this theological presentation of the resurrection he speaks of "putting on immortality."[128] In other places he defines the resurrection as "future immortality" or "blessed immortality."[129] And, when discussing one of his central ethical principles, meditation on the future life, he refers to it both as a meditation on immortality and a meditation on the resurrection.[230] This interchangeable use of immortality and resurrection implies that Calvin consistently used both as synecdoches for the future, heavenly life of humankind and perceived the two to be closely related to one another. Both are essential to the Christian faith in his view and both are witnessed to it in scriptures.[131] For this reason, Calvin accuses both the Libertines, who denied the resurrection of the body,[132] and the Anabaptists, who denied the immortality of the soul,[133] of departing from the truth of Christianity. Seeing no absolute contradiction between immortality and resurrection, Calvin would find Oscar Cullman's argument that immortality is a Greek notion incompatible with the biblical doctrine of resurrection quite odd.[134]

But if Calvin, from the perspective of humankind, sees immortality and resurrection as closely related to one another, he does not conflate the two. He perceived clearly the distinction between immortality and resurrection, not only as two different stages in the process of restoration but also as distinct doctrines. He notes from time to time that while certain philosophers may have been able to know something of the immortality of the soul, none was able to penetrate the more difficult doctrine of the resurrection.[135] Unlike the immortality of the soul, for which several signs remained in humankind, the resurrection of the body has no such witness.[136] It seems to be a higher doctrine available only to believers. Curiously, the perspective of God as redeemer does not appear when Calvin discusses immortality and resurrection. He does not present the two as standing in contradiction to one another, as he does with the body and soul, the enslaved and free wills, earthly and heavenly wisdom, and the destroyed and perfect image. He simply maintains a clear distinction between the two as stages and as doctrines. His primary view of the relation between immortality and resurrection is that from the perspective of humankind. In this view immortality and resurrection appear in continuity with one another as the penultimate and ultimate stages of humankind's restoration to its eternal inheritance. From this viewpoint, it is obvious that it is the resurrection of the body which is superior to the immortality of the soul and not vice versa.

Quistorp's conclusion that Calvin emphasized the resurrection of the body in spite of the fact that he preferred the immortality of the soul is not supported by all the texts.[137] As we saw in the foregoing paragraph, Calvin at times points directly to the superiority of the doctrine of resurrection to that of immortality, echoing his preference (demonstrated in chapter 3) for Christian philosophy over earthly philosophy. Nor is Quistorp's analysis of Calvin's doctrine as an incoherent combination of Greek dualism and biblical realism supported. He claims that

> The Biblical contrast of the present and future aeon is to this extent even in Calvin *identified* with the metaphysical antithesis between the temporal and the eternal, the earthly and the heavenly, the bodily and the spiritual. Hence he thinks of the future life preeminently as a heavenly and spiritual life which definitely begins at death with the liberation of the immortal soul, and which is completed in the immediate vision of God without the mediation of the humanity of Christ. . . . But we saw that the spiritualizing tendency in the eschatology of Calvin was constantly interrupted and rectified by the influence on his teaching of Holy Scripture with its concrete hopes, especially in regard to the resurrection of the flesh as the resurrection of this body. The orientation of Calvin's eschatology (and of his theology) as a whole towards the general resurrection preserves its Biblical character, even though that character is seriously threatened by the other aspect of his thought.[138]

The analysis of the temporal and eternal lives in Chapter 1 and the analysis of Calvin's view of the body and soul and immortality and resurrection in this chapter make it difficult to accept Quistorp's conclusion that Calvin conflated Greek dualism and the holistic anthropology of the scriptures. It also calls into question Schulze's claim that the *only* difference between Calvin and Plato on this point is that Calvin paid more attention to the resurrection of the body.[139] Calvin's view of the resurrection body is not a "foreign element" in his otherwise dualistic anthropology.[140] Rather, it is a constant element of his consistently eschatological anthropology. It stands to-

gether with the immortality of the soul as an essential description of
the future life of humankind.

Conclusion

In *The Spirit of Medieval Philosophy* Étienne Gilson delin-
eates two major ways in which medieval Christian theologians were
able to reconcile the soul and body and the immortality and resurrection. First, one could follow Augustine and adopt Plato's views of
the immortality of the soul. The difficulty with this, as he points out,
is that Plato's view of the immortality of the soul is not wholly
compatible with the Christian insistence on the unity of the soul and
body. Theologians who use this view run into the problem of defin-
ing the self as a "soul using a body" and allowing this definition to
remain as "somewhat of an alien body" in their theology.[141] The
result is that they denigrate the body and do not adequately present
the resurrection. The second approach attempts to avoid these difficulties caused by the use of Plato's definition of the self by employing Aristotle's view of the self. The solution of Aquinas, for instance,
is to speak of the self as a substantial unity in which the soul is the
form of the body. The advantage of this position is that although the
entire person constitutes the substance, it is the soul (the form)
which confers that substantiality upon the whole. This view of the
self as a complex substance does away with the dualistic tendency
inherent in the view of the self as two different substances which are
united temporarily.[142] The difficulty with this view is that it can lead
to a denial of individual immortality.

In the Middle Ages Christian theologians attempted to steer a
path between the Scylla of dualism and the Charbydis of the denial
of immortality in their anthropologies. Various directions were
taken. Some followed Augustine by affirming both Plato's views of
immortality and the biblical view of the whole self. Some followed
Avicenna, arguing both that the soul was an individual immortal
essence and that it was joined to the body as the form of matter.
According to Gilson it was Thomas who gave the "less facile" solu-
ton, since he successfully maintained both the immortality of the
soul and the unity of the soul and body.[143] Though he offers no
criteria for this assessment of Thomas, Gilson implies that Thomas's
solution is the only one that does not crash on the rocks of dualism or
the denial of immortality. It could be argued, however, that Calvin's

solution to the problem of the soul and body and immortality and resurrection also steers a safe path between the two. While Calvin places himself in the Augustinian tradition by adopting the definition of the self as a combination of two different substances, he interprets this holistically rather than dualistically. The mystery of the self as soul and body is analogous for him to the mystery of Jesus Christ as divine and human: both are complex unities in which the two elements are distinct but never separated from one another. His view of the soul as a created, immortal essence; his complex view of the relation of the soul to the body as similar and in unity, as unequals, and as contradictories; and his view of the resurrection as the consummation of immortality all point in this direction. Using the thesis of perspectivalism, we have seen that Calvin: emphasizes the created nature of the soul at one time, its immortal essence another; affirms and denies the immortality of the soul; emphasizes the unity and similarity of the body and soul, the superiority of the soul, and the contradiction between the body and soul; and affirms the immortality of the soul after death of the body and the resurrection of the body as the consummation of salvation. If this perspectival solution to the problems of Christian psychology is not as neat as Thomas Aquinas's Aristotelian one, it is at least as distinctive.

Notes

/1/   Heinrich Quistorp, *Calvin's Doctrine of the Last Things,* trans. Harold Knight (London: Lutterworth Press, 1955), pp. 51–54, 59, 60 [hereafter referred to as *Last Things*].

/2/   Partee, *Calvin and Classical Philosophy,* pp. 61–65; Babelotzky, *Platonische Bilder,* pp. 108–38.

/3/   Schulze, *Meditatio futurae vitae,* pp. 71–89; Quistorp, *Last Things,* p. 62.

/4/   Battenhouse, "The Doctrine of Man," p. 468; Quistorp, *Last Things,* pp. 81, 101.

/5/   Ibid., p. 101.

/6/   See appendix 5 for a detailed listing of these scholars.

/7/   *CO* 7: 111 *(Briefve instruction).*

/8/   *CO* 47: 289 (John 12:25); *Co* 48: 45 (Acts 2:27).

/9/   *CO* 49: 558 (I Cor. 15:45).

/10/   *CO* 7: 112 *(Briefve instruction); CO* 48: 418 (Acts 17:28). See also chapter 2, pp. 38–42. *CO* 7: 128 *(Briefve instruction).*

/11/   See chapter 1, pp. 18–22.

/12/   *CO* 31: 303 (Ps. 31); *CO* 49: 427 (I Cor. 7:39); *CO* 34: 100 (s. 74 on Job 20); *CO* 35: 558 (s. 2 on Ez.); *CO* 33: 684 (s. 55 on Job 14); *CO* 31: 103 (Ps.

9:12); *CO* 45: 410 (Luke 16:23): *CO* 7: 114 *(Briefve instruction); CO* 33: 675
(s. 54 on Job 14).
/13/   See chapter 2, pp. 50–54.
/14/   *Scandals,* p. 61 *(OS* 2: 201).
/15/   *CO* 7: 179 *(Des Libertins).*
/16/   *CO* 7: 186 *(Des Libertins).*
/17/   See chapter 2, pp. 76ff.
/18/   *CO* 53: 92 (s. 8 on I Tim. 1). See also *CO* 53: 621 (s. 2 on I Tim. 6); *CO*
33: 348 (s. 28 on Job 7); *CO* 7: 180.
/19/   *CO* 33: 491 (s. 39 on Job 10).
/20/   *CO* 34: 456 (s. 98 on Job 27); *CO* 33: 206, 348, 674–75.
/21/   *CO* 44: 401 (Mal. 1:2); *CO* 48: 418 (Acts 17:28).
/22/   *CO* 44: 401 (Mal. 1:2).
/23/   *CO* 33: 162 (s. 12 on Job 3).
/24/   *CO* 7: 180 *(Des Libertins).* This argument is also used against the
Platonic view of *metempsychosis,* since Calvin believes that it is God, not
our memory of a former life, that gives our souls reason, *CO* 33: 542.
/25/   *CO* 33: 622 (s. 50 on Job 13).
/26/   *CO* 33: 491–92 (s. 39 on Job 10); *CO* 49: 381 (I Cor. 5:5).
/27/   McNeill 1: 56–57, *Inst.* 1.5.5 in *OS* 3:48–49.
/28/   McNeill: 1: 184–85, *Inst.* 1.15.2 in *OS* 3: 174–75. (Emphasis mine.)
/29/   *CO* 33: 490.
/30/   *CO* 34: 467 (s. 98 on Job 27).
/31/   *CO* 55: 274 (I Pet. 4:7); *CO* 55: 473 (II Pet. 3:4); *CO* 55: 476 (II Pet.
3:10).
/32/   *CO* 33: 518 (s. 41 on Job 10); *CO* 50: 61 (II Cor. 5:3).
/33/   *OS* 3: 174 *(Inst.* 1.15.2).
/34/   *CO* 31: 103 (Ps. 9:12); *OS* 3: 48–49 *(Inst.* 1.5.5); *OS* 3: 174–76 *(Inst.*
1.15.2). See also *OS* 3: 47–48 *(Inst.* 1.5.3, 4).
/35/   Battenhouse, "The Doctrine of Man," p. 425.
/36/   Schulze, *Meditatio futureae vitae,* pp. 71–89. Quistorp, *Last Things,*
p. 62 and p. 193, n. 1. Babelotzky refers to it not as a dualism but as a
dichotomy, *Platonische Bilder,* p. 108, and emphasizes only the radical
distinction between the soul and body in Calvin's theology, ibid., p. 106ff.
/37/   Partee, *Calvin and Classical Philosophy,* p. 51.
/38/   Ibid., pp. 62–65.
/39/   Balke, *Calvin and the Anabaptist Radicals,* p. 305. Oddly enough,
Balke does not dwell on the soul-body relation at all in his treatment of the
Psychopannychia, pp. 304–8.
/40/   Émile Doumergue, *Jean Calvin: Les hommes et les choses de son
temps,* 7 vols. (Lausanne: George Bridel, 1897–1910), 4: 308.
/41/   Margaret Miles, "Theology, Anthropology and the Human Body in
Calvin's *Institutes of the Christian Religion,*" *Harvard Theologial Review* 74
(1981): 311, 316.
/42/   Ibid., p. 323.
/43/   McNeill 2: 1486, *Inst.* 4.20.1 in *OS* 5: 472.
/44/   *CO* 35: 320. See also *OS* 3: 174 *(Inst.* 1.15.1).
/45/   McNeill, 2: 998–99, *Inst.* 3.25.7 in *OS* 4: 446.

/46/ *CO* 35: 531 (s. 1 on Ez.).

/47/ *CO* 35: 469 (s. 151 on Job 39).

/48/ CO 33: 657 (s. 53 on Job 14).

/49/ CO 33: 649 (s. 52 on Job 13).

/50/ OS 3: 409 (*Inst.* 2.10.8). See also OS 3: 332 (*Inst.* 2.7.6), where he claims that God provides a law for human bodies as well as souls, a sure indication of divine grace!

/51/ OS 4: 356 (Inst. 3.20.44).

/52/ *CO* 27: 203 (s. 84 on Deut. 12); OS 4: 356 (*Inst.* 3.20.44); CO 35: 408–9 (s. 151 on Job 39).

/53/ *CO* 6: 593 (*Excuse à Messieurs les Nicodémites*) [hereafter referred to as *Excuse*]; CO 6: 611 (*Excuse*); CO 49: 400 (I Cor. 6:20).

/54/ CO 33: 676–77 (s. 54 on Job 14); OS 3: 274 (Inst. 2.3.2).

/55/ McNeill 2: 997, *Inst.* 3.25.6 in OS 4: 441. For the emphasis on the whole person and the sinful condition of human existence, see also: *CO* 49: 235 (Rom. 12:2); *CO* 49: 400 (I Cor. 6:20); *CO* 33: 545 (s. 44 on Job 11).

/56/ *Commentary on I Corinthians* 15:49 in Fraser, 9: 341 (*CO* 49: 560).

/57/ See chapter 2, pp. 42–47.

/58/ CO 52: 179 (I Thess. 5:23); CO 33: 545 (s. 44 on Job 11); CO 51: 190–91 (Eph. 4:4).

/59/ *CO* 49: 562–63 (I Cor. 15:53).

/60/ See Bernard McGinn, ed., *Three Treatises on Man: A Cistercian Anthropology* (Kalamazoo, Mich.: Cistercian Publications, 1977), Introduction.

/61/ *OS* 3: 182–83 (Inst. 1.15.2).

/62/ Calvin rejects this not because it is philosophical but because it is trivial and often misleading. There is evidence for this in the fact that he has no qualms about using and approving of other philosophical views of the soul, such as immortality. See chapter 3, pp. 95ff.

/63/ OS 3: 184 (*Inst.* 1.15.6).

/64/ OS 3: 210 (*Inst.* 1.15.7).

/65/ *CO* 36: 432 (Is. 26:9). He claims that this is an alternative of utter simplicity which is within the capacity of all to understand. *CO* 38: 462 (Jer. 24:7).

/66/ *OS* 3: 183 (*Inst.* 1.15.6).

/67/ CO 40: 30 (Lec. on Ez. 1:4).

/68/ *CO* 49: 136 (Rom. 7:25). Plato's tripartite division of the soul envisions the charioteer as reason, that sovereign part of the soul which directs the two lower parts of the soul, the spirited element and the irrational element, *Phaedrus* 246a–7, 253–54e). In the *Timaeus* this tripartite division is further complicated by Plato's division of the soul into an immortal part (reason) and a mortal part (the two horses). Plato does not use this view of the divisions of the soul consistently, however. The later Platonists, such as Plotinus, dogmatized this view. Aristotle in the *De anima* distinguishes five levels of the powers of the soul. In descending order they are: reason, locomotion, perception, desire, and nutrition. These five were transmitted in the tradition as a three-fold division of the rational, vegetative or sensitive, and nutritive souls. The rational soul contained the intellect and the will; the sensitive soul the five external senses and the three internal senses (common sense, imagination, and memory); and the nutritive soul the powers of growth and reproduction.

/69/   *CO* 49: 145 (Rom. 8:9).

/70/Ibid.

/71/   *CO* 49: 341 (I Cor. 2:11).

/72/   *CO* 36: 432 (Is. 26:)); *CO* 45: 37 (Luke 1:46); *CO* 38: 462 (Jer. 24:7); *CO* 55: 49 (Heb. 4:12); *CO* 40: 458 (Ez. 18:32).

/73/   *CO* 52: 178–79 (I Thess. 5:23).

/74/   *CO* 55: 49 (Heb. 4:12).

/75/   *OS* 3: 177 (*Inst.* 1.15.3).

/76/   *CO* 23: 66 (Gen. 3:9).

/77/   This is an important argument against those who accuse Calvin of attaching the doctrine of the resurrection of the body as an addendum to a Platonic, dualistic anthropology. See pp. 176ff. of this chapter.

/78/   *OS* 3: 176 (*Inst.* 1.15.2).

/79/   *OS* 3: 174 (Inst. 1.15.2).

/80/   *CO* 33: 488–89 (s. 39 on Job 10).

/81/   *CO* 35: 128 (s. 128 on Job 24).

/82/   *OS* 3: 174 (*Inst.* 1.15.2).

/83/   McNeill 1: 435, *Inst.* 2.10.8 in *OS* 3: 409.

/84/   *OS* 3: 176 (Inst. 1.15.3).

/85/   *CO* 9: 597 (*Response à un Hollandois*).

/86/   *Psychopannychia* in *Tracts and Treatises*, 2: 427–28.

/87/   *CO* 7: 180; *CO* 47: 47 (John 2:19). See also *CO* 33: 490 (s. 39 on Job 10); *CO* 50: 60–64, 65 (II Cor. 5:1); *CO* 55: 452 (II Pet. 1:14); *CO* 7: 113 (*Briefve instruction*); *CO* 7: 126 (*Briefve instruction*) in which he says this: "[T]here are three states of the soul. The first when it is in the body, as in a tabernacle; the second after death, as at the gate of the temple; the third in heaven with its glorious body."

/88/   *CO* 52: 161 (I Thess. 4:3); *CO* 7: 180 (*Des Libertins*); *CO* 33: 515 (s. 41 on Job 10); *CO* 33: 488–89 (s. 39 on Job 10).

/89/   *CO* 33: 210 (s. 17 on Job 5); *CO* 50: 60–65 (II Cor. 5:1); *CO* 33: 674 (s. 54 on Job 14).

/90/   *CO* 33: 205, 208 (s. 16 on Job 4).

/91/   *CO* 50: 60–65 (II Cor. 5:1).

/92/   *CO* 33: 206, 208 (s. 16 on Job 4).

/93/   *CO* 33: 205 (s. 16 on Job 4).

/94/   *CO* 33: 210 (s. 17 on Job 5); *CO* 7: 126 (*Briefve instruction*).

/95/   *CO* 33: 488–89 (s. 39 on Job 10).

/96/   *CO* 33: 728 (s,. 58 on Job 15); *CO* 33: 292 (s. 23 on Job 6); *CO* 33: 624 (s. 50 on Job 13); *CO* 35: 128 (s. 128 on Job 34).

/97/   *CO* 55: 214 (I Pet. 1:8–9).

/98/   *CO* 49: 234 (Rom. 12:1): *CO* 7: 111–13 *Briefve Instruction*).

/99/   *CO* 9: 809–10; *CO* 55: 452 (II Pet. 1:14); *CO* 33: 674 (s. 54 on Job 14); *CO* 7: 113 (*Briefve instruction*); *CO* 40: 539–40 (s. 2 on Ez.).

/100/   In his commentary on II Cor. 4:16, for instance (*CO* 50: 58), Calvin notes that the outer person is not restricted to the body alone, but refers to all that has to do with the present life:

"For the apostle intended everything that has to do with this present life to be included. He here speaks of two men and we are to think of two kinds of life, an earthly and a heavenly. The outer man is the continuance of our earthly life and consists not only of youth and good health, but also riches, honor, friendships, and other such good things. Thus, when we suffer decrease or loss of these things, which are needed for the maintenance of our present life, our outward man so far perishes. Since we are too much concerned with these things, as long as everything goes according to our wishes, the Lord takes away from us bit by bit those things that engross our attention and thus calls us back to meditate on a better life. It is necessary that our present life should perish that the inner man may begin to come into his own, for the more earthly life declines, the more heavenly life advances, at least in believers. For the wicked the outward man also decays, but there is nothing to make up for it. But in the sons of God this decay is the beginning and almost the cause of their regeneration. He says that this happens daily because God is continually active, stirring us up to think on the life to come. Would that it would take deep root in our minds that we might make continual progress amidst the perishing of the outer man!"

See also *CO* 33: 286 (s. 23 on Job 6); *CO* 51: 186 (Eph. 3:17).

/101/   *CO* 33: 170 (s. 13 on Job 3).

/102/   "We see that we are held here as in a prison, as long as this body envelops us we are slaves to sin," *CO* 33: 627–28 (s. 50 on John 13); "He signifies by this that there is no better way to move toward perfection and to withdraw from the servitude of sin than to leave his body where he is held captive as if in a prison," *CO* 7: 204 *(Des Libertins)*. The true mourning of Christians should be for those things due to their "prison and servitude to sin," *CO* 33: 144 (s. 11 on Job 3). *CO* 50: 62 (II Cor. 5:4); *OS* 3: 458 *(Inst.* 2.13.4); *OS* 3: 339 *(Inst.* 2.7.13); *OS* 4: 29–30 *(Inst.* 3.2.19); *OS* 4: 150 *(Inst.* 3.6.5).

/103/   *CO* 49: 134 (Rom. 7:24).

/104/   *CO* 33: 511 (s. 41 on Job 10).

/105/   *CO* 49: 111 (Rom. 6:12).

/106/   *CO* 49: 107–8 (Rom. 6:6).

/107/   *CO* 55: 271 (I Pet. 4:1); *CO* 55: 266 (I Pet. 3:18–19); *CO* 33: 345 (s. 28 on Job 7); *CO* 40: 244 (Ez. 11:19–20); *CO* 55: 274 (I Pet. 4:6); *CO* 50: 84 (II Cor. 7:1); *CO* 23: 779 (s. 3 on Gen. 22); *OS* 2: 271–72 *(Inst.* 2.3.1).

/108/   *CO* 49: 128 (Rom. 7:14).

/109/   Calvin appears to be as clear as Melanchthon on this issue. See *Loci communes theologici* in *Library of Christian Classics,* ed. Wilhelm Pauck (Philadelphia: Westminster, 1969), 19: 130–32.

/110/   *CO* 47: 13–14 (Jn. 1:14); but see *OS* 5: 387–89 *(Inst.* 4.17.30).

/111/   *CO* 7: 124 *(Briefve instruction); CO* 49: 514 (I Cor. 13:12); *OS* 3: 186 *(Inst.* 1.15.2); *CO* 55: 265–66 (I Pet. 3:19). Flesh can also mean for Calvin not the sinful life but the temporal life. *CO* 48: 44 (Acts 2:26); *CO* 49:

557 (I Cor. 15:43); *CO* 55: 54 (Heb. 4:15); *CO* 49: 398 (I Cor. 6:15); *CO* 49: 399 (I Cor. 6:17); *OS* 3: 458 (*Inst.* 2.13.4).

/112/   McNeill, 2: 987, *Inst.* 3.25.1 in *OS* 4: 432, "So long as we are confined to the prison house of the flesh; we are away from the Lord." McNeill 2: 1012, *Inst.* 4.1.1. in *OS* 5: 1, "Shut up as we are in the prison house of our flesh, we have not yet attained angelic rank. God, therefore, in his wonderful providence accomodating himself to our capacity, has prescribed a way for us, though still far off, to draw near to him." *CO* 34: 178 (s. 75 on Job 22), "For what is our principal lodging? This body here. If a man could have grand palaces, the most sumptuous in the world, it is certain that he would not stay in prison always. Thus, the proper lodging of each is his body and we see what fragility there is there. What solidity [*fermeté*] is there in it? There is nothing but corruption and rottenness. What must we do then? We must tend towards that celestial building, that is, we should ask to be restored that the word of God will dwell in us and that we will be in his temples and that what in us now is corruptible and transient will be renovated and that we will be in this restoration what has been promised to us. . . . Since flesh and blood cannot inherit the kingdom of God, what is corruptible in our nature must die so that we may be thoroughly renewed and restored to a state of perfection. That is why our body is called a prison in which we are held captive."

/113/   *CO* 49: 145 (Rom. 8:10).

/114/   See Torrance, *Calvin's Doctrine of Man*, pp. 26–28.

/115/   McNeill 1: 482, *Inst.* 2.14.1 in *OS* 3: 458–59. Also *CO* 48: 51–52 (Acts 2:38); *CO* 48: 26 (Acts 2:2).

/116/   To assume that Calvin was constrained to take this position in order to remain a "biblical theologian" is an anachronism.

/117/   McNeill 2: 1001, *Inst.* 3.25.8 in *OS* 4: 448.

/118/   *CO* 49: 537 (I Cor. 15:1)

/119/   *CO* 35: 127 (s. 128 on Job 34).

/120/   *CO* 51: 160 (Eph. 2:1); *CO* 49:145 (Rom. 8:10ff.)

/121/   *CO* 49: 543 (I Cor. 15:18–19); *CO* 52: 164 (I Thess. 4:13); *CO* 49:545 (I Cor. 15: 21–22).

/122/   By restoration Calvin does not mean a return to the state of existence in the garden of Eden but a raising of the believer to an even better state of existence than that enjoyed by Adam and Eve, that future life promised to Adam and Eve from the beginning. *OS* 4: 448 (*Inst.* 3.25.8); *CO* 33: 216 (s. 17 on Job 5); *CO* 49: 535 (I Cor. 15:35); *CO* 49: 557 (I Cor. 15:44).

/123/   *CO* 47: 59 (Jn. 3:7).

/124/   McNeill 1: 687, *Inst.* 3.6.3 in *OS* 4: 149.

/125/   *CO* 49: 547–48 (I Cor. 15:26). Torrance presents a similar interpretation of Calvin in *Kingdom and Church*, pp. 141–42.

/126/   Two other places where he joins immortality and resurrection are: *CO* 48: 508 (Acts 23:8); *CO* 45: 604 (Harm. of Gospels, Mt. 22:23).

/127/   McNeill 2: 990, *Inst.* 3.25.3. in *OS* 4:435.

/128/   *OS* 4: 446 (*Inst.* 3.25.7); *OS 4: 440* (*Inst.* 3.25.7); *OS* 4: 434 (*Inst.* 3.25.3), where he says that if there were no resurrection our condition would be more pitiable than that of all other mortals.

/129/   *CO* 49: 561 (I Cor. 15:51); *OS* 3: 419 (*Inst.* 2.10.19).

/130/   *OS* 4: 172 (*Inst.* 3.9.2); *CO* 52: 164 (I Thess. 4:13); *OS* 4: 434
(*Inst.* 3.25.1); *OS* 4: 454 (*Inst.* 3.25.10); *CO* 33: 689ff. (s. 55 on Job 14).
    /131/   *CO* 49: 536 (I Cor. 15:1).
    /132/   He argues this against the Libertines in *CO* 49: 537 (I Cor.
15:1); against the Manichees in *OS* 4: 444–45 (*Inst.* 3.25.7).
    /133/   See pp. 157ff. of this chapter.
    /134/   Oscar Cullman, *Immortality of the Soul or Resurrection of the
Dead* (London: Epworth Press, 1958), pp. 15–16.
    /135/   *OS* 4: 435 (*Inst.* 3.25.3); *CO* 50: 63 (II Cor. 5:6); *CO* 49: 536 (I
Cor. 15:1); *CO* 50: 60–61 (II Cor. 5:1). Not even Plato, who "recognized
man's highest good as union with God" knew of the resurrection, *OS* 4: 433
(Inst. 3.25.2). And even the Jews, who knew of the future, heavenly life,
were not aware of the resurrection, *CO* 48:41 (Acts 2:25).
    /136/   Calvin does not say this with total consistency, however, for in
the *Institutes* 3.25.5 (*OS* 4: 439) he remarks that the funeral rites of the
pagans show that they have some witness of the resurrection. This is the
only place I have found in which Calvin says this.
    /137/   Quistorp, *Last Things*, p. 133.
    /138/   Ibid., p. 193. (Emphasis mine.)
    /139/   Schulze, *Meditatio futurae vitae*, p. 86. See also Partee's discus-
sion of Calvin's view of immortality and resurrection *Calvin and Classical
Philosophy*, pp. 62ff. Partee simply repeats Schulze's view that the difference between Calvin and Plato is that Calvin teaches the resurrection,
ibid., p. 64. On the whole, his discussion does not go beyond that of Schulze
and his conclusions remain, at best, suggestions, as for example the following statement: "One can argue more plausibly that the discussion of the
immortality of the soul and the resurrection of the body in Calvin can no
more be separated than the discussions of God the Creator and God the
Redeemer," ibid., p. 65.
    /140/   Walter Zimmerli, Introduction to the 1932 edition of *Psycho-
pannychia* in *Tracts and Treatises*, 2: 6. Reference taken from Partee,
Calvin and Classical Philosophy, p. 65, n. 80.
    /141/Étienne Gilson, *Reason and Revelation in the Middle Ages* (New
York: Charles Scribner's Sons, 1938), p. 174. There is a great deal of
similarity in Zimmerli's "*ein fremdkörpor*" and Gilson's "alient element."
    /142/   Ibid., p. 188.
    /143/   Ibid.

CONCLUSION

> [I]t is not very sound theology to confine a
> man's thoughts so much to himself, and not
> to set before him, as the prime motive of his
> existence, zeal to illustrate the glory of God.
> For we are born first of all for God, and not
> for ourselves.
>
> *Reply to Sadoleto*

Calvin's Anthropology?

Even to mention "Calvin and anthropology" in one breath
requires some justification, for Calvin's own statements and those of
many of his interpreters suggest that the very phrase "Calvin's
anthropology" may be an oxymoron. As this quotation from the
Reply to Sadoleto indicates, and decades of scholarship have concluded, John Calvin, like his Protestant predecessor Martin Luther,
is a theocentric Christian theologian *par excellence*. Thus, he is to be
either praised or blamed primarily on the basis of his rigorous and
distinctive contribution to the doctrine of God (theology proper or
strict theology). Whatever thoughts he may have had on the doctrine
of humankind serve only the purpose of developing the central and
dominant doctrine of the glory, majesty, or sovereignty of God. This
bias in the interpretation of Calvin's theology is shared by church
historians, Renaissance historians, historical theologians, and systematic theologians alike.

This theocentric interpretation of Calvin's theology, with its
correlative neglect of Calvin's anthropology, must be challenged.
Calvin never intended theology and anthropology to be mutually
exclusive. Just as for Augustine God and the soul belong together, so
for Calvin the knowledge of God and the knowledge of humankind
belong together, as the famous first sentence of the *Institutes* declares: "Nearly all the wisdom we possess, that is to say, true and
sound wisdom, consists of two parts: the knowledge of God and of

ourselves."[1] Anthropology as well as strict theology is an essential part of the heavenly philosophy. These two parts, however, are not equal in value. Though in the sentence immediately following the opening of the *Institutes* Calvin acknowledges that while these two parts "are joined by many bonds, which one precedes and brings forth the other is not easy to discern,"[2] the remainder of that chapter is an argument for the precedence of the knowledge of God. As he remarks in his conclusion to the chapter, "however the knowledge of God and of ourselves may be mutually connected, the order of right teaching *(ordo recte docendi)* requires that we discuss the former first, then proceed afterward to treat the latter."[3] Though "the knowledge of ourselves not only arouses us to seek God, but also, as it were, leads us by the hand to find him,"[4]

> it is certain man never achieves a *clear* knowledge of himself unless he has *first* looked upon God's face, and then descends from contemplating him to scrutinize himself. For we always seem to ourselves righteous and upright and wise and holy— this pride is innate in all us—unless by clear proofs we stand convinced of our own unrighteousness, foulness, folly, and impurity.[5]

Knowledge of God and knowledge of ourselves, both essential to the heavenly wisdom, must be rightly ordered or they will lead the person astray. And the right order requires that knowledge of God take logical and ontological precedence over knowledge of ourselves. As he explains in the *Reply to Sadoleto*, zeal for God does not preclude zeal for humankind; rather, it places it in proper perspective.

> But since He taught that this zeal ought to exceed all thought and care for our own good and advantage, and since natural equity also teaches that God does not receive what is His own unless he is preferred to all things, it certainly is the part of a Christian man to ascend higher than merely to seek and secure the salvation of his own soul.[6]

Examination of ourselves does lead to contemplation of God, in whom we live and move, but without the proper knowledge of God there is no true knowledge of ourselves.

Calvin's concern to order rightly the knowledge of God and the knowledge of ourselves reveals his commitment to their mutual connection in theology. It points to what the five chapters of this study have demonstrated in detail: that the knowledge of humankind is an essential and ever-present element of Calvin's theology. The phrase "Calvin's anthropology," therefore, far from an oxymoron, is a most adequate description of Calvin's theology. Further, the adjective "theocentric" is not the best choice to describe accurately the distinctive character of Calvin's theology. Rather than a circle with a center of *theos*, Calvin's theology is an ellipse with two foci, *theos* and *anthropos*. One could accurately refer to Calvin's theology as "theocentric" only if that term were taken to underscore the ontological and epistemological *priority* of God and the knowledge of God as described above. However, since this term usually connotes either an exclusive focus on the doctrine of God or an interpretation of the doctrine of humankind as synonomous with the doctrine of sin, it is perhaps wiser to use another term to describe the distinctive character of Calvin's thought. Since Calvin is neither an anthropocentric nor a theocentric theologian, and since a fundamental distinction between the perspective of humankind and the perspective of God pervades his doctrine of humankind, it is perhaps more accurate to describe his anthropology as "perspectival."[7]

The Dynamic Perspectival Structure of Calvin's Anthropology

Once we begin to speak of Calvin's anthropology, however, the question immediately arises of how we are to interpret it. In the past decades conflicting interpretations have been offered. By far the most common is that which presents his doctrine of humankind as a brief prelude to or synonomous with his doctrine of sin. Tillich's comment in his survey *History of Christian Thought* exemplifies this.

> The doctrine of God is always the most decisive thing in every theology. For Calvin the central doctrine of Christianity is the doctrine of the majesty of God. Calvin states more clearly than any of the other reformers that God is known in an existential attitude. *For him human misery and divine majesty are correlated. Only out of human misery can we understand the divine majesty, and only in light of the divine majesty can we understand human misery.*[8]

Dowey's incidental remarks on Calvin's anthropology and Torrance's full-length-study *The Doctrine of Man* exemplify this also.[9] Other surveys and studies have interpreted Calvin's anthropology as more closely related to the doctrine of creation than the doctrine of sin, for example Stauffer's *Création et providence* and Partee's *Calvin and Classical Philosophy.*[10] Still others, noting both the creation and fall emphases on Calvin's anthropology, have concluded that Calvin's doctrine of humankind is ambiguous at best, internally inconsistent at worst. Paul Pruyser, for example, speaks of Calvin's "anthropological realism, a viewpoint which accepts some basic functional polarities in man and conceptualizes them as a network of lines of conflict."[11]

It is the conclusion of this study that the distinctive character of Calvin's anthropology is less adequately understood when it is interpreted *primarily* in terms of the doctrine of sin (the thesis of pessimism), the doctrine of creation (the thesis of optimism), or a combination of these two (the thesis of contradiction); it is more adequately understood when it is interpreted in terms of the distinction between the human and divine perspectives and its variations in the doctrines of creation and redemption (the thesis of perspectivalism). As Calvin remarks offhandedly in *Concerning Scandals,* "[n]o matter what subject is under consideration, making certain distinctions usually sheds a great deal of light on it."[12] This is certainly true of Calvin's theology when the subject is humankind. No matter which particular aspect of anthropology Calvin is considering, the dignity of humankind, the *imago dei,* reason, the will and human freedom, or the relation of the soul to the body, a fundamental distinction is present. From the perspective of God as creator, all lines and details of the portrait of humankind appear in absolute contrast to each other, black against white. From the perspectives of God as judge and redeemer, all details of the portrait appear in absolute contradiction to one another, again, black against white. But from the perspective of humankind, all lines and details of the portrait appear in relative comparison to one another, as varying shades of grey. When the subject of humankind is viewed thus, in light of a fundamental distinction between the perspectives of God and humankind in its two major variations in the realm of creation-eschatology and the realm of soteriology, a complex portrait of the self emerges. From the perspective of God as creator, humankind appears with all temporal creatures as a black botch of nothingness standing in stark contrast to the blinding light of the eternal creator.

From the perspective of humankind, on the other hand, humankind appears as the spot most brilliantly reflecting the light of the eternal creator in the entire temporal creation. Contrasted with God it is a black hole in space; compared with the rest of creation, it is a single star shining brighter than all the galaxies and angels put together. But the portrait is not yet complete. From the perspective of God as judge, Calvin paints humankind as a solid black mass of iniquity in contradiction to the purity of God. From the perspective of God as redeemer, he paints humankind (those who are the elect) in the pure and shining image of Jesus Christ. And, from the perspective of humankind, this time in its soteriological variation, Calvin paints humankind in comparison with the rest of creation as a mottled grey work of art, which, though dulled by sin, still reflects some of the creator's glory in its reason and will, soul and body. Standing over against God it appears as one huge ignorant and guilty person; standing within the creation it appears as the creature with the inviolable gifts of understanding and will.

The juxtaposition of these divergent views of the self results in a complex sixteenth century portrait of humankind. Calvin does not paint a harmonious portrait of the self from one eternal perspective. Rather, painting more like El Greco than Botticelli, he fills the canvas with a multitude of scenes drawn from various perspectives. Here we see humankind as a snail crawling before the eternal creator; there humankind as the masterpiece of creation; here we see a worm before the eternal judge; there the perfect human being Jesus Christ; here we see Cato; there Diocletian. There is no one focal point on the canvas. The eye is constantly drawn from one image to another in an almost dizzying way.

Though the portrait contains conflicting perspectives, it is, nevertheless, a unified whole. Its unity, however, is not that of logical consistency. Rather, its unity is that of a complex ordering of parts, one that joins contradictory yet complementary perspectives in order to describe accurately a complex reality. Viewing Calvin's portrait of humankind, one is left with the impression that the human being is an essentially mysterious creature that must be described from conflicting viewpoints. Just as the phenomenon of light requires both the wave and particle theory to be described accurately, so human existence requires both the perspective of God and the perspective of humankind to be described accurately.

It is the fundamental distinction between the perspective of God and the perspective of humankind, then, that unifies Calvin's dizzying combination of diverse perspectives in his rich portrait of humankind. It has been the primary aim of this study to uncover the fundamental distinction between the perspective of God and the perspective of humankind in its two major variations in the doctrines of creation and redemption that pervades Calvin's anthropology; and, to argue for the greater adequacy of the thesis of perspectivalism for interpreting his anthropology as a whole and his view of the specific anthropological issues of the *imago dei*, reason, the will, and the soul and body. If this dynamic perspectival structure is not taken into consideration, the distinctive complexity of his portrait of humankind will be missed. Focusing on his statements made from the perspective of God, some interpreters will highlight the misery of humankind in sin and its glory in Jesus Christ. Others, focusing rather on Calvin's statements made from the perspective of humankind, will highlight the dignity of human beings in his anthropology. Still others, noting both kinds of statements in Calvin, will conclude that he is internally inconsistent or only practicing expert exegesis. As the analyses in chapters 2–5 have shown, each of these interpretatons, though partially correct, fails to uncover the complex depth, order, and unity of Calvin's distinctive, dynamic perspectival anthropology.

Notes

/1/   McNeill 1: 35, *Inst.* 1.1.1 in *OS* 3: 31.
/2/   Ibid.
/3/   McNeill 1: 39, *Inst.* 1.1.3 in *OS* 3: 33–34.
/4/   McNeill 1: 37, *Inst.* 1.1.1 in *OS* 3: 32.
/5/   McNeill 1: 37, *Inst.* 1.1.2 in *OS* 3: 32. (Emphasis mine.)
/6/   *Reply to Sadeloto*, p. 58 (*OS* 1: 463).
/7/   It is my belief that this thesis concerning the distinction of the human and divine perspectives in its variations has implications for the adequate interpretation of other doctrines in Calvin's theology (such as justification and sanctification, grace and works). It has been the aim of this study, however, to argue *only* that this distinction enables us to interpret Calvin's anthropology more accurately.
/8/   Tillich, *History of Christian Thought*, p. 263. (Emphasis mine.)
/9/   See the discussion of both these texts in chapter 2, pp. 50–61.
/10/   See the discussion of these texts in chapter 2, p. 67 n. 51 and chapter 3, pp. 100ff.
/11/   Pruyser, "Calvin's View of Man," p. 56. Even Pruyser concludes, however, that "the purest self is the theocentric self, subordinate to God's sovereignty, with the distinct coloring of self-abasement yet without low self-esteem," ibid., pp. 53–54.
/12/   *Scandals*, p. 12 (*OS* 2: 168).

APPENDIX I

HOMO IMAGO DEI, HOMO MICROCOSMOS, AND HOMO MIRACULUM

The long analysis of the various controversies over Calvin's understanding of the *imago dei* in chapter 2 demonstrates the importance this particular traditional model of humankind had for Calvin in the formation of his own anthropological configuration. It is this model and no other that serves as the sun around which the other models revolve. A brief look at his use of the *homo micro-cosmos* and *homo miraculum* models will confirm this.

Calvin is no stranger to the traditional *homo microcosmos* model of humankind. Surprisingly enough, he uses this ancient model with some frequency. In the thirty-ninth sermon on Job, his most sustained statement on anthropology outside of the *Institutes*, he uses it to interpret humankind's special place and role in the universe.

> God, in a manner of speaking, looks at himself and con-templates himself in men; it is not without reason that he regards all that he has made and finds it good. It is the case that man is the principal and most excellent work there is among all creatures, for God wanted to display in him that which he placed in only small portions in the heavens, the earth, and in all animals. He did this in such a way that man is said to be a *little world*, since it is there that we see so many admirable things that we are bound to be astonished. Since this is so, we should always be persuaded that God contemplates his work in us, that he will be moved and inclined to be good to us and maintain us. [1]

It may appear that Calvin is using this model here in a straightfor-ward, traditional way to indicate that humankind reflects all aspects of the cosmos. But Calvin has another meaning in mind when he employs this model in his sermon. For him it does not connote a reflection of the entire cosmos in the traditional, ancient sense. Rather, the model of the microcosm refers to a miniature theatre in which all sorts of miracles *of God* are displayed in a most vivid way. If the world itself is a theatre of *God's* glory, a common theme in Calvin's theology, then humankind as little world is a smaller theatre, but one with a larger and better repertoire.[2]

Calvin, both here and elsewhere, uses the *imago dei* model to interpret the microcosm model. Thus, for Calvin to say that humankind is a microcosm means that the human being is a preeminent specimen of *God's* wisdom, power, and justice.[3] It is not a microcosm because as a rational soul it has the potential to imitate God's wisdom, power, and justice by actually knowing all things or becoming all things. Rather, it is a microcosm because, as the specially chosen image of God, humankind as a whole is the showplace and recipient of God's wonders and gracious benefits.

That this is what Calvin has in mind when he uses the term "microcosm" or the model becomes more evident when his combination of the microcosm and Asclepian *homo miraculum* model is considered. He describes humankind as "a rare example of God's power, goodness, and wisdom," containing "within him enough miracles to occupy our minds, if only we are not irked at paying attention to them."[4] He is using the microcosm and *miraculum* models to point to the power of God and the beauty of God's gifts to human beings rather than the potential of human beings. This focus on the power and gratuity of God rather than on human potential is an astounding inversion of the *homo miraculum* model. He identifies the *miraculum* not as humankind, but as the condescension of the glorious creator to the creature: "Whoever is not astonished and deeply affected at this miracle [*hoc miraculum*] is more than ungrateful and stupid." In this inversion of the Asclepian model so popular in the Renaissance, Calvin underlines the initiative and glory of God and the lack of merit on the part of human beings. When he uses the models of *homo microcosmos* and *homo miraculum*, then, Calvin refers either to humankind's reflection on the glory and grace of the benevolent Father God or to the limitations of the creature in relation to the creator and his miracles.

The conclusion I draw from this analysis of Calvin's use of *homo microcosmos* and *homo miraculum* is this: Calvin's controlling model in his new anthropological model is that of the *imago dei*. He certainly uses the other two traditional models.[6] And he also uses ontological language in his anthropology. For example, he occasionally speaks of the "degrees" or "levels (*rengs*) of being.[7] Calvin's use of these other anthropological models and the ontological language, however, is controlled by his own understanding of the *imago dei:* it is the sun around which these other planets revolve.

Notes

/1/   *CO* 33: 481 (s. 39 on Job 19). See also *CO* 32: 278 (Ps. 119: 139); *CO* 23: 25 (Gen. 1:26).

/2/   *CO* 48: 414 (Acts 17:26); *CO* 23: 11–12 (Arg. to Gen.). For Calvin's more common view of the entire world as the theatre of God, see *CO* 23: 32 (Gen. 2:2).

/3/   See *CO* 23: 25 (Gen. 1:26): "Multa quidem sunt in hac corrupta natura quae possint contemptum inducere: verum si omnia rite expendas, est homo eximium quoddam inter alias creaturas divinae sapientiae, iustitiae, et bonitatis specimen: ut merito a veteribus dictus sit [*microcosmos*]." And in *CO* 33: 481 (s. 39 on Job 10) he uses the more common definition of microcosm: "Or est-il ainsi que l'homme est le principal ouvrage et le plus excellent qui soit entre toutes les creatures, Dieu à voula là desployer ce qu'il n'avoit mis qu'en petites portions et au ciel et en la terre, et en tous animaux: tellement que l'homme est appellé comme un petit monde, que là nous voyons tant de choses admirables qu'il faut qu'on soit estonné." Later in this same sermon, however, he points out that this status of humankind as the microcosm or the "ouvrage" of God means that it is "un ouvrage si excellent" that "là . . . on peut voir ta sagesse, ta vertu, ta bonté inestimable pour te glorifier. . . . ." ibid.

/4/   McNeill 1: 54, *Inst.* 1.5.3. in *OS* 3: 46–47. See also *CO* 48: 416 (Acts 17:27), where he says: "Certain of the philosophers called man a microcosm because, above all the other creatures, he is a proof of the glory of God, full of countless miracles as he is."

/5/   *CO* 31: 91 (Ps. 8:4). A moment later he repeats this identification of the miracle with God's providence: "hoc mirum esse quod Deus assidue de hominibus cogitat," ibid., col. 92. See also *CO* 33: 487 (s. 39 on Job 10), where he insists that the true miracle is our very existence as creatures "manufactured" by God. The very fact that humankind is a miraculous creature shows that it is *God's* works which are wonderful and marvelous. See also *CO* 23: 24 (Gen. 1:24). Here and elsewhere Calvin uses metaphors for humankind that connote products or works of art created by manufacturers or artists (cheese, tapestries, coins, weavings, etc.). It seems to me that this underlines his emphasis on God as the great artist and humankind as the masterpiece or marvelous creation of this artist.

/6/   He makes use of other models of the self in addition to the *homo miraculum* and *homo microcosmos* models: "petits rois," *CO* 33: 359 (s. 29 on Job 7). In his commentary on Genesis 1:24 Calvin also adapts the model of the self as the bond of the universe to his view of humankind as the created image of God: "Ergo non minus in hac parte miraculum quam si

Deus creare ex nihilo coepiesset quae indigeat, sed ut melius consociet singulas mundi partes cum ipso universo, *CO* 23: 24.
/7/ E.g., *CO* 51: 620–21 (s. 30 on Eph.). It is when Calvin is using the relative, comparative perspective of humankind that he uses such language to speak of the different degrees of creation. From this perspective humankind appears as "lower" than the angels, *CO* 41: 459 (s. 13 on Dan.); *CO* 33: 725 (s. 58 on Job 15); *CO* 34: 257 (s. 82 on Job 21) but "higher" than the animals, *CO* 33: 359 (s. 29 on Job 7; *CO* 31: 95 (Ps. 8:8). Babelotzsky notes this language of ontological hierarchy, calling it "ein Echo der im Gefolge der grieschen Philosophien enstanden Vorstellung vom Menschen als einem Mikrokosmos sein. . . . ," *Platonische Bilder*, p. 92. He is more correct in this than Dowey, who denies that Calvin accepted any metaphysical views, *Knowledge of God*, pp. 7–8. My thesis is that Calvin does use the ontological language of the hierarchy of being. However, this language is secondary in importance to the language of the *imago dei*. Furthermore, his view of the ontological hierarchy of creation is only part of his view of the place and role of humankind in the universe, that part seen from the relative perspective of humankind. The perspective of God leads to quite a different view of the role and place of humankind in the universe. For example, if from the perspective of humankind it appears that humankind is lower than the angels but higher than the animals, from the perspective of God it appears that humankind is higher than all of creation, including the angels, *CO* 33: 360 (s. 29 on Job 7). As he comments on Hebrews 2:16 (*CO* 55: 33), we are superior to the angels because, as the elected image of God, we are the recipients of the liberality of the heavenly father: "Quod ergo nos angelis praetulit, non factum est excellentiae nostrae, sed miseriae respectu. Quare non est nos esse angelis superiores gloriemur: nisi quia ampliore misericordia, qua indigebamus, nos prosequutus est coelestis pater, ut tantum bonitatem in terras effusam angeli ipsi ex alto suspicerent." For both sides of this view of the *imago dei* model itself, see pp. 38–42 of this work. Because Calvin sees humankind as microcosm and as *imago dei* both in its relations to the entire universe and in its special relationship to God, Torrance is incorrect in concluding that for Calvin "Man *cannot* be understood by his relation to the world. It is not from below man that man can be understood but from above man. Therefore, we must not commence with the elements of the world, but with the Gospel which sets Christ alone before us with His cross and holds us to this one point. That means of course that there can be no naturalistic understanding of man, for that would involve an inversion of the very order of creation, and would run directly counter to the divine purposes of grace upon which the whole of creation depends," *Calvin's Doctrine of Man*, pp. 24–25. (Emphasis mine.) In his chapter entitled "Man's Place in Creation," therefore, Torrance says very little about the nobility of humankind in relation to the animals and the earth and almost nothing about humankind's relationship to the universe. This is a misleading, one-sided presentation of Calvin's anthropology at this point, since Calvin speaks *both* of humankind's relation to the other levels of creation from the perspective of humankind *and* humankind's special relationship to the creator and Christ from the perspective of God. (I have tried to show this in the discussion of the controversies on pp. 38–42 of chapter 2.)

APPENDIX II

CALVIN ON HUMANISM (*STUDIA HUMANITATIS*)

Calvin often contrasts "heavenly science" with the "human sciences" and heavenly wisdom with all "letters."[1] All human arts and sciences are so much smoke and empty speculation in his view, and therefore to be avoided by Christians. In the same way he contrasts Christian theologians and all humanists (*gens de lettres*), whether they be "papists," Platonists, or simply "grammaticasters." One need not look far in Calvin's works to find contemptous remarks of such "learned" men. In his *Excuse à Messieurs les Nicodémites*, for instance, he takes the "Platonists" to task for being such humanists that they "almost turn Christianity into philosophy."[2] This particular group of scholars is dangerous, he claims, because they "imagine Platonic ideas in their heads, concerning the way to serve God, and thus excuse the majority of foolish Papist superstitions."[3] Having made the connection between foolish humanist scholars and the approval of "papist" superstitions, he moves quickly to this surprising conclusion:

> [I] would prefer that all human sciences be exterminated from the earth to their serving as the cause of cooling the ardor of Christians and turning them from God. But there are many scholarly people who have fallen asleep in this speculation; that it is enough to know God and understand the right path of salvation, and then to determine in their own offices how things should be.[4]

This and other such rejections of all the new arts and sciences of his day, and their practitioners, if taken out of context, present Calvin as an enemy of humanism (*studia humanitatis*). However, once again Calvin evades the charge by employing his shifting perspectives.

Calvin does indeed condemn all human arts and sciences and all *gens de lettres* without remainder. But, his condemnation is

made from the perspective of God as redeemer and it is not the only
judgment he makes. His condemnation is a condemnation not of the
liberal arts and sciences in themselves, but of the improper use of
them by certain *gens de lettres.*

> For whatever knowledge and understanding a man has *counts
> for nothing unless* it rests upon true wisdom; and it is of no
> more virtue for grasping spiritual teaching than the eye of a
> blind man for distinguishing colors. Both of these must be
> carefully attended to: (1) that knowledge of all the sciences is so
> much smoke *apart from the heavenly science of Christ;* and (2)
> that man with all his shrewdness is as stupid about understand-
> ing the mysteries of God by himself as an ass is incapable of
> understanding musical harmony.[5]

And again

> And yet this science that all men desire is nothing but pure
> vanity for there is nothing solid about it. Saint Paul says that
> one may take for knowledge what men wish to be their doc-
> trines, because it serves their purposes. But people say, "There
> is a wise man," or "There is a well-educated *[bien lettré]* man,"
> when a man simply knows how to inflate himself and strut
> about like a peacock. Such men may have a reputation, but in
> spite of that all this science is nothing but insane babbling *if it
> is not founded on Holy Scripture.* Because the perfection of our
> wisdom is to be taught by God and to live within our limits;
> when we follow that which God is pleased to show us, that is
> enough for us.[6]

Though a person has the reputation of *"grande science,"* this is no
guarantee that she or he will follow the simple truth of God. In fact,
those who cling only to earthly science and despise the heavenly
science are far from the gospel and to be avoided.[7] From the
perspective of God as redeemer, all human arts and sciences are
empty adornments of the self. All people of learning are nothing
before the redeemer. It is the simple and humble, those who have
learned to be always "little schoolchildren" before God, who are
truly educated for life.[8] Calvin's contempt for letters and people of
letters and his contradiction between earthly science and the heavenly science are to be understood from within the perspective of
God as redeemer, therefore.

But this is not the only qualification which must be made if we
are to understand fully Calvin's view of the humanist arts and

sciences. To this negative assessment from the perspective of God as redeemer, he adds a positive assessment from the perspective of humankind. From this perspective Calvin does not contrast the heavenly and human sciences, but distinguishes them as lower and higher types of wisdom which flow from one source.[9] And, instead of the absolute distinction and contradiction between the two, it is the unity of the two which comes to the foreground. Calvin's approval of the humanist arts and sciences as part of the infinite wisdom of God can be seen in his reference to the heavenly philosophy or wisdom as the "heavenly science."[10] His use of the same term to refer to heavenly wisdom and the flourishing humanist arts and sciences underlines his view of the unity of the two in God. Seen from this relative perspective, astronomy, medicine, sculpture, painting, and civil government all appear as gifts of God to all people, believers and unbelievers alike.[21] These lower sciences and arts are given to enhance the present life together on earth. As such, they must be acknowledged and used, by Christians as well as others. It is only when they are confused with the heavenly science, and therefore not used for their intended purpose, that they are to be condemned.[12]

Therefore, if understood and used properly (i.e., directed toward the service of God and the heavenly wisdom), all legitimate arts and sciences are acceptable and even a requirement for life on earth. Thus, just as Calvin is able to interpret Christian simplicity to include a knowledge and use of rhetoric, so he is able to interpret Christian foolishness to include a knowledge and use of the humanist arts and sciences.

> By "being fools" we do not mean being stupid; nor do we direct those who are learned in the liberal sciences to jettison their knowledge and those who are gifted with quickness of mind to become dull, as if a man cannot be a Christian unless he is more like a beast than a man. The profession of Christianity requires us to be immature, not in our thinking, but in malice.[13]

Knowledge of the liberal arts and sciences, then, is not incompatible with the foolishness of the gospel, provided it is rightly used and acknowledged. In fact, Calvin stresses the positive nature of these arts and sciences so much that at one point he argues that even to deny the positive value of these external aids for the common life on earth is to deny God's providential plan for the salvation of particular

persons. God can make use of all proper ways to lead men and
women to knowledge of Christ, even knowledge of the liberal arts
and sciences. It is only "fantastics," therefore, persons totally devoid
of reason, who want to abolish "all letters and knowledge" and who,
"under the shadow of the simplicity of the gospel" would "prefer
there to be no science at all in the world."[14] God calls and redeems
the educated and the uneducated; the discrimination of the Anabaptists against the lettered is just as bad as the humanists' and philosophers' discrimination against the unlettered, therefore.[15] Christians should recognize God's grace in the intelligence of all educated
persons and in the burgeoning of the liberal arts and sciences.[16] And
in their gratitude, they should make use of these gifts in their
callings, always in the service of one God and always with humble
recognition that these gifts are of no value for salvation.

Calvin heeded his own advice to Christians and gave due
recognition to humanist scholars and to the liberal arts and sciences.
In the same treatise in which he condemned the "Platonists" and all
gens de lettres, he duly notes that not all *gens de lettres* are guilty of
the excesses and abuses he has described.[17] And in the *Commentary on Acts* he distinguishes between two types of humanists, those
who are curious and don't respect the word of God, treating it like a
profane novelty, and those who reject the word of God.[18] The
former, in his opinion, are not hopeless. And Calvin admits, though
he does not use this term, that there is such a thing as a Christian
humanist. His definition of the "Christian humanist" serves as a tidy
summary of his assessment of the liberal arts and sciences from the
perspective of humankind:

> . . . [P]hilosophers or dialecticians who do not convert Chris-
> tianity into philosophy or abuse the sciences which God re-
> vealed to the world in order that they may serve as aids and
> instruments of the truth, and who do not think that the truth of
> God, which the scriptures call invincible, is so weak that they
> can in the end supress it with beautiful appearances of reason
> or subtle subterfuges.[19]

Calvin himself fits this description.

Because of Calvin's varied assessments of humanist scholars
and of the liberal arts and sciences, those scholars who describe
Calvin's attitude toward humanism as one of blanket rejection are
inaccurate. He rejects those humanists who abuse their learning by
using it to reject or distort the gospel. And he rejects all arts and

sciences, when they lead away from God.[20] But it is clear in the *Excuse* that he is condemning the abuse and not the thing itself. This is also true in two other works, *Concerning Scandals* and the *Reply to Sadoleto*. As I noted earlier, the latter treatise is the work of one Christian humanist in response to another. Calvin does not fault Sadoleto for being a humanist, a man of great learning. On the contrary, he praises him as a man whose "excellent learning and distinguished eloquence [have] deservedly provided [him] a place among the few whom all who would be thought studious of liberal arts look up to and revere."[21] There is no reason to believe that Calvin is practicing his sarcasm on Sadoleto here, for he agrees with his opponent that Christian humanism is a legitimate vocation. He does not attack Sadoleto's humanism per se, but rather his abuse of his learning in the service of false truths. Calvin accuses Sadoleto of being unworthy of the name "humanist" precisely because he has fooled simple people with the arts he has learned; this is action "unsuitable to the character of one who has been polished by all kinds of liberal learning."[22] He also charges him with adding philosophy to Christianity, which for Calvin is the mark of a "Platonist." Sadoleto has used the knowledge of philosophy he has to add to the gospel's simplicity and confuse less learned folk. In other words, he has not kept the scriptures as his Lydian stone, but has mixed it with philosophy in an undiscriminating way.[23] Sadoleto is to be spurned not because he is a humanist, but because he did not apply the cardinal rule of Christian theology: to keep the heavenly science above all human sciences and use the latter as handmaidens only. Because he has mixed the heavenly and the earthly in this way, he has created an "indolent theology," a common result among those "who have never had experience in serious struggles of conscience."[24] Thus, Sadoleto's brand of Christian humanism is as distorted and misleading as pagan philosophy and Anabaptist fantasies. If he had properly distinguished between the heavenly and the earthly sciences and directed his learning to the truth of God, he would have been a proper Christian humanist.

Calvin's evaluation of humanism *(studia humanitatis)* is as varied as his judgment of individual humanists. From the perspective of God as redeemer, all such studies are found wanting. However, from the perspective of humankind, many of these studies, especially rhetoric, astronomy, medicine, and political science, appear as gifts which it is blasphemous and even idolatrous to reject.[25] The answer to the question, "Was Calvin a Humanist?," is not simple, then, even if we restrict the meaning of humanism to *studia humanitatis*. Within the broad coherence of the dynamic perspectival structure based on the distinction between human and divine perspectives, Calvin both champions and undercuts the liberal learning of his day.

Notes

/1/ *CO* 9: 809–10; *CO* 35: 125 (s. 128 on Job 34); *CO* 51; 599; *CO* 32: 634 (Ps. 119).
/2/ *CO* 6: 600 *(Excuse à Messieurs les Nicodémites)*.
/3/ Ibid.
/4/ Ibid.
/5/ *CO* 49: 324–25 (I Cor. 1:20). (Emphasis mine.)
/6/ CO 53: 649 (s. 54 on I Tim. 6:20–21). (Emphasis mine). See also *CO* 49: 429 (I Cor. 8:1).
/7/ *CO* 49: 324, 326 (I Cor. 1:20)
/8/ *CO* 33: 201–2 (s. 16 on Job 4).
/9/ *CO:* 32: 633, 634 (s. 13 on Ps. 119).
/10/ *CO* 9: 808.
/11/ *CO* 3: 634 (s. 13 on Ps. 119); *OS* 3: 257 *(Inst.* 2.2.14); *OS* 3: 101 *(Inst.* 1.11.12); *CO* 23: 100 (Gen. 4:20).
/12/ *CO* 31: 633–35 (s. 13 on Ps. 119).
/13/ *Scandals*, p. 18 *(OS* 2: 172). See also *CO* 32: 322 (Ps. 127:1).
/14/ *CO* 46: 326 (s. 27 on Harmony of the Gospels).
/15/ Ibid. See also *OS* 4: 70 *(Inst.* 3.3.14).
/16/ *OS* 3: 258 (Inst. 2.2.15); *CO* 36: 483 (Is. 28:26).
/17/ *CO* 6: 600 *(Excuse à Messieurs les Nicodémites)*.
/18/ *CO* 48: 406 (Acts 17:18); see also *CO* 6: 600.
/19/ *CO* 6: 601 *(Excuse à Messieurs les Nicodémites)*.
/20/ Carlos M. N. Eire is essentially correct in his interpretation of Calvin's attitude toward the Nicodemites, arguing that Nicodemism was a much more complex phenomenon than is usually assumed by scholars, "Calvin and Nicodemism: A Reappraisal," *Sixteenth Century Journal* 10 (1979): 45–69, p. 69. The implication is that Calvin's response was much more complex, also. This study has tried to show the structures in Calvin's own thought which enabled him to respond with complexity and consistency to such "amorphous" and internally diverse groups.
/21/ *Reply to Sadoleto*, pp. 49ff. *(OS* 1: 457ff).
/22/ *Reply to Sadoleto*, pp. 49ff. *(OS* 1: 460).
/23/ *OS* 1: 465–66 *(Reply to Sadoleto*, p. 53).
/24/ *Reply to Sadoleto*, p. 78 *(OS* 1: 477).
/25/ For his references to medicine and political science see *CO* 7: 245, 246 *(Des Libertins)*; *CO* 33: 608 (s. 49 on Job 13). Calvin's references to rhetoric (in the context of the Renaissance debate on truth and eloquence) and his references to astronomy (in the context of the Renaissance debate on

astrology, magic, and science) are so numerous and intriguing that they deserve separate studies of their own.

/26/ For a helpful discussion of Calvin's debt to humanism in his theological method, see E. David Willis, "Rhetoric and Responsibility in Calvin's Theology," in *The Context of Contemporary Theology*, eds. Alexander J. McKelway and E. David Willis (Atlanta: John Knox, 1974), pp. 43–63.

CALVIN'S DOCTRINE OF PROVIDENCE

I have deliberately chosen to describe the set of problems discussed in chapter 4 in terms of the relationship between human freedom and divine providence since the traditional designation of "Grace and Free Will" is too narrow to describe the range of problems considered here. The relationship of human freedom to the grace of universal providence and sanctification is just as much an issue for Calvin as the relationship of human freedom to the grace of election and justification. Since it is usually only the latter two that are discussed under the heading "Grace and Free Will," I have decided not to use this terminology. Also, Calvin himself uses the specific term "providence" as the heading under which each of these different manifestations of grace falls. By providence Calvin refers in general to the gracious activity of God in governing the world. In his treatise *Against the Libertines* he distinguishes three types of this providential governing of the world: universal providence, particular providence, and special providence.[1] By universal providence Calvin understands that universal operation of God in the entire universe by which God governs all creatures according to the properties created in them. By particular providence he understands God's ability to govern by interrupting the laws of nature used in universal providence. And by special providence he understands God's governing of the world as redeemer, by using events to afflict the wicked and comfort the blessed. Neither Calvin nor his interpreters are consistent in their use of labels when referring to the different types of providence. Partee chooses to examine only what Calvin calls universal and particular providence, adopting those labels.[2] Stauffer, in his major work on Calvin's doctrine of providence, *Création et providence*, departs from Calvin's terminology by speaking of general (universal) and special providence. By general providence he refers to the "order of nature" and by special providence the governance of the human race by grace.[3] Verhey adopts Calvin's threefold distinction and uses it consistently.[4]

I have chosen to honor Calvin's distinctions between the types of providence of God but to alter his terminology for the sake of greater clarity. There are two major divisions in God's providential governing of the universe that follow Calvin's distinction between God as creator and God as redeemer. Thus, I speak of creative providence and redemptive providence in Calvin's theology. Each of these two is further distinguished into two parts. God's creative providence governs the whole of the world through the laws of nature and particular events and persons against or without the laws of nature. I speak of these two types of creative providence as universal and particular providence, respectively. God's redemptive providence governs the whole of the human race toward the end of final salvation of the cosmos and those individuals united to Jesus Christ, i.e., the church. I speak of these two types of redemptive providence as general and special.[5] Using these terms, I examine Calvin's view of divine government and human freedom in a number of different areas, including the issue of election and justification and free will and the use of universal providence and sanctification and morality and responsibility. It is because each of these issues falls under the general heading of "providence" that I have titled chapter 4 "Divine Providence and Human Freedom."

It is curious that the doctrine of providence has for so long held second place in the interest of Calvin scholars to the doctrine of predestination. The recent works of Partee (*Calvin and Classical Philosophy*) and Stauffer (*Création et providence*) may signal a growing interest in providence. This can only be welcomed as a more accurate understanding of Calvin's theology. Calvin's concern with providence pervades his commentaries and sermons as well as the *Institutes*. This fact has been hidden by scholars who turn only to 1.16–18 of the *Institutes* when discussing his doctrine of providence in the *Institutes*, for example. While Calvin does explicitly develop his doctrine here, he also develops it in 2.4–5 (on sin), 3.8–11 (on the Christian life), and 4.20 (on civil government). That these discussions also fall under the general rubric of divine government and human freedom is shown in chapter 4.

Notes

/1/   CO 7: 186–98 (*Des Libertins*, ch. 14); see also CO 8: 347–49 (*De praedestinatione*, ch. 10); CO 36: 215 (Is. 10:2).
/2/   Partee, *Calvin and Classical Philosophy*, pp. 46, 95–96.

/3/ Stauffer, *Création et providence*, pp. 268ff. This could be because Stauffer examines only the sermons and not Calvin's treatises and the *Institutes*, where he is more systematic in his presentation and terminology.

/4/ Verhey, "Against the Libertines," pp. 190–205.

/5/ My use of these two adjectives is limited to this context. It is common in Calvin literature to find them used also for general and special revelation and common and special grace. There is no exact parallel here, however, between what I am calling general providence and common grace or general providence and general revelation. Common grace and general revelation are the parallels of what I have called universal and particular creative providence, and general redemptive providence. Special grace and special revelation are the parallels of what I call redemptive providence, in its specific form alone.

CALVIN'S DOCTRINES OF PROVIDENCE AND ELECTION

The Relationship between Special Redemptive Providence, General Redemptive Providence, and Creative Providence

Niesel has said that "[t]he church is indeed the real object of the divine providence. In this we clearly recognize the focusing of Calvinistic teaching about creation and providence in the revelation of God in Jesus Christ; for the church is the body of Christ."[1] Though he does distinguish between the church as the real object and the final end of God's providence, Niesel is inaccurate in his emphasis on the doctrine of the church within the doctrine of providence in Calvin. As I tried to suggest briefly in appendix 3, pp. 207–09 above, Calvin is concerned with the entire range of issues that fall under the heading of divine government and human freedom. He is clear that the providence of God has as its object the entire universe and the whole of the human race.[2] He does not say that the church is the real object of divine providence and the rest of the human race or universe only the false or (to use the Barthian adjective) shadow object of God's providence. Nor does he suggest that we focus on God's special redemptive providence to the exclusion of the other forms of providence.[3] His point in calling the care of the faithful the "special" providence of God is an epistemological rather than an ontological one. God's providence, though existing and capable of perception everywhere, is best perceived (and therefore acknowledged) in the mirror of Christ and his body, the church.[4] The faithful, therefore, are more accurately described as the "chief theatre of the divine providence" than as the "real object" of God's providence.[5] And as such, the church has a special mission in the world: to acknowledge, interpret, and confess God as the benevolent provider of the world. For "although God does not foretell the future to us, he wishes us to be eyewitnesses of his acts and to propound their causes wisely."[116] God's special redemptive providence, then, is but a set of spectacles through which to view God's continuous, active, and omnipresent providential care for the world.[7] This should be kept in mind as we examine the relation of human freedom to the various forms of special redemptive providence, election and justification as well as sanctification.

Notes

/1/   Niesel, *Theology of Calvin*, p. 74.

/2/   *CO* 31: 349 (*De praedestinatione*, 10.13).

/3/   This is what Niesel does in *Theology of Calvin*, pp. 61–79.

/4/   *CO* 48: 49 (Acts 2:23); *CO* 31: 330 (Ps. 33); *CO* 29: 241 (s. 1 on Sam. 1); *CO* 45: 289 (Mt. 10:29); *CO* 31: 337 (Ps. 33); *CO* 23: 257 (Gen. 18:18).

/5/   *CO* 8: 349 (*De praedestinatione* 10.13).

/6/   *CO* 23: 258 (Gen. 18:18). In his commentary on Psalm 33, for instance, Calvin does not say that God's providence does not exist outside the church but that it is more hidden there than in the church. All those who look at God's providence in the mirror of the church, then, know that God is not cold and indifferent but an active and caring "pilot of the world," *CO* 31: 337.

/7/   The allusion to Calvin's view of the special revelation of the scriptures as the "spectacles" through which the general revelation in nature can be read in the *Institutes* 1.6.1 (*OS* 3: 60) is deliberate since there are parallels between his view of creative and redemptive providence and general and special revelation. See p. 209, n. 5.

CALVIN'S *PSYCHOPANNYCHIA*

We argued in chapter 5 that while Calvin's anthropology retains a spiritualizing tendency, it is not dualistic. This conclusion concerning Calvin was supported with evidence taken from the *Institutes*, his sermons, and several theological treatises, including the *Psychopannychia*.[1] An important question is raised by the use of this latter treatise: Does the *Psychopannychia* support or contradict Calvin's view of the soul and body, immortality and resurrection, in his later works? This treatise, which Calvin wrote in 1534, two years before the publication of the first edition of the *Institutes*, but did not publish until 1542, has been the subject of great controversy among Calvin scholars. Ganoczy concluded that this early work bears a "forte empreinte de cette philosophie dualiste" and that "Par son exaltation du spirituel en face du corporel, elle révelait 'des tendences' Neo-Platoniciennes."[2] Doumergue agrees, adding that Calvin "sensibly modified" his language and even his ideas when he discussed the same topic of the 1559 edition of the *Institutes*.[3] In other words, Doumergue admits that Calvin is a dualist in the *Psychopannychia*, but uses this treatise as an example of Calvin's transformation from a humanist in his early years to an evangelical theologian in his mature years.[4] Battenhouse also agrees that the treatise is dualistic, but he draws quite a different conclusion from this than Doumergue: "In his earliest theological work, the *Psychopannychia*, Calvin clearly elucidated the difference, and different origin, of man's body and soul. Thus, the dichotomy between spiritual and temporal authority rests in Calvin's anthropology, in fact, in his very doctrine of creation."[5] In other words, he uses the treatise to support his claim that Calvin was and remained a dualist. Babelotzky refuses to take sides on this issue, but his brief comment on this treatise supports Battenhouse's and Doumergue's claim: "Auch die weiteren Anklänge an platonisches Gedankengut in der

Psychopannychia lassen sich praktish alle aus dem *Phaidon* erklären."[6]

Other Calvin scholars assert that this treatise, far from being dualistic, actually is consistent with Calvin's mature anthropology. Partee, for example, simply quotes the *Psychopannychia* along with Calvin's later writings without arguing for this use.[7] Torrance also uses the *Psychopannychia* as one of his major sources in his exposition of Calvin's eschatology in *Kingdom and Church*. Torrance refers to the work as a "significant work in eschatology,"[8] which indicates "even at this early stage those elements which came to be so prominent in his mature exposition of eschatology."[9] The terms Calvin uses in this treatise form his preaching and instruction from its appearance until his death.[10] In other words, Torrance considers this work to be representative of Calvin's mature, evangelical theological work. To his credit, Torrance does mention that the language of this treatise has been interpreted as evidence of Calvin's Stocism.[11] Instead of arguing against this interpretation, however, he simply asserts that the evidence for this "cannot be substantiated"[12] and that "The discussion in the *Psychopannychia* makes it abundantly clear that deliverance from the prison of the body or the flesh, means the resurrection of the body to a *better nature. . . .*"[13] Quistorp agrees, stating that later Calvin

> scarcely changed the thoughts contained in it; we find them recurring in the relevant sections of the *Institutio* and indeed just in the final edition of 1559 in which the eschatological chapter, *De resurrectione ultima*, appears in quite new form; likewise in the appropriate sections of his scriptural exegesis. Sometimes we find formulations which are identical with those in the *Psychopannychia*.[14]

More recently Willem Balke, in *Calvin and the Anabaptist Radicals*, investigated the bibliographical problems of this treatise. He reports that Calvin refrained from publishing this treatise from 1534 to 1542 on the advice of other Reformers. Bucer, Olivetan, and Fabri considered the work immature and on this ground urged him not to publish it. In response, Calvin revised the treatise. Capito suggested delaying publication of the revised treatise because he feared it would stir up even more trouble between the Reformers and the Anabaptists. Finally, however, all urged him to publish it as a defense of the biblical teaching on the soul.[15] While Balke does not discuss the problem of dualism in this treatise, by this and other evidence he supports the view that *Psychopannychia* is not inconsistent with Calvin's later works. He also shows, for instance, that Calvin's later (1544) treatise, *Briefve instruction contre les Anabaptistes* is an extended reworking of the *Psychopannychia*, some sections being merely excerpts from the earlier treatise (e.g., *CO* 7: 114–29).[16] He also provides evidence from Calvin's letters and prefaces that Calvin himself understood this text to be wholly consistent with his later works.[17]

Neither group of Calvin scholars, those who point to the similarities and those who point to the differences between the *Psychopannychia* and Calvin's later works, is wholly correct, though the former are more correct. The *Psychopannychia* is different from Calvin's other anthropological works. However, the difference is one of clarity rather than contradiction. The difference in terminology is obvious. First, he seems to present the body as an impediment to the spiritual life:

> But since human life on earth is a warfare (Job vii. 1), those who feel both the stings of sin and the remains of the flesh, must feel depression in the world, though with consolation in God—such consolation, however, as does not leave the mind perfectly calm and undisturbed. But when they shall be divested of flesh and the desires of the flesh . . . then at length will they rest and recline with God. . . .[18]

He speaks consistently in this treatise of the body as a prison[19] without complementing this language with the language of appreciation for the body as a tabernacle and temple. He even denies that the body is the image of God.[20] Also, he uses Plato's myth of the cave to speak of the great difference between the body and soul.

> The body, which decays, weighs down the soul, and confining it within an earthly habitation, greatly limits its perceptions. If the body is the prison of the soul, if the earthly habitation is a kind of fetter, what is the state of the soul when set free from this prison, when loosed from these fetters? Is it not restored to itself, and as it were made complete, so that we may truly say that all which it gains is so much lost to the body? Whether they will or not, they must be forced to confess, that when we put off the load of the body, the war between the spirit and the flesh ceases. In short, the mortification of the flesh is the quickening of the spirit. Then the soul, set free from impurities, is truly spiritual, so as to be in accordance with the

will of God, and not subject to the tyranny of the flesh, rebelling against it.[21]

Here and elsewhere he appears to be conflating Plato's conflict of the soul and body with Paul's conflict of the flesh and spirit.[22] Furthermore, his entire emphasis in this treatise is on the immortality of the soul as an essence capable of existing independently of the body.

Calvin's emphasis on the immortality of the soul as an independent existence can be explained by the limited context of his polemic against the Anabaptists. This treatise was not intended to represent Calvin's entire position on the relation of the soul to the body but only to prove the immortality of the soul after the death of the body.[23] Calvin's apparently uncritical adoption of the language of Platonic dualism can be interpreted as faithful, though somewhat loose presentations of his holistic anthropology. This can be shown on the basis of the *Psychopannychia* alone. First, Calvin maintains in this treatise that the terminology he is using is taken from Scripture and not philosophy,[24] even the language of the body as a prison. Second, his language about the body as an impediment to the soul in many cases can be read in terms of his view of the body as a synecdoche for the temporal life which is but a stage on the way to the completed salvation of the resurrection.[25] That this is so may be supported by his claim that the body itself is not evil.[26] It may also be supported by the analogy he draws between the distinction between earth and heaven and the distinction between the body and soul. "Had they a particle of sense they would not prattle thus absurdly about the soul, but would make all the difference between a celestial soul and an earthly body, that there is between heaven and earth."[27] Third, even his statement that the image of God "cannot possibly be understood of his body, in which, though the wonderful work of God appears more than in all other creatures, his image nowhere shines forth,"[28] is not as obvious a contradiction of his later view of the *imago* as has been thought.[29] For as he explains in the same paragraph, it is only the soul which can properly represent God, who is spirit. As a bodily image "ought to express to the life all the traits and features, that thus the statue or picture may give an idea of all that may be seen in the original, so this image of God must, by its likeness, implant some knowledge of God in our minds."[30] A few sentences later he remarks that the image was not in humankind until Adam had been completed by the gift of the soul from God. It seems to me that Calvin's polemical context must be kept in mind here for an accurate interpretation of this passage. He explains the point of this entire discussion by saying, "Here, however, I do not insist, lest it should become a ground of quarrel. All I do wish to obtain is, that the image itself is separate from the flesh."[31] Because he is arguing against the Anabaptists that the soul is distinct from the body, he here ties it to the argument concerning the *imago dei* and the distinctiveness of humankind. He makes the same point against the Anabaptists in the *Briefve instruction*.[32]

Fourth, Calvin's apparent conflation of the soul/body dichotomy with the spirit/flesh contradiction of the scriptures is only apparent. Calvin makes his reader aware of the fact that he knows, supports, and understands the difference between these two:

> For when Paul says that "the spirit lusteth against the flesh," (Gal. 5:17), he does not mean that the soul fights with the flesh nor reason with desire; but that the soul itself, in as far as it is governed by the Spirit of God wrestles with itself, though in as far as it is still devoid of the Spirit of God, it is subject to lusts.[33]

Also, his later use of the body as a synecdoche for sinful existence appears here, though in somewhat less clear form:

> He [Paul] no doubt calls the body the mass of sin, which resides in man from the native property of the flesh; and the spirit the part of man spiritually regenerated. Wherefore, when a little before he deplored his wretchedness because of the remains of sin adhering to him (Rom. vii.24), he did not desire to be taken away altogether, or to be nothing, in order that he might escape from the misery, but to be freed from the body of death, i.e., that the mass of sin in him might die, that the spirit, being purged, and, as it were, freed from dregs, he might have peace with God through this very circumstance; declaring that his better part was held captive by bodily chains and would be freed by death.[34]

Finally, Calvin's view of the immortality of the soul as a preliminary stage in the journey toward the full perfection of salvation in the resurrection is also present in this treatise.[35]

On the basis of the *Psychopannychia* alone, then, it can be argued that this treatise is not an example of Calvin's early humanist dualism. Not only can his apparently dualistic terminology be interpreted to be consistent with his holistic anthropology as outlined in this work, but also many of the theological arguments he puts forward in the *Psychopannychia* can be shown to be the same arguments he uses later in his life. For example, his acknowledgement of the scripture's variety of meanings for the soul and his rejection of the definition of the soul as a vital force of the body are found here.[36] Also, the argument against substantial immortality of the soul which Calvin used against the Libertines is present here.[37] And, his emphasis on the unity and similarity of the body and soul as recipients of God's grace, also an argument he used against the Libertines, is present here.[38] To the textual evidence of the *Psychopannychia*, considered in itself and in its similarity to Calvin's later works on the soul and body, one could add a final, more speculative and psychological argument. It seems highly improbable to me that if Calvin believed the *Psychopannychia* to be inconsistent with his sermons and the *Institutes* that he would have allowed it to be published. It was not like him to risk the clarity of the truth of the gospel for the sake of scholarly ambition.

It is my conclusion, on the basis of these three reasons, that the *Psychopannychia* does not reflect a dualistic anthropology any more than any of Calvin's other works, even though it does exhibit his spiritualizing tendency. This is the justification for quoting it alongside the *Institutes* and sermons in chapter 5.

Notes

/1/   In *Tracts and Treatises*, 2: 414–90.
/2/   Alexandre Ganoczy, *Le Jeune Calvin: Genèse et évolution de sa vocation réformatrice* (Wiesbaden: Franz Steiner Verlag, 1966), p. 37, n. 134, p. 123.
/3/   Doumergue, *Jean Calvin*, 4: 312, n. 2.
/4/   Doumergue, *Jean Calvin*, 4: 312ff.
/5/   Battenhouse, "The Doctrine of Man," p. 425.
/6/   Babelotzky, *Platonische Bilder*, p. 50.
/7/   Partee, *Calvin and Classical Philosophy*, chap. 5, "Soul and Body in Calvin's Anthropology."
/8/   Torrance, *Kingdom and Church*, p. 90.
/9/   Ibid.
/10/ Ibid.
/11/ Ibid., p. 92.
/12/ Ibid.
/13/ Ibid., p. 93.
/14/ Quistorp, *Last Things*, pp. 55–56.
/15/ Balke, *Calvin and the Anabaptist Radicals*, pp. 26–28.
/15/ Ibid., p. 28.
/17/ Ibid., pp. 29–30.

/18/   *Psychopannychia* in *Tracts and Treatises*, 2: 433.
/19/   Ibid., 2: 439, 442, 429, 266.
/20/   Ibid., 2: 422.
/21/   Ibid., 2: 443.
/22/   Ibid., 2: 425, 434, 455, 467, 429.
/23/   See chapter 5, pp. 157ff.
/24/   *Psychopannychia* in *Tracts and Treatises*, 2: 418, 420.
/25/   Ibid., 2: 425 and 432 especially.
/26/   Ibid., 2: 422, 425, 448.
/27/   Ibid., 2: 444; see also ibid., 2: 430.
/28/   Ibid., 2: 422–23.
/29/   See chapter 2, pp. 42ff.
/30/   *Psychopannychia* in *Tracts and Treatises*, 2: 423.
/31/   Ibid.
/32/   See chapter 5, pp. 159ff.
/33/   *Psychopannychia* in *Tracts and Treatises*, 2: 422.
/34/   Ibid., 2: 439–40.
/35/   Ibid., 2: 441, 442, 449.
/36/   Ibid., 2: 420, 422, 419, 451.
/37/   Ibid., 2: 457, 468, 478.
/38/   Ibid., 2: 474.

SELECTED BIBLIOGRAPHY

Primary Sources

CALVIN

Calvini opera selecta. Edited by Peter Barth and Wilhelm Niesel. 5 vols. Monachii: Kaiser Verlag, 1926–36. [Cited as *OS*.] Each passage is cited by volume and page number first, followed in parentheses by the book, chapter, and section numbers of the *Institutes of the Christian Religion*.

Ioannis Calvini opera quae supersunt omnia. Edited by Wilhelm Baum, Edward Cunitz, and Edward Reuss. 59 vols. Brunsvigae: C. A. Schwetscke, 1863–1900. Vols. 29–98: *Corpus Reformatorum.* [Cited as *CO*.] Each passage is cited by volume and column first, followed in parentheses by the title of the work. The exegetical and homiletical works are identified as lectures (Lec.), sermons (s.), or commentaries, and are referred to by biblical texts as well as by volume and column.

MISCELLANEOUS

Budé, Guillaume. *De Transitu Hellenismi ad Christianum.* Edited by Maurice Lebel. Editions Paulines. Sherbrooke: University of Sherbrook, 1973.

Correspondence des réformateurs dans les pays de langue française. Edited by A. L. Herminjard. 9 vols. Geneva, Basel, Lyon, and Paris: H. Georg, 1878–1893.

Translations

CALVIN

A Reformation Debate: Sadoleto's Letter to the Genevans and Calvin's Reply. Edited by John C. Olin. Translated by Henry Beveridge. New York: Harper & Row, 1966; reprint ed., Grand Rapids: Baker Book House, 1976.

Academic Disourse. Translated by Dale Cooper and Ford Lewis Battles. *The Hartford Quarterly* 6 (1965): 76–85.

Calvin: Theological Treatises. Translated by J. K. S. Reid. Philadelphia: Westminster Press, 1954.

Calvin's New Testament Commentaries. Edited by David W. Torrance and

Thomas F. Torrance. Grand Rapids: Wm. B. Eerdmans, 1960—Vol. 4: *The Gospel According to John*, translated by T. H. L. Parker; Vol. 6: *The Acts of the Apostles*, translated by John W. Fraser; Vol. 8: *The Epistles of Paul to the Romans and Thessalonians*, translated by Ross Mackenzie; Vol. 9: *The First Epistle of Paul to the Corinthians*, translated by John W. Fraser.

Concerning the Eternal Predestination of God. Translated by J. K. S. Reid. Greenwood, So. Car.: Attic Press, 1975.

Concerning Scandals. Translated by John W. Fraser. Grand Rapids: Wm. B. Eerdmans, 1978.

Genesis. Edited and translated by John King M.A. 1847; reprint ed., Edinburgh: Banner of Truth Trust, 1975.

Institutes of the Christian Religion. Edited by J. T. McNeill. Translated by Ford Lewis Battles. 2 vols. Philadelphia: Westminster Press, 1960. [Cited as McNeill.] Each translation used is cited by volume and page number first, followed by the book, chapter, and section numbers of the *Institutes*, followed by the corresponding volume and page numbers of *OS*.

Letters of John Calvin. Edited by Jules Bonnet. 4 vols. Vols. 1–2 translated by David Constable. Edinburgh, n.p., 1855. Vols. 3–4 translated by M. R. Gilchrist. New York, n.p. 1858.

Psychopannychia. In *Tracts and Treatises*, 2 vols., edited by T. F. Torrance, translated by Henry Beveridge, with an Introduction by Walter Zimmerli. Grand Rapids: Wm. B. Eerdmans, 1958. 2: 414–490.

Secondary Sources

Babelotzky, Gerd. *Platonische Bilder und Gedankengänge in Calvins Lehre vom Menschen*. Wiesbanden: Franz Steiner Verlag, 1977.

Baker, Herschel. *The Dignity of Man: Studies in the Persistence of an Idea*. New York: Harper & Row, 1961.

Battenhouse, Roy W. "The Doctrine of Man in Calvin and Renaissance Platonism." *Journal of the History of Ideas* 9 (1948): 447–71.

Battles, Ford Lewis. "The Sources of Calvin's Seneca Commentary." In *Courtney Studies in Reformation Theology I: John Calvin*. Appleford: Sutton Courtney Press, 1966. Pp. 38–66.

Bauke, Hermann. *Die Probleme der Theologie Calvins*. Leipzig: Hinrichs'schen, 1922.

Bíeler, André. *La pansée économique et sociale de Calvin*. Geneva: Georg et Cie., 1961.

——. *The Social Humanism of Calvin*. Translated by Paul T. Fuhrmann. Richmond: John Knox Press, 1964.

Bohatec, Josef. *Budé und Calvin: Studien zur Gedankenwelt des französischen Frühhumanismus*. Graz: Böhlau, 1950.

——. "Calvin et l'humanisme." *Revue Historique* 183 (1938): 207–41 and 185 (1939); 1–104.

Bois, Henri, "La Prédestination d'apres Calvin." *Revue de Metaphsique et Morale* 18 (1968): 669–705.

Boisset, Jean. *Sagesse et sainteté dans la pensée de Jean Calvin*. Paris: Presses Universitaires de France, 1959.

Borgeaud, Charles. *Calvin: Fondateur de l'académie de Genève*. Paris: Armand Colin et Cie., 1897.

Bourrilly, E., ed. *Calvin et la Réforme en France*. Aix-en-Provence: Faculté Libre de Théologie Protestante, Imprimerie Paul Roubaud, 1959.

Bouwsma, William. "Calvin and the Crisis of Knowledge in the Renaissance." *Calvin Theological Journal* 17 (1982): 190–211.

———. "The Two Faces of Humanism: Stoicism and Augustinianism in Renaissance Thought." In *Itinerarium Italicum: The Profile of the Italian Renaissance in the Mirror of its European Transformations*, dedicated to Paul Oskar Kristeller on the occasion of his 70th birthday. Edited by Thomas A. Brady, Jr. Leiden: E. J. Brill, 1975. Pp. 3–60.

Breen, Quirinus. *Christianity and Humanism: Studies in the History of Ideas*. Edited by Nelson Peter Ross. Grand Rapids: Wm. B. Eerdmans, 19868.

———. *John Calvin: A Study in French Humanism*. 2nd ed. Grand Rapids: Wm. B. Eerdmans, 1968.

Cairns, David. *The Image of God in Man*. 2nd ed., rev. London: Collins, 1973.

Calvetti, Carla. *La Filosofia di Giovanni Calvino*. Milan: Societá Editrice "Vita et Pensiero," 1955.

———. "I presupposti filosofici della doctrina calvinistica del 'servo arbitrio.'" *Rivista di filosofia neo-scolastica* 44 (1952): 301–33.

Doumergue, Émile. *L'Ascétisme et l'intellectualisme de Calvin*. Mantauban: Imprimeries Cooperative, 1909.

———. *Jean Calvin: Les hommes et les choses de son temps*. 7 vols. Lausanne: Georg Bridel, 1897–1917.

Dowey, Edward A., Jr. *The Knowledge of God in Calvin's Theology*. 2nd edition. New York: Columbia University Press, 1965.

Ganoczy, Alexandre. *Calvin: Théologien de l'église et du ministère*. Paris: Les Editions du Cerf, 1964.

———. *Le Jeune Calvin: Genèse et évolution de sa vocation réformatrice*. Wiesbaden: Franz Steiner Verlag, 1966.

Gerrish, B. A. *Grace and Reason: A Study in the Theology of Luther*. Oxford: Oxford University Press, 1962.

———. *The Old Protestantism and the New: Essays on the Reformation Heritage*. Chicago: University of Chicago Press, 1982.

———. *Reformers in Profile*. Philadelphia: Fortress Press, 1967.

Gilson, Étienne. *Les Idées et les lettres*. Paris: Librairie Philosophique J. Vrin, 1932.

————. *Reason and Revelation in the Middle Ages*. New York: Charles Scribner's Sons, 1938.

————. *The Spirit of Medieval Philosophy*. Translated by Alfred Howard Campbell Downes. The Gifford Lectures for 1931. New York: n.p., 1940.

Hall, Basil. *John Calvin: Humanist and Theologian*. 2nd ed., revised. London: Cox & Wyman, 1967.

Harbison, Elmore Harris. *The Christian Scholar in the Age of Reformation*. New York: Charles Scribner's Sons, 1956.

Harkness, Georgia. *John Calvin: The Man and His Ethic*. New York: Abingdon, 1958.

Haydn, Hiram. *The Counter-Renaissance*. New York: Harcourt, Brace, & World, 1950.

Hermans, Francis. *Histoire doctrinale de l'humanisme chrétien*. 4 vols. Paris: Casterman, 1948.

Higman, Francis. *The Style of John Calvin in his French Polemical Treatises*. Oxford: Oxford University Press, 1967.

Leclerq, Jean. "Pour l'histoire de l'expression 'philosophie chrétienne.'" *Mélanges de Science Religieuse* 9 (1952): 221–26.

Lefranc, Abel. *Les Grands écrivains de la Renaissance*. Paris: Librairie Ancienne Honore Champion, 1914.

————. *La Jeunesse de Calvin*. Paris: Librairie Fischbacher, 1888.

Linder, Robert. "Calvinism and Humanism: The First Generation." *Church History* 44 (1975): 167–81.

McClelland, Joseph C. "Calvin and Philosophy." *Canadian Journal of Theology* 11 (1965): 45–53.

Marcel, Pierre. "La Prédication de Calvin àpropos du livre de M. Richard Stauffer." *La Revue Réformée* 29–30 (1978–79): 1–53.

Miles, Margaret Ruth. "Theology, Anthropology, and the Human Body in Calvin's *Institutes of the Christian Religion*." *Harvard Theological Review* 74 (1981): 303–23.

Mooi, R. J. *Het Kerk- en Dogmahistorisch Element in de Werken van Johannes Calvijn*. Wageningen: H. Veenman und Zonen, 1965.

Niesel, Wilhelm. *The Theology of Calvin*. Translated by Harold Knight. Philadelphia: Westminster Press, 1956.

Nixon, Leroy. *John Calvin's Teachings on Human Reason*. New York: Exposition Press, 1963.

Oberman, Heiko A., ed. with Brady, Thomas A., Jr. *Itinerarium Italicum: The Profile of the Italian Renaissance in the Mirror of its European Transformations*, dedicated to Paul Oskar Kristeller on the occasion of his 70th birthday. Leiden: E. J. Brill, 1975.

Parker, T. H. L. *John Calvin: A Biography*. Philadelphia: Westminster Press, 1975.

Partee, Charles. *Calvin and Classical Philosophy*. Leiden: E. J. Brill, 1977.

————. "The Revitalization of the Concept of 'The Christian Philosophy' in Renaissance Humanism." *The Christian Scholar's Review* 3 (1973–74): 360–69.

Pruyser, Paul. "Calvin's View of Man: A Psychological Commentary." *Theology Today* 26 (1969): 51–68.

Quistorp, Heinrich. *Calvin's Doctrine of the Last Things*. Translated by Harold Knight. London: Lutterworth Press, 1955.

Rudnick, Sandra Dell. *From Created to Creator: Conceptions of Human Nature and Authority in 16th Century England*. Ann Arbor: University Microfilms, 1963.

Schulze, Martin. *Meditatio futurae vitae: Ihr begriff und ihre herrschende Stellung im System Calvins*. Leipzig: Dieterich, 1901.

Smits, Luchesius. *Saint Augustin dans l'oeuvre de Jean Calvin*. 2 vols. Assen: van Gorcum, 1958.

Spitz, Lewis. *The Religious Renaissance of the German Humanists*. Cambridge: Harvard University Press, 1963.

Stauffer, Richard. *Dieu, la création et la providence dans la prédication de Calvin*. Berne: Peter Lang, 1978.

————. "Dieu, la création et la providence dans l'oeuvre homilétique de Calvin," *La Revue Réformée* 27–28 (1976–77): 196–207.

————. "Plaidoyer pour une lecture non-Calviniste de Calvin." *Revue Réformée* 30 (Supplement, 1979): 2–11.

Stendahl, Krister, ed. *Immortality and Resurrection: Death in the Western World, Two Conflicting Currents of Thought*. New York: Macmillan Co., 1965.

Torrance, T. F. *Calvin's Doctrine of Man*. London: Lutterworth Press, 1952.

————. *Kindgom and Church: A Study in the Theology of the Reformation*. London: Oliver & Boyd, 1956.

Trinkaus, Charles. "Renaissance Problems in Calvin's Anthropology." *Studies in the Renaissance* 1 (1954): 59–80.

Verhey, Allen D. "Calvin's Treatise 'Against the Libertines.'" Translated by Robert G. Wilkie and Allen D. Verhey with an Introduction by Allen D. Verhey. *Calvin Theological Journal* 15 (1980): 190–219.

Walker, Williston. *John Calvin: The Organiser of Reformed Protestantism, 1509–64*. 3rd ed. New York: Schocken Books, 1969.

Wallace, Ronald. *Calvin's Doctrine of the Christian Life*. Grand Rapids: Wm. B. Eerdmans, 1952.

Wencelius, Léon. "Le classisisme de Calvin." *Humanisme et Renaissance* 5 (1938): 231–46.

Wendel, François. *Calvin: Sources et évolution de sa pensée religieuse*. Paris: Presses Universitaires de France, 1950.

————. *Calvin et l'humanisme*. Paris: Presses Universitaires de France, 1976.

Willis, E. David. *Calvin's Catholic Christology: The Function of the So-Called "Extra Calvinisticum"* in Calvin's Theology. Leiden: E. J. Brill, 1966.

————. "Rhetoric and Responsibility in Calvin's Theology." In *The Context of Contemporary Theology*. eds. Alexander J. McKelway and E. David Willis. Atlanta: John Knox, 1974, pp. 43–63.

AXLING

A Christian Presence in Japan

AXLING
A Christian Presence in Japan

LELAND D. HINE

THE JUDSON PRESS, VALLEY FORGE

AXLING: A CHRISTIAN PRESENCE IN JAPAN

PREFACE

"THE BEST AND NOBLEST LIVES are those which are set toward high ideals; and the highest and noblest ideal that any man can have is Jesus of Nazareth," said René Almeras, a French clergyman of the seventeenth century. Such an idealist was Dr. William Axling, who lived toward the high ideal set by Christ. Faith in God gave him courage to carry out Christian idealism. He was not a mere visionary, but a true idealist who expected hardships and sufferings, and yet pressed forward to attain goals set before him.

Coming to Japan, he was sent first to the northeastern section of the main island as an evangelistic missionary. When there occurred the great famine of 1905, immediately he conducted relief work and visited on foot the starved and sick. His service of loving-kindness brought such a benevolent and reviving effect upon the people that the Department of the Imperial Household honored him with official commendation.

Then he moved to Tokyo, where he started the Baptist Tabernacle which flew a banner of social evangelism; this was the first institutional church ever founded in Japan.

After graduating in 1928 from Colgate Rochester Divinity

School, the alma mater of Dr. Axling and my father Dr. Yugoro Chiba, I became an associate to Dr. Axling at the Tabernacle. In this capacity I acted as director of its branch, the Fukagawa Christian Center which was located in an industrial slum district; Dr. Axling later moved to this district to live. "Old Man." That was what I called him because of our intimacy and he called me "Sam." We went around together visiting homes in need with words of love and encouragement and with gifts, even in sweltering summers and freezing winters.

"Old Man" wanted to be perfect, just as the Christ of God was perfect. His command of Japanese was excellent. Yet he wrote out his sermons and read the drafts to me, asking me to make corrections freely. When his sermon was delivered, it was a masterpiece. He often addressed a Japanese audience, saying "We Japanese," so that sometimes people listening to him behind the scenes took him to be a Japanese.

Beauty of character was a point he stressed quite often in his talks. Again, he quoted that scripture passage in Philippians 4:13, "I can do all things through Christ which strengtheneth me." He himself attained beauty of character through the power of faith in Christ, and was an outstanding missionary evangelist, educator, social worker, promoter of international peace, and leader in the ecumenical movement. All the beauty, glory, and merit of his life in Japan we cherish in our hearts as we continue to serve the cause which he left for us to continue.

I express my sincere appreciation to Dr. Leland Hine for taking the painstaking effort to write this biography of Dr. William Axling whom I knew all my life, with whom I was associated for eleven years during his fifties and sixties, and who was, to me, the dear "Old Man."

ISAMU CHIBA

Tokyo, Japan

CONTENTS

INTRODUCTION

THIS BOOK GREW FROM A PLAY, *The House at Fear's End,* by Louis Wilson, of the drama department of California Baptist Theological Seminary. Researching for the play convinced Mr. Wilson that a full-length biography of William Axling should be written.

He began the process and asked me to help. Later, when his interest turned to other things, I completed the work, using his valuable material and his continuing advice and assistance.

A multitude of others also have assisted. Mr. Axling's friends and relatives in America and Japan have graciously taken time to write down memories and share insights. Theodore Livingston, B. L. Hinchman, Miss Ada L. Nelson, and Nobua Tokita have read the manuscript and corrected several mistakes. Officers of the American Baptist Foreign Mission Society, especially Miss Hazel F. Shank, who at the time was reorganizing mission records, have been most helpful. Various secretaries at California Baptist Theological Seminary worked beyond hours at typing.

My wife, Eileen, has assisted in research, read the manuscript, and been very patient during the many hours consumed by the project.

With abundant assistance from these and many others, this book has emerged. It tells the story of a man who, to an amazing degree, lived his life by faith in God as revealed in Jesus Christ. This man lived his Christian life and rendered his Christian ministry during the first half of the turbulent twentieth century, and in the first Asian country to thrust itself into the modern world. In the history of foreign missions, he belongs between the pioneer who established a beachhead and the modern missionary who stands as an adviser to the rising indigenous churches. In mission theory, to a remarkable degree, he combined mission and ministry, evangelism and service, proclamation and action.

Most of all, he was a warm human being—with amusing and sometimes irritating foibles, but also with an awesome strength rooted in his single-minded dedication.

Combining the efforts of many, I have tried to tell the story of William Axling.

LELAND D. HINE

1. SON OF A PIONEER

THE UNION PACIFIC LOCOMOTIVE gave several vigorous puffs of black smoke. Slowly the "Eastbound" drew away from Gothenburg, a whistle-stop station in western Nebraska. Waving goodbye from the platform was stocky, black-bearded N. E. Axling—or Nils Axling—and his graying wife, Karen. Both were as Swedish as the name of their town.

Had there been an Old Testament prophet in the crowd, he might well have proclaimed, in typically symbolic language, and to the amazement of all, "This train is leaving for Japan where my chosen servant will preach to thousands and receive high honors from the Emperor."

Waving from the window was the unlikely subject and ultimate fulfiller of such a prophecy—Nils' fifteen-year-old son, William. Far from thinking of Japan, he could hardly believe the present. His frugal father was sending him to business school—and by train! For the moment, excitement and anticipation drowned all else. Yet, deep down inside William felt that he was running away. He was trying to escape parental pressure for his conversion to Christianity.

On the surface William knew that business school would help

him to take advantage of the opportunity that was opening up before him. By 1888 Nils Axling owned a sizable amount of real estate and was developing a farm-management business. The Axlings' close friends, the Andersens, also needed someone to help them in business affairs. Matt Andersen, soon to marry William's sister Emily, operated a farm-implement store, in which young William had been employed.

Canny Swedish common sense had made a good start in settling and developing the Gothenburg region. Smart young men among the coming generation needed only some technical knowhow in order to push on to the next level of progress. Nils wanted his son to be in on the coming prosperity.

Why, then, did William feel that he was running away? All he needed to do was to make a profession of faith in Christ, announce his conversion, and go about his work as an accepted, even favored, member of the community. Although he was not a conformist, neither was William a typical teen-aged rebel. If he had ever heard of the then popular agnostic, Robert Ingersoll, he was not a devotee of his. He evidently did not have even the normal young man's desire to sow some wild oats.

A psychiatrist could have abstracted two rather strong resentments against the church which were locked in this quiet young man's subconscious—or perhaps even in his unspoken consciousness. His father's habit of long preaching tours had caused the family genuine hardship as well as loneliness. Also, he harbored all of the frustrated fury possible for a teen-ager against the Swedish Baptist Church in Oakland, Nebraska, and the officials of that denomination who had revoked his father's ordination.

Even though these resentments were real, they were only very indirectly responsible for William's behavior. His resistance was rooted in other soil. In sum, his positive feelings toward Christ, the church, and the Christian way of life far outweighed the negative. What this serious young man feared was his own sense of responsibility. He knew that he could not take Christian decision lightly. He knew that becoming a Christian would lead him into a life even more demanding than that of his father. Later he expressed his resistance: "If I became a Christian I should offer myself as a missionary to the heathen world. This was disgusting to me and led me to plunge into a busy life in order to drown this conviction."

And so he was off to business school. Almost nothing is known of this year in William's life. The school has long since disappeared. Probably because in retrospect he looked upon this excursion as one of rebellious flight from his appointed task, William seldom referred to it. The experience left an indirect mark in prudent management of his own affairs and careful administration of mission funds.

By the fall of 1889 William was back in Gothenburg working in Matt Andersen's store. Near the end of September of that year the dread event happened, but when it came it was not particularly dramatic. A traveling evangelist was staying in the Axling home and holding services in the Swedish Baptist Church. The Axlings did not belong there, but sometimes the children attended. There is no reason to suppose that the preacher was unusual. William had heard the same message in the same American revivalistic manner hundreds of times. This time, however, his defenses crumbled. To the end of his days the to-be-renowned Dr. William Axling would testify, "I don't remember his name, I never saw him again, but he converted me."

Even as the conversion experience was not unusually dramatic, the outward change was not immediate. Yet the transformation was complete. Life's challenge now lay in the enlargement of the Christian cause in a foreign land rather than in the economic development of Nebraska. One day this small-town boy from mid-America would be granted an audience with the Emperor of Japan in honor of his many contributions to that country. That night, however, squirming on the hard bench in the little frame church, William was more frightened than elated.

In the Horatio Alger literary tradition of William's youth, one could choose many rags-to-riches themes to characterize the life of William Axling: from the slums of Omaha to honorary citizen of Tokyo; from son of immigrant to defender of immigrants; from fugitive from evangelism to missionary evangelist; from store clerk to confidant of diplomats. Also, as in any good Horatio Alger story, there were many adversaries. William's story, however, is much more realistic. His battles are more genuine, his character is more ambiguous, and his victories are more uncertain.

But, first, from what soil did this success story spring? Both his parents were born in a tiny hamlet among the fiords of northern Sweden. Nils Axling contributed his share to the community

as a cobbler. In most ways he played his role in life as genera-
tions before him had done. In one serious aspect, however, he
deviated from the standard of his fellow townsmen. For some
reason, now lost, he began a serious personal study of the Bible.
This endeavor led him to break with the state church and become
a Baptist.

To Nils, this experience was not a mere change of religious
affiliation. It was a revolutionary change of belief and life. His
overwhelming convictions overcame the reserve of his Lutheran
training, and, without any theological preparation, he began to
preach. Like so many who have found faith in a new way, he
intolerantly assumed that no one in the state church could have
a genuine religious experience.

Six days a week he continued to work at his trade, but evenings and Sundays found him preaching in his own town and
as far as his legs could carry him into other remote villages.
Predictably, the state clergy accused this upstart lay preacher of
heresy. Many of his hearers, some of whom were old friends and
neighbors, agreed. Hot tempers rose above the cold climate—
sometimes to physical violence. On one occasion he was stoned
until believed dead and thrown into a thicket.

While growing persecution limited Nils' opportunities for
preaching, and dimmed his enthusiasm for Sweden, rising propaganda from United States railroads and ship companies was
painting a rosy picture of a paradise across the sea. Also, the
Axlings were encouraged by many of their countrymen from
Norway-Sweden who at that time were responding to the Yankee
invitation. At the same time that economic depression and political unrest pushed, inflated promises pulled toward this new opportunity. So for the Axlings, America seemed to offer personal
freedom, economic opportunity, and a fruitful mission field
among their fellow Swedes.

In 1866 rugged, strong-minded Nils and his courageous, dutiful
and largely like-minded, wife Karen packed their few transport-
able belongings and, with their two daughters (three-year-old
Emily and baby Amanda), set out for America. So began the pilgrimage that determined the birthplace, the boyhood locale, and,
to a large degree, the cultural and emotional context in which
William Axling was reared.

Travel was not easy in those days, especially for the poor.

Immigrant boats were only a small step above the slave ships. After being processed like so many cattle for entry, there was still a long trip to final settlement. Swedes, however, were more fortunate than some. Customs officials were more congenial to them than to southern Europeans. Most often there were friends or interested countrymen to give helpful hints.

For the Axlings, the inland trek began with a crowded freighter making its way up the Hudson River to Albany, New York. From there a barge took them through the Erie Canal to Buffalo. This water transportation was slower, but cheaper, than the train. In Buffalo they sought the least-expensive rail fare to Chicago.

The first brief resting place for the Axlings was a shared home in the growing Swedish community on Chicago's north side. In contrast with the ceaseless motion which they had experienced since leaving home, Chicago provided relief. Compared with their quiet home, though, Chicago was anything but tranquil. In 1866 the city was in that awkward stage between frontier town and commercial city. Most of its over one hundred thousand residents from widely diverse ethnic backgrounds were living in drab, look-alike frame houses that were spreading without plan inland from Lake Michigan. Factories, stores, and other public and business structures were placed somewhat indiscriminately among the homes. The city was a beehive of noisy, confused activity—both legal and illegal. The successful already were building their mansions, and the failures were filling the giant flophouses. The Swedes, like other immigrants, were creating their ghetto, segregated from their fellow townsmen by language and custom as well as location. Those, like the Axlings, who belonged to a sect church, were isolated from their brethren as well, because most of the immigrants were members of the state church of Sweden. Although there was no active persecution, and common needs in a strange land reduced tension, folk like the Baptists felt a strong need for an organized church for social as well as religious reasons.

Very shortly after their arrival, Nils Axling joined with three other Swedish Baptist ministers in establishing the first Swedish Baptist church in Chicago. This tangible evidence of missionary opportunity made the rigors of the journey seem worthwhile.

But the truly challenging missionary adventure lay farther west. There numerous Swedish homes and communities were deprived of even minimal religious care. Just incidentally, lonely Swedes of the Lutheran state-church background could be won to the Baptist cause more easily than those who were living in a settled parish. From Karen's point of view any excuse to leave the din of Chicago was a good reason.

The first stop on the way west was Rock Island, Illinois. This bustling river settlement was already a strong Swedish community, and the headquarters for the Swedish Baptist operation. The first conference organized by that denomination was not in the homeland, but in this frontier settlement, in 1856.

In Rock Island, Nils returned to his European pattern—mending shoes during the week and preaching on weekends. Nearly every Friday evening he packed a bundle of Swedish-language tracts and Bibles, along with a few provisions, and trudged off across the rolling plains in search of lost Swedish souls. He traveled unbelievable distances over Illinois and across the river in Iowa. Besides making personal visits at lonely farmhouses, he frequently preached in village homes and schoolhouses.

Since there were no hotels or eating places, he was entirely dependent upon the hospitality of the often poverty-stricken settlers. Frequently he slept in his clothes upon the cold, damp ground. Late Sunday night or Monday morning he returned home and to the workbench. With some variation, this pattern continued until late in Nils' life.

His success, or at least his determination, caused the Illinois-Iowa Baptist Association, in 1869, to invite Nils to become its missionary. The frugal Swedes may also have taken into account the fact that he was one of those rugged individualists who believed that a minister should not take pay for his work. He could be counted upon to refuse the $600 yearly salary received by his predecessor! They were right. Nils accepted without pay.

Accepting an official position meant mostly that Nils traveled farther and spent less time at home. On June 24, 1869, he helped organize a church in Oakland, Nebraska, some sixty miles northwest of Omaha. While refusing direct pay, he did allow the congregation to assist him in buying a farm in the area. As soon as possible his family (which now had grown by the addition of a son, Albert) moved to the farm.

From September, 1871, to July, 1872, Nils added the pastorate of the Oakland church to his farm work and slightly curtailed

missionary travel. During this time, the first William Axling,
usually referred to as Willie, was born.

The barely established Axling family was no match for the depression which descended on the United States in 1873. The end
of the Franco-Prussian War had caused a drastic reduction in
farm prices, which in turn wrecked the whole economy. Unable
to meet his obligations, Nils was forced to surrender his first
piece of American real estate.

For the first time since they had started their western trek, the
Axling family retreated slightly—to Omaha. Here Nils could gain
some income from his old trade and secure cheap housing in the
"Gopher Town" section. More tragedy came early in 1873 with
the death of Willie.

This was the chain of events which determined the place and
circumstances of the birth of William Axling, in what he preferred to call "the slums of Omaha."

He was born on August 6, 1873, and, in defiance of adverse
circumstances, was named William. Quite unknown to the new
baby or his proud parents, six months and two days earlier, Dr.
Nathan Brown had arrived in Yokohama to begin the first permanent Baptist missionary work in Japan.

William spent his first six years in these surroundings. His use
of the word "slum" is a typically slight exaggeration by which
he hoped to dramatize his identification with those to whom he
later ministered in the slums of Tokyo. Gopher Town was not a
slum in the modern sense, even though the residents were desperately poor and the housing was the least adequate in the city.
The area received its name from the practice of digging rooms
out of an old river bluff and enclosing the open side with a sod
wall. The result was as functional as the sod huts on the prairie,
but more sophisticated town folk did not consider these proper
houses.

Yet the social stigma of living in Gopher Town did not seem
greatly to damage the naturally bright, optimistic William. By
the time he was able to leave the house without adult supervision, there were many playmates and countless possibilities for
adventure along the Missouri River. Besides, the depression,
which lingered until 1879, left few of Omaha's seventeen thousand citizens with conspicuous affluence which the poor could
compare with their desperate plight.

As a matter of fact, among the poor, William's father made a better living than most, and as a lay preacher he was considered something of a professional man. His mother, also, had proved her adaptability to frontier living by becoming a midwife. Her quiet efficiency, calm courage, and developing skill made her a favorite among the Swedish women. Though little William may not have understood what her urgent secret missions were about, he basked in the obvious respect which his family enjoyed.

The Axlings had one more dwelling place before final settlement in Gothenburg. On September 20, 1879, the Oakland church asked Nils to assume its pastorate. In the light of improving economic conditions, the elder Axling decided to try again. This time he staked an eighty-acre tree claim near Oakland. His call to the pastorate probably followed this arrangement to support his family in the area.

The pastor-church relationship began auspiciously. During the calendar year 1880, fifteen new members were added, bringing the total to a then very respectable seventy-nine—"a figure which was not exceeded for many years." The same year the congregation erected its first building, which served until 1919.

Taken as a whole, however, the years at Oakland were unhappy for William and disheartening for the family. From the boy's point of view, conditions there were much worse than in Omaha. Two sisters and a not-too-congenial brother were no replacements for the host of friends he had left behind him in Omaha.

For the first time William became aware of poverty. Eighty years later he could still remember a "three-times-a-day dish of corn mush and bitter, unrefined sorghum." A family project was going into the fields with his mother "to pick up cow chips, our only fuel for cooking and heating."

Nils still refused to receive pay for his ministerial duties and still insisted on taking his evangelistic tours as well as caring for the local flock. Had he spent more time on the land, or accepted payment from the church, life might have been easier.

The most crushing blow, however, came from members of his own flock. A bitter controversy led to his resignation, a split in the church, and a censure by his own denomination. Undoubtedly, Nils was partly to blame. He could have avoided much controversy by spending more time developing the local church, which in turn would gladly have paid him for his services. Yet, once the controversy began, Nils could be more accurately described as a "fanner of the flame" than "a pourer of oil on troubled waters."

As in most church quarrels, particularly in that day, the debate soon became theological. Nils was considered a heretic on two counts. First, he believed that communion should be open to all Christians, regardless of denominational affiliation or even baptism. Second, he believed that those who had not had a full chance to accept the gospel would be given an opportunity after death. He did not reject the idea of hell, but believed that all would have a chance to accept the gospel.

The first count was serious, but the second was intolerable. The great enemies of frontier preachers from colonial days had been the Deists, their children the Agnostics, and their cousins the Universalists. All these doubted hell, and the last named believed that everyone eventually would be saved. No encouragement or compromise with such people could be allowed. The fact that no one involved in the debate really understood the issues did not inhibit pastor, parishioners, or denominational officials. Like many uneducated farmer-preachers, Nils loved speculative theological debate. Also, like most untrained persons, he was absolutely sure of his opinions. His opponents were of the same kind.

In July, 1882, Nils resigned. The church minutes with characteristic understatement read simply, "It was decided to call a pastor who could devote his entire time to the work of the church." As usual, however, the matter was not so easily settled. Many of Nils' followers left the church. In March, 1883, A. P. Ekman, general missionary of the Swedish Baptist Conference, was called in to adjudicate. Thirty members of the church were excluded, and the name of Nils Axling was removed from the list of approved Swedish Baptist ministers.

William, apparently, was not told the details until several years later. Nevertheless, the warmth and the approval which he had felt from the community in Omaha were now replaced by hostility and rejection in Oakland.

Nils responded to this reproof as a typical American pioneer. He made plans to move farther west. As for his evangelistic activity, a man who had been stoned and left for dead in Sweden was not likely to be told what to do or to preach.

In the spring of 1883 the Axling family made its last long move. As soon as the spring rains were over and the mud ruts turned to dust, the Axlings loaded their possessions on a wagon and started west once more. Nils had filed a homestead claim about twenty-five miles west of the Swedish settlement of Lexington. Already he and some Swedish friends had made plans to found a village.

Karen, who was unusually frail that spring, came later by train. The rest of the family covered the some 250 miles, taking turns walking and riding on the lumber wagon. They spent the nights on the trail, and Emily and Amanda prepared the meals over open fires. The last Axling daughter, eight-year-old Lydia, helped as she could.

This time the Axlings experienced economic success. The depression was over, the Indian threat had diminished, and the Union Pacific Railroad provided adequate transportation. Nils and his associates chose a spot thirty miles east of the junction of the North and South Platte Rivers, a mile north of the river on the railroad and at a Pony Express station. They laid out town lots and chose the name of Gothenburg. Although true affluence was long in coming, the Axlings were never again in dire want.

William was not quite ten years old when the family settled in Gothenburg. He made his final break with the town shortly after his nineteenth birthday. Thus, these important years of mature decision he spent in a barren frontier town as the son of sturdy pioneer Swedish parents. Years later he wrote:

> Here among the endless sand hills and the sweeping prairie, the writer spent his boyhood. The only vegetation was sand burrs and cactus, among which rattlesnakes flourished like fleas on a dog's back. The night noises were the coyotes' wild screech. During the day antelopes and wild horses roamed in droves across the plains. Occasionally a stray buffalo was silhouetted across the western sky.

The frontier, however, was not all romance. The grinding poverty, the endless work, the lonely isolation—the few institutions, objects, and processes of culture—all brutalized men and crushed women. Life was easier in the towns than in the country, but not much. No social planner would have chosen Gothenburg during the 1880's to mature a cosmopolitan internationalist with great appreciation of strange cultures and deep understanding of widely diverse persons. Yet this is what happened in William's case.

Many of the pioneers refused to be overwhelmed by the hostile environment. What they lacked in abundance they made up in a clear grasp of essentials. Many, like the Axlings, had come halfway round the world for a chance to build a life and a society according to their ideals. The values of their old culture, often romanticized by distance and preserved in folklore, provided one element for the new. The American dream and hope for the future provided a second element. Even though cultural advantages were few, the experience of living in a Swedish community in an American setting provided a cross-cultural experience in itself.

Gothenburg, like most frontier towns, early provided two creative institutions—the one-room schoolhouse and the box-like church. Looking back, William perceived three influences which molded him, "the one-room schoolhouse, the little church, and the Christian home—my debt to each is incalculable."

His two strong parents unquestionably made the most significant impact upon William's personality. His brother Albert, always physically weak and epileptic, died three years after the family arrived in Gothenburg. The three sisters were congenial, but completely overawed by the powerful parents. The community remembered them as "three awfully good daughters" who grew up to be "very good Christian women."

But those parents! Tall, black-bearded Nils was a person who threw all of his keen natural intelligence, rugged strength, and stubborn determination into everything he did. In temperament he was stern, distant, and absolutely inflexible. If he ever admitted to being wrong, there is no record of his doing so. His unquestioned confidence in his own opinions made communication difficult, particularly after his hearing failed. Intense personal pride revealed itself both in the yearly photograph which he always contrived to have taken and in his carefully blackened beard. Yet his moral integrity and determined pursuit of his goals won the respect of nearly all and the affection of some. His softer side showed most clearly whenever he learned of a Swede down on his luck.

Karen was a worthy helpmate. In that patriarchal society she seemed to be a perfect wife—apparently compliant to her husband's every wish, a faultless housekeeper, a conscientious mother. Her temperament was quiet, self-effacing, tender, and gentle. In the community she was regarded as an angel of mercy at a time of birth, illness, or death.

Though frail in body, Karen was in spirit every bit as rugged as her husband. The steel in her soul revealed itself not only in her ability to fill the demanding role of pioneer wife but in the way she kept her own integrity. For instance, even though she understood English, she always refused to speak what she considered to be a "harsh, alien tongue." By this means she assured herself that she had not entirely surrendered to the rude ways of the American frontier. As a side effect, William learned the connection between feeling and language and many of the sensitive nuances of communication.

Karen had her weaknesses also. Her standards of housekeeping and personal behavior were rigidly high. Neighbors called her "cranky, particular." Her acts of kindness, though genuine, were carried out with the clearly implied expectation that the recipient would rise to the standard of the giver. Nor was Karen uncorrupted by pride. As family circumstances improved, she knew exactly how to reflect their rising status without criticizable ostentation.

Both parents were deeply religious. There was something of the air of a prophet about austere Nils. His religious convictions, untroubled by formal study, were held in that absolute form possible only for the uneducated. Young people dreaded his long, dogmatic sermons, but his realistic understanding of the Swedish immigrant made him an effective evangelist among his people. His gift he used faithfully.

William's own mature assessment of his parents was concise: "Father did the preaching, Mother did the living." His mother always remained his ideal of Christlikeness. Gothenburg neighbors agreed. As one wrote, "Dr. William Axling has inherited wonderful characteristics from his mother—his gentleness, patience, and ability to take whatever came." For good or ill, William was the son of both his parents. The well-meaning, constant pressure of gentle Karen's perfectionism was as much responsible for his excessive sense of duty as were the more obvious demands of his father. Both parents encouraged the development of a fierce pride and a determination to express that pride in socially acceptable ways. Both laid upon him a heavy sense of obligation, which drove him at times to impossible tasks. Both also helped to develop his integrity, devotion to others, and dedication to the cause of Christ.

Among the family practices, one which had special impact upon William, was the "prophet's chamber." Like so many deeply Christian pioneers and rural families in America, the Axlings set aside a room in their house which was made available to "any Protestant evangelist who visited and served the settlement." Undoubtedly Nils' own experience of sleeping on the hard, cold ground while on his rounds added zest to the ceremony. According to William, "furloughing missionaries, regardless of their denomination, were greeted with double welcome and given the use of that prophet's chamber and a seat at our frugal table." William traced his early missionary interest to his contact with these visiting missonaries.

Knowing what William Axling became, it is easy to find molding influences in his early life. His friends and neighbors during his early years did not think he was unusual. Most of the ten years in Gothenburg he spent as a normal boy and teen-ager of that day and place. He fished in the Platte, hunted in the sandhills, and walked both alone and with friends over countless miles in every direction. If remembered at all, it was as a quiet, friendly, energetic youth. He seemed a bit more serious than the average boy, but his love of practical jokes dispelled that image. His nieces found him something of a nuisance, especially when he insisted on riding them home from school on the handlebars of his bike. The years at Gothenburg were good years in many ways. Once again he felt the protective warmth of belonging to one of the highly respected families of the town.

In many ways, William Axling remained, all of his life, an outgoing, friendly Nebraska boy. He never became too old to sit in awe of nature, too sophisticated to marvel at man's achievements, too learned to wonder at God's providential care, or too jaded to delight in a dish of ice cream.

That September evening when he finally decided to become a Christian, the most serious struggle of his young life was solved. Still the way ahead was very uncertain.

2. STUDENT

How DOES ONE BECOME A MISSIONARY? William was not too sure. Even those occasional missionary occupants of the prophet's chamber had not been very helpful to him at that point.

Sometimes William dreamed of jumping a train to San Francisco, stowing away on a freighter, and making his own way to some exotic land. He would be a lay preacher on the model of his father. In more sober moments, however, his naturally practical mind sought ways of becoming an appointee of some mission agency. Although he was fuzzy on such details, he knew that being an effective missionary required education. His own study had stopped with the eighth grade, the highest offered in Gothenburg, plus a year in business school.

But that was not his only problem. The year 1889 was a very poor time for a young man in Nebraska to begin a new career. A long real-estate boom and period of agricultural prosperity had ended two years before. The boom, promoted by railroad propaganda and supported by eight years of adequate rainfall, had ground to a halt. Great optimism had been supported by an unreasonable theory that cultivation had favorably changed the climate. For the ten years following 1887, however, the climate disproved the theory. By 1891 the population of Nebraska was in retreat. That year saw over eighteen thousand prairie schooners cross the Mississippi River, headed back east into Iowa.

The Axlings were affected by the hard times, but not dislodged. Their roots now were deep enough to stand the storm. Nevertheless, the shock of the depression was sufficient to make the loss of a strong man with business training a serious blow if William were to leave home to become a missionary.

Then, there was Father! William's awe for Nils was a compound of respect and fear. William's conversion would cause the older man pleasure. Nevertheless, William knew that in typical paternalistic fashion Nils expected his only son to take over the family affairs and provide for the parents in their old age. Nils never doubted that his plans for his family were identical with God's will. How was William, a dutiful son, to overcome the father's objection? No one ever sat down and reasoned with Nils Axling.

For two more years, William fought his inward battle in silence. He even kept his conversion secret. Matt Andersen's store and his father's accounts occupied his time. Only his closest friends sensed that he was becoming quieter, even a bit withdrawn. Whenever questioned he passed it off with, "Oh, I didn't sleep well last night."

In the middle of July, 1891, William suddenly took the next step. On a Sunday afternoon, Nils was baptizing a group of converts in the nearby Platte River. At the end of the service he intoned the traditional, "We have done as was commanded and still there is room."

William suddenly walked forward and was baptized. The only reaction was a slight tightening of the muscles in the father's face. That night Nils seemed unusually at peace and the mother's eyes were slightly moist. Nothing was said. These rugged folks had never learned how to show affection without betraying weakness.

Even then, William did not join a church. His attendance, though quite regular, was divided between the Swedish Baptist and the newly formed Methodist Church. By this time he knew the whole story of his father's expulsion from the Swedish Baptist denomination. Seeing his father's continued missionary work made it easy for him to distinguish between Christian faith and institutional loyalty. His lifelong refusal to engage in theological debate and his broad ecumenical tolerance may well have been rooted in his father's experience.

By baptism, William reconfirmed his decision to become a missionary, and within the week he announced his plans to enter foreign service. Even more alarming to the elder Axling was William's determination to seek an education to prepare himself for the ministry.

Nils exploded. He directed his attack not against missionary service but against an educated clergy. Internally, he was against the one as much as the other—for William, that is. But even Nils could see the inconsistency of a man who had spent much of his life preaching, and much of his substance supporting churches, evangelists, and missionaries, objecting to giving his son to Christian work.

On the other score, however, Nils was uninhibited. Both at home and throughout the town he released a torrent of words against the principle and practice of an educated clergy. It was an educated clergy that had ruined the state church! He claimed, "God himself gives words to the true man of God. One who trusts in Christ does not need to depend on books. The Spirit fills the mouth of the true prophet." On and on went the argument. Some, especially the less-reverent youth, wondered why God had not been more effective with Nils.

Providentially, the Methodists recently had called a young pastor with whom William could talk, and the two spent many hours together around the kitchen table in the parsonage. These conversations clarified the training necessary for a man who hoped to do missionary work in the coming twentieth century. Most important, William had found a sympathetic, knowledge-able person upon whom he could lean—a wise person who gave William a leadership position in the newly organized youth program, the Epworth League.

An unexpected amount of support came from home. William received a lesson in the strength of quiet women. As Nils blus-tered and sulked, as he argued and ignored, Karen made unmis-takably clear where her convictions lay. She supported her son's ambitions unwaveringly. More timidly, the sisters also drew to themselves some of their father's wrath by supporting their brother.

The year was terribly unhappy for all. Finally, in the fall of 1892, without being reconciled to his father, William made the break. He entered the preparatory school at the University of Nebraska, and after two years he was ready to enroll in the university proper.

In 1892, Lincoln was hardly a metropolis, and the university was not a rival of Harvard. From the perspective of Gothenburg, however, the town did have its attraction. The year before, a colorful young resident, William Jennings Bryan, had been elected as Democratic representative to Congress. In 1894, Bryan conducted a brilliant, if unsuccessful, campaign for the Senate. Lincoln, and probably William, witnessed the most important debate of Bryan's campaign, one which discussed the tariff.

In 1896 Lincoln was brimming with national and world discussion. Its silver-tongued orator was carrying the Democratic banner for the Presidency of the United States. This was a crucial election. Reform programs, which had been developed and promoted by the Grange and Farmers' Alliance, and furthered by the Populist Party, were that year adopted by the Democratic platform and its standard bearer. However, when Bryan went down in defeat, the program went with it. Effective, progressive reforms were forced to wait for the rise of urban liberals.

Low tariff, cheap money, and anti-imperialism strongly appealed to the sensitive William. These ideas seemed to favor the poor and the oppressed. They led the way toward a lessening of world tensions. To espouse these ideas was to embrace the cause of humanity, he felt.

Positive response to humanitarian liberalism, however, had the effect of adding to William's sense of guilt. His family had become a part of the establishment. They now owned rather than rented land. They received rather than paid interest. Cheap money tended to reduce their land and wealth, which by Nils' death amounted to a modest rural fortune of over fifty thousand dollars. If he had known the trend of his son's thinking, Nils would have been confirmed in his fear of education.

The attraction toward a humanitarian liberalism had a second source. In 1894 Lucinda Burrows, vivacious daughter of Jay Burrows, also matriculated at the University of Nebraska.

Jay Burrows had become a leader among the Nebraska liberals. Born in New York state, he had begun a newspaper career before the Civil War. During the war his wife had moved with her parents to Iowa. After his discharge, Jay also went west and settled in Benton County, Iowa. It was here that Lucinda was born on August 6, 1873. In 1880 the family moved to a farm near Fille, Nebraska. Later, Jay became president of the Nebraska Farm Alliance. In 1889 they moved to Lincoln, so that Jay could assume the editorship of the *Alliance,* an influential weekly paper expressing the liberal point of view.

As Lucinda grew to womanhood she followed her mother's religious leanings and became a member of the Baptist church near Fille. When the family moved to Lincoln, she transferred her membership to the First Baptist Church of that city. From early childhood Lucinda was motivated by a deep Christian faith, which expressed itself in her concern for others. In her person and attitude she blended the faith of her mother and the social activism of her father. While a student of the university she sought out a Negro church where she could teach a Sunday-school class.

As in the case of William, eventual missionary work was the goal which brought Lucinda to the university. Quite naturally, then, the two met at gatherings of the local chapter of the Student Volunteer Movement.

Although this phenomenal organization had many roots, it can be traced directly to a meeting of 251 college students invited by D. L. Moody to meet at Mount Hermon in 1886. Before this first conference closed, one hundred young people had volunteered for missionary service. Such success encouraged the leaders to send representatives to campuses in the United States and Canada. The first year's results were 2,200 more missionary recruits. By 1890 a strong network of chapters on college and university campuses had spread across North America. With the effective leadership of John R. Mott, this organization did more than any other agency to recruit missionaries and disseminate missionary information among college students.

William got his chance to attend his first missionary convention as a representative of his chapter to the national conference held at Lake Geneva, Wisconsin, in 1894. The movement supplied both William and Lucinda with current facts about missions, strengthened their commitment, and provided opportunity for fellowship. (Some of the fellowship took place after approved hours, with shades drawn, so that university authorities would not discover that men and women were still together!)

The common life goal which brought William and Lucinda together formed a basis for a growing relationship. Their conversations began to be sprinkled with personal references. They discovered the likeness of their backgrounds in the hardships of frontier life, and similarities in their seemingly different struggles. Lucinda was trying to Christianize the social conscience of her father, while William was trying to humanize the austere religion of his.

Most important, the two found in each other a profound affinity, based in common sensitivity to the needs of others and in absolute commitment to God's will. Acquaintance grew into friendship, friendship into courtship, and courtship eventually into marriage.

Financially, university life reminded William of the hard times in Oakland. As the rural depression widened into a business panic in 1893, money was very hard to come by. In those years Nils would have found difficulty in supporting a college student. He did not try!

Enterprising William put together a strenuous support program. For food, during the first year, he worked in a restaurant five hours a day, five days a week, plus seven hours on Sunday. To pay for a room, he worked as a janitor. Finally, he did clerical work on Saturdays to provide for incidentals. Later, he became a janitor for the university with responsibility for the music building. Since classes were held in the evening, the cleaning was done between 10 P.M. and midnight. The furnace, which was also a part of his responsibility, had to be started between 4:00 A.M. and 5:00 A.M. during the winter months.

The university years also provided William with an opportunity to try his ministerial wings. He first joined the YMCA evangelistic band, a team of young men who visited nearby churches to hold services. From the start William was a favorite speaker. Little experience was needed. He could easily make his own variation on themes he had heard all his life.

Wider experience came in 1895 when William assumed the summer pastorate of the Free Baptist Church at Antelope Center, Nebraska. Shortly after arriving in Lincoln he had joined the Free Baptist Church. This was his first formal church membership.

Recognizing the potentiality of its new member, the congregation licensed him to preach. The summer opportunity followed naturally.

This first pastorate was characterized neither by success nor by failure. William performed his Sunday and weekday duties for two months and returned to college with a total offering of eleven dollars, minus train fare.

During the next school year William began attending the First Baptist Church with Lucinda. His maturing understanding of the missionary task convinced him that splinter groups, such as the Free Baptists, were inadequate to meet the worldwide challenge. The result was a change of membership into what is now known as the American Baptist Convention. William and Lucinda then belonged to the same church.

The new relationship quickly opened wider opportunities. A new license to preach was followed by a call as student pastor of the First Baptist Church in David City. Although the fifty-mile distance confined most of his activities to the weekend, for the first time William had full pastoral responsibilities resting upon his shoulders.

Any doubts that William may still have harbored about his fitness for the ministry were swept away by this experience. The leading layman, H. L. Batsy, called him "one among a thousand." His most obvious professional ability emerged as "an able teacher, a strong preacher, and a soul-winning evangelist." Some wished that the young pastor would give more time to the Sunday school and supervise church finances more carefully. Nevertheless, with a preacher like William, a long-suffering small church like David City could not afford to complain about minor difficulties, especially as the young man's leadership qualities other than great preaching began to emerge. Old members were amazed at the patience, sympathy, and insight with which he handled personal problems, and at the quiet persistence with which he pursued his goals.

William did not realize how much Lucinda had come to mean to him until a serious illness forced her to leave the university. At about the same time her mother died. Lucinda returned to the Burrows farm where her father was then living. As her strength returned she kept house and later taught school in order to earn money to return to college.

During his last two years of college, William found the gruel-ing work schedule made more unbearable by the added weight of loneliness. Not that he and Lucinda had ever had an extensive social life. Occasional strolls and joint work on committees for the church and the Student Volunteer Movement were all they could afford in either time or money. Separation denied even these pleasures. They continued to correspond, but seldom saw each other.

William received his A.B. degree on June 10, 1889, after an undistinguished college career. The college experience had ex-tended his linguistic understanding to German, Greek, and Latin. Instead of meeting the requirement of infantry drill, he made up other academic work. This change of program may well have reflected William's growing distaste for war.

With a college degree secured, William searched frantically for funds to follow his former roommate William Elmore to the Rochester Theological Seminary, Rochester, New York. With little more than train fare collected, he rushed off an application on September 7, 1889. He was accepted and became one of the fourteen members of that year's entering class.

Seminary was a dynamic experience for William Axling. Hori-zons expanded for the Nebraska youth with awesome rapidity. Buried feelings and half-identified thoughts came into meaningful focus. As he expressed it, "the courses under dedicated professors, the comradeship with like-minded students, and the atmosphere of the institution opened up to me a totally new world—intel-lectually and spiritually."

Two faculty members, particularly, caught William's imagina-tion. The first was president of the seminary and prominent Bap-tist theologian Augustus H. Strong. During the time William was a student, Dr. Strong was trying out in class the material for his durable *Systematic Theology*. Dr. Strong was also an outstanding advocate of, and frequent speaker for, the foreign-mission enter-prise. William never departed from the Christ-centered theology of missions taught by his mentor. He also responded to the spirit of his teacher, a spirit expressed to the Ecumenical Missionary Conference in New York, in 1900: "When I hear the word 'Go' I hear no arbitrary command. . . . He imparts to us his own longing to redeem; he reveals to us the heart of God. . . . He takes our little boats in tow on the broad current that sets in the direction of that one far-off divine event at which the whole creation moves."

William's second most influential teacher was Walter Rauschenbusch, church historian and social-gospel advocate. Although Dr. Rauschenbusch was still teaching in a German seminary, William attended some of his classes. In these classes, William began to put together his commitment to Christ and his concern for the earthly struggles of man. The young student's heart and mind leaped forward in assent and confirmation on hearing his teacher say such things as he later wrote in A *Theology for the Social Gospel:*

> Theology is not superior to the gospel. It exists to aid the preaching of salvation. Its business is to make the essential facts and principles of Christianity so simple and clear, so adequate and mighty, that all who preach or teach the gospel, both ministers and laymen, can draw on its stores and deliver a complete and unclouded Christian message. When the progress of humanity creates new tasks, such as world-wide missions, or new problems, such as the social problem, theology must connect these with the old fundamentals of our faith and make them Christian tasks and problems.

Under such stimulation William became a serious student. He was one of the privileged few who were allowed to read with the president "an approved work of German theology." Dr. Strong considered him "the best scholar in his class."

Activistic William did not spend all of his seminary years in study. Again, as in college, he was forced to earn his own way. Some help came by a loan from the New York Baptist Union for Ministerial Education. Also, as in college, he became a member of an evangelistic team. After this group spent a weekend in Ontario, New York, the congregation was so greatly impressed that it called William as pastor.

Many of the trademarks of Axling's ministry became evident during his two and one-half years at Ontario. Twenty persons were won to Christian commitment and baptism. A number of these were from a class of boys which he taught. Although he was still young, people trusted him with their personal problems and responded to his patience and persistence. His temperament made it possible for him to set a high standard before his people without alienating their affections. By general consent "the church was lifted to a higher spiritual standard."

The open, tolerant, cooperative spirit so typical in Axling's later work was evident also in Ontario. Although he was a convinced Baptist, William was never narrowly sectarian. The small upstate New York town was impressed by the young Baptist pastor who could work so effectively with all Christians. The Presbyterian minister commented: "I have always found him ready and willing to cooperate with us in our church work. I believe him to be liberal-minded and possessed with that particular tact which will enable him to labor successfully with people of other denominations."

The young Axling also had his somber side. Young and old alike noted the degree to which "the wrongs of the world saddened him and often weighed heavily upon him." As he spent each weekend making his pastoral rounds on a battered bicycle, even children were moved by the "all-too-often sad expression on his face." Then, as always, however, William's essential optimism, confident faith, and obviously positive devotion to Christ were dominant.

While William was busy in seminary, Lucinda returned to the university where she earned her teacher's certificate in June, 1900. While completing her course she also worked with a prominent woman physician. Through that experience she earned money and acquired some knowledge of medicine, which she hoped might be used on the mission field. The following year she taught school in Lincoln.

No one knows just when William and Lucinda became formally engaged. At least from the time of her illness it was commonly understood that they would be married and go together as missionaries. Both worked toward that end.

Sometime during 1900 they applied to the American Baptist Missionary Union, as the American Baptist Foreign Mission Society was then known. Lucinda's application was processed by the woman's board. Although the young couple had often talked of going to Burma, on being asked whether he had a preference for a field of labor, William answered, "No decided preference at present." Later in the application he agreed to go wherever his services were needed, "after consultation and proper consideration of my adaptability for that field." When asked whether he acquired a new language with ordinary facility he answered, "Yes, I think so."

Finally, the spring of 1901 brought the end of school days. When William finished seminary, the missionary board asked the young couple to go to Boston for an appointment. As soon as she had finished her teaching obligation, Lucinda headed east.

The marriage took place in the little church in Ontario, May 21, 1901. The congregation proudly decorated the building with white lilacs, and the women prepared a lunch. One of William's college roommates, who was also a fellow seminary student at Rochester, Steven Cory, officiated. Each of the local ministers was on hand to offer a toast.

After the service the newlyweds traveled to Boston where they received formal appointment. On the return trip they stopped off in Northfield, Massachusetts, for a missionary conference. Here in an atmosphere congenial with their student volunteer days, they spent what passed for a honeymoon.

In fulfillment of a former agreement, the couple returned to Ontario for the months of June and July. Understandably, however, in those days, William and Lucinda were giving their best thoughts to preparing for what they fully expected would be their life's work in Burma. In the middle of July, however, a letter came from the mission board: "Our committee has voted, designating you to work in Japan."

3. A FIRST-TERMER

JAPAN! As THEY HAD STROLLED along the streets of Lincoln, ridden
on the train to Boston, relaxed at the missionary conference in
Northfield, and sat in their temporary quarters in Ontario which
served as their first home, the young Axlings had ranged the
world in their missionary discussions. They had pictured themselves in many places: Burma, India, Assam, China, and Africa.
Always, however, they had returned to Burma. Somehow, Japan
had never figured in their plans.

When they left Boston, they knew that their destination was
not finally set. As good soldiers they had agreed to go anywhere
the board had a need. Secretly, both had harbored some question
about the possibility of Burma. But Japan! After a few days of
discussion, thought, and prayer, William wrote his answer to
Dr. Thomas Barbour, foreign secretary of the American Baptist
Foreign Mission Society. He expressed both his surprise and his
disappointment: "I did so much want to go to some intensely
dark and needy spot." Nevertheless, personal desire could never
stand in the way. "If the committee feels this is God's field for
me, . . . I shall gladly consecrate my life to the very best service
of which I am capable in Japan."

In reply, Dr. Barbour assured the young missionaries that their desires would be respected. It was still possible that the Stedmans, who had spent many years in Korea, might decide to change to Japan. If so, the Axlings could be relieved, and Burma would be the next choice.

In the midst of his letter, Dr. Barbour slipped in some good advice to the young, overzealous Axling: "As to the choice of a life involving personal hardship and discomfort, while the true Christian will not avoid this, I do not think the spirit of Christianity requires that it should be sought."

Further negotiations seemed to settle the matter in favor of Burma, and the Axlings were to sail in September. On Sunday, July 29, the Ontario church said farewell to their pastor and his wife. Lucinda was surprised to discover how much these people had come to mean to her in so short a time. She felt her throat tighten as the congregation joined hands, forming a circle around the sanctuary, and sang, "God Be With You Till We Meet Again."

Next stop was Lincoln. Reunions and farewells mingled with a rush of activity. The First Baptist Church, in which the Axlings kept their membership, and from which they received support until retirement in Alhambra, California, had planned the ordination of William to the gospel ministry. Much time was also spent in collecting gear—part of which was sent on its way to Burma.

Only one dark cloud hung over the anticipation of those days. Nils had not yet been reconciled to his son's decision. A letter carefully composed with Lucinda's help was ignored. Nevertheless, plans were made and followed to spend a few days in Gothenburg before heading for the field. On the happy side of the visit was the evident approval which severe Karen gave to daughter-in-law Lucinda.

While William was renewing old friendships and introducing his new bride in his home town, another letter came from the executive board of the mission society. They were assigned to Japan! William's patience was near exhaustion. Gradually, he had come to accept the idea of Japan, but continued uncertainty was annoying—especially since some baggage had already been sent to Burma. The anxiety of the first-term missionary was beginning to get to him.

In spite of their displeasure, however, the Axlings raised no serious objections. After one more farewell, this time at the Swedish Baptist Church in which William had been converted, they set out for San Francisco and Japan. The congregation sang "Throw Out the Life-Line."

The long train and boat trip gave the Axlings time to read about their unexpected field of labor. Fortunately, they had saved much of the Student Volunteer literature, in which they could search out pertinent data.

Study confirmed William's opinion. Japan was not a land of primitive savages. After being reopened to the world by Commodore Matthew Perry in 1854, Japan had made rapid progress by the selective adoption of Western ways. At first, Western powers imposed special influence treaties upon Japan, as they had upon China. These reduced Japan's sovereignty. This trend, however, was stopped by a rapidly rising group of young leaders who recognized that Japan's sovereignty could be maintained only by modernization. These men were mostly sons of the Samurai class, whose old position would have compared roughly with the knights of medieval Europe. Between 1860 and 1890, amazing progress was made against the old feudal structure by centralizing the government, building a modern military organization, and transforming the economic structure. Commissions were sent abroad to study methods and structures of Western society.

By 1901 Japan was well on the way to taking its place among the modern nations. The central government was supreme. The legal system had been modernized, the currency and banking structures overhauled, and an ambitious plan of education launched. In addition, modern medicine was being taught and practiced. The great powers were forced to take note when Japan defeated China in 1895 and took a leading part in quelling the Boxer Rebellion of 1900.

The Axlings' search for missionary data revealed many interesting facts: The Christianity introduced into the islands by the Roman Catholics in the sixteenth century had now been eradicated. In modern times, Jonathan Goble, a sailor with Commodore Perry, had returned in 1860 to establish a Free Baptist mission endeavor. Following the treaties of 1859, which regularized the position of foreigners in Japan, the Presbyterian, Episcopalian, and Dutch Reformed churches of the United States all appointed missionaries for Japan.

The Free Baptist effort was soon discontinued. In 1873 Dr. Nathan Brown established a continuing Baptist work in Yokohama. This amazing man, then sixty-six years of age, had already served in Burma and Assam. He learned the language quickly and began producing Christian literature. His was the first translation of the entire New Testament into the Japanese language.

Although, in 1901, relatively few Japanese were Christians, the church was well established. By 1900 there were 42,451 Protestant believers in Japan. The number of institutions was impressive. Nine colleges and universities, plus a number of theological training schools, schools to train for medical care, as well as industrial and lower-level schools were supported by the various missions. In 1900 the American Baptist Missionary Union was supporting fifty-six missionaries in Japan on nine stations. They had successfully organized twenty-seven churches, only one of which was self-supporting. The Baptists operated one theological school and had seven national ministers in the field. They also had several other schools operating at various levels.

The missionary picture, however, was not all bright. For ten years Protestantism had been declining. The reverses came partly because all of the missions had overreached themselves in the previous decade, and partly because the Japanese were reacting against the rapid spread of this Western religion. During the 1880's Japan had accepted, somewhat uncritically, all things Western, and in that decade the church had profited from this general acceptance. Many Japanese had turned to the missionaries to learn Western languages. By 1890, however, the well-to-do, at least, could learn these languages elsewhere. Now that this need was not so great, Buddhist anti-Christian activities were allowed, or even encouraged.

While disappointment continued, the Axlings felt a growing excitement as their ship approached Yokohama. Surely this land presented many challenges for dedicated young people. Maybe they would be instruments in the hands of God to get Christianity moving again.

Hearts beat faster as the ship moved into the harbor. Travel posters had pictured a glorious view of Mount Fuji in the background. Overcast skies, however, denied them this pleasure.

At last the boat docked. Many people were there to meet friends and business associates, but no one seemed to be looking for new missionaries. Nevertheless, in his usual unperturbed manner, William secured their luggage and made his way to the Baptist Mission office. After being admitted, he introduced himself:

"I am William Axling and this is my wife Lucinda."

"Oh."

"Did you expect us on a later boat?"

"Expect you for what?"

"I am William Axling, the newly appointed missionary for Japan."

"We were not expecting a new missionary." [*Pause.*]

"I do remember reading about a William Axling being appointed to Burma, but we have not received any new men."

After producing identification and a letter from Dr. Barbour, which Lucinda happened to have in her purse, the missionaries were finally convinced. They offered embarrassed apologies, and the humor of the situation overcame them all.

The next day the Axlings were introduced to the girls in the Soshin School. Long after, one of them remembered the new Americans as "young and beautiful." Mrs. Axling sang a song, "Moment by Moment."

After a brief stay in Yokohama, the Axlings moved to Sendai, in Northern Japan. About one hundred miles by rail north of Tokyo, this city of 800,000 residents was a missionary stronghold. Some thirty missionaries and wives, representing several denominations, resided there. The city also boasted three Christian colleges.

The Baptist work in the North was then under the direction of Ephraim H. Jones, an able veteran of seventeen years. His new recruits needed no coddling. They immediately applied themselves to language study and were almost too willing to turn a hand to any possible task. Shortly after the Axlings arrived, Mr. Jones mentioned William in a letter, describing a preaching place he had established on the road between town and some military barracks. In part, the letter read: "Brother Axling, who is not able to preach yet, has his part to go out in the street stopping the passers-by, and pushing a tract into their hands, kindly urging them to stay and listen for a while." Within a few months, William was touring with Mr. Jones the many outstations located in this northern district. Most young missionaries are enthusiastic, but the Axlings were unusually so. Mr. Jones was especially impressed by William's determination "to know the people, as well as their language."

William was delighted by these trips. Here was all the "darkness" he had longed for. Sendai was not only the last stronghold of Christian missions to the North. It was also near the edge of Japan's Westernization program. It did not take William long to realize that Japan's modernization was not yet completed. Many of the government programs were only on paper, and some, which were a reality, were often administered with slight concern for the human beings involved. Among the urban poor and in rural districts conditions were still quite primitive—most of the people were uneducated, and many were superstitious.

By the end of the first year William was enthusiastic about Japan. But Sendai was too tame! Why sit idle among so many missionaries when the need was to be found farther north? William's attention was fastened on Morioka. This city of thirty-five thousand had no foreign missionary. Years before, Baptists had begun a church there, but after Thomas Poate was forced to leave in 1890, a few converts had struggled, not very successfully, to keep the Christian witness alive. Mr. Jones, who stopped there occasionally, was of the opinion that "a resident missionary in the town could, . . . put new life into that large and important district."

As William and Lucinda discussed the frustrations of first-term inactivity, they convinced each other that they were ready for larger responsibility. So, on October 7, 1902, they composed a letter to Dr. Barbour. In it they described the need and referred to Mr. Jones' opinion. After painting a picture of the valiant, but almost overwhelmed, Christian fellowship in Morioka, Axling wrote: "My heart yearns to be able to put my shoulder against their shoulder and to be able to *keep* it there long enough to enable them to experience the sensation that they are not fighting their battles alone."

After detailing the feasibility of their plan for housing and finance, William gently reminded Dr. Barbour that the Axlings had changed their plan to fit into the board's need: "I am glad I am in Japan, but I shall never feel satisfied until I get in vital touch and within helping distance of this neglected part of our field."

Mr. Jones added his voice to the Axlings' in favor of transfer. Even though an itinerant Japanese evangelist, Mr. K. Taketa, gave some time to the church, a constant missionary presence might well tip the scales in the whole area.

The executive committee of the board faced a hard decision. Unquestionably, the arguments were sound, and the board did not want to deny the wish of the promising young missionary couple. The hard facts were, however, that William was needed to replace Mr. Jones on his upcoming furlough. Ideally, an experienced man should have taken Mr. Jones' place, and the Axlings should have been sent to Morioka. But no such experienced man existed.

Once again the Axlings swallowed their disappointment and applied themselves to the task at hand. Lucinda had become quite effective in the musical program and could assist in teaching the women and children. William now restricted his traveling in order to concentrate on language study.

Always lurking in the back of any new missionary's mind is the question of health. Will his body adjust to the radical change of climate, diet, and way of life? In the hot, humid summer of 1903, William became desperately ill. He was only a fair patient. He could voice his thanks to God for "all those long days laid aside with him." More honestly, he fretted to Lucinda: "Untold opportunities all around us and I am only holding down my pillow."

Morioka was now out of the question. No one would allow an ill man to go so far from a trained physician. Determined not to go home, William forced himself to carry many responsibilities in Sendai, while Mr. Jones traveled throughout the field. In February, William went to Tokyo for an operation which improved his condition considerably.

By spring the battle seemed won. Relieved, William wrote home of "one of the most desperate struggles of my life, namely the struggle to regain my health without going home. It has taken all of the grit, all of the courage, all of the will power that I could command."

Spring never seemed better to William than in 1904. As the ice and snow of northern Japan's severe winter began to melt, strength began to return to his weakened body. With health he knew he could serve. For about a year now he had been timidly practicing his Japanese within the Christian fellowship. After his first attempt he wrote to President Strong, of Rochester Theological Seminary: "It was not a very extended talk, however, and the three-year-old child in the front row could have done much better with only one-tenth of the agony."

In April, the Axlings were finally allowed to move to Morioka. The board removed its restrictions, and the local authorities allowed his settlement on the condition that he would offer English classes.

One would never have guessed that William had been ill. During the first year the church building was repaired and moved to a better location. A preaching station was opened in the heart of the city, two new centers were opened in outlying districts, and four members of the church left to attend the theological school in Yokohama. Axling's amazing ability to inspire the aid of the Japanese was proved by his raising all the money for the improvements from local sources, "a mighty stimulus toward self-support in the future."

Mrs. Axling was equally effective. She was soon supervising four Sunday schools as well as teaching English classes. One of her girls enrolled in the school at Sendai to prepare herself to become a Bible woman.

In September, 1904, William attempted his first public speaking to a non-Christian audience. He chose a street corner in the town of Tono for the first attempt. Though his ability was far short of the precise command of the language which he later attained, he came home exulting, "Though the chains are still on, I have been able to work them loose to some extent."

Part of Axling's success followed upon his ability to catch the attention of the total community. Moving the church made it more noticeable. He never did hide the fact that he had a camera, apparently the first one in the community. His bicycle, the first with rubber tires in the region, provided publicity as well as transportation. He was never bashful about approaching the leaders of the community. After all, he was an ambassador of the King with important news.

His publicity usually paid off. In Morioka, the principal of the police school asked him to teach the Bible to student policemen because the principal thought, "they ought to know what Christianity is and what it teaches."

Axling's fame also increased the size and quality of his English classes. Many of his students were teachers from the local normal and commercial schools. Others were from prominent families. Since almost all were non-Christian, William considered this an evangelistic opportunity.

Whenever William left Morioka and journeyed through the countryside or visited the smaller villages, his reception was sharply different. The old fear of a foreigner, still strong, fed by new stories of Western imperialism, made this mild young man in their midst seem dangerous and subversive. Buddhist priests further stirred up the people. Frequently rowdy young men, fortified with *saki*, broke up meetings. Children and sometimes adults occasionally pelted William and Japanese Christians with stones. William was reminded of the stories his father had told him of Swedish persecution.

Encouragements in Morioka hardly offset the disappointments in the field. Frantically William sought a means to break through. How could he shake off the devil's mask which the imagination of his hearers seemed to place over his face? As an anxious first-termer, he feared any failure. Could he make it? Was he worthy of the investment of Christians at home?

One cold winter night the crisis came and passed. All day long he had tramped through the snow and cold. Two attempts at holding meetings had ended in failure. An ugly crowd had almost turned into a dangerous mob. Late that night he turned into a small Japanese inn, paid his fee, and prepared for bed. As he lay down upon the straw floor and drew the thin quilt over him, despair gripped his soul. How could he sleep on the hard floor with insufficient cover to keep him warm? "Oh God," he cried, "if I cannot rest in a local inn, how shall I continue my work?" For a long time he lay struggling with his feeling. Hot tears rolled down his cold cheeks. Even prayer seemed impossible. Suddenly, however, the words of his favorite hymn, "Nearer, My God, to Thee," began to move slowly through his mind. Then he remembered the story of Jacob, who had a vision of heaven's nearness as he rested his head upon a stone pillow. Slowly the power of reassuring prayer returned, and quiet sleep followed.

Shortly after this experience two unexpected events began to melt the stubborn opposition. The first was the Russo-Japanese War.

The steady rise of Japan toward being a world power made an eventual clash with Western interests in the Far East inevitable. The first came with Russia. England, all too happy to have Russia's eastward expansion checked, sided with Japan and effectively isolated Russia from all possible allies. In February, 1904, Japan attacked Russia. In quick succession she won several land and sea battles. Russia, far from defeated, was unwilling to pursue an unpopular war at a time when she was threatened by internal revolution. Japan, while seemingly victorious, had severely strained her meager resources. Both countries then gladly accepted President Theodore Roosevelt's offer to mediate a peaceful settlement. This was accomplished in September, 1905.

The war definitely established Japan as a world power. For the first time since the Middle Ages an Eastern nation had, by force of arms, forced a Western nation to accept terms. The first modern nation in Asia had been born.

But how did the war help Axling? First, the success of this adventure vindicated the Westernizers in Japan. If Western tools could bring success, maybe Western ideas should be entertained.

Second, most Protestant missionaries were from America or Britain, countries which had supported Japan. The missionaries themselves were almost improperly sympathetic with the Japanese effort. A Baptist, C. W. Hill, was typical. He supported the war because, "although Japan's people are still largely non-Christian, her national ideals and policies are based on Christian principles, and her development and leadership will without doubt conform to the best ideals of Christian civilization."

Third, during the years of military buildup the missionaries had given a considerable amount of attention to converting military personnel. They were successful not only with enlisted men but also with several officers, such as Rear Admiral Uriu. This fact was widely publicized.

Finally, the behavior of the Japanese Christians enhanced the Christian image. They were active in their expressions of loyalty, and outstanding in their bravery on the battlefield. At home they outdid all others in caring for sick and wounded soldiers. With the active help of missionaries, they also cared for soldiers' families and needy civilians who were being overlooked by an overtaxed government.

The Emperor responded by making the first public recognition of the presence of Christians in the nation. Following his lead, other government officials took many occasions to praise the Christian contribution. The common people took note both of their leaders' statements and of the acts of mercy performed by the "Jesus People."

Axling found difficulty in seeing anything good in war. Yet, as he mingled with the people and noted their changing attitudes, he concluded that "God is again going to make the wrath of man to praise Him, and that this present war is going to mean more for the spread of Christianity in Japan than any other historical event since the introduction of Christianity into the empire."

The second event which melted opposition and expanded Axling's missionary opportunity was another of those ambiguous circumstances by which Christianity so often moves forward. The intense human suffering of the famine which gripped northern Japan in the winter of 1905-1906 certainly was not God's will. Nevertheless, Christianity was advanced and William Axling learned many valuable lessons through this tragedy.

No stranger to crop failure and hardship, he was appalled by what he saw. Day after day he went out to do what he could. Night after night he returned home sick and bewildered. Lucinda worried as her still physically weak husband turned away from her carefully-prepared meals, saying, "I can't eat; I feel wicked. You have no idea the pictures that rise to my mind every time I raise my fork to my mouth."

William joined with other missionaries in the area to do what could be done. All facilities were open to provide shelter. Each missionary besieged his home agency with pleas for help. Axling led in the formation of the Foreign Committee on Relief, which sent a more general appeal to the American people for help.

This latter appeal came to the attention of President Theodore Roosevelt. On investigation, he discovered that the Japanese Government was very desirous of not appearing weak before the world. Finally, a carefully worded statement was issued by the President, urging the American people "to help from their abundance their suffering fellow man of the great and friendly nation of Japan." It was discreetly mentioned that Japan was undergoing "a calamity such as may occasionally befall any country."

In response, large sums were contributed through the Red Cross and directly to the Foreign Committee on Relief. Axling and his associates showed great wisdom, as well as compassion, in distributing these funds. In so doing they worked closely with many government agencies. As a result, a bond of mutual confidence and respect was established. Always grateful, Axling wrote: "The closer I get to the officers of this prefecture and their methods, the greater grows my wonder and admiration for the complete records and intimate knowledge which they have of the people they have under their official care."

The authorities were amazed at the unselfish interest of these foreigners, and their eyes were opened to the depth of human suffering, which was sometimes hidden from their official eyes. Together they worked out an informal partnership, which not only helped in that crisis but also afforded opportunity for Axling to learn methods which he employed effectively throughout his later ministry.

William's fertile mind devised means of assistance which went beyond direct relief. One work project emerged from a conversation with the governor of Iwate Prefecture. Axling had often noted the old castle, with its neglected grounds, which stood in the middle of Morioka. If the Nambu family could be persuaded to donate this center of their ancient feudal glory, and if the government would provide some funds, a beautiful park could be built. The immediate benefit would be much-needed employment. After negotiations, William acquired some American relief money, and the park was built.

By the time the famine was over, very little active opposition to the Christian message remained. Officials were friendly, the educated classes were more tolerant, and the common people were less suspicious and distrustful of Christianity.

William took special satisfaction in the fact that "it silenced the outcry of the Japanese socialists, that Christianity cares for only the soul of men, and does nothing to help them in their struggle for food."

Nearing the end of their fifth year in the field, William and Lucinda Axling were beginning to lose their first-term jitters. They knew that they could communicate the Christian message to the Japanese. They were gaining confidence that their brand of simple evangelical faith and positive Christian action would work.

Although Lucinda had not been as widely involved in the

famine relief as her husband, she had discovered her own ways of showing the relevance of the gospel. She said: "I decided that if they were not interested in my work, I would interest myself in theirs. One means of doing this was the establishment of a cooking class, which reached about a dozen girls not before touched by Christian influence."

Often Western cooking seemed as strange as the gospel. One problem was to encourage the girls to stir the cream back into the milk, rather than skim off "that nasty yellow stuff." Modern anticholesterol advocates probably would agree with the girls.

In spite of growing confidence, one agonizing problem remained—health. Though William was usually able to keep about his work, many relapses followed his first illness. The famine was too much. While carrying all the extra work of relief, he insisted on increasing his evangelistic ministry in order to take advantage of improving climate. But the work was not all. William's sensitive soul was crushed by the mass of human suffering. His frustration was increased by what he described to Dr. Strong as the "downpull" of a heathen culture and a very difficult language.

As fall approached in 1906, William was trembling on the verge of complete physical and nervous collapse. With both hands, however, he clung to the assurance he had received that night in the rural inn. Surely God was still near. Finally, however, his doctor insisted, "Bill, I am sending you home; you cannot wait for your normal furlough. It is your only chance to continue in Japan."

On November 17, 1906, the Axlings sailed for home. As Japan disappeared over the horizon, William turned to Lucinda and said, simply, "God will bring us back."

4. NEW POSSIBILITIES

EVEN THE PACIFIC OCEAN had enlisted in a conspiracy against William Axling. If ever he needed a quiet, therapeutic cruise, it was in 1906. Instead, the roughest crossing of his long career intensified his already acute suffering.

It could have taken an intrepid prophet, indeed, to walk up to that broken little man sailing back to the United States and declare, "William Axling! The missionary statesman of Japan!"

His internal struggle was intense. Was he finished at thirty-three years of age? Thirty-three! If his life was ever to count, he *must* go forward now. Maybe he should settle for a quiet pastorate in America. But had not his success in Japan confirmed his call as a missionary? Certainly his suffering was slight beside what he had observed the past winter. But what good was a man who spent half his time in bed? Had he misread the vision that night in the country inn? Was it not enough that he had tried, and now he should go home and accept a less demanding task? Oh, if the doctors could only find some specific ailment which could then be treated and cured.

When William landed in San Francisco it took all his strength to grasp a ragged corner of reality. He meekly followed Lucinda's decision to accept the invitation of Mrs. Anna Johnson to spend some time at her home.

In the quiet seclusion of the Johnson ranch near Chatsworth, California, William began to find stability. Improvement still eluded his grasp, but the slide toward disintegration was stayed. As he began to accept, at least for the moment, the impossibility of action, he turned seriously to that "blessed service" of intercessory prayer. Perhaps for the first time, Japan and Christian work there meant more to him than anything else in all the world.

A physician in Chatsworth, unable to find any organic illness, assured William that he would be able to return to the field within a year. Hope returned, but not strength.

After several months with Mrs. Johnson, the Axlings decided to visit Gothenburg. Partly the trip was a discouraging experiment, against the doctor's advice, to test William's strength.

Now that a year had passed with no significant improvement, William agreed to enter a sanitarium at Battle Creek, Michigan. This interesting institution had been reorganized by Dr. John Harvey Kellogg, brother of the cornflakes promoter, especially to treat cases like William's. In 1907 doctors were using a combination of rest, exercise, and diet, along with baths and mechanical and electrical devices for massage and stimulation.

Soon William began to improve. Within three months he was able to walk two or three miles a day, "with less fatigue than that many blocks formerly caused."

Walking was not the only exercise for which William used his returning strength. Before anyone quite knew how it had happened, he was holding Christian services for patients and personnel. He also delivered an address on conditions in Japan to the students of the Seventh Day Adventist medical college.

The mission board needed no medical report to know that William was recovering. A stream of letters asking for a return sailing date, and filled with ideas for creative new forms of ministry, spoke eloquently.

As returning health made sustained thought possible, William spent hours searching for improved ways to advance the mission cause in Japan. Again and again the example of the institutional church returned to his mind. Progressive churchmen in America were developing these enterprises to meet the needs of America's growing inner-city problems. The idea was to use the church as a complete social center, which could provide education, practical training, and medical services seven days a week.

William, however, was too wise to think of transplanting the American institutional church to Japan. What he wanted was a thoughtful adaptation of many of its features. Why could not the church be used many hours each day of the week? Does evangelism need to wait for Sunday? How could one care for the needs of new converts in a non-Christian land with the limited program then being carried on? Would not evangelism be more effective if it rested on the base of Christian service to the needs of men? He vividly remembered the response to the gospel which had followed famine relief in northern Japan.

After much thought, Axling described his ideas "in a nutshell" to Dr. Barbour:

> Time is too precious and the opportunities are too golden for churches out there, (or here for that matter) to be in the harness only one day in the week. The work of proclaiming the gospel to the unsaved should be constantly going on, and our churches and converts and inquirers should have a place where they can go at any time that will be thoroughly Christian in its atmosphere, a help to their Christian experience, and an object lesson in Christian service.

William's thinking coincided with a current concern of the American Baptist mission in Japan. At the time, Baptists in Tokyo were facing many urgent problems. Large numbers of Baptist converts from outlying provinces were flocking to Tokyo as students and workers. The poorly equipped Tokyo Baptist churches were unable to keep the predominantly young, new converts from drifting away, either to other denominations or even from the Christian cause. A mission conference held in Tokyo decided upon the advisability of constructing a well-equipped and strategically located building which would serve as a conference center, provide for social events, and function as an evangelistic station.

Construction of what was to be known as the Central Tabernacle Building began in the fall of 1907. Beyond general objectives which they hoped to accomplish, apparently no one had a very clear idea as to how the new structure was to be operated. Or, perhaps more accurately, there were several plans of operation at least half formed in the minds of different persons.

While in Japan attending the mission conference, Dr. Barbour shared the interest and concerns of William Axling and urged his appointment as director of the new venture. Those who knew the record of Axling's first term joined in the recommendation.

As the signs of spring began to appear in 1908, William was recovering his old spirit. While others still had reservations, he was sure that he would return to Japan. A less-convinced mission board gave guarded assurance. Meanwhile, the happy couple were reunited through the generosity of his sister, Amanda, now Mrs. Ernest Bihl, who took the Axlings into her home near Chicago. Here the careful program of rest, exercise, and diet continued to work its healing wonders.

Expecting to get their new assignment at any moment, the Axlings went to Gothenburg in the fall. How pleasant was this return to the scene of William's childhood! The confidence he had gained by his first-term experience was no longer clouded by bad health. He spent hours walking about the town and out to the rolling hills by the Platte. At many familiar spots he paused and reminisced about boyhood struggles and the marvels of God's goodness.

Those days were made especially sweet by a reunited family. While still critical of an educated clergy, Nils now accepted his son and was proud of his distant mission. The older man had softened considerably. While William was in Japan, a delegation from Oakland had made its way to Gothenburg to apologize to Nils and invite him back into fellowship with the Swedish Baptist Church. Nils accepted the apology, but remained aloof from the denomination.

Lucinda, rather than William, faced a severe struggle on this visit. By this time it was evident that her desire for a child was not likely to be fulfilled. Several times she had suggested adoption. Nils was on her side. While they were staying in Gothenburg, he contrived to let Lucinda care for a baby from the orphanage which he had helped to found in Holdridge, Nebraska.

William, apparently, vetoed the adoption. Whether his uncertain health, or his sense of dedication to the missionary task, or some combination of reasons prevailed, is not known. At any rate, childlessness was one of the burdens Lucinda agreed to bear.

In mid-November the word came: "That Rev. and Mrs. Axling be designated to carry on the general work centering in the Tabernacle in cooperation with one or more Japanese workers."

They were to be residents of Tokyo! William would have the opportunity to try out his new ideas. Lucinda swallowed her disappointment and sent the baby back.

William was fully conscious of the strategic importance of Tokyo. Always sensitive to world events, he knew that Japan had been moving rapidly forward in its international status. During the two years he had been gone, Japan had become a party to important agreements with France, Russia, and the United States. He knew Japan's passionate determination to fulfill these agreements. He also understood how fast Japan must develop in order to maintain her progressive image. The inevitable drive to bring reality up to the image would center in Tokyo. The fortunes of Japan would be determined by the decisions made there and by the youth trained in that city—and he would be there!

On December 1, 1908, the Axlings headed back to Japan and the exciting new possibilities.

As William devoured every scrap of information about conditions in Japan, he learned that Christian work was prospering. Only the shabby treatment of Japanese nationals in the United States had raised a major obstacle. In October, 1906, the San Francisco Board of Education had ordered Japanese, Chinese, and Korean children to attend separate Oriental schools. The Japanese, naturally proud of their rapidly rising world status, objected.

President Theodore Roosevelt, with characteristic brusqueness, threatened to send federal troops into California. In a calmer mood he persuaded the school board to rescind its action in return for a promise to seek a limitation of immigration. The result was the so-called Gentlemen's Agreement which checked the flow of Japanese laborers into the United States. Only parents, wives, or children of those already resident could enter. Since Japan was making an all-out effort to build up her industrial and military strength, she welcomed restrictions which would keep her people home. Nevertheless, Japanese people deeply resented the racial implications of the whole affair. This resentment was sometimes taken out on missionaries.

Such damaging prejudice on the part of their countrymen only intensified the Axlings' resolve to fashion such an example of Christian love and compassion that the Japanese could understand the gospel.

Their work was waiting for them. The Tabernacle, which had been dedicated September 20, was already operating. Mr. C. H. D. Fisher, the man who had supervised construction, was giving general supervision along with his regular duties. Mr. Yoshikawa, a Japanese evangelist, was the only full-time staff member.

William liked the building at once. Its floor plan was a trapezoid measuring fifty-four feet across the front and extending back ninety-six feet to a width of thirty-six feet in the back. In the front, easily accessible from the street, was an evangelistic room designed for nightly meetings. Several rooms of various sizes lent themselves to social gatherings, lectures, and club meetings. A number of these were equipped with sliding or folding doors opening into an auditorium, which, when thus expanded, would accommodate 1,200 people. At the rear of the lot was a parsonage for a Japanese worker.

First, the Axlings looked for an available Japanese house in the neighborhood. They secured one at Ura 6 Surugadai-Cho. As they moved in, they felt that they truly were residents of Tokyo.

Putting the Tabernacle building to work was the major task of William's second term. While crossing the Pacific he had practically memorized the policy statement drawn up by the Japan Conference and sent to him with his appointment. He felt that the core of the matter was stated in Resolution No. III: "That arrangements be made for aggressive Christian effort through evangelistic services, evening classes, social efforts of suitable nature, etc., under the direction of a missionary and a Japanese evangelist in consultation with the Board of Control." How anxious he was to put the flesh of his ideas on the bones of that directive!

Within a short time William also discovered inherent difficulties. Some of these he shared with Lucinda.

"Loue, not everyone is going to agree with our work."

"What do you mean, Bill?"

"Some expect the Tabernacle to become a permanent Billy Sunday revival tent. Others want us to spend most of our time in social service."

"I haven't mentioned it before, Bill," offered Lucinda, "but I get the feeling that many at the mission office expect us to run a conference center for the promotion of everyone else's program."

"I'm sure you are right," chuckled William.

"What will we do? We can't please everyone."

"We will do our best to accomplish in the Tabernacle what we think Christ would do."

To others William revealed none of his misgivings. Everywhere he spoke of "the providential leadings that have brought this enterprise into being and have been so numerous and unmistakable that this fact is written large in luminous letters of light."

Without hesitation the Axlings went out to prove this interpretation to be true.

Most urgent and demanding greatest immediate attention was program development. Regular evangelistic services were already in progress. These Axling expanded. As a pattern developed every other month a well-advertised evangelistic campaign lasting about a week was held in the large auditorium. Whenever possible, well-known speakers such as Seimatso Kimura, often called the Japanese Moody, were featured at these meetings. The objective was to attract persons who had never before heard a Christian message.

Every night, except when a campaign was in progress, briefer evangelistic services were held in the smaller room set aside for that purpose. Occasionally, first-timers would stop in at these meetings, but they usually attracted persons who had heard but had not yet decided. William, or one of the staff, usually conducted these meetings.

By 1912 Axling had reinforced the evangelistic program by a class for inquirers who wanted to make a more serious study of the faith. Whenever possible he taught this group himself.

Combined, these three approaches constituted a comprehensive and continuing program of direct evangelism. But direct evangelism was not enough. In spite of the best efforts of Axling and his staff, thousands streamed by the Tabernacle unaware and unconcerned. There was no persecution as in the North— only a vast sea of indifference.

In an attempt to penetrate this indifference, as well as to offer needed services, the Axlings zealously expanded the Tabernacle program. A reading room was opened. A social room was made available to church and community groups. Of great importance was an evening school, which offered courses for those who worked during the day. Mr. H. B. Benninghoff, from Waseda University, served as principal. He and William persuaded all available Baptist personnel in the area to take turns offering courses.

Quite early, a Saturday night series became a fixture. Outstanding men from all walks of life were invited to speak. Usually they were successful lay Christians who could exhibit the reality of Christian faith in secular occupations. William boasted: "These messages have covered a scope as wide as the reach of Christianity itself." Probably no other Tabernacle program was as effective in reaching the student population, or in advertising the work of the Tabernacle to prominent Japanese.

An unsuccessful attempt was made to secure a residence hall which, under the sponsorship of the Tabernacle, would have provided a sort of YMCA for young men coming to the city. Though no building was found, the effort gave William a "deep insight into the conditions in which multitudes are compelled to live." Many youths, after laboring long hours in school or factory, returned to a five-by-eight room. The only escape was one of the "ten thousand brilliantly lit places of sin where there is life and action and music and merriment." William soon discovered that these places conspired to break down "the moral fiber of many a young man isolated among Tokyo's two million people."

William chose the only immediate remedy at hand—an extensive expansion of the social activities at the Tabernacle. Here young people could come for healthy conversation and amusement. Loneliness was chased away, and the monotony which drove many to sin was relieved.

Lucinda worked as hard as William. Her efforts were aimed primarily toward the needs of women and children. Young women as well as young men were flocking to Tokyo. Lucinda, aided by Japanese Bible women, reached out through several Bible classes, an afternoon school for homemakers, and systematic neighborhood visitation. A special group met to discuss the problems of young single women in the big city. An afternoon was given to a children's club for the "hundreds of children whose only playground is the street and for whose souls no one seems to care." After great difficulty a permit was secured to open a kindergarten-nursery for the children of young working mothers. When this venture opened in 1912, it was immediately faced with a long waiting list. Its capacity of fifty-six was far too small.

Directing the expanding activities of the Tabernacle along

with building and supervising staff was only one aspect of William's work. The original directive under which he operated suggested the possibility of inviting a church to use the facilities of the Tabernacle. After surveying the situation, William agreed. At that time, the five hundred Baptist Christians in Tokyo were divided among seven poorly equipped churches. Not only could the Tabernacle provide a superior building for a church, but William hoped to keep his work at the Tabernacle church-centered.

Helped by William's patient negotiations, the First Baptist Church and the Independent Baptist Church united to form the Central Baptist Church. The resulting 109 members of the new church made a good choice in calling Rev. Nakajima as pastor. The combined strength of the two congregations, plus the better facilities and location, achieved immediate success. Attendance, which ran between 100 and 125 for the first year, was higher than that of any other Baptist church in Tokyo.

The initiation of a program and the establishment of a new church proved to be far easier than the development of administrative policy. Many factors were involved. All missionary endeavors suffer from multiple control—the home board, the field missionaries, the national church, and the local institution. The Tabernacle as a new venture accentuated the problem. The separate organizations of the church and the Tabernacle compounded it.

Axling, a strong advocate of Japanese direction of the work, believed that his fellow missionaries were unwilling to yield their control. Many a night he fretted to Lucinda: "We cannot expect a highly civilized and very sensitive people like the Japanese to put their best into an enterprise run by foreigners. Didn't we experience that in the North? Remember how they responded as soon as we appointed a consulting committee and took them seriously into the work? Even if it doesn't work well at once, how can we hope to build a church here unless we give the Japanese leadership experience?"

Although Lucinda fully agreed with her husband's view on this subject, her response in these conversations was largely of the soothing "Yes, dear" variety.

Control of the Tabernacle was placed in a board of control made up of three missionaries elected by the Japan Missionary Conference, three Japanese elected by the Japanese Convention, and the resident missionary. This was a fine arrangement, except that the Missionary Conference insisted that the board had jurisdiction of the physical plant only. The conference took the view that the program was the sole responsibility of the missionary, who should report only to his fellow missionaries and to the home board.

William's objections seemed to fall on deaf ears. He told how he had opened even the financial records to his Japanese Consulting Committee in the North. He argued that cooperation could be expected only when all "no-trespass signs were taken down" and "both parties have as full a knowledge as possible about the facts."

As he grew bolder he chided older missionaries: "'You know that the time is long past in Japan for any institution to be centered around a missionary, or a group of missionaries. Moreover, in the Christian church in Japan today you can find both in the pew and in the pulpit men who are our peers in scholarship, consecration, and devotion."

When traditionalists asked why he had accepted his position if he did not agree with the policy, he retorted that he assumed the board of control would be just that. Whenever anyone pressed too hard, he would pull out his battered copy of the October, 1905, issue of the *Baptist Missionary Magazine* and say: "My position has always been clear. This is what I wrote early in my career: 'that the native Christians should furnish the leaders and take the leadership of Christian work is the ideal in all lands. In Japan, moreover, it is the actual and one of the inevitable features of effective work. It is inevitable because Japan will not tolerate and does not need foreign leadership.'"

All of these arguments were also written to the home board, along with this assurance, which shows that Axling was not completely free of a sense of Western superiority!

And yet, lest I be misunderstood, let me say this, that there is still great need for the missionary and missionary work in Japan. There is preeminently a need for a tactful, considerate, consecrated missionary at the heart and center of every Christian enterprise and institution in Japan. The contribution which he can make is still an absolute necessity in the work of evangelizing this empire.

To a large degree, Axling got his way and the supervision of the total work was given over to the board of control. With William on their side, the three Japanese members carried the greatest weight. According to William, the change "had the effect of causing the Japanese to rally around the Tabernacle and its work." Yet the ensuing policy was not always wise. For instance, the board failed to insure the building, with the result that everything was lost in the 1913 fire.

Equally difficult was the relationship between the Tabernacle and the Central Baptist Church. In this case William could not blame the policy of mission versus national church.

There was, however, another built-in conflict of interest. On the one hand, the churches which combined forces to move into the Tabernacle apparently looked upon their decision as a shrewd deal whereby their expenses could be cut and more missionary money would become available. On the other hand, however, one reason the missionaries desired a church in the building was to help defray expenses.

Nothing wearied Axling more than these administrative squabbles. Yet few affairs demanded more of his time. He always erred by placing too much confidence in expected good will, rather than in strict administrative principles. When he proposed a joint administration, the conference objected on the ground that the church was not ready for equal partnership. They also feared that the Tabernacle might be reduced to an adjunct of Central Baptist Church, rather than continuing to serve the denomination as a whole.

In this case Axling could not wait for the slow process of negotiation. As the church was not paying its bills, he recognized and discouraged "the temptation to lean upon the Tabernacle." Then, in the emergency he drew up a preliminary plan which recognized two separate institutions and laid down rules for their operation. Both parties accepted definite budgetary goals. After the plan was in effect, Axling could report with much relief: "The relationship between the Tabernacle and the Central Church is most harmonious at the present time."

Living in Tokyo brought its expected opportunities. During his first term in the city his personal involvement was less extensive than he later enjoyed, but he was where the action was. The 1911 Three Religions Conference took place in Tokyo. Axling, like others, was startled when Christianity replaced Confucianism and took its place with Shintoism and Buddhism as one of the informally recognized religions of Japan. He felt the deep shock when Emperor Meiji the Great died in 1912. The struggle between old conservatives and a small group of liberals, ranging from antichristian to socialists, was going on around him.

From the very beginning Axling was more than an observer. In spite of occasional differences of opinion, his Baptist brethren recognized his practical wisdom, his enormous capacity for work, and his effectiveness as a team man. As a result, they began placing him on many boards and committees. Most important in this period was his chairmanship of a joint board formed to unify Baptist theological education in Japan. Baptist work in Japan, as in America, was divided between that supported by what we now call the American Baptist Convention and the Southern Baptist Convention. The American Baptists had a seminary in Yokohama and the Southern Baptists had one in Fukuoka. The joint board was charged with the responsibility, first, of combining these schools and, second, of exploring the possibilities of developing a great Christian university with a department of theology.

The possibility of eventual merger of all Baptist work in Japan excited Axling's imagination. On every possible occasion he proclaimed "the absolute need for all Baptist workers—foreign and Japanese—to look upon the field as one and work together, with one mind and one heart." His exhortations rang from pulpit and printed page: "Let the distinctions of North and South be sunk in the deepest depths of oblivion, and let us, as a united force, work together for the extension of Christ's kingdom from Kyushu to Hokkaido."

Whenever anyone asked him how the project was going, Axling replied, "Everyone feels that this marks the beginning of an era of great and better things for our Baptist work in the Empire."

In the fall of 1910 the new institution opened in Tokyo, with twenty-five students. Dr. W. B. Parshley, who had been president at Yokohama, became president of the new institution. Dr. Yugoro Chiba, president of the Southern Baptist institution, became dean. Of the eight faculty members, four of whom were missionaries and four Japanese, only one was a Southern Baptist. Even Dr. Chiba had his strongest affiliations with the American Baptist Convention.

Despite the heroic efforts of Axling and others, however, the venture did not succeed. Missionaries of the American Baptist Foreign Mission Society and most of the Japanese wanted to push forward toward further union in educational enterprises with other Christian institutions. The missionaries of the Southern Baptist Convention, while not opposed in principle, wanted to be sure where these trends would lead.

Then, too, Tokyo was not well located for the Southern Baptists. By comity agreements they labored in southern Japan. After a trip to the South, William acknowledged that he had not before realized "the tremendous sacrifice which our Southern friends have made" in moving their theological education to Tokyo. He was sure that they would gain in the long run by the unified effort, but realized "the largeness of vision" which they would need.

Neither side had quite enough vision. By 1918, union effort was discontinued by mutual agreement. Axling remained chairman of the board of the American Baptist school.

Probably nothing ever gave Axling more pleasure than speaking. His style was in the older oratorical tradition, with its high-blown phrases and frequent alliterations. A powerful voice, backed by a persuasive personality, moved audiences long after his style became obsolete. As he perfected his Japanese, he became a popular preacher and lecturer.

Among Axling's mounting responsibilities was that of field mission treasurer. This office brought him into all financial discussions and made him responsible for several administrative decisions. His natural frugality was intensified by the necessity of spreading the always-too-few missionary dollars over the always-too-many demands. His Japanese colleagues, who usually viewed him as an ally, considered him unnecessarily parsimonious.

One of his duties was to work out a budget for the student dormitory at the Baptist Seminary in Tokyo. The students presented a list of needs through their representatives, one of whom was K. T. Shiraishi. Every time he met with Axling he was solemnly informed that the mission budget had been tightened and that economies must be made. The student name for Axling became "Stingy Sensaei."

Eight years later, Mr. Shiraishi was a self-supporting student at Hartford Theological Seminary in Connecticut. Shortly after his arrival, an unexplained monthly check began arriving from the American Baptist Foreign Mission Society. Only later did he learn that his unknown benefactor was William Axling. Mr. Shiraishi then discovered Axling's "true personality." "For he has made very careful use of missionary money, but he is very generous with his own money."

Had the nationals only known it, William had two faces where missionary money was concerned. Always against waste, either personal or institutional, he was deeply convinced that the mission must spend much more money if it ever hoped to accomplish its purpose. In a letter to Dr. Barbour, pleading that the executive committee authorize a large short-run expenditure of money to get the Tokyo Baptist churches off the ground, he named churches and amounts needed. The center of his argument was:

> For a year and a half I have been studying our own and the work of other denominations here in Tokyo. I find that where we have put in ten dollars other denominations have put in thousands of dollars. Especially is this true when it comes to equipment. As far as I have been able to learn, without exception, every church in Tokyo that is today a strong, self-supporting church is so because in the beginning it was helped to get on its feet in the erection of an attractive, adequate building. Every church that has not been helped in this way is just where our churches are—putting up a tremendous fight to keep from dying out. . . . Unless we generously help our churches in the matter of equipment they will be in ten years just what they are today.

Quite likely the executive committee wished to respond to Axling's suggestion. Unfortunately, however, strong denominational pressure to establish new churches and to show immediate evangelistic results forced the spending of the meager funds available as they were doing. As a result, the Baptist work in Japan continued to be very widespread and usually rather thin, lacking firm indigenous support.

By 1910, Axling was in frequent demand as a speaker at Bible conferences and conventions. Not only Baptists, but other denominations, interdenominational groups, the YMCA, and secular organizations called upon him.

Best of all was the "unspeakable privilege" of evangelistic preaching. His first conspicuous success as a campaigner came during a cooperative evangelistic effort which attempted to enlist every Baptist church in the Japanese Empire. William was chairman of the committee and the evangelist for the Southern Baptists in the Lieu Chiu islands.

A mass movement erupted. To the invitation to follow Christ, whole families and whole neighborhoods responded. All sixteen members of one family became Christians. The apparent ease with which people turned to Christianity caused William to question their sincerity until he mingled with them in their homes and in the market places. There he was convinced by "a light in their faces which shines not on land or sea, a light absent from the faces of their neighbors and friends."

The most dramatic event of the second term was the terrible fire which destroyed the Tabernacle, on February 20, 1913. This fire was a part of what it meant to live in crowded Tokyo.

The Axlings were awakened at 1:30 A.M. by the clanging of the fire bells. As they ventured out into the cold night air, the frantic, pushing crowd warned them that they faced no ordinary fire. As they made their way to Misaki-Cho, their eyes fell first on a mass of flames where the Salvation Army Student Hostel stood across the street from the Tabernacle. The Tabernacle was still untouched. For a few moments they hoped. Then the fierce wind changed, blowing the full force of the heat from surrounding fires against the front of the building. Almost at once "spurts of smoke burst from under the hot tiles of the roof." The fire department was busy elsewhere. Within a half-hour the building was gutted.

Unable to save anything from the Tabernacle, the Axlings retired to the comparative safety of the Sarah L. Curtis home, one block south of their own house. There from the third floor they helplessly watched the carnage. Hundreds of homes were all burning at once. A solid wall of flame pushed a wave of frightened, helpless humanity before it. Lucinda was overcome by the grandeur of such a calamity. Why do beauty and tragedy seem so close?

Another change in wind direction saved the Axlings' home and finally made possible the containment of the fire.

While the embers were still hot, people began returning. Temporary huts and shacks served for homes and shops, and within a few months housing in the area was better than before.

However, at the time when the Tabernacle was most needed, it was destroyed. A crude shack placed on the premises served inadequately. Rented facilities were no better. William was determined to rebuild the Tabernacle so that it would be able to stand in the face of any disaster.

While the rest of the community was rebuilding, William threw his energies into planning for a new and better building. Characteristically, he had spoken in glowing terms of the old building. Actually, however, experience had shown many weaknesses. Not only should a new Tabernacle be fireproof, but it should have a more effective design as well.

All of William's promotional abilities came to the fore. Articles, speeches, letters, and conversations were all employed to carry the message that "the Tabernacle is the only church in this city of two million people that is trying to meet the needs of people along modern lines of church work with a day and night program throughout the week." Obviously, such an enterprise should be continued and expanded.

Astutely William marshaled the testimony of other Christian groups to his cause. As chairman of a commission on city churches, preparing for the forthcoming regional conference set up by the Continuation Committee of the World Missionary Conference of Edinburgh, in 1910, William had been directing a survey to determine urban needs in Japan. He let it be known that he had discovered that many of the old and experienced missionaries in the larger cities of the Empire were convinced that work such as the Tabernacle was doing was just what was needed to meet adequately the situation in their respective cities.

While waiting for authorization and funds to rebuild, the board of control decided to construct a rough lumber-and-galvanized-metal shack measuring twenty-four by forty-two feet. In this facility Axling continued on a limited scale the night school, kindergarten, children's clubs, nightly evangelistic meetings, and Sunday school. The afternoon school for young women was held in the Axling home.

Gradually, all parties concerned became committed to the idea of an adequate building, and machinery was set in motion to raise money, both in Japan and in America. Part of the burden was lifted when the Alumni Association of the Divinity School of the University of Chicago accepted a pledge for $30,000.

Early in 1914 William's health was again in danger of collapsing. The horror of the fire, the strain of keeping the Tabernacle program going under difficult circumstances, the endless committee meetings for the seminary and for fund-raising, the heavy administrative load, and frequent speaking engagements became too much. William began to complain that under the pressure of so many responsibilities no man can do his best work. He himself could have relieved some of the load by learning to say "No!"

This time Axling was able to overcome his bodily weakness. He forced himself to return to the routine of rest, exercise, and diet that he had learned at Battle Creek. As he put it, "With a tightening of the grip on the will and some bottles of Sanatogen," he came through.

Construction began on the building in the summer of 1914, and as soon as the work was progressing satisfactorily the board decided that the Axlings should take their furlough. Thus their third term could begin with the opening of the new building.

So, in December, 1914, the Axlings started home for a well-earned rest. This time a calm Pacific reflected their contented mood.

5. THE GOLDEN YEARS

"Loue, listen to this!"

The words broke into Lucinda's daydream as she gazed out over the rolling Pacific. She had spent most of the second day of their journey back to Japan in the fall of 1915 just thinking about what had happened in their lives during the last term in Japan and what might lie ahead of them.

"What is it, Will?"

"I have been reading Dr. Rauschenbusch's *Christianity and the Social Crisis*. He published it only a few years after I left seminary, and it is exactly the kind of thing he used to say in class. Listen to this:

> The fundamental contribution of every man is the change of his own personality. We must repent of the sins of existing society, cast off the spell of the lies protecting our social wrongs, have faith in a higher social order, and realize in ourselves a new type of Christian manhood which seeks to overcome the evil in the present world, not by withdrawing from the world, but by revolutionizing it."

"How well he expresses it!" exclaimed Lucinda.

"Doesn't he, though? And, Loue, that is what we are going to help to happen in Japan. She is ripe for it. Listen again:

If this new type of religious character multiplies among the young men and women, they will change the world when they come to hold the controlling positions of society in their maturer years. They will give a new force to righteous and enlightened public opinion, and will apply the religious sense of duty and service to the common daily life with a new motive and directness."

The years 1915-1931 were good years for the Axlings. The August before returning to start their third term, each had observed a forty-second birthday. Their health was good, their spirits were high, and each was secure in the knowledge of tested abilities. As a bonus, few couples have known such mutual commitment, or have had the opportunity to share so completely in a common task.

Also, during these years William's ideal of a Christian nation seemed attainable—a nation in which such large numbers of leading citizens would carry their faith into their daily lives that all structures and institutions would be guided by Christian principles. In such a nation it would be more natural for men to turn to God than to evil. Such a nation would so sweeten international relations that peace might someday become a reality.

Westerners who know that that kind of optimism died with World War I may well be bewildered by the Axling of the 1920's. He sounded and acted like the optimists of the late nineteenth century. But in Japan his hope had some base. Neither William nor Japan was deeply affected by the first world war. With little effort or risk Japan picked up the Far Eastern German colonies and considerable international prestige. William, aside from comments on a shrinking missionary force blamed partly upon the war, largely ignored the conflagration.

In Japan, as the leaders of the old oligarchy, who had brought their country into the modern world, began to die, there was a real possibility that democratic liberals would take over. These men embraced all that was good in Western democracy and hoped to avoid its pitfalls. Some were Christians and nearly all were extremely open to Christian ideals. In general, they represented a business faction which hoped for the economic rather than the military advancement of their nation.

If this faction could win politically, if their Christian interest could be cultivated, and if a solid Christian base could be established among the people, then Axling's ideal was possible. Accordingly, the many and varied activities in which he engaged during these years had a unity of direction from that perspective. Everything he did was calculated to make confession of Christ both possible and meaningful to Japan.

His successes were imposing, and yet his failures even enough to overwhelm most men.

As planned, the Axlings arrived back in Japan shortly after the opening of the new Tabernacle building. The furlough year had been spent resting in Honolulu, fulfilling a comparatively moderate speaking schedule which included the Northern Baptist Convention annual meeting in Los Angeles, and resting again in Gothenberg. In acknowledging the welcoming celebration given him in Japan, William said, "We had a fine time in America, but getting back is the best part of all."

Nearly all of Axling's contribution to Japan was rooted in the Tabernacle. Except for his first term and last tour, it was his primary responsibility. At the Tabernacle he worked out his philosophy and practice of missions. It was there that his performance gave substance and validity to the words he spoke and wrote.

As soon as they could make their way, William and Lucinda went to inspect the new building. There it stood as they had planned and imagined—three stories of reinforced concrete with an artificial stone front. On the roof was a not-quite-completed garden, designed to make up for the lack of a park in the area. Inside, twenty-nine rooms of various sizes would accommodate a diversified program. The auditorium, though smaller than before, could be expanded to accommodate six hundred persons.

Immediately, Axling began planning a week-long dedication for early in 1916, which would both publicize and launch the full program of the Tabernacle. Each day was carefully planned to catch the attention of a specific group. In order to insure good publicity, the first day, Friday, January 14, was Press Day. Both the Japanese and the international press came, inspected the building, learned of the projected program, and wrote good stories. Many also returned to cover the remaining proceedings.

Saturday, Dedication Day, was expected to state clearly the central purpose of the whole enterprise. Highly respected Dr. Chiba, of the Theological Seminary, preached a sermon in which he called on the directors and staff to "remember that in all your work your supreme purpose must be to lead men and women to Christ and fashion them in his likeness."

Baptist Day dramatized the total Baptist enterprise in the city. Axling himself spoke, pleading for a great forward movement "under the initiative and leadership of Japanese leaders." With great satisfaction he noted that this Sunday meeting brought together the largest group of Baptists ever to meet in Tokyo up to that time.

On Monday, great effort was made to attract all elements of the immediate area to Community Day. The Commercial Club of Kanda Ward sent an official delegation. This time the major address was given by Baron Sakatani, a former minister of finance.

Social Service Day, held on Tuesday, drew the largest crowd. The superintendent of Municipal Charities in Tokyo asked that special invitations be sent to fifty persons interested in social work so that "they might have an opportunity to see and hear what a Christian church is attempting to do." One of the principal speakers, Professor Ryutaro Nagai, of Waseda University, declared: "Christ and his gospel are the only panacea for the socially sick and disorganized world."

On Wednesday, Education Day attracted a much smaller but thoughtful group of students to hear Dr. S. Motoda, of the Episcopalian Rikkyo College, and Dr. Kaginosuke Ibuka, of Presbyterian College.

The week was concluded with a return to the central religious theme of Evangelistic Day. The speaker this time was Colonel Gumpei Yamamuro, of the Salvation Army.

Axling estimated that over twenty-three hundred people, many of whom had never before heard of the Tabernacle, attended. In addition, messages of congratulation or recognition were received from many church, political, and social leaders in Japan. The minister of education, the government official with primary responsibility for religious institutions, wrote: "The fact that the Tabernacle will undertake to alleviate some of the social ills of the community is the matter on which the state should congratulate itself. If you are able to fulfill your religious mission and at the same time do away with some of the evils of the social fabric of Japan, it will be a great blessing to the nation."

From public utterances, at least, those "luminous letters of light" in which Axling had first read the providential place of the Tabernacle in God's plan never waned. Every year was the best year, and the next year always held new promises. Very often, however, other missionaries and colleagues could not find adequate justification for the boundless optimism which William expressed.

But if Axling's description of the accomplishments and possibilities of the Tabernacle revealed his tendency to overstatement, his labors there adequately expressed a compensatory factor. His vision never idled his hands. What he hoped for he strove for.

In other words, the Axlings worked hard. William was convinced that the Tabernacle had a strategic opportunity to show to the church and to the nation the way toward a Christian Japan. Every detailed activity, every frustrating problem, and all of the bone-wearying days of near drudgery caught some reflection of divine glory from his certainty.

By the third term Axling understood the needs of his district, which he correctly surmised were typical of much of urban Japan. The Japan of the future was being molded and often disillusioned and corrupted by the hard realities of city life. The children of this younger generation often were neglected by the working mothers. This class also often fell prey to disease and human exploitation. Loneliness, frustration, and a too-often unsuccessful search for new values were constant unwelcome companions.

In attempting to meet these needs, much of the earlier program was kept and expanded in the new building. Something was happening from 7:30 A.M. until 10:00 P.M. seven days a week. On Sundays, Central Baptist Church filled the day with activities of worship, Christian education, and a youth program.

Weekdays began when working mothers dropped off their small children for a day nursery. A bit later, over one hundred children gathered for kindergarten. At 3:00 P.M. the roof garden was thrown open to serve as a playground. Children's clubs held at various times for different age groups rounded out the regular children's program. Other special interests included a daily vacation Bible school and summer camping.

Adult activities on weekdays began with an afternoon class for young women. Learning English was the chief attraction for those who were free to come at that time. The Bible was the textbook.

In the evenings, even the expanded facilities seemed inadequate. Although the program was changed occasionally to meet shifting circumstances, the core continued to be night schools, Bible classes, and evangelistic meetings. Major attention was always given to youth. Young working men and women were given opportunity both to improve their ability to live in the city and to discover Christian values by which to live. Students in the many surrounding schools were offered Bible classes. Apprentices, young boys bound to learn a trade at about twelve years of age, were given a chance to continue school at night.

Special features included an expansion of the Saturday night lecture series; free legal advice to the exploited poor; a working man's club to relieve monotony; a man's friendly society, which was a sort of rescue mission operation; and a visiting nurse, who traveled into the surrounding area to help meet health problems.

Increasingly, the Tabernacle became a community center. A game room and reading room were available to all. Any civic-minded group could use the building as a meeting place. Whenever an epidemic threatened, the Tabernacle would be thrown open for the city as an inoculation center. The total program, however, was permeated by the evangelistic purpose of winning persons to Christian commitment, and each evening ended with an evangelistic service.

By 1919 Axling could write: "The Tabernacle has reached the state in its development where the main emphasis has to be put on the deepening rather than the broadening of its work."

While his eyes were always fixed on the long-range goal of a Christian Japan, Axling was always extremely sensitive to immediate personal needs. This personal concern saved the Tabernacle program from becoming sheer activism. William's humble humanity effectively reached even those on the fringes of the program, as Mr. Seizo discovered.

Mr. Seizo was proud of being known as a rough character who had earned the right to be called by the name of the legendary drunkard Yasube. Often he was called "Hated Yasube."

One day Mr. Seizo stopped by the Tabernacle to pick up his grandson from Sunday school. There he met an unusual foreigner in formal Japanese dress who introduced himself as Mr. Axling.

During the following months the two men met several times. Axling went to Mr. Seizo's home to inquire whenever his grandson missed Sunday school. Axling never failed to greet him when they met on the street. On occasion, Mr. Seizo came to hear this strange foreigner preach and was amazed at his grasp of literary Japanese. It shamed him somewhat that this foreigner could speak the language better than he.

On one Easter morning they met on the street. Axling greeted Mr. Seizo and asked cheerfully, "How is your wife?"

Mr. Seizo was irritated. Why should this man trouble his conscience when he was on the way to the wine shop? "The old hag still exists," he snapped.

William smiled. "My old woman," he said, "told me to give you her greetings."

Mr. Seizo turned abruptly and, without even the slightest bow, almost fled down the street. The words burned in his mind, "my old woman." He thought again and again: "He spoke on my level, because he wanted to come close to me. Close to me, drunken Yasube."

After this encounter, Mr. Seizo began coming to a Bible class. He learned from Dr. Axling about the Son of God, who was born in "a filthy, smelly horse stable," and he understood because a great person, a Doctor of Theology, would stoop to call his esteemed wife "my old woman."

Mrs. Axling, who in those days gave full time as director of the women's and children's work, had the same touch. Her special concern was with the young women who in the city were thrust from the usual shelter of the Oriental home and community. Many of these girls were overwhelmed by the strange, rough, crude world they found. At the Tabernacle and in Lucinda they found an oasis of strength. One girl spoke for many when she sat down as soon as she returned from the evening school and wrote: "My heart was so full of gladness and joy that I must write and tell you about it before I go to bed." After describing the temptations of the day, she explained what the Tabernacle meant: "The air of the classroom, the teacher's loving sympathy and kindness, the hymns and Bible lessons and prayers, were all so different that I can never forget it."

The seven-day-a-week program put the building to efficient use, but exacted a frightful toll from the staff. As programs multiplied and expanded, the staff grew. By 1919, in addition to the Axlings, there were eleven full-time and ten part-time workers. In the late 1920's, there were twenty-six full-time and seven part-time staff persons. Still there were never enough hands to perform all the tasks.

Most of those who carried the staggering burdens of work at the Tabernacle were Japanese. True to his principles, Axling placed as much responsibility on the nationals as the mission board would allow. In 1919, Tota Fujii assumed extensive executive functions. This capable young Japanese Baptist had gone to America, where he worked his way through William Jewell College and then acquired a master's degree at Brown University. William delighted in his "earnest spirit and devotion to the work." Frequently, he referred to his coming as a "real milestone in the history of this institution." By 1925 Mr. Fujii was able to assume total responsibility while the Axlings were in the States for the Japanese Reconstruction Campaign.

Tension, however, was not entirely missing. No large staff is ever able to work long, hard, and often discouraging hours without friction. Sometimes the staff felt that Axling received too much credit for what they did. William also worried: "I am greatly troubled when I see my name so prominently linked with the Tabernacle in the publications at home." He always went out of his way to praise his Japanese colleagues and desired "that they should receive full credit for the contribution which each is making to the success of the Tabernacle work."

The sheer force of Axling's own devotion, concern, and Christian spirit did more than anything else to keep the project going. He never forgot the important days, nor neglected to minister to the sorrows of his "choice group." Always at Christmas there was a party. Whenever someone was ill, Axling would leave the festivities a little early and, with a box of cake in his hand, make his way to the bedside of a sick friend.

Despite all this, however, the best efforts of all concerned sometimes met with failure and tragedy. Axling accepted responsibility for these as quickly as he tried to give credit to others for success. One day a little boy, intent on flying a toy airplane, disobeyed the rules and climbed over the fence of the roof garden. In a moment of carelessness he fell to his death.

The grief which this accident caused Axling left a deep impression upon the staff, particularly the children's worker, Rev. Yutaka Matsudiara. William made several visits to the boy's home, but he never could find adequate words to express himself. One day he said to Mr. Matsudiara, "Now I understand the true meaning of why the Japanese commit suicide, by hara-kiri as an expression of apology."

On September 1, 1923, Axling's determination to be ready for the next disaster bore fruit. Two minutes before noon on that fateful day, a catastrophic earthquake hit the Tokyo-Yokohama area. Within five minutes about two-thirds of each city was destroyed. Before the clouds of dust from falling walls had settled, they were joined by smoke from spreading fires. Almost simultaneously a typhoon blew in from the sea and fanned the already uncontrollable fires into a raging furnace. The official count placed the death toll beyond 330,000. The Axlings were still on vacation when the disaster struck. Miss Amy R. Crosby, who was staying in the Axling home, watched the fire sweep down the opposite side of the street. She and the house were saved by a sudden change of wind direction.

Mr. H. Saito, then a student at the Theological School and a caretaker for the Axling home, joined others of the Tabernacle staff in doing what could be done. He told Axling: "I did my best to rescue the children running about the burning city. All of us were filled with a power beyond our own strength."

Axling returned immediately. He was met by refugees, "hundreds of thousands of them, stunned, terror-stricken, white-faced, fleeing hither and thither," attempting to escape "that hell of fire and fear." Once again the sights and sounds of raw human suffering cut deeply into William's sensitive soul. Husbands and wives, parents and children, were searching frantically for one another through the rubble, digging for charred remains and fearfully asking for news. Above the sights and smells day and night hung the weird wail of the searchers.

Defeated again! This was his first reaction when Axling arrived at the gutted Tabernacle. The walls were standing and the floors secure, but there was no labor to clear the rubble, and there were no tools nor building materials to make even temporary repairs. Defeated! And the need was so great for a center for the distribution of food, clothing, and medicine!

Help came from an unexpected source. A young Shinto priest,

convinced of the integrity of the Tabernacle work, appeared next morning with twenty-four non-Christian young people and volunteered their services.

William was stunned. "You know, I have looked upon you and your shrine across the way as my chief competition," he confessed.

The young man smiled. "I am afraid you do not have a convert," he replied. "Yet I find Shintoism impotent in such an emergency. May I help you serve the people?"

For several days all twenty-five men, forgetful of their own losses, gave their best time, energy, and thought to the exhausting task of clearing away debris. The priest continued to help for two months.

Another non-Christian neighbor, a physician, who, through years of observation, had become convinced of the value and sincerity of the Tabernacle work, also offered his services. He made possible a free dispensary. The gallery of the auditorium was turned into an emergency hospital with thirty beds and a crude operating room.

Beyond a solid building and an excellent local reputation, the Tabernacle had another asset in William's growing contacts and reputation. He was able to acquire food, medicine, and money. From the treasury of the Imperial family came eighty thousand yen. The Japanese Government made the Tabernacle an official center through which Japanese and American relief supplies could be dispensed.

The whole Tabernacle staff, now regathered, threw all their efforts and talents into the task. One immediate, urgent need was for milk to feed babies whose mothers were no longer able to keep them alive. As if by magic, Axling acquired a large supply of evaporated milk. After a day of dispensing this life-giving fluid, Mr. Saito reported, "These mothers worshiped me, putting their hands together as we do in worship and prayer."

Old sugar bags were spread on the third floor of the Tabernacle and others were used for partitions. Many families were given temporary shelter in this "sugar-bag town."

William Axling had built well. This time the Tabernacle became a tower of physical and spiritual strength in a time of trouble. Yet social service was never allowed to crowd out the evangelistic thrust. Christian literature was distributed along with the food. This was never done as a condition, or with any obligation, but as a part of the Christian response to disaster. Weekly meetings were held in which many persons, including the neighborhood physician, became Christians.

One of the refugees brought to the Tabernacle was a little orphaned girl named Haruko. When no records could be found, Mr. and Mrs. Fujii took care of the little five-to-eight-year-old girl. Later the Axlings opened their home. Although they never adopted her, they became her legal guardians and to all intents and purposes her parents.

Some of the Axlings' friends, such as Miss Kishi Abe, a Bible woman at the Tabernacle, saw the potential difficulties and were very much against the arrangement. However, Mrs. Axling's deep maternal love overcame the objections, and they kept Haruko and brought her up. As is common in relationships between parents and children, both joys and sorrows followed during the years in which Haruko grew up.

As soon as the emergency was met, William turned his energies toward rebuilding. With characteristic breadth of vision, he pleaded with Americans to accept the opportunity to rebuild and expand the facilities serving the Baptist cause in the damaged area. About one-half million dollars was needed just to restore the churches and other buildings.

Axling wrote articles in Baptist publications, corresponded with friends, and spent much of his 1924-1925 furlough trying to raise money. Recognizing that the mission board was already in debt, he hoped to inspire Baptists to a mighty effort. Sometimes he chided American Baptists for giving nine million dollars for the great home field and for the vast work on ten foreign mission fields while the Shintoists of Japan, out of their poverty, spent a million on the building of one single shrine.

But Americans in the 1920's were enjoying their private pleasures. So, little money was raised, and the Tabernacle was merely repaired, with an annex added on the back. Even then, most of the money came from an appreciative Japanese Government and from Japanese philanthropists. The Tabernacle had won its place. There an authentic word could be spoken—a fact which was often more readily understood by the non-Christian Japanese than by the church in either America or Japan.

In 1928, Axling wrote of his disappointment in his annual report:

Five years have passed since the Tokyo-Yokohama area was laid waste by earthquake and fire. During this period most of our churches in this section have worried along in temporary shacks which offered little protection in summer rains and winter winds. The memberships of these churches have been engaged in a desperate effort to rebuild their homes and places of business. The constituency in America has, for the most part, turned a deaf ear toward the appeal for funds to reconstruct the broken Baptist line in this strategic center.

The already heavy financial and work burden of the Tabernacle was increased in the fall of 1924 by the opening of a branch in Fukagawa. This area contained one of the more dismal of Tokyo's slums. Located on very low land, its frail buildings were severely damaged or destroyed by every typhoon. The 1923 earthquake had been disastrous. Large quantities of debris from other parts of the city were dumped in the area. This action helped raise the level of the land, but left the people more miserable than ever. Honest workmen and vicious degenerates were fighting with huge rats for existence against disease and starvation.

The city authorities asked Axling to establish a branch in Fukagawa. Axling, Fujii, and Miss Crosby began at once to seek ways and means. Before they could act, however, the United States Congress passed the Immigration Act which excluded the Japanese, and Japanese reaction made it almost impossible for Americans to acquire property.

At last a lot was rented and filled with five feet of debris in order to raise the level above the tide. Here a refugee shelter, donated by the Board of Health, was erected, and a day nursery was begun.

With the help of the government funds and gifts from Japanese philanthropists, a two-story wood structure was erected in the fall of 1924. Just before he left for America, Axling was approached by an American women's medical group asking permission to house a relief project in the new center. They would supply two women physicians and operate a free dispensary. Mr. Fujii successfully negotiated an agreement.

Once again, Axling and his staff exhibited their ability to bring together various goodwill groups to serve human need. In this case government officials, Japanese philanthropists, a nonsectarian medical group, and the Christian staff from the Tabernacle cooperated in harmony. As it developed, the program at Fukagawa was similar to, but less extensive than, that at the older location. It became, according to Axling, "an out and out Christian institution, combining community-betterment work with an aggressive program of evangelism."

Although never a rigorous theorist, Axling knew what he was about. He believed that all Christians were called to do the works of Christ and to proclaim his salvation. When Christians were faithful in these two activities, he was sure that individuals would be transformed, that society would be changed, and that God's will would be done on earth as it is in heaven.

In a widely circulated pamphlet, *A Day in the Tokyo Tabernacle*, published in 1923, Axling made what is possibly his fullest statement of missionary policy. His concern for action and proclamation are both clearly stated. First is a beautiful expression of the Christian presence in the midst of human need:

> The Tabernacle aims to become a community center. We are endeavoring to plant ourselves deep down into the life of the little world that surrounds us. We strive to make its problems our problems. We yearn to become the rallying center for the life of our environment, a help, a haven, a home, an inspiration, an incentive to a higher and larger life to all the members of our community.

Then a little later, follows a declaration of the evangelistic thrust:

> But everywhere and all the time we strike the evangelistic note. Christ is humanity's greatest need and the Gospel is the World's greatest message. Evangelism runs like a golden cord through our whole program and gives direction and definiteness of purpose to all our activity. All our work is shot through with the Gospel message. We are not satisfied simply to "fill up the small gaps of a thousand minor needs." We dare not be neglectful of these needs. But infinitely more "we are here to fill up one appalling emptiness with the glorious presence of the Lord Jesus Christ."

Axling never developed a theory which carefully explained the relationship between these two. As a result, he was criticized both by conservatives who could not accept his preoccupation with social service, and by liberals who could not understand his simple evangelism. To Axling, the two always stood side by side —each incomplete without the other. He refused to subordinate one to the other. Both in his person and in his ministry they were united. He could not conceive of a fully Christian ministry with either missing.

In the Tabernacle, Axling worked out his understanding in practice. From the Tabernacle, his influence radiated into much of Japan.

"What the Tabernacle attempts for Kanda Ward the church should do for Japan and the world." With this statement of his thesis, William Axling focused a discussion at the annual missionary conference.

"What do you think the Tabernacle does for its ward?" asked one.

"We have not always done too well," said William, "but we aim to establish points of vital contact with each section of that little world, and to infuse that contact through and through with Christian ministry and the Christian's message."

"Quite an order," snapped another.

"Seriously, Bill," questioned the first, "how realistic is your aim? I am not denying that you have won many to Christ and have done good works, but have you really influenced the ward?"

"Not as much as I wish, but I think there was a real difference between the response of our community to the fire of 1913 and the earthquake. Did I ever tell you about the Shinto priest?"

"Several times!" commented the second, in an audible aside.

"But, Bill, most of us have more than we can do just keeping our heads above water," interjected a third. "At this point we can't extend our ministry much beyond snatching brands from the burning."

"That is just the problem," replied William, firmly. "We have so often boasted that the Baptist dollar possesses particular power as a convert-getter that we are caught in our own snare. After forty years we find that we have run over vast districts with the gospel message, but have failed to build strong, aggressive, indigenous churches that are able to take up the work and carry it on to completion. We have, in no small numbers, led individuals here and there to a Christian discipleship, but have failed to form strong Christian communities that will transform the social order."

The discussion remained unresolved. Another public meeting took precedence.

With characteristic simplicity, William analyzed and evaluated the mission situation in Japan. With characteristic dedication, he gave all of his time, strength, and wisdom to backing up his convictions, both at the Tabernacle and in an ever-widening ministry.

Axling believed that Japan was ripe for Christian plucking. Victory, however, would not be easy. The battle could be lost, but success was possible. As he saw it, success depended upon several factors. First, there was need for a bolder, broader, more vigorous Christian effort, centered in Japanese leadership. Second, Japanese liberals needed to see the truth and functional value of Christianity and how it could aid in their own struggle for power against the reactionary militarist. Third, Christians in America needed to recognize the value of a strong Japan in the East, and to support policies which would strengthen the hands of the liberals. Most of all, America needed to prove herself a Christian nation, so that Japan, too, might become one. It was in the pursuit of the second and third of these objectives that Axling became a statesman.

Axling never believed that the Christianizing of a nation would lead inevitably to the conversion of every individual. He was sure, however, that many more people would find personal faith in such a culture. Also, his conception of Christianity included the promoting of God's will on earth in the social structure and among the nations, as well as the rescuing of individual souls for heaven.

Many missionaries and American Christians rejected Axling's basic presupposition. That is, they did not believe that Japan was about to become Christian. They noted that fewer than 1 percent of the population had professed Christian faith. They doubted that the infant church was close to being able to assume wide responsibility. Some, building on a pessimistic view of history, hoped only to rescue a few souls before the catastrophic end.

Axling would have none of it. "Japan stands at one of God's great creative hours," he shouted from every soap box available to him. The tone was set by a 1916 pamphlet, *The Triumph of the Gospel in Japan.* He reminded the pessimist of the older 1868 Imperial edict against Christianity: "As long as the sun shall continue to warm the earth, let no Christian be so bold as to come to Japan. And let all know that if the Christian's God himself shall violate this command, he shall pay for it with His head." Axling insisted that Christian progress in Japan should be measured against this background, rather than by some standard derived from a modern Christian nation.

Axling never tired of detailing gains achieved and possibilities ahead. True, Japan had first tried adopting Western materialism without its spiritual dynamics. Some had "boasted that they were building in the Orient a great secular state, into which there should go nothing but the genius and intelligence of man," but this attempt had failed. Now "Japan is in the midst of a far-reaching religious awakening," Axling wrote.

Acknowledging that the masses of people still held to old pagan faiths, and that these faiths also were experiencing a revival, Axling argued that a vital Christianity had the best chance to win. He pointed to the discussion groups being conducted in high places, in which Christianity was considered a live option. On the part of the youth: "They tell us, by the hundreds they tell us, that when they turn to Buddhism and Shintoism they find them fountains without water, cisterns that are dry, systems without a life and without a dynamic."

Axling amassed and used the testimonies of many prominent Japanese who were sympathetic to Christianity to show a favorable trend. In typical fashion, he accepted the trend as proof that "Christianity in the Japanese Empire is a triumphant force. The gospel is winning the day. Jesus Christ is marching in triumph across the land and is gripping the hearts and transforming the lives of the people everywhere."

Without waiting for everyone to accept his basic assumption —that Japan was ready for Christianization—Axling pushed on to make his other points. The time had come for a broader missionary policy, pursued on a cooperative front with Japanese leadership. These ideas were not new to Axling, but his greater prestige gave them more weight and his extensive writing gave them a wider hearing.

A paragraph from a 1921 pamphlet, *On the Trail of Truth About Japan,* well expresses his idea of the kind of ministry needed:

Only a Christianity with an evangelistic fervor and a social passion can meet the present needs. The simple program of the earlier days must be broadened and enlarged so that the church may function efficiently and with saving healing power amidst the complexity of Japan's modern life. Preaching there must be, by men whose hearts are aflame and whose souls are aglow. But the gospel must be given hands and feet and incarnated in lives of lowly ministry that the common people and those who toil may understand. The individual is the unit, and the church will get nowhere until it seeks and saves him, but it must also take homes and institutions and communities into its heart and strive for their salvation if it is going to do effective kingdom building in the Japan of today.

Always, Axling urged that this work be guided and conducted as much as possible by the Japanese themselves.

Even the boldest, most creative ministry, Axling came to believe, would never succeed on a large scale unless the Japanese liberals could win control, and America could prove itself a Christian nation by its policy. This conviction propelled Axling into the realm of statesmanship.

Axling's first book, *Japan on the Upward Trail,* issued by the Missionary Education Movement of the United States and Canada, in 1924, placed his concerns in wider historical perspective. Numerous articles and addresses reinforced his theme.

The pamphlet established his method of using extensive quotes from Japanese prominent in politics, business, education, and the church to buttress the point he was trying to make. Often the statements were reports of private conversations between Axling and these persons. His extensive contacts on all levels of society, which he had established during his twenty years in Japan, gave his words convincing quality.

Several ideas kept recurring in his statements. Japan's record of past wars, while regrettable, was no worse, and probably better, than that of any other modern nation. Japan's current mood and future plans were peaceful. This peaceful attitude was insured by the rising power of the people. According to Premier K. Hara: "Public opinion is becoming a potent force in the life of the nation. This means peace, for the people are demanding peace."

A peaceful future for Japan was further insured by an educational system which, according to Professor Yoshino, of the Imperial University in Tokyo, was 80 percent on the side of democracy. "Practically all of the younger professors in these institutions are lined up in the same way."

Building on these two factors—a growing power of the people and a democratically educated youth—Axling saw "a rising tide of liberalism." Nevertheless, there were dangers. The old militarists were still powerful. They exploited every aggressive and non-Christlike act in America to discredit the liberals. America's behavior at this important juncture was, therefore, critically important. America had become the ideal model for the liberals and was, of course, the land from which most of the missionaries came.

In view of these facts, America would do well to forgo any aggressive actions in the Pacific, such as "the monstrous military dock which is building at Honolulu." Also, discrimination against the Japanese nationals in the United States would be disastrous, both for the immediate spread of the gospel and for the long-range development of Japan.

Finally, long before most Americans, Axling realized that the future of mankind as well as of the church was to lie in the East and with the nonwhite people. Enlightened self-interest, as well as loyalty to the cause of Christ and the ideals of democracy, called for a positive policy toward Japan. Japan was crucially important, because she was the first Asian nation to become modern.

In addition to his general writing and speaking, Axling became directly involved in two sensitive issues of Japanese-American relations during the 1920's. The first was the Washington conference on the limitation of armaments, and the second was the Immigration Act of 1924.

The Washington conference was called by Secretary of State Charles Evans Hughes for November 11, 1921, to discuss limitation of naval armaments and to establish agreement on Far Eastern policy. The United States hoped to head off a developing arms race, stabilize territorial claims in the Pacific, and shift commitment to the Open Door Policy for China from its own shoulders to an international agreement.

In the spring of 1921, Axling, who was on furlough, was asked to share his understanding of the Japanese situation with the State Department. His writing and lecturing had already established his reputation as a careful and sympathetic interpreter. Also, Secretary of State Hughes, a prominent Baptist layman who had served as the first president of the American (then called Northern) Baptist Convention, knew of Axling.

The conviction grew in several quarters that the presence of Axling at the conference would be helpful. Many prominent

Japanese knew him and had confidence in him. He was also widely known among Christian people in America. He could do much to interpret American feeling to the Japanese delegation and to express the Japanese position to the American public.

Axling was delighted. He saw the conference as a return of hope after the American rejection of the League of Nations. As he saw it: "For three long years idealism had been lying prostrate with her face in the dust. In that daring proposal Secretary Hughes took her by the hand, raised her to her feet and bade her hold her head erect." If this conference went well, the Japanese liberals would be strengthened and the cause of Christ extended in the whole Far East.

The mission board extended his furlough so that he could attend. Officially he was an accredited news correspondent for *The Baptist*. With typical boldness and tenacity, Axling used every avenue open to him for the furtherance of peace.

The influence of one semiofficial person at a great international conference is almost impossible to measure. Probably Axling's greatest success was with the Japanese delegation. Early in the conference, he met with Prince Tokugawa, the head of the delegation, and in the days that followed he had conversations with other Japanese dignitaries. Whenever he felt it advisable, he sent memoranda, which were always gratefully acknowledged. Through these contacts he helped to interpret American feeling toward Japan and gave hints as to how Japan could present itself in a better light. Specifically, he urged the Japanese to be more open and less secretive about their legitimate interests, and shortly afterwards the Japanese delegation issued a forthright statement which helped to clear the air. Though always sympathetic to the Japanese cause, Axling insisted that fine words "have to be followed up by deeds."

With less overall success, Axling expended much time interpreting the Japanese side to Americans. Before and during the conference he spoke before service clubs, chambers of commerce, university groups, at West Point, and in the conference chambers of the United States House of Representatives. He spoke also in many churches. One week took him to Boston, Massachusetts; Providence, Rhode Island; Rochester and Ithaca, New York; Toledo and Cleveland, Ohio; Harrisburg, Lewisburg, and Chester, Pennsylvania; and Wilmington, Delaware.

Axling's interpretation of the importance of the conference was summarized in eight articles published in *The Baptist* and made available to other periodicals in the United States, Britain and Japan. In these articles the missionary-statesman described the legitimate security and self-interest needs of the Japanese in the Far East, and argued for an enlightened American policy which would strengthen the hands of the Japanese moderates. Throughout, he interpreted the Oriental approach, which demanded slow, deliberate action, and he explained the time necessary for the Japanese delegates to clear agreements with their home Government. Occasionally, he also warned that "yellow journalism," with its "glaring headlines" of "crisis and conflict and deadlock," was detrimental to the spirit of the conference.

Unquestionably, Axling's efforts broadened the understanding of many, but there is no evidence that they created even a small groundswell of popular support for a more progressive foreign policy in the Pacific. His was only one of a few voices crying in the wilderness. There was much anti-Japanese feeling in America, fanned by racial prejudice and by those who wished to exploit their special interest in the Far East. Even men like Russell H. Conwell, carried along by the groundswell of these attitudes, spoke against disarmament on the grounds that Japan was our enemy, waiting to sweep down on the Pacific Coast, shell its cities, and wipe out its people. Such talk fed militarism, both in Japan and in America.

By maintaining contact with them and publishing their activities, Axling became a focal point for many of the unofficial goodwill groups, both Japanese and American, who were seeking to influence the conference. One of *The Baptist* articles was titled "Forces that Function in the Background." By the use of rather shaky statistical methods, Axling tried to dramatize the fact that ten million American Christians were praying for the conference. He listed the many representatives of Japanese Christian peace and commercial groups in Washington who were working in the interest of peace. Most picturesque was Madame Yajima. "On her face," wrote Axling, "glows eternal youth in spite of the fact that the winds of ninety winters have beat upon it." She came with a prayer for peace signed by ten thousand Japanese women, which she called "the mobilization of the hearts of Japanese women in favor of peace."

Axling soon discovered that the assumption of a prophetic role inevitably raises antagonism. His pamphlet and addresses, including "Ten Telling Facts About Japan," before the annual meeting of the Northern Baptist Convention in Des Moines, Iowa, aroused racists and supernationalists—some of whom were Baptists.

Most difficult to take was the opposition of his own colleagues. A few days before the Washington conference was to open, the executive committee of the mission in Japan cabled its response to the board's suggestion that Axling's furlough be extended:

> Executive Committee approve if it is absolutely necessary in view of the American situation. The general opinion seems to be Rev. William Axling's report conveys erroneous impression with regard to situation. Mission cannot accept the responsibility for what he says. Besides Dr. Axling needed here.

When Axling received a copy of the cablegram, his eyes widened in disbelief. After rereading it, he then turned and read it to Lucinda.

"Oh, Bill, what does it mean for us and for our work in Japan?"

"I don't know, Loue, I don't know. What can they have heard to make them think I have misrepresented the situation?"

"You do sometimes overstate the good in a situation," Loue offered, a bit timidly.

"I know, I know, but I have to. You heard Conwell stirring up the people against Japan. You read the papers. Someone has to dramatize the other side."

"Are you sure that you are not leading people astray, Bill? Do you really think the liberals can win?"

"Loue, you know that I warn people that I am taking the positive side; that I am telling them what can happen if we rise to the occasion. In fact, it is happening. The rise of Takahashi to the Premiership proves it. You remember how he attacks the militarists. Now he is Premier."

After a few days of self-questioning, in which he went about his work "stunned and dazed," Axling wrote a long letter to his colleagues. In it he explained his objectives, described with much detail the care with which he had checked his impressions with prominent Japanese and Americans, reported his activities, and expressed sorrow for the apparent rupture of relationship. But, he added:

I did not look forward to any such work as that which I have been called upon to do. I did not seek it. It was not work which I would choose. My heart yearns to be back in my little nook in Japan. To me the whole thing from the beginning is of God. I dare not fail him.

It is a great heart sorrow to me that I do not have the sympathy and confidence and prayers of my fellow missionaries in the work which I have been trying to do. I thought I had; to find that I have not is a disappointment that is bitter indeed. But to me my duty is clear and I go on—lonely in the feeling that you are not back of me—but strong in the consciousness that I have been doing and am now doing what God has laid upon my heart as the only thing that I could do and look Him in the face in the special situation in which I find myself.

Many of his colleagues were not convinced that the liberals were winning, or that whether they were or not was any business of the church. Nevertheless, William Axling was not easy to put in his place. The work at the Tabernacle was a shining example and his convictions were unshakable. So Axling finished his work in Washington with his usual optimism. According to the final paragraph of *The Baptist* series:

Aside from agreements reached and treaties signed this conference has put international cooperation on the map. It has established the principle of limited armament. It has set a precedent of substituting consultation in international affairs for conflict. It has erected high barriers against the possibility of war between the four great powers that dominate the Pacific. It has paved the way for a better understanding between nations East and West. It has demonstrated the power of the people and the efficiency of open diplomacy. It has put the dynamic of faith behind international agreements instead of force. It has made the calling of similar conferences inevitable. It has established cordiality as the big word among the nations and has made the path of peace a broader and safer highway for humanity. Here is a story of progress in the ironing out of international problems unparalleled in ancient or modern history.

For the next two years, Axling lived in the glow of this conference. His liberal friends were coming to the fore in government. Japan's policy toward China was softening. Military strength and military influence were being reduced. The church was healthy and growing in this favorable atmosphere. The meaningful official response to the suffering caused by the 1923 earthquake was further evidence that Japan was absorbing Christian ideals.

Then came the news of May 26, 1924. Axling was at his desk in the Tabernacle when word came. Mr. Fujii came in quietly and placed a newspaper on his desk. Axling read in shocked unbelief: "The U. S. Congress has passed the Japanese Exclusion Act."

"Oh, no! Tota!" After a long pause, "I am sorry. I apologize for my people."

"We know that you or other truly Christian people are not to blame."

"I am afraid many professing Christians are in favor."

"You forget that I spent much time in America," said Mr. Fujii, smiling faintly.

"I know, I know, and again I apologize," responded Axling, his voice flat and weary. "What do you think this will mean, Tota?"

"We know that America has a great immigration problem. She has a right to limit those who enter. The thing that hurts is the discrimination. We are not being treated like others. Most Japanese will take it as an insult to our race and our culture. It will both hurt the liberal forces of our country and slow the spread of Christianity."

William straightened in his chair. "Abraham Lincoln once said, 'Nothing is settled until it is settled right.' This thing must not be allowed to stand."

"This thing" had been a long time coming. The forces opposed to immigration, especially the so-called "new immigration" from Southern and Eastern Europe had been gaining for some time. In 1921 the first quota act was passed, providing that immigration from any country must not exceed a number equal to 3 percent of the persons from that country who were residents of the United States in 1910. The object was to limit overall immigration and to insure continuity of established ethnic mixtures. The anti-immigration forces were still not satisfied. The 3 percent still allowed over one-third of a million persons to enter the United States in a year. Also, by using the 1910 date, many persons were allowed to come from Southern and Eastern Europe.

In addition to the nationwide trend, the anti-Japanese crusade on the West Coast had reached a new level of hysteria. Several anti-Japanese societies, a number of newspapers, and several politicians were circulating all kinds of fantastic scare stories about the Japanese taking over California and eventually the whole nation. For example, it was claimed that the Japanese owned five thousand acres of the best land in Merced County. A check showed that they, in fact, owned only 395 acres of farm land and thirty-six town lots. It was claimed also that Japanese births in California were three to one over white births. Investigation, however, showed that white births outnumbered Japanese by more than twenty-five to two. The birth rate among Japanese women residing in America was high only because most of them were of child-bearing age.

This anti-Japanese group joined forces with those opposing the "new immigration" and passed the 1924 act. The base date was moved back to 1890 and the quota cut to 2 percent. In addition, the law completely denied the Japanese any quota on the grounds that those who could not become citizens should not immigrate to this country. Actually, there had been comparatively little Japanese immigration after the Gentlemen's Agreement of 1907. Also, the new base made the possible number of Japanese negligible. The irrational fears of prejudiced persons were satisfied at the cost of insulting the proud and sensitive Japanese people.

Reaction in Japan was immediate, widespread, and bitter. As quickly as possible, Axling got in touch with some of his influential friends. Baron Y. Sakatani responded frankly: "To the lover of peace this legislation has deplorable possibilities. It will add fuel to the fires of the militarist. In the years yet unborn, 'Remember the Exclusion Law' may easily become their rallying cry. Generation may pass the word onto generation and poison the will to outlaw war."

"Do you think it is possible," queried Axling, "that after an initial excitement, this may be looked upon as an unimportant element of internal American policy?"

"Of course it is a question of American domestic policy, but its influence will reach far out into the highways of international intercourse."

"How do you feel about the racial overtones?"

"As you will know, this is the center of the matter. If this thing is left to take its course, the world may be divided into two big camps, the 'white' and the 'colored,' or the 'Asians' and the 'Westerners,' and all that we had hoped for, perpetual peace and world brotherhood, will be gone forever."

"What do you think must be done?"

"Personally, I still have faith in America. I cannot understand the attitude of the American Congress. All the Americans whom I know are of a different type and are true to that nation's past ideals. I cannot but believe that eventually the American people will do the right thing in this important matter. . . . America has inflicted the wound. She alone can heal it."

From every place and from every level of society the response was the same. A high school teacher reported watching boys and girls take the pictures of Washington, Lincoln, and Wilson, who had been esteemed as heroes, down from the walls. They marched together out to a hill, buried the pictures, and said, solemnly: "Let us bury our ideals with our betrayed sweetheart, and let us build an imperishable ideal of eternal peace in the land of the rising sun."

On the whole, the blame was placed on Congress, but some observers were more discerning. Mr. M. Zumoto, a member of Japan's Parliament, told Axling: "No single event in the long history of our intercourse with America has shocked and pained us so deeply as this unnecessary affront hurled upon us by the National Congress of the United States. . . . The great fact stands out, that behind Congress are the great masses of American people, who doubtless approve what their Congress has done. . . . The men of Congress are keen politicians. They would not have acted in the way they have unless they were assured that their constituency would approve."

Hoping to change that constituency, Axling sought ways of influencing his countrymen. One way came through the Federal Council of the Churches of Christ in America. It published Axling's booklet *Japan Wonders Why* and helped sponsor a speaking tour in America.

The booklet followed the familiar Axling method. After stating in simple terms the issues, and quoting extensively from prominent Japanese, it ended with an appeal for justice for the good of the Christian cause and the world.

In explaining the issue, Axling stated eight basic facts which undermined the arguments for the exclusion law. Some of his statements dealt with Japanese behavior. Japan did not exclude any race or people from her land. Americans or any other persons could become citizens of Japan. Japan had lived up to the Gentlemen's Agreement and was not seeking permission for extensive immigration. American companies could buy land in

Japan, and individuals could acquire 999-year leases. The dual citizenship principle, whereby Japanese living in America were considered Japanese citizens until specifically released, was not peculiar to Japan. Other facts cited made it clear that Japan's objection was grounded upon the racial and cultural insult to the Japanese people. Since the 2 percent quota granted to other nations would have allowed only 146 immigrants a year, prejudice seemed the only possible reason for exclusion.

Finally Axling appealed to right-thinking Americans to demand revision of the law. Failure to do so would be disadvantageous to the already harmed Japanese church. "The racial discrimination in that legislation has caused multitudes of Japanese to question the right of the Christian faith to pose as a world religion, and to doubt the sincerity of Christian brotherhood."

Of equal importance for the gospel in Japan and for the world was the "stunning setback" of the liberal movement. The liberals, who stood for democracy and took America as a model, were hurt, because "Through this legislation America has discredited and disheartened the leaders of this movement, handicapped their progress and added new fuel to the dying fires of the reactionaries, the militarists, and the ultra nationalists."

Axling spent several months in the United States presenting his plea in person. He also used the time to seek money for repairing the earthquake damage. Neither project, however, was very successful.

After traveling extensively about the country and speaking 165 times before all kinds of groups, Axling wrote his colleagues in Japan: "The best people in America see the situation in its true light, sense the wrong which has been done, and are supporting us in our effort to have this wrong made right."

The major response seems to have been respectful, but bland. Except for a few Ku Klux Klan members who demonstrated against his meetings and a few sensitive persons who were working with him in this endeavor, most listened with mild interest. Japan was little known and far away. After all, the law had been passed and signed by the President. What could be done? Apathy, that greatest enemy of righteousness, won the day.

Axling's planned itinerary ended with a tour of the West Coast and a message before the annual meeting of the Northern Baptist Convention in Seattle. The prospect of his making a frontal attack on the exclusion cause on the West Coast, where anti-Japanese feeling was hottest, sent a shock wave through the religious and business community.

The men charged with raising missions funds on the West Coast, A. W. Rider and F. W. Harding, convened a conference of clergy and laity to prepare a strategy. The all-day meeting produced the following night letter sent to Paul E. Alden, associate secretary of the American Baptist Foreign Mission Society:

> Influential groups here, containing some of our constituency, which opposed restriction law and now works actively for better Japanese-American relations, believe, if Axling suggests reopening immigration question, he would arouse powerful race hostility from group now controlling extensive publicity channels, only postponing attainment of objective they and Axling seek. If Axling confines himself to reconstruction and need of better relations between countries, omitting critical and propaganda aspects of campaign, this group can cooperate. Otherwise they consider his coming a disservice to Japan. Brinstad and Tingley concur. Have arranged meeting Axling and this group with Brinstad and Tingley in San Franciso March sixth to give Axling opportunity knowing actual situation on Pacific Coast. Can you secure Axling's cooperation? Assuming same am setting up according program. Leave for Seattle Thursday night. Letter follows air mail.

The mission executives, however, who had cleared Axling's return to America, were not about to have him silenced. After checking with his superior, J. H. Franklin, Mr. Alden replied with a night letter of his own:

> Unwilling Axling keep silent on question on which Northern Baptist Convention and our Board have taken strong position. See convention resolution page two hundred fifty-one last convention annual. Our usefulness in Japan depends largely on our loyalty to such pronouncements. In view of Axling's widely known attitude it would be impossible avoid questions and newspaper interviews and refusal to discuss immigration question would cause serious misunderstanding on both sides of the Pacific. Very desirable Axling secure first hand understanding of Pacific Coast. Cancelling engagement Philadelphia enable him attend conference San Francisco, March sixth. Advise he be booked only where cordial invitations extended with knowledge attitude of Convention and board trusting him in conference with pastors to meet situation wisely.

While the telegraphic communications were going on, the then somewhat slow airmail letter from F. W. Harding was making its way to New York. This letter was based largely upon the opinion gained through a conference with F. N. Lynch, Baptist leader and vice-president of the San Francisco Chamber of Commerce. Mr. Lynch, who carried major responsibility in developing Japanese-American trade, had been active in opposing the passage of the legislation. He and his associates, among others working for improvement of Japanese-American relations, had arranged for Japanese warships to visit San Francisco. On that occasion they spent $10,000 in entertaining the sailors.

Mr. Lynch, speaking for the Chamber of Commerce, "which includes some of the finest Christian men in the city," was sure that any agitation on the immigration question would worsen the situation. It "would only stir up most powerful hostility from such organizations as The Native Sons of the Golden West and from labor organizations." Japanese-Americans would suffer and the gulf between the two countries would become wider.

This letter from Mr. Harding also urged Axling to talk of the need for reconstruction, to speak in general about improved relations between the two countries, and urge better treatment of Japanese in America. Finally: "Of course, if Axling should feel that he could not modify his message in line with the advice given by the best friends Japan has on the coast, and who thoroughly understand the condition here, we can cancel all dates. I hope though we can sail right ahead."

Other communications followed, piling up the evidence that "the best friends of Japan" were against stirring up the immigration issue. As names such as Lynch and Corwin S. Shank, of Seattle, began to multiply, the board officials took a second look. While they still believed "thoroughly in the position taken in our first telegram," a conference with Axling and others concluded that no definite position should be taken until after Axling met with the San Francisco group on March 6.

The stand of the society caused "a lot of running around," trying to arrange an acceptable program. Businessmen's clubs on the whole were closed. One meeting was arranged before a small audience—"one given to deeper thought"—a union meeting of several theological schools. Thus was the issue neatly removed from the centers of power to a harmless theological discussion.

When Axling met with West Coast leaders he ran into a solid wall of unanimous opinion against raising the issue of the exclusion clause. Any criticism of Congress was considered harmful to all aspects of Japanese-American relations. Right or wrong,

Axling was convinced that the West Coast friends of Japan were sincere in their belief. That night he wrote to the board: "All things being considered, therefore, it seems to me that the only thing to do is to fall in line. . . ."

As he probed a bit, Axling found that unanimity stopped with the opinion that the law should not be attacked at the present time. Some believed that the law was just and should stand. Others believed that it should be changed and might possibly be changed in the future. Some wanted controversy kept at a minimum so that church budgets would not suffer. Others were concerned about the sale of goods.

In any event the "hard-headed, clear-thinking, practical-minded businessmen" won. They were practical. The idealist, who thought of practicality upon a larger scale than the immediate value of trade, or even of the immediate effects upon the Japanese living in California, was silenced. More accurately, Axling's message was muted. The "practical" way led straight to the Pacific theater of World War II. Where a full Christian acceptance of the ideal would have led, no one can ever know.

Axling spoke many times on the West Coast, but his cause was already defeated. After much behind-the-scenes shuffling, he was given a spot on the last day of the national convention program, at 8:30 on Sunday evening.

This message, "The Peace of the Pacific and the Peace of the World," was one of Axling's truly prophetic utterances. With an accurate sense of history, he stated that "the drama of human life has been staged around the world's seas." After a brief review, he declared: "Our age is witnessing another shifting of the seas. Today the era of the Pacific stands at its dawn." He then stated flatly: "The big things of the coming countries are not going to happen in Europe. They will be staged around the Pacific."

The speech then called on Americans, especially Christian Americans, to respond to the new reality. Axling pointed out that peace in the Pacific depended upon American attitudes and actions as much as anything the Japanese might do. He concluded on the note that only in Jesus Christ could East and West find a common bond of brotherhood as sons of a common Father. He was willing to pay the price of being accused of anti-Americanism by his fellow countrymen or of being accused by the

Japanese of attacking Japan for the sake of making his message clear because, "There are some things worth living for and fighting for even at the risk of being misunderstood or misjudged. There are some things worth dying for. This is one of them."

Because this address is so significant in showing Axling's views at this time, views that were far ahead of his own time, large sections of it have been included in the special section which immediately follows this chapter. For anyone who accepted Axling's thesis, apathy was inexcusable and business as usual a crime.

A few days later the Axlings were once more on an ocean liner headed back for Japan. William's reputation as a missionary-statesman was fully established even though his cause was lost for his own generation at least.

THE PEACE OF THE PACIFIC AND THE PEACE OF THE WORLD

(Portions of the address delivered by Dr. William Axling at the Northern Baptist Convention, Seattle, Washington, July 5, 1925.)

Today the Pacific stands at the fork in the road of its destiny. I am not an alarmist but we are living in an hour that calls for straight thinking and frank speaking. For the sake of the world and its future, let us not blink the fact that a prodigious peril is rearing its head out in the Pacific area. . . .

For four centuries the world was a white man's world. The story of the extension of his sway East and West, North and South during those four hundred years is the most dramatic story in legend and in life. There are proud pages in that story. There are also pages that are dark. There are pages of heroic service and of uplifting and enrichment of stranded and stagnant peoples. There are also pages of cruel encroachment and selfish aggression.

But the story of the white man's expansion is a closed chapter. . . .

The tragic blunder of America's exclusion law with its racial discrimination lies right here. It discriminates on racial grounds against Japan and the Orient and challenges their right to equality in the world's life and challenges their right to equal treatment as between nation and nation. . . .

This law has needlessly raised momentous issues between the Occident and the Orient as they stand facing each other in the mid-Pacific. It has done more than any other event in recent years to crystallize race consciousness all up and down the awakening Orient. It has deepened the feeling and the fear that the occidental will not, in a crisis, give the oriental full-orbed justice and a square deal.

Let us never forget that the peril hovering over the Pacific is not a "yellow peril." It is a peril of the white man's making. A peril that the white man can banish by putting the sweetening spirit of justice and fair play into his dealings with the oriental people.

Another element in the peril which is at present stalking across the Pacific is the damning psychology of fear. It was fear that caused the world war and slew eleven million of this generation's finest and fairest youth. Today this demon of fear is at work on both sides of the Pacific.

America has no need of launching goose-step days and war games in the Pacific in order to drive fear into Japan's soul. It is there already. America for sixty years and more was the incarnation of Japan's dreams and hopes and ideals. America was the guiding star in Japan's sky. She was all that Japan in her heart of hearts yearned to become as a nation.

Today to many thoughtful Japanese—I am not speaking about her jingoists and militarists—America with her immeasurable resources in men and money throws a threatening shadow across Japan's path. Why this change? Alien land laws, anti-naturalization Supreme Court decisions, abrogation of the Gentlemen's Agreement, a racial exclusion law, national mobilization day, citizen's military training camps, and the maneuvers of our fleet in the Pacific, these have built up in the Japanese mind a radically different America from the America of Washington and Lincoln's time. The America of that early day Japan understood. The America of today is a riddle to her mind. . . .

Still another peril in the situation is the fact that communists the world around are eager for an American-Japanese war. They found that the world war opened the way for their cause in Russia and to a greater or less degree in all of the European nations. America and Japan are the two capitalistic nations that at the present bar their onward march. For this reason the wavers of the red flag want war and they want it soon.

I repeat. The Pacific stands today at the fork in its path of destiny. Here will be staged the most titantic

William and Lucinda Axling in Japanese costume during their first term of service in Japan.

Haruko, the orphaned Japanese girl who was adopted by the Axlings after the earthquake in 1923.

A view of the devastation created by the earthquake and fire which gutted the Tabernacle in 1923.

"that he might create in himself one new man in the place of the two, so making peace, and might reconcile us both to God in one body through the cross."
Ephesians 2:15-16

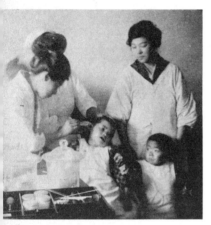

Fukagawa Dispensary

FUKAGAWA CHRISTIAN CENTER

Dispensary Waiting Room

Roof Garden

Japanese Christian Fellowship Deputation which visited the U.S. in 1941.

In order to continue his policy of living among the Japanese which he began in the prewar years Axling purchased this residence when he returned to Japan after the Second World War.

Dr. and Mrs. Axling receive one of the many honors which were given to them at their Farewell Reception hosted by the Japanese Baptists in 1954.

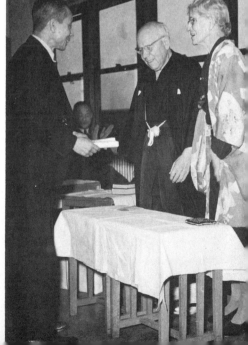

Dr. William Axling working at his desk. (Used by permission of **Shufo no Tomo.**)

William Axling spent many boyhood years in this house in Gothenburg.

struggle of human history or here will be witnessed a normal expansion wondrous in its scope and wondrous in its influence upon the world's life. . . .

What Japan needs just at this time is a demonstration of America's fine sense of justice, her passion for peace and her will to outlaw war. Japan needs a concrete staging of President Coolidge's challenging utterance on the day of his inauguration when he said that 'America is about to substitute friendship and understanding for the old standard of dealing with other countries by terror and force.' The translation of this noble utterance into concrete action on the part of the American nation would clear the way for peace and brotherhood across the Pacific area.

Again, if peace on the Pacific is to be built according to Christ's pattern, justice and fair play must be cornerstones in the structure. Not long since a friend of Japan in Washington, D. C., wrote to his Japanese friend in Tokyo saying, "The immigration law is America's last word on the matter. America will instead try to help Japan in other ways, through charity and through education." Can you imagine an attitude more distasteful than this to a high-spirited and self-respecting people? The Orient does not want charity; it wants justice. . . .

Again, Jesus was a master in sensing the inner worth of another soul. Appreciation will pave the way for peace in the Pacific. Too long has the white man drugged himself with the delusion that he was born to rule the world. Too long have we allowed our "superiority complex" to befog our thinking and govern our attitude toward the colored peoples. . . .

Do you want to massacre a multitude of America's fairest youth in a vain attempt to deny the fundamental fact that today men West and East are equals in the world's common life? A flaming fact which God has written in letters of light in the personalities of men everywhere and all over the life of our shrinking modern world. . . .

America, in spite of her tremendous resources in

men and money, cannot write this chapter of peace alone. Japan cannot write it alone. This great goal can only be reached when America and Japan, standing together in the high consciousness of God-given mission, march out as colleagues and work together in a cooperative relation.

Japan and the Orient do not want paternalism or patronage. They want partnership. They do not want condescension but comradeship as between man and man and in the world's work.

Once more, anew we must sense and sound abroad Christ's eternal truth that, regardless of place and race, men are kith and kin of God. Bearing the image of the eternal in their hearts, men East and West are sons of a common Father, members of God's great world family.

Anew we must sense and sound abroad Christ's eternal truth that there is no East and there is no West in the heart of God. There is no East and no West in Christ's great glowing soul. He drew no color line. In the face of every man he met he saw the marks of a son of God, highborn and high-destined and possessing a personality packed with potential power.

In a word, if there is to be peace in the Pacific that shall stand the strain and the stress of the years yet unborn, this area must be brought under the sway of Christ and of his dynamic ideals. Not America first. Not Japan first. But Christ first. America for Christ! Japan for Christ! The Pacific for Christ!

Thus in the last analysis the building of the structure of peace across the Pacific is the church's task. For a God-consciousness must precede the brother-consciousness. Only when men learn to say "Our Father" from their heart of hearts, will they be able to say "Our brother."

A new sense of God must clear the way for a new sense of brotherhood among men. East and West men must re-think God, re-discover God, re-explore God, re-experience God before they can found a far-flung brotherhood.

To this end it is just as important to Christianize America as it is to Christianize Japan. The two processes must go hand in hand. There must not only be new ideas and new ideals but a new heart and a new creature on both sides of the Pacific before peace and brotherhood can reign. We must aim at nothing less than that of building across the Pacific a brotherhood rooted in God and centered in Jesus Christ.

Some of you may be saying in your soul, "He has attacked America." Nothing has been farther from my thought. I have not forgotten that I am a son of America's soil. I have not lived in Japan so long that I have lost my love for my native land. My soul is still stirred by a strong sense of love and loyalty when I see that old flag of ours. I have spoken as an American but as a Christian American who for twenty-four years with growing concern has been studying the situation from both sides of the Pacific.

At the close of this convention Mrs. Axling and I are returning to Japan. Out there I will be attacking the men who only think yellow and are seeing red across the Pacific. There I will be laying this whole problem, from the oriental point of view, upon the hearts and consciences of the Japanese people. And out there some will say, "He is attacking Japan."

This is a part of the price that must be paid for peace. But there are some things worth living for and fighting for even at the risk of being misunderstood and misjudged. There are some things worth dying for. This is one of them.

Others may call the message of the evening an empty dream. If so, my soul is fired with hope. For I remember that the world's dreamers have been its torch-bearers and its trail-blazers. Some man has dreamt, and out of his dream has leaped a challenging ideal that has started humanity off on a new and higher trail.

Back in creation's dawn God dreamt a dream of a redeemed race. In the fullness of time Christ came as the incarnation of the Divine Dreamer and the fulfiller of his dream. Christ dreamt a dream of a world where his kingdom would come and where he would reign as the Prince of Peace and towards the fulfillment of that dream the whole creation moves. . . .

6. WIDENING HORIZONS

"THY WILL BE DONE, on earth as it is in heaven" was the prayer and guiding light of William Axling's life. For this to happen, men must find personal faith and learn to do God's will in society. But according to Axling, for these things to come to pass a second prayer of Jesus needed to be answered. Jesus asked the Father that all Christians might be one "even as thou, Father, art in me, and I in thee, that they also may be in us, so that the world may believe that thou hast sent me."

To Axling, whose faith was never parochial, the work of Christ was always one, whether in Gothenburg, Nebraska; Ontario, New York; Tokyo, Japan; or elsewhere in the world. This spirit, coupled with his growing prominence, opened many doors of service within his own denomination, in the total mission endeavor in Japan, and in the worldwide Christian community.

Many of these doors to larger service opened into the endless committee meetings and the routine administrative tasks which plague most ecumenical activity. As any experienced ecumenical worker knows, most of the time is spent dealing with frustrating trivia; but, as anyone who comprehends the accomplishments of the modern ecumenical movement knows, the overall results have been of utmost benefit to modern Christianity. Few other men and no other Baptist contributed so much to the early stages of interchurch relationships in Japan.

As early as 1918 Axling, who had so successfully mastered the Japanese language, was asked to direct a school to which all major denominations sent appointees for language study. This project appealed to him, because his own proficiency had cost dearly. Hard study had been one cause of the breakdown during the first term. When he came to Tokyo, with the help of Mr. Fujii, he obtained the services of Rev. Shingi Ojima as tutor. Axling continued on the board of the language school until the end of his career.

The National Christian Council was brought into being with far broader objectives of interchurch cooperation. Axling served on the organizational committee in 1922. Explaining his involvement to the mission board, he stated that the purpose of the council was "to represent the whole Christian community and to serve as a clearing house for all phases of Christian work in the Empire."

Axling served as one of the secretaries of the council for many years. Gradually the new organization absorbed the functions of the older missionary-dominated Federation of Christian Missions and became the most important cooperative Protestant enterprise in the islands. This work was made possible by the plodding faithfulness and wise advice of men like Axling.

Slowly, Axling began to move out into wider ecumenical circles. When he was in the United States in 1925, the Foreign Mission Convention invited him to speak on the gospel in an Oriental city. This gathering had been called by the Foreign Mission Conference of North America for the purpose of deepening missionary commitment in the days after World War I when interest in missions was slipping badly in America. In his address to the group Axling, of course, drew directly on the practice and theory of the Tabernacle.

In July, 1926, Axling substituted for the ill Methodist Bishop K. Uzaki at the meeting of the International Missionary Council in Sweden. He was one of twenty-seven world Christian leaders who came, charged chiefly with the task of planning for a much larger world conference to be held in Jerusalem two years later. At this meeting, Axling attracted some news coverage by a statement that Soviet Russia was the only power which had practically solved the race issue. Several Orientals who had traveled in Russia quickly agreed. Although Axling always looked upon communism as a major foe of Christianity, he often used the Communists' sense of dedication to their cause and certain of their acts to shame Christians and democratic nations into action.

As the Jerusalem meeting approached, Axling was chosen in his own right as one of the eight delegates from Japan. This conference was the most representative of worldwide Christianity which had gathered up to that time. Nearly one-fourth of the 240 delegates were from the younger mission churches. Five of the eight from Japan were Japanese.

The time and place were impressive. They met during the Easter season on the Mount of Olives, surrounded by the holy places of Christianity's birth. Housing was provided in tents and temporary wooden barracks, reminding the delegates of the church's pilgrim journey. Sessions were held in a sanitarium built by German Protestants but occupied since World War I by the British—a sharp reminder of growing world tensions. The program honestly faced the many important issues confronting modern missions. Axling noted: "We are facing one of the most critical and crucial hours in the history of Christian missions. It was no accident that the Jerusalem conference coincided with this hour."

The packed fifteen-day program, exhausting to many, was a delight to Axling. Most of his concepts and commitments concerning missions were confirmed, clarified, and expanded. He was thrilled by the degree to which world Christian leaders shared his fears and his dreams.

A major section was given to a study of race relations. The consensus agreed with Axling that "no problem today is so worldwide in its reach and so packed with danger and dynamic as the problem of race relations." Most saw the problem addressed to Christians: "It is the duty of Christian forces everywhere to learn more fully the mind of Christ on the problem of interracial relations and to press forward boldly the realization of permanent worldwide understanding."

The special problems in urban and rural areas, the challenge of industrial change, and the threat of growing secular attitudes which were analyzed by the conference confirmed Axling's observations. Rufus M. Jones, the Quaker thinker and leader, clearly identified secularism as the chief enemy. He declared: "No student of the deeper problems of life can very well fail to see that the greatest rival of Christianity in the world today is not Mohammedanism, or Buddhism, or Hinduism, or Confucianism, but a worldwide secular way of life and interpretation of the nature of things."

In the face of these problems, neither Jones nor Axling advocated otherworldly escapism. As Axling expressed the alternative in a report to *The Baptist*: "The conference declared 'its conviction that the gospel of Christ contains a message not only for the individual soul, but for the world of social organization and economic relations in which individuals live.' "

The Jerusalem meeting was the first major Christian conference to deal extensively with the relationship between Christianity and the non-Christian religions. The older attitude of utter rejection, "disdain and intolerance," was increasingly difficult to hold in the light of modern knowledge and deeper understanding of world religion. Trying to interpret the changing attitude to his American Baptist constituency, Axling wrote, "We have labeled them false faiths. Gradually, however, a new attitude has evolved. Real religious values have been discovered in these systems."

This growing appreciation of other faiths caused some to question the validity of the whole mission endeavor. Not so for Axling, nor for the majority of his fellow conferees. Recognizing values in others, or weakness in Christians, did not cloud the central place of Christ, who "in his life and through his death and resurrection disclosed to us the Father, the supreme reality, as almighty in love, reconciling the world to himself by the cross."

Finally, the conference agreed with Axling in recognizing the central importance of an indigenous church. Outstanding national leaders, representing every major mission from every field, were present and heard. Axling was enthusiastic: "At Jerusalem the older and younger churches met as equals. They shared each other's wisdom and experience, they looked out at the vast unfinished task as partners."

The trip itself was one of the rich experiences of Axling's life. It was his first visit to Palestine, and on the way back he made a side trip to Burma, where he had wanted to go as a youth.

Traveling companions included old friends such as Charles W. Iglehart, a district superintendent of the Japan Methodist Church, and August K. Reischauer, of the Presbyterian Church.

New friendships also were formed. Rev. Michio Kozaki, of Japan's Congregational Church, was secretary for the group. This young man shared a cabin with Axling, and the two became close friends. Axling fell to calling him his "kid brother." Through the years the chance phrase took on real meaning.

Side trips added interest and more than expected amusement. Immediately after the conference, Axling took a tour of the Holy Land with Dr. John A. Mackay, of Princeton University, and Doctors Reischauer and Iglehart. At the Sea of Galilee the men hired a boat and crossed the lake for a period of devotion. On the other side they separated for silent meditation.

After a short time, Dr. Iglehart's meditations were interrupted by an unbelievable sight. There was the dignified Axling stripped down to his shorts doing a strange dance in which he was shaking his trousers with one hand and striking at an invisible foe with another. For a moment he thought Axling must be reenacting the story of the demoniac! Dr. Iglehart grabbed his camera and snapped a picture. As he stood up, he felt *his* first few flea bites before he was overrun. The men had accidentally chosen the ruins of an ancient stable as the site of their devotion. The boatman, recognizing what had happened, refused to allow them to sit on the seats going back to Capernaum. Huddled in the bow of the boat, they continued to search for real and imagined fleas.

An indirect result of the Jerusalem meeting was the publication of a social creed. For some time, Axling and his friends in the National Christian Council had been discussing guidelines for a Christian society. Their ideas were reported to, and discussed by, the conference. After the delegates returned they sponsored the publication of a statement which presented a strong Christian declaration for social justice.

A broad, irenic spirit brought Axling into working relationship with all factions of the Japanese Christian movement. Although he thought of organizational structure as a necessary tool in establishing the kingdom of God, he opened the auditorium at the Tabernacle to Kanzo Uchimura and his nonchurch movement. In return, Axling often spoke at the nonchurch gatherings. This cooperation, of course, did not imply complete agreement.

Axling began the publication of a monthly magazine, *The Religious World*, in 1912, because "of the two Japanese religious magazines that are read by pastors and evangelists, one is rationalistic in its teaching and its influence and the other is rabid in its opposition to organized Christianity—the church."

Axling's horizon continued to widen in the area of evangelistic preaching. By the 1920's he was one of the most effective non-Japanese speakers in Japan. In addition to one-night stands, he was often called upon for long evangelistic campaigns in Baptist and other churches. Many of the most prominent of Japan's Christian leaders were won to Christ under his preaching. The testimony of Dr. H. Saito, who later became one of the most prominent Baptist leaders in Northern Japan, is typical:

> About 1918, when I began attending the Osaka Baptist Church, I heard a sermon preached by a foreigner at a special evangelistic meeting. He spoke so earnestly and enthusiastically and so moved me by his speech that I could not sleep that night. That person was Dr. Axling. The next year, much against the wishes of my family, I was baptized. My strong determination was created by the power of that sermon preached by Dr. Axling.

The most grandly conceived Japanese evangelistic campaign of the 1920's was known as the Kingdom of God Movement. The idea sprang from two sources. The first was the desire of the National Christian Council to promote a broadly based evangelistic effort. The second was the fertile mind of Toyohiko Kagawa. While Kagawa was in prayer on Easter Day, 1928, the inspiration came to him. For some time he had been convinced that Christianity would remain powerless in Japan until it numbered at least one million persons. His idea, therefore, was to launch a campaign with the slogan "A Million Souls Movement."

When asked, Kagawa agreed to combine his movement with the plan of the National Council. The result was the Kingdom of God Movement, with its motto: "Thy Kingdom Come: In my Heart, and in the World." The goal was to win a million people to the Christian faith. The method was to be preaching and social action designed to penetrate all levels of Japan's society. Especially it was hoped to reach the lower classes.

Axling, who found the aims most congenial to his own interests, was at the center of the movement from the beginning. He was one of the two secretaries on the central committee and was probably the most used foreign speaker.

The central committee shaped general strategy, provided speakers, produced literature, and raised funds. District committees did the same for their localities.

Strategy called for large mass meetings with internationally famous speakers, smaller evangelistic campaigns in every church, training conferences to prepare lay evangelists, and occupational evangelism directed toward city workers and rural residents.

Efforts of direct evangelism, while they fell short of expectations, were fairly successful. The training of lay evangelists was the least satisfactory and may account, at least partially, for the failure of the movement to approach its goal.

Most creative was the attempt at occupational evangelism. Unlike most mission fields, Japan's small Christian following was composed largely of the intellectual and upper middle classes. Astute observers, such as Kagawa and Axling, realized by 1927 that neither the church nor the liberal forces were going to conquer Japan unless significant numbers of the common people were soon won over.

In the cities, rather unsuccessful conferences were planned to bring together factory workers and the Christian employers for a frank discussion of capitalism, labor conditions, wages, and related problems. Axling stated the aim as a desire to find solutions for these problems, "in harmony with the teachings and spirit of Christ." If these solutions could be found, laborers convinced of Christian concern would be open to the gospel message.

For the rural areas, specialists in rural work were brought together in a conference, and plans for the peasant gospel schools were formulated. Thirty such schools, which brought together fifteen to twenty-five young men for a week to ten days, were held in the first six months of 1931. In these schools the students received intensive training for Christian and community leadership. For the first time, solid progress was made in rural areas for the cause of Christ. Unfortunately, events proved that the movement had come too late.

The actual campaign started January 1, 1930, and reached its height during the first two years. About two-thirds of the Protestant churches were in some way involved.

By mid-1932, the movement was in decline. Probably the rising tide of fascism, more than any other factor, impeded its progress. Although it had failed in its ambitious goals, Axling's evaluation was correct: "Aside from the direct evangelistic results, this movement inaugurated a new era of cooperation among the Christian forces in Japan." In so doing, the movement held up Christ to the nation in a very powerful and persuasive way. But the nation was already looking in other directions.

7. THE TROUBLED YEARS

"DRAWING NEAR TO DAI NIPPON. How I love her! And how much I have suffered because of some of the things she has done since September 18, 1931! God guide her, I passionately pray."

"A new term of service equals a new opportunity to make good. God match me for this new chance."

Thus the fifty-nine-year-old Axling expressed his feelings to his diary as he made his way back toward Japan in February, 1933. He and Lucinda both were fifty-nine years old. Thirty-one of these years they had spent in Japan. They were now heading back for what might well be their last tour of duty. The possibility that William might reach his goal of a Christian Japan now seemed further away than in 1915. Yet, never one to pause in the face of difficulty, he would give his all. What he had lost in physical vigor since 1915, he had more than offset in experience, wisdom, and prestige.

What is more, his effectiveness had increased as he had assumed many of the characteristics of the Japanese people. Not only was he now known for his sympathetic understanding of Japan's national problems, but his manners and mannerisms had taken on an authentic Japanese flavor. Like the Japanese, he was intensely emotional, but had learned the Oriental art of complete control of external expression of these feelings. His continued study of the Japanese language enabled him to make the fine distinctions between synonymous ideograms possible only to learned Japanese. On many occasions, when a majority of the Japanese appeared in Western clothes, Axling showed up in traditional Japanese dress. Then, too, by the 1930's, advancing age gave him the appearance of an Oriental wise man.

Now, as the Axlings sat together on the boat, William turned to Lucinda and began to express his hopes and fears. Her response was animated but shallow. Something of the old cutting edge was gone. Lucinda could no longer reflect critically his deepest concerns. The team was not what it had been. While William's strength continued almost unabated, Lucinda had failed greatly. Neither her mind nor her body had fully recovered from the devastating attack of meningitis six years earlier. At the time, her bouncing back just in time for William to go to Jerusalem had seemed a miracle. Later it was evident that the disease had exacted a price for giving up its victim. After a few moments, William fell silent and began to reflect on the past furlough.

It had been a busy time, even by Axling's standards. The usual reunions were shadowed by the fact that both of his parents were now gone. The usual and diverse speaking schedule included fifteen state conventions. National officials, who also attended many of these meetings, were chuckling over a typical Axling idiosyncrasy. At nearly every meeting he began: "I had planned a sermon for today, but while I was praying this morning, the Lord laid a new message on my heart. I feel constrained to change my topic." Then he would proceed with essentially the same message at each convention. What he described probably happened the first time and he wished to preserve the drama of that situation for each new audience. The message dealt with the crisis and urgent opportunities in Japan.

In the middle of his furlough, Axling traveled to Herrnhut, Germany, to attend the triennial meeting of the International Missionary Council. Again he was a representative of the Japan Christian Council. The place could not have been more appropriately chosen. In 1932, all countries were gripped in a worldwide depression. Fascism and communism had reared their ugly heads. Western civilization was beginning to lose its nerve and thrust, and the whole mission project was being called into question. In Herrnhut two centuries earlier, Count Zinzendorf had revitalized the Moravians with his pietism, and, they, in turn, had stimulated all Protestantism to undertake the world mission.

The sixty persons representative of world Protestantism met very much aware of the roots of the effort and painfully conscious of the challenge of their time. Axling wrote of struggling with the "titanic issues which the Christian movement is facing throughout the world today." The delegates listed, particularly, the "ruthless economic and industrial development" and a "militant crusading communism and alarming restrictions of freedom of religion and missionary activity being imposed" by many governments. So the delegates were driven to a renewed effort to "discover the divine resources" and release these for the Christian cause and the good of the world.

The answers of the conference were familiar to sensitive Christians throughout the ages: The proclamation and practice of a full gospel of personal redemption and social justice. The encouragement of indigenous churches so that Christ might speak in his mighty power directly to all peoples and cultures rather than being strained through a western sieve. A greater spirit of unity and love among the divided Christian groups, that the world's needs might be met and the gospel heard. In a word, the answer was a full surrender to Christ and his way of life.

The proclamation of the conference was clear, but few in the church and fewer in the world were listening. This neglect was tragic, because Axling probably was correct when he wrote: "The International Missionary Council, under God, has been raised up for such an hour as this. It is the only organization that Protestant Christendom has that surveys the field as a whole, plans for the work as a whole, and furnishes the Protestant churches throughout the world the necessary machinery for cooperation and unity on a worldwide scale."

Hardly had Axling returned from Germany when a new blow fell. The Laymen's Foreign Missionary Inquiry had completed its review of missionary methods and accomplishments. The publication of a summary of its report, *Rethinking Missions*, was causing a furor throughout Christian America. Virtually all conservative Christians and many moderates and liberals felt that the study brought into question the whole missionary enterprise.

The American Baptist Foreign Mission Society, deeply troubled over the possible impact of the book on its constituency, asked Axling, as one of its senior missionaries, to give an evaluation. He reached New York City on November 19, 1932, the day after publication. By prearrangement, a copy of the book was waiting in his hotel room. He spent the next forty-eight hours in a careful analysis of the report.

On the basis of this study, Axling wrote a statement for the board which was published in a pamphlet, *The Appraisal Appraised*. Like most missionaries, he felt that the study group had not spent time enough getting under the surface and correctly evaluating what missionaries had accomplished. Depending upon a nonmission research group to collect data, and a brief visit largely independent of working missionaries, had given the commission a certain objectivity, but at the cost of empathy. Axling commented: "I miss the sense of humility and awe which, it seems to me, should grip men who are tracing the steps of the redeeming, recreating Christ across a century of India's, China's, and Japan's life. . . ."

Even more serious to Axling was the publicity which the report had received. From the newspapers one could well assume that a prestigious committee headed by the great William E. Hocking, of Harvard University, had discredited the whole missionary enterprise. Such an impression would lead orthodox Christians to question the integrity of their missionaries, and others to reject all missionary activity. The report, in general, ". . . furnished an alibi for pastors, laymen, and laywomen who had been looking for a chance to get out of the game."

On the other side, Axling could see much good in the report. It brought together a great mass of data and focused attention on many valid missionary problems. He agreed that Christianity must learn to relate more positively to other world religions and to Eastern culture. While some feared this necessity, Axling had learned that the Japanese religions sometimes became ". . . a sort of Old Testament, out of which they can move forward and upward" to Christ. His experience indicated that in any open interchange between Christianity and other faiths, ". . . the more outstanding Christ appears and the more unique and supreme becomes his place in the picture."

Axling also discovered that the commission, at many points,

saw the future of missions much as he saw it. They emphasized the need for training national leadership and developing indigenous churches, that the "foreignness about our churches and Christian institutions" might be removed. The mission enterprise must move beyond sheer evangelism to a "full ministry to the whole life of the whole man." Also, the scandal of a Christian following consisting of fewer than 1 percent of the population, but divided into dozens of denominations, must be removed.

Like most missionaries, Axling was distressed by the criticism of missionary personnel. Characteristically, however, he responded by confessing his own insufficiency and the weakness of many other missionaries. Then he went on to name many outstanding men on the foreign field. He fully agreed that quality was more important than quantity for missionary personnel and hoped that future appointees would be carefully chosen and ". . . trained for and sent out to fill definitely designated posts."

In general, Axling was disappointed that the commission had not understood the validity of pioneer methods, and had failed to see that forward-looking missionary societies, such as the American Baptist Foreign Mission Society, were already implementing the positive suggestions. Most of all, wrote Axling, "I miss a great, glowing soul in the report. There is no fire, no passion. Unharnessed and undirected emotionalism is dangerous and deadly, but when a divine passion ceases to pulsate through this foreign mission enterprise, it is doomed."

Although approaching his sixtieth birthday, William Axling lacked none of that fire or passion, nor was his emotion undirected. To him Christ was the answer—the answer to individual need and the only one who could give direction to life and bring love and justice among men and in society. While an individual could be redeemed, he could not reach his full potential apart from contributing to, and receiving from, society. To Axling, man's private life and the multitude of its relationships were of one piece, but never whole until in relationship to Christ.

On the way back to Japan, Axling stopped in Hawaii to proclaim his message in a campaign sponsored by the Kingdom of God Movement. He delivered thirty-three addresses in less than a month's time.

Then it was on to Japan. While Axling was still on the boat, the kind of double news so characteristic of this period in his life reached him. There were the telegrams of welcome from Japanese Christians and institutions. These expressed warm regard, deep confidence, and boundless hope. Then there was news of the alarming slide of the nation toward fascism.

The means by which Japan sought to fulfill its destiny had changed radically in September, 1931. At that time the Japanese military units stationed in Manchuria, without the approval of the civil government, and probably without orders from their own command, began a war which reduced that area to a colony of Japan. While the struggle between the democratic liberals and the military reactionists did not start or end in 1931, this incident can be called a turning point. The course was set by which Japan was to become Fascist at home, an aggressor abroad, and an Axis ally during World War II.

Why did Japan take this course? The reasons are complex. Knowledge of some of the factors is necessary to an understanding of Axling's stance and work. First were the international pressures. Japan needed resources and trade in order to live. Because she was a latecomer among modern nations, these were difficult to attain except at the expense of some other powerful country. During the 1920's Japan established her place among the nations of the world. Then came the worldwide depression, beginning with the crash of 1929. This disaster shook the great industrial powers, who had vast areas and resources under their control. Japan's very existence was threatened. The lesson seemed to teach that peaceful agreements were no substitute for spheres of influence based on power. Economic disadvantage was made more galling by the racial discrimination practiced by Western nations.

The liberals, on their part, made several mistakes. Like liberals of all ages, they became impatient with the slow pace of the people—particularly the rural folk, whom they despised as hopelessly backward. An intelligent understanding of democracy was limited almost entirely to the middle class in the cities. The Japanese liberals also overreacted to the danger on the left, including communism. In order to crush this radicalism, they allowed cruel repression of mildly leftist students and exalted the mystic position of the Emperor as a demigod who stood above the government, demanding unreasoned obedience. This tactic was later used by the militarists when they came to power.

Finally, an irresponsible fringe, more concerned with their personal freedom than with the great issues of the nation, expressed their freedom in behavior shocking to conservative rural society. The *maga* and *mobo* ("modern girl" and "modern boy"), the beatniks of the day, while not large in numbers, could be used by the reactionaries as examples of what Japan would become if liberal ideas prevailed.

The militarists, on their side, had never given up. When the forces of the army and the navy had been cut back during the 1920's, it was often possible to place retired officers as heads of schools, especially in small towns. Through these schools, the youth were indoctrinated in the ideals of the militarist. Many of the older generals and admirals leaned heavily toward the views of the financial leaders. By the 1930's, a new breed of young officers was coming to the fore. Many of these were sons of small landowners and even peasants who felt threatened by the ideological changes, and who had received very little benefit from economic progress. The vast majority of enlisted men were peasants. In the military, they moved from the ranks of the forgotten, downtrodden class to become the honored protectors of the Emperor. Military service was a way to instant prestige. The militarist understood the peasant and his problems, and he had a sincere, though materialistic, desire to improve his lot.

After September, 1931, the militarists moved unremittingly toward absolute control. They distributed anti-Western propaganda. They used the race issue extensively, promising to free Asians from Western colonialism. They also attacked the corrupting Westernizing influence of the liberals at home. They excused terrorists on the basis of the supposed threat to Japanese nationalism by the liberal internationalist. They kept parliamentary government, but reduced it to a powerless debating society of those who now claimed to speak for the Emperor. Thus, step by step Japan became Fascist. Anyone who stood in the way was assassinated. Cabinet followed cabinet in bewildering succession.

While still in America, Axling published in *The Baptist* a very frank appraisal of the situation, called "Japan in Upheaval." In that article, he described the staggering problems which Japan faced in "troubled and turbulent times." At the root was overpopulation, which had been blown up to crisis proportion by the general world depression and foreign pressures against Japan in the form of restrictive immigration, high tariff, and various other trade barriers. As a result, 80 percent of Japan's ever-growing flood of graduates could not find work. The laboring class, always poverty-stricken, was in desperate straits. Peasants, accustomed to live at a subsistence level, were now falling below that line.

Not all blame was laid on outside conditions. Axling made it quite clear that "within Japan corrupt politicians and grasping capitalists must bear much of the responsibility for the under currents and cross currents which are sweeping with such havoc across the nation's life. . . ."

In these muddy waters, both the Fascists and the militarists were fishing for control. At first, as Axling saw it, the Fascists supported the older liberals against a flood of Communist propaganda. As soon as their power increased, the Fascists turned against the liberal politicians and capitalists "on the ground that the corruption of the one and the greed of the other make them inimical to the state."

In 1932, the issue still was not clear. Axling sympathized with the Fascists in their desire to remove corruption and in their program to bring greater justice to the people. He feared, however, a coalition of the Fascists, all ultranationalists and ultra-patriots, with the militarists. This is, of course, what happened.

Axling ended the article and began his new missionary term with a stubborn optimism. His ideals were correct and his God was powerful. He and other Christians were called to give their all to make the good possibilities a reality. As he stated it:

> Japan's present pains are birth pains. She will emerge out of these agonies with a chastened soul and a more just economic and social order. Is it a mere matter of chance that at this critical hour in her history a Kagawa should have come on the scene and the Kingdom of God Movement come to the birth, both pointing her to Christ and his gospel as the only way out?

Almost as soon as he returned, Axling sought a platform from which to restate his ideals, and from which he hoped to begin to gather the Christian forces of Japan for a stubborn battle against the rising forces of evil. This opportunity was provided by the twenty-fifth anniversary of the founding of the Tabernacle.

November 18, 1933, was the chosen date. Axling used to the fullest his flare for dramatizing his work through prominent

Japanese. Some of the luster, however, was dimmed by the fact that many of Axling's contacts had lost, or were losing, their prominent places to the new regime. One of his oldest friends in high places, Baron Y. Sakatani, highlighted one of the most creative thrusts of the Tabernacle ministry. He said: "The social work conducted by the Tabernacle under the leadership of Dr. Axling became a forerunner or a model for subsequent social enterprises in Japan. . . ." The laymen's study of missions had suggested that, since the church could not meet the vast needs of the world, pilot projects which might stimulate local officials to action would be more effective. This the Tabernacle had done.

The then American ambassador to Japan, Joseph Clark Grew, came to the celebration somewhat reluctantly. Whether the reason for this reluctance was his busy schedule, or uncertainty about the wisdom of identifying American policy with the well-known Axling internationalism, is unknown. Whatever it was, he gave a good speech commending the Tabernacle for exhibiting the modern church attitude which "looks upon a disease as something to be cured, misery as something to be alleviated, ignorance as darkness to be dissipated." He added that all of this was done at the Tabernacle while "seeking to fulfill its primary object, the regeneration of souls. . . ."

Dr. Axling himself took the occasion to restate the purposes of the institution. From the beginning, he said, "three shining goals" had been held before the staff. The first was a yearning to "gear our Christian faith to actual life and put on a demonstration of its meaning in terms of concrete action." The second was "a consuming desire to render a full-orbed service, ministering to the total life of the people of our community." The third was to build a better world through "the building of better men," which could only be done by bringing them into "'vital relationship with God through Jesus Christ."

In 1933 the Axlings moved into a small Japanese-type house which they had built in Fukagawa on the property of the Christian Center. The house, large enough for the family and for holding small group meetings, was completed for about fifteen hundred American dollars. Even though Axling cheated a bit with an American-type bathroom and double doors, he felt that the home proved what he had insisted for years, "that there is no need whatever to build expensive foreign-type residences."

The frugality expressed in building the house was character-istic of the Axlings. Lucinda spent hours making and repairing clothes. William was seldom seen in a shirt that was not frayed at the cuffs. When missionaries came to Tokyo for meetings, they hoped they would not be assigned to the Axlings. Food was plain, and often not plentiful. An extra guest usually "meant that the slices were a little bit thinner," rather than the addition of another dish. Also, the gas heaters were always turned very low, leaving the house cold. In the morning, "Uncle Billy," as Axling was affectionately called, would rise and stand over the stove, reading his Bible. Women missionaries bustled around, helping Lucinda, partly to keep warm. They would have liked to talk, but felt they must not interrupt morning devotions.

Few blamed Uncle Billy. They knew he had suffered much with the Japanese through many disasters, and "it kind of hurt him to have more than the rest." They just hoped that when they visited the area they would be able to stay somewhere else.

Most important, this "home by the side of the road" was an attempt to stay close to the people. The detachment of growing prominence bothered Axling. Here he was again with the poor-est people. While he could still spend only a small amount of time visiting in their homes, he prayed that his and Lucinda's very presence would speak. "May our living in this industrial, under-privileged section show whose we are and whom we serve and mean much to our neighbors."

Identity with slum-dwellers had its limits. Friends enjoyed teasing Axling about the double locks on his front door, and the additional lock on each internal door. "If you love and trust the Japanese so much, why all of these precautions?" they queried. Axling would always grin a bit sheepishly and reply, "I love even the men who are attempting to steal, and I can best show my love by leaving them no opportunity to be tempted."

As in the past, Axling's primary responsibility was at the Taber-nacle and its extension, the Fukagawa Christian Center. He main-tained his office at the Tabernacle. Mr. Fujii carried nearly all of the day-by-day responsibility at the Tabernacle, and Mr. Isamu Chiba, son of Dr. Chiba, president of the seminary, directed the Christian Center.

The Axlings had known Sam, as they called Isamu Chiba, from birth. They had followed his career with interest. After he was graduated from William Jewell College and Rochester Theological Seminary, he joined the Tabernacle staff in 1928. Sam, with great affection, referred to Axling as his "old man." When he was planning marriage, he asked Axling to officiate. Rather timidly, he asked if Dr. Axling would use a service which he himself had written during his seminary studies. Without hesitation, the understanding older man complied. Axling also showed his respect by often asking Sam to correct the Japanese in a manuscript of a sermon he was preparing.

The depression added greatly to the needs that the Tabernacle desired to serve, and at the same time sapped its resources. About one-quarter million people in Tokyo were hit directly or indirectly by unemployment. Attempting to supply basic shelter, tents were erected on the grounds of the Christian Center. Crude floor boards and stoves were provided to combat the bitter cold through the winter. In 1931 the Christian Center supplied over six thousand free lodgings and fifteen thousand free meals. As the depression deepened, every department of the Tabernacle was strained by its policy of trying to meet every individual and community need with a definite program of Christian service.

By 1937 the financial situation was acute. While employment picked up at the advent of the war with China, funds dropped drastically. Money for Axling's work, much of which had come from the Imperial household, the Department of Home Affairs, and the city of Tokyo in recognition of social-service reform, was almost cut off. It also became more difficult to raise money from individuals in Japan. Under this stress Mr. Fujii almost demanded that Axling accompany him on the many necessary money-raising expeditions.

At the same time, the American Baptist Foreign Mission Society had been gradually cutting its contributions from 10,000 to 2,640 yen a year. While much of the cut reflected shrinking mission funds, part of it followed a questioning of the Tabernacle work. Some powerful voices were insisting that the project should become self-supporting.

Axling was caught in the middle of the debate. No one argued more strongly for indigenous control and self-support than he. Yet he felt that the Tabernacle was an exception because in America, or any other country, institutions engaged in that kind of work were rarely self-supporting. He produced figures showing that Methodist institutions of a similar nature received a far larger percentage of their budget from America. He argued that any attempt at a full-orbed ministry in a depressed area must depend upon endowment funds or other contributions, or cease to exist.

Apparently, some on the field and at home thought that the Tabernacle should reduce its services to what Central Baptist Church could support. The great thrust of the time was for evangelism and strengthening of local churches. Axling strongly approved this goal. He did, however, plead that the Tabernacle was winning more converts at less overall expense than any other Baptist institution in Japan. He also asked, "Are the Baptists so weak and so reduced in economic strength that a work such as the Tabernacle must be sacrificed?"

In the face of the emergency, Axling and his staff strained every nerve to keep from reducing services. All expenses were cut to the absolute limit. Salaries were lowered and working hours lengthened. The project was maintained, but at a terrific cost to the staff.

The extra strain was partly responsible for igniting the smoldering administrative controversy which always had plagued the Tabernacle operation. In essence, the problem was correlation of the activities and responsibilities of the Tabernacle and Central Church—both autonomous institutions using the same building. As tension arose, the Tabernacle became just one more storm center in the troubled years. On November 2, 1935, Axling expressed his frustration in his diary: "Have I spent thirty years building a temple of contention?"

As sides were taken, one faction wanted the church to assume the functions of the Tabernacle. Another faction thought that the church should make a larger financial contribution to the work, but did not consider the church qualified to direct the complex social program. Whenever Axling met with the Tabernacle trustees or the officers of the church, it was the same story. Each side accused the other of breaking faith, justified itself, and complained bitterly of conditions and personnel. The sensitive Axling took much of the blame. "The fault," he said, "falls on me, because of setting up a dual organization."

As it developed, Mr. Fujii became the central figure in the controversy. He was fully committed to the social program of the

Tabernacle, was highly competent in his work, and strongly distrusted the ability and the spirit of the church leadership. From his point of view the church had been partially subsidized by the Tabernacle through the years.

On its part, the church leadership felt that Mr. Fujii was not sufficiently concerned with the Christian aspects of the work. If he got his way, the church officials were sure they would be either excluded from the Tabernacle or forced to pay high rent.

Axling, who was "stunned and driven to despair" by this attack on Fujii, made it clear that he would "stand by him until the last." With his steady, unquestioned commitment, Axling found it difficult to understand why "Christians failed to work together."

Finally, in 1937, an open explosion came. Because of government pressure on all Christian groups, efforts were being made to clarify and secure land titles by placing properties under holding companies clearly controlled by Japanese. Fujii seized this opportunity to gain control of the building by a board completely congenial to the Tabernacle program. The Central Church, if it stayed, would remain as a renter, with no legal rights.

This maneuver caught Axling off guard. At the time, he was trying to persuade the home board to accept Japanese-controlled holding companies, but he certainly did not want to see the church excluded. At a meeting held March 22, 1937, the board of trustees voted to ask Fujii to resign. Axling was forced to agree that Fujii's action was unjustified. Privately, he referred to this as "the bitterest day of my life. After eighteen years of working together! Tragic!"

Although he was finally forced to oppose Fujii, Axling expressed his own sense of responsibility by resigning as a member of the Tabernacle board.

Axling's hope of settling the issue in Japan was frustrated when Fujii appealed his case to the foreign board in New York. Courteously, he sent a copy of this appeal to Axling. In response, Axling prepared a statement for the board and a reply to Fujii. A review of the history of the two institutions made it clear that the church had a right to exist without paying rent. It did have a moral obligation to help with expenses. This it had not always done adequately. At no time was the Tabernacle considered to be only a social-service institution. Money had been raised for an institutional church, and without the church the Tabernacle would become an entirely different institution.

As he looked back, Axling saw how unwise he had been in creating a double-headed organization. All of the work should have been kept under the church. "But," he said, "our eagerness to see the Central Church self-supporting blinded me to the dangers involved." Knowing that the total endeavor could not become self-supporting, he had hoped to make clear what part was being subsidized. The result was "separate program, conflicting interest, and divided loyalty."

Sadly, Axling saw that all sides had failed "in their attitudes and conduct and we are all responsible for the present impasse." But his most serious shortcoming lay at another point: "my failure and inability to fuse a more Christlike attitude and spirit among those related to this situation. The fundamental cause of our problem has been, and is, a lack of humility, love, forbearance, and a spirit of forgiveness. We have utterly failed to be Christian."

In a sense, of course, he was right. Nevertheless, more careful administrative policies would have helped. Axling never excelled as a day-by-day administrator. He always expected everyone to share his sense of dedication, his largeness of heart, and his ability to overlook irritations along the way, so that the final goal might be reached. Then, too, Axling often escaped the little irritations by traveling to distant places to hold meetings, or by trotting off to an exclusive club to give an address.

Fellow missionaries, as well as Japanese co-workers, often felt that Axling expected too much of them. He never said so directly, but the assumption of his speech and actions tended to reflect on them. Those who knew him well could see chinks in his armor. For example, more than one missionary had traveled with Axling, slightly ashamed of his heavy baggage, only to discover the unencumbered Axling quite willing to share his friend's extra blanket.

This unyielding posture of rectitude had its compensating side. Axling always supported his colleagues. He never engaged in missionary feuds or wrote letters to weaken the position of a colleague. Almost always he refused to impute a wrong motive to any man.

When one was in trouble, he could always depend on Axling for sympathetic understanding, if not defense. When J. S. Kennard was accused of leftist sympathies, it was Axling who recognized his ability and suggested that he might fit as a teacher in the Philippines. When a teacher at Kanto Gakuin was divorced and remarried, everyone turned against him. Axling alone pleaded for tolerance and understanding.

Actually, the Tabernacle controversy was not settled. A sort of truce took the place of a solution until the building was sold during the second world war. Both Mr. Fujii and Dr. Axling continued to work at the institution.

About the same time, Axling's domestic tranquillity was shattered by their foster daughter. The little refugee Haruko, who had become their foster child after the 1923 earthquake, was now an adolescent. When she met Axlings at the boat as they returned from America, in 1933, William was startled. "How Haruko has grown!"

The maturing of a child, which nearly always surprises parents, was an unusual shock to the Axlings. Haruko never quite fitted into that dedicated household. Probably no child could. The deep, tender, and abiding love which the Axlings had for each other was based more firmly in their mutual commitment to the mission task than in their purely personal relationship. The latter was also very real, but there was never time to develop it. The child was not quite sure that she was included in this family relationship.

On their part, the Axlings were never completely comfortable with Haruko. Childlessness was one of Lucinda's greatest disappointments, which she never expressed freely or fully. William almost never mentioned the subject. One time, in 1936, after returning from visiting the Chibas, who had just lost a second child, he commented, "A childless home is a lonely place, but it is hard to have them and lose them."

But his home was not childless. There was Haruko. By one of those queer twists of fate, however, the Axlings' love for Japan distorted their relationship to the person closest to them. They were determined that she remain thoroughly Japanese. Never once did she accompany them to America, nor was she allowed to share the American side of their life.

Haruko felt rejected. She learned, however, to get compensatory benefits from an indulgent Lucinda. The result was a marginal existence. Enough benefits came her way from living in the Axling home that she was looked upon as spoiled. Yet she did not feel the security of belonging.

William's busy schedule was one factor that prevented a close relationship from developing with his foster daughter. He did often plan to be there for special occasions, such as a birthday. He was certainly concerned about her. As he realized that womanhood was approaching, he often prayed, "God keep her true."

About the time the Tabernacle controversy was developing, the first serious signs of adolescent rebellion appeared. Axling was shaken. He was unable to talk with his friends about it, but in his diary he recorded: "Had a heart-breaking scene with Haruko. How hard it is for human nature to keep going straight!"

Later the situation calmed. In 1936, Haruko requested church membership. What a joyful day in the Axling household! The baptism took place September 26, 1936. "For years we have prayed and waited for her to take this character-determining step!"

Haruko was a pretty child, with a pleasant personality, who grew into an attractive young woman. While singing in the choir at Fukagawa, she met a fellow choir member, Mr. Okada. When she was about twenty years old, she married this promising young architect. Three children were born to this marriage.

Probably the Christian Center provided the most personal satisfaction for Axling during this period. Even before they moved to the area he usually made his way there for the evening service. Afterward he spent much time directly with the people around the center. Frequently through the winter he traveled with Sam from house to house, distributing clothing, fuel, and the Christian message.

Often these excursions brought more pain than pleasure. In Fukagawa he never overlooked the Japanese custom of visiting one's neighbors between Christmas and New Year's Day. After this experience in 1933, he wrote: "Called with Chiba on sixty or more families. The sights seem terrible. What would Jesus do? What would he have me do?" In spite of personal pain at such sights, it was characteristic of Axling to try to do what Jesus would have him do, and this gave him satisfaction.

A somewhat more frivolous satisfaction, by Axling's standards, was golf. In the spring of 1934, when he was approaching sixty-one years of age, he took up this diversion. Up until this time his one recreation had been walking. Walking was his favorite means of transportation. When forced by long distance to take the train, it was not unusual for him, after arrival, to strike out across the countryside on a six-mile hike. His friends were accustomed to hearing him remark, "I've just got to get out and walk."

The decision to become a golfer was made in typical Axling fashion. "After long study and prayer, I took steps to take up golf to keep physically and spiritually fit." From time to time he complained about the frustrations of his new sport. He wrote: "I begrudge the time and the expense." There is probably no connection, but it is interesting to note that the militaristic rigorists had designated golf as a decadent, rich man's game. There was something of the mild protester in Axling.

As Axling's actual work at the Tabernacle lessened, the slack was more than taken up by other activities—both Baptist and interdenominational. Recognized as an elder statesman by both Japanese and missionaries, he was called upon to perform numerous official and unofficial duties. He was honest when he stated: "Missionaries and Japanese alike embarrass me with their confidence."

Most important among his official duties were the chairmanship of the board of trustees of Kanto Gakuin and the chairmanship of the executive board of the East Japan Baptist Convention. This convention represented the work that American Baptists sponsored in Japan. As chairman of the executive board, Axling found that many of the problems in and among the churches came to him as they would to an executive secretary in the States.

Many hours of Axling's "free" time were consumed in writing and speaking to an ever-widening audience on a variety of subjects. Unquestionably, he enjoyed his popularity and delighted in expanding opportunities. Yet these increased openings only added a new dimension to the difficult question Axling was always asking: "What shall I do with my life?" He found it almost impossible to say no to any request.

By 1934 Axling was complaining: "There is no end of requests for articles from all kinds of periodicals." These articles ran the gamut from devotional sermons to interpretations of the international situation. Given Axling's inclusive view of the Christian faith, there was no sharp difference in his treatment of the various subjects.

In addition to periodical articles, Axling published his most widely-read book, a biography of Kagawa, in 1932. This was translated into many languages, including Arabic. The next fall, Kagawa asked Axling to translate his book *Christ and Japan* into English. For many months, every spare moment was given to making Kagawa speak idiomatic English. After spending most of one Sunday on the project, Axling emerged to ask Loue, "Was the Sabbath kept or broken by this activity?"

As requests for articles came in a steady stream, invitations to speak came in an overwhelming flood. Often for months at a time, he spoke on an average of once a day.

In that these activities kept him from direct ministry with people, he was troubled. After finishing one writing assignment, he asked, "Have I become a man with a pen, rather than a personality with a message?" In speaking he could feel the immediate response, but he even questioned this activity with close friends. "I have spent all day working on addresses—words, words. How many words I utter! May my life speak louder for my Lord." Of course, there is no record of his ever turning down an article or speaking engagement unless he had an unavoidable conflict.

Knowing that Fujii and Chiba were operating the Tabernacle and Christian Center, the American Baptist Foreign Mission Society asked Axling to give general supervision to the work in northern Japan. Persons responsible for that request probably were either unaware of his many other involvements or unsympathetic toward them. This was in 1933, when the Steadmans, who had carried on the work in the North, were forced to return to America.

With characteristic vigor, Axling attacked the new responsibility. Most of his efforts consisted of evangelistic meetings and conferences with local leaders. The work was not easy. The center of the northern field was 330 miles from Tokyo. Many of the stations were on remote branch rail lines. In order to save time and money, Axling frequently traveled by night, sitting up in a day coach, so that he might spend the day on the field. For a man in his sixties, such a journey was quite an undertaking.

The one who objected most to this arrangement was Lucinda. Though she still taught a Bible class and did some children's work, she was no longer fully employed. She was lonely. Also, she worried about William's health. Her warnings, which at times became nagging, were brushed aside by her unperturbed husband.

Whenever he was away, Axling wrote at least a postcard to Loue every day. When he returned, she greeted him excitedly and asked to be told what had happened. William, however, always exhausted, wanted only to rest. When he was out, he gave himself completely to anyone he met. But when he came home he "just kind of slumped." Even if there were company he would sit in a corner and say nothing. When Lucinda was equally involved in missionary activity, this was all right. As she withdrew from active participation, however, it made her furious.

Axling had little difficulty in transferring his missionary theory and practice back to the rural areas. Soon a stream of observations and advice was flowing to New York. He had the same vision for a Christian witness in rural Japan that he had developed in the city. He discovered that the churches in the North were struggling for existence. "If there is no missionary resident on the field," he wrote, "we will probably be able to hold the present line, although even that is not going to be easy at some of the centers."

Within a short time, Axling decided on the kind of missionary who was needed. He should be a man who would "stimulate and encourage these faithful workers to make the most of a great rural opportunity." Specifically, he should be "a compelling personality and a great growing soul" and also trained at Cornell in agriculture. In other words, a young rural Axling!

One of the delights of returning to the North was the opportunity to renew association with Mr. H. Saito, who had been converted by Axling in an evangelistic meeting in Osaka. Later as a bewildered young man, Mr. Saito had gone timidly to the Tabernacle, where Axling spotted him. "Oh, Mr. Saito, welcome to Tokyo!" Mr. Saito could hardly answer. "He still remembers me —me, such a little insignificant person," he thought. Axling took him into his home, helped him get into the seminary, and gave him experience at the Tabernacle. They became fast friends.

Now this friendship was deepened when Axling learned that Mr. Saito was trying to establish a dairy school as a means of practical help and Christian witness. Axling was one of the first to encourage the plan in the face of many doubters.

The execution of the plan was overtaken in 1934 by serious crop failure and attendant famine in the North. Mr. Saito needed land for his school. When an ideal plot became available, he and his friends were utterly without money. Time was of the essence. In bold faith they borrowed 500 yen, with the promise to return it within a few days. Mr. Saito bought the land, but what then?

Without any real plan, but backed by the prayers of his two friends, Mr. Saito went to Tokyo. Early one morning he arrived at Dr. Axling's home in Fukagawa. While he was hesitating, deciding whether or not to knock, Axling opened the door.

"Well, Mr. Saito, welcome to my home!"

"I am sorry to call so early and unannounced."

"Strange, very strange," Axling was smiling and shaking his head. "You know I was just praying in my morning devotions. I was concerned about what to do with 500 yen I received yesterday from my book about Dr. Kagawa. Then the northern farmers came to my mind, and now here you stand."

As soon as he could find speech, Mr. Saito told Axling of his need for exactly 500 yen. Axling invited him in. They read one of his favorite Scripture verses, Philippians 4:19: "My God will supply every need of yours." Then they prayed together.

Renewed responsibility in the North, the scene of his early ministry, brought back to Axling many memories. The most painful was the famine. Because of his previous experience he was asked to survey the situation for the National Christian Council and then to direct some aspects of relief work. Once more he was exposed to mass raw human suffering. In five villages he found over fifty thousand people in desperate straits. "80 percent of the primary children are anemic, and infant mortality has jumped to 30 percent."

Once again his robust health was threatened. During the winter of 1934 he was forced to spend several days in bed with his eyes bandaged. The next fall he was fighting a "serious nervous slump" which kept him from his work for almost a month. Soon, however, he was again able to "get a grip on myself" and carry on.

A more serious threat to his continued ministry came as a result of an accident. On August 29, 1936, while helping to carry a heavy swimming float up the beach, he fell and the float landed on his throat. Breathing became exceedingly difficult and his voice was completely gone. In great pain, he was rushed to the hospital in Sendai where he spent thirty-four days. It was October 15 before he received the first medical assurance that his voice would likely return.

During those two and one-half months Axling suffered both emotionally and physically. The diary records the conflict:

September 1: "We live in deed and not in words. I have lived too much in words. Now I face the possibility of a voiceless future. Have I preached my last sermon?"

September 15: *I have been pleading to God for another chance.* He has given me so many. Will I make any more of this if it is given? There must be a *last* chance."

September 17: "For 21 voiceless days I have swung back and forth from hope to fear, confidence to mere despair, regarding the outcome of this fight to get back my voice. God knows—that is enough."

September 23: "I have talked too much, both to God and man, and not listened enough. Thus, the loss of the voice seems a tragedy, a chance to learn the art of listening."

September 30: "How my faith varies with every wind that blows! When prospect of recovery is good, faith unfurls its banners, but at every setback its flags fly at halfmast."

October 3: "Put myself in Dr. Isobe's care, but he is simply an agent. God can heal. He is still the Great Physician."

One year after the accident, Axling wrote: "A year ago today, I faced the end of things but God has given me another chance. How easily we look upon our common blessings as commonplace!"

Letters bearing good wishes and assuring prayerful concern came from all over the Empire. Many, such as Fujii, made the trip to bring love and greetings in person. If Axling had ever entertained doubts concerning the regard with which he was held by the Japanese Christians, the experience of the accident swept them away. Also, faithful Loue, "utterly forgetful of her own limited strength," came to his side and stayed most of the time.

Although he recovered, speaking continued to be difficult.

While preaching he could force himself, but sustained conversation was tiring. Two years later he was well enough to request and receive a two-year extension beyond retirement age. Not that he doubted the capabilities of his colleagues. The day before his accident he had lunch with Rev. and Mrs. Marlin D. Farnum. Afterward he commented: "Fine folks like these enable one to grow old confident that the future will be in good hands." He just was not ready to quit!

One aspect of the 1930's which heartened Axling was a growing ecumenical activity. When he went to Japan in 1901, the lines of division between the denominations had been sharply drawn and there was little fellowship between different groups. Gradually, joint evangelistic campaigns, missionary fellowships, and then the National Christian Council opened the way to cooperation. Although progress was rapid in the 1930's, even this achievement came as much from civil pressure as from Christian love.

Axling was among those who threw himself on the side of unity. Most inexcusable to him was the separate work maintained in Japan by Northern and Southern Baptists from America. These two groups had divided Japan between them, and each had developed churches, schools, publications, and all of the necessary denominational machinery. The Japanese could see no sense in this arrangement. When people moved from one section of the country to another, they felt "the absurdity of trying to change and act differently when no difference exists."

On special occasions "Japanese Baptists have shaken hands across that imaginary dividing line and good-naturedly asked each other why they were divided into two camps." In 1939 a joint committee worked out a plan of merger. Axling, who was widely acceptable to both groups, played a major role in this accomplishment.

The union was ratified in January, 1940, at Himeji, and went into effect on the first of April of that year. It brought together thirty-six churches sponsored by Northern Baptists and twenty-three sponsored by Southern Baptists. Even though many Japanese Baptists and missionaries on both sides desired union, the action was unquestionably hastened by the impending bill for control of religious bodies. This bill was expected to require at least fifty churches for a denomination to register as a legal religious body.

The accelerating progress in wider denominational cooperation was even more of a mixed blessing—mixed because of government pressure and often tainted by growing world tensions. For better and worse, Axling was involved at almost every level. He continued as an officer of the National Council, served on several committees, and represented Japanese Protestants at various functions both at home and abroad.

At times he was hopeful, as when he came home one night and wrote in his diary: "Attended a meeting on church union and able to make some suggestions which seemed helpful. It is great to be in where history is being made." Other contacts left him discouraged and uncertain: "How earnestly Jesus prayed for the unity of his followers, and how indifferent we are about it!"

On three occasions Axling traveled to other lands to represent Japanese Christianity. The first, in 1935, which took him to China as a fraternal delegate from the Japan National Christian Council, was the most depressing. War was two years off, but relations between the two countries were severely strained by Japanese economic imperialism. Three years earlier the Chinese Christian Council had refused to acknowledge the presence of the Japanese representatives. This time, however, they were received.

With his usual dogged optimism, Axling drove ahead, seeking to cement relationships in Christ. He accepted the cool Chinese reception as "a wonderful welcome." As often as possible he spoke publicly and privately to Chinese Christians. His contagious faith broke through, and he discovered: "It is easy for Christians to understand each other, but how hard for nations." Although barely submerged hostility, which he continually encountered, hurt Axling deeply, it drove him to greater effort. On the way home he thanked God for the "opportunity and privilege of speaking a word for Christ, the only solution for racial and international problems."

After that experience Axling made two other short trips to China, attempting to set up retreats of Christians from the two nations. These were to provide an opportunity for closer relationships to develop. The first was to be in China, with Japanese representatives, and the second was to bring Chinese to Japan. But war canceled the plan seeming to deny Axling's frequent prayer: "O Father, bind these two nations to each other."

A second major journey took Axling to the All-Philippine Christian Conference in 1937. This time he was invited because of his reputation in ecumenical circles, rather than as a formal representative from Japan. After the conference he remained in the Philippines for a five-week evangelistic and lecture tour.

Traveling to one of these lectures became quite an adventure. The pilot of the small plane hired to transport him lost his way, ran out of fuel, and was forced to make two emergency landings in the sea. A routine six-hundred-mile four-hour trip stretched into 1,100 miles and twenty-four hours. Axling emerged with his usual smile and gave his lecture as though nothing had happened.

The young Philippine church left a favorable impression on Axling. He approved as a forward step the recent change from the loosely organized National Christian Council to the Philippine Federation of Evangelical Churches, to which only denominations could belong. The speed with which indigenous leadership was being developed also pleased him, though he wondered whether the mother church might not be withdrawing her support too fast.

Axling especially sought out and preached to Japanese groups living in the Philippines. The attendance was small, but interest good. Here, as in other places, he found Japanese living abroad difficult to reach with the gospel. Their attention was too exclusively absorbed by "fighting for prestige and wealth."

The true breadth of Axling's ecumenical spirit was revealed on this journey. It happened that the Roman Catholic Church had held one of its great world eucharistic conferences in Manila just before the Protestant gathering. Axling's report of this event was both a criticism ("may not go deep in its impact") and an appreciation: "This congress also demonstrated on a large scale the unity and solidarity of the Roman Catholic Church. Here men of every race, nation, and class were of one mind, motivated by one purpose, and moving toward one goal." On the boat he had personal contact with several priests and lay Catholics who were traveling to the conference. His final evaluation of this experience was that "life is too short and the opposing forces are too powerful for friends of Jesus to be fighting each other."

The third journey took Axling to Madras, India, as a representative from Japan to the meeting of the International Missionary Council, in 1938. He also served on the planning committee, which originally had expected the meeting to be in Hangchow, China. However, as soon as the undeclared war broke out between Japan and China, the other members realized that the site would have to be changed, or the conference canceled.

As late as September 15, 1937, the eternally optimistic Axling wrote to Dr. John R. Mott, pleading that a change not be made too quickly. Axling went on to express his hope that a settlement might be reached before the time of the conference. If this happened, he wrote,

> The Christians of Japan and China should take advantage of the earliest possible opportunity to get together and unite their forces in creating a new atmosphere and in building better relations between these two nations. What finer opportunity could they find for doing this than the proposed World Christian Conference!

The committee overruled this option, since to wait would force a canceling of the conference if peace did not come. The majority felt it imperative that world Christianity should consult and speak in the midst of a determining world situation.

Lucinda and Mrs. Iglehart, of the Methodist mission, both accompanied their husbands on what proved to be a most pleasant voyage and conference. Axling's chief contribution was an extensive report to the evangelistic section on the Kingdom of God Movement. In spite of the satisfaction he felt in his participation in the conference, Axling felt that he was under a shadow. Japan had forced the moving of the conference by an undeclared war.

At least one dream came true in the troubled years. The United Church of Christ in Japan (the *Kyodan*) was born. The day the Baptists voted to join, Axling confided to his diary: "For years I have dreamt and urged one Christian church in Japan, and I didn't expect to see it realized in my lifetime. A miracle!"

But when it came, the miracle was viewed by some as a trick of the devil. The actual process of unification began in April, 1940, while Axling was in America on furlough. At that time the long-threatened Religious Bodies Law went into effect. For the first time Christianity was fully and legally recognized as one of Japan's religions. And, like the others, it was brought under a specific regulation. In many ways this law clarified what was previously a difficult relationship, guided by over three hundred overlapping and erratically enforced laws.

The bill did not require unity, but specified that no denomination with fewer than fifty churches or five thousand members would receive recognition. From the government perspective, it was justified. The other official religions, Buddhism and Shintoism, included millions in single organizations. Why should the small Christian following be split into so many parts?

The law also required greater Japanese control. This, too, seemed reasonable. By this time other aspects of Japanese life had learned what was helpful from the West, had made adaptations to Japanese culture, and were controlled by Japanese. Why should the church still depend on foreign capital and personnel? This dependence was especially noticeable in schools, where a major portion of the budget came from abroad and many departments were headed by missionaries.

Finally, the Japanese assumed that the government had not only the right but the responsibility to supervise the religious life of its people. Religion was one factor to be used for the good of the Japanese state. This had always been the Japanese view. The liberals looked upon Christianity not as an autonomous faith but as a source of morality for the people. The only thing that changed with the rise of the militarists was the purpose to which religion was to be put.

Although no poll is available, probably a sizable majority of Japanese Christians were in favor of church union. Denominational distinctions which had grown out of developments in the West meant little to them. Missionaries were more evenly divided, with possibly a majority doubtful.

Previous attempts toward unity had developed only a fairly effective council of churches. Steps beyond this were blocked by institutional inertia and endless theological discussion which similar attempts elsewhere met. The strong push of the new law was welcomed by many national leaders and by at least some missionaries, including Axling.

In spite of much willingness from within and strong pressure from without, the task of unification was not easy. In September, 1940, the National Christian Council passed a resolution committing the churches to complete self-support and to autonomy in such areas as setting policy, owning and governing property, and administering all ecclesiastical affairs. The Council went on to resolve the quick establishment of a union of all churches into a single body. All except a few small groups agreed to move ahead toward the creation of a united church. Subcommittees were established to settle the problems of structure, finances, creed, and policy.

January 21, 1941, Axling wrote: "Visited committee drafting bases of united church. Having rough sailing. Why is it so difficult for Christians to get together? Christ knew it would be and prayed for them."

The pressure of time precluded the development of a complete statement of faith. The first declaration of purpose, however, included enough to establish the overwhelmingly orthodox purpose of the founders: "The triune God, Father, Son and Holy Spirit, as revealed in the Holy Bible, forgives sin, justifies, sanctifies and endows with eternal life those who believe through the atonement of Jesus Christ, who died for the sins of the world and rose again."

Undoubtedly, the most immediate problem was to find a means of responding to government policy which was openly aimed at making the church a constituent part of Japanese solidarity. "Make your Christian faith stronger by following closely the way of traditional Japanese moral teaching, and thus contribute your share to the future of the Japanese empire," exhorted a statement in Constitution as one of "the life principles of this Kyodan."

That the church might become truly indigenous was desirable. That it become only a tool of Japanese fascism was not. It seems useless to argue whether the United Church became the first while escaping the second. Axling, as usual, saw the positive. July 15, 1941, he wrote: "The United Church takes over the N.C.C. headquarters and much of its work. Thus, Christianity becomes indigenous and part and parcel of Japanese life." Others, however, saw Japanese cultural and national aims swallowing the Christian faith. Whether Japanese Christians were more blindly patriotic than Christians of other lands is questionable. Actually, war and defeat stunted the development and changed the course of the Kyodan so quickly that no one knows what would have happened under more normal circumstances.

On June 24-25, 1941, the founding assembly was held, at which thirty-four Protestant bodies united. At first there were eleven "blocs," representing denominational families, whose delegates made up the Board of Counselors. In the end only two of the

Episcopalian bishops joined. Most members came from the Presbyterian, Methodist, Congregationalist, Baptist, Lutheran, and Disciples groups. The various denominations retained some liberty of belief, church order, and activity.

The structure of the church, in conformity with both governmental intentions and Japanese character, was highly centralized and autocratic. The director had almost absolute power to appoint, discipline, and dismiss both pastors and department heads. He also controlled finances and property. The director was elected by the General Assembly of the Kyodan and approved by the Minister of Education.

As before stated, no one knows what might have happened had the Kyodan been able to live a more normal existence. Stephen Neill's evaluation is about as far as one can go: "The record of Japanese Christians during the war is a mixture of heroism and subservience of perplexed loyalties and sorely tested fidelity. The wonder is not that the Kyodan accomplished little, but that under the conditions of its existence it was able to accomplish so much."

Axling's appraisal, written in October, before the war broke out, is interesting:

A year ago Protestants of Japan made an epic-making decision to establish a united church. This dream is now a reality. Events since prove that if Japanese Christians had not dared to venture to assume self-support and establish a united front, the Christian movement here would have gone into eclipse. The Japanese Christians have moved out and occupied the Christian line and are holding it.

Although Axling, like others, disapproved of governmental interference in Christian affairs, he believed that the church would be able to withstand these influences best as a *united* church. He also believed that a truly indigenous church was possible only through a uniting of all the Christian forces.

Nothing distressed Axling during the 1930's as much as the relentless rise of the militarists and the rush of the nations toward the second world war. These developments spelled defeat for his dream of a Christian Japan. His reputation as a missionary-statesman assured him a voice, but the removal of his friends from office robbed him of direct influence. Nevertheless, he continued to keep in touch with his old friends, was active in such organizations as the Japan-American Society, and continued to interpret Japan's needs and actions to Americans, both in writing and in speaking.

The last-named task became increasingly difficult. Japan's methods were indefensible. On the other hand, as world tension increased, a blind nationalism was capturing America, as well as every other country.

Axling continued to acquaint Americans with Japan's legitimate interests, described the good aspects of Japanese leadership in Asia, and urged that Japan not be censured for doing as other nations had done during their periods of development. Privately, Axling still desperately hoped that American recognition of Japan's problems would ease tensions sufficiently to allow a return of the liberals to power. They, too, would seek Japanese ascendancy in the Far East, but by more acceptable methods.

Two pamphlets published in 1938 summarized his arguments. *Toward an Understanding of the Far East Crisis* was a rather general treatment. *Light and Shadows in North China* was written after he traveled through that area with a group sponsored by Japanese businessmen.

In the first pamphlet, Axling clearly delineated Western and American responsibility for the crisis. According to Axling, Japan had been forced to take drastic measures when she attempted to break out of the economic web which Western imperialism had thrown about her islands. She was goaded into a radical response by discriminatory immigration legislation and by United States racial attitudes, exhibited by policies such as rejection of the racial-equality clause in the Treaty of Versailles.

While not approving Japanese imperialism, he reminded Americans that each Western country had risen to prominence by exploiting weaker peoples. "It ill behooves those nations to hang on to their holdings with one hand and point an accusing finger at Japan with the other."

Japan's leaders, Axling believed, felt a sense of "manifest destiny." They considered themselves called upon to save Asia for the Asians. The arguments they were using were very similar to those used by the United States when it forcibly took land from Mexico. Of course other Asians did not see it this way, any more than Mexico agreed with the United States' rationale for pushing to the Pacific.

The pamphlet *Light and Shadows in North China* recognized

the sufferings caused by the war and the abuses by many of the Japanese civilians who were crowding into North China to exploit the situation. It also stated that the Japanese military government was putting much thought and effort into relief and reconstruction. While not condoning Japanese aggression, Axling took the position that China had not been free, nor was she capable of solving her own problems. He believed that it was better for Japan to take the lead in the building of China than for the West to continue in that role.

All of Axling's semipolitical pronouncements during this period were pro-Japanese, but they did not condone militaristic behavior. Power politics could never solve the world's problems. "Unless all of us have a vital sense of kinship, a living sense of affinity and a flaming passion for brotherhood and are bound together by this deeply rooted spiritual bond, every other tie will be superficial and temporary. . . ."

But Axling was not guilty of a Pollyanna attitude. Mere good feelings and friendship were not enough. "Economic justice," he said, "implemented in a fair distribution of the earth's area and its natural resources, must be realized." Even this would be insufficient without a ". . . God-implanted consciousness of identity and kinship between nations. . . ."

In all these writings also, far more than most men of his time, Axling recognized the real and growing threat of communism in the Far Eastern situation. He realized that reforms must come and justice be established or communism would take over. He saw Japan, in spite of its many weaknesses under the militarists, as the one force which could stop communism.

Criticism was inevitable. The mild displeasure and apathy which had greeted his previous ventures into international affairs was now replaced by angry protest. Among the charges was one that his pamphlet *Light and Shadows in North China* was published and distributed by the Japanese government. In answering this charge, Axling made it clear to Dr. J. W. Decker, then mission secretary, that he had "taken precautions to safeguard my independence and integrity, and not to get entangled in partisan attitudes or political situations." He wrote the pamphlet because he did not approve the general report of the group with whom he had toured North China. Rather than his compromising, the businessmen had accepted his interpretation and published his pamphlet. Axling pointed out that many prominent missionaries were using both of his pamphlets to instruct their constituencies in Great Britain and America.

More grievous was a document prepared by a group of missionaries to China which was presented to, and made available by, the American Baptist Foreign Mission Society. This report, highly critical of Axling's interpretaton of the situation, concluded that he was making "a laughingstock of himself" by his support of Japan.

"Such expressions are hard and hurt, hurt terribly, but they are good discipline. It does one good to see himself as others see him." Thus Axling expressed himself to his diary in a lonely hotel room the day he received a copy of the document. It came after he had spent several disheartening months of furlough trying to persuade Americans not to paint "the Japanese blacker than the truth."

He was trying to paint honestly. Repeatedly he made it clear that he had no love for the militarists, but "I still believe in Japan and have an unutterable love for the Japanese people." The Japanese side also needed to be heard. "It is not easy to paint the picture so that it will be neither whiter nor blacker than the truth," he sighed, "but someone should try, though it is an unpopular thing to do in these days."

After studying the document, he came to a sad conclusion. He and Mrs. Axling were already on extended time beyond retirement. He wrote a letter of resignation so that the board would not be embarrassed. "The feelings of an individual must not be allowed to jeopardize the interests of such an organization," he wrote. His sixty-seven years rested with unaccustomed heaviness upon his shoulders that April day in 1940.

The mission board supported Axling in his right to speak and enabled him to return to Japan. The board's action, however, did not imply approval of his stand. Dr. Decker wrote to him, expressing the viewpoint which had come to be held by even friendly, informed Americans:

I know that you and many others feel that Japan's adherence to the Axis was a step forced on her by the opposition of the United States. However, I am compelled to take a contrary view. It seems to me that the United States has been more patient and hesitant in the steps taken than has been true of any great nation with similar power in the history of the world. . . . Please do not think my attitude has changed, for it has not. I am very conscious of Japan's real needs, that our country has been smug, complacent and selfish in the enjoyment of our ample place in the sun, but it will do no good to hide our faces from the other side of the picture. . . . I write to you frankly because I appreciate you and your viewpoint.

A deeply disturbed William Axling returned to a turbulent Japan in the fall of 1940. Outside of rendering some help in the formation of the United Church, he felt that he was on the sidelines, helplessly watching a life's work go down the drain. What could be done was the responsibility of the missionaries led by Field Secretary Martin D. Farnum and by Japanese leaders, such as Mr. Fujii and Mr. Chiba. His advice was still sought, but all important events seemed now determined by blind forces leading toward war.

One last, desperate effort to ward off destruction was made by Japanese Christians who had absorbed the aspirations of men like Axling. They planned to send a deputation to American Christians in an effort to build bridges of understanding.

Axling was asked to join them. Shaken by his recent experience of rejection, however, he resisted. His well-known stand might offend both Americans and the Japanese. Also, acceptance would mean leaving Lucinda behind. When he broached the subject she was adamant. Of course, he should go.

"I will miss you very much," she said, "but you have to do what God wants you to do."

"But, Loue, you complain about my trips here in Japan."

"This is different. They aren't always necessary, but who understands Japan and can speak for her the way you can? No one, and you know it."

William looked long and admiringly at his wife. What a faithful and dedicated woman she was! Yet he was worried. What if war should separate them? Could either of them bear it?

Then, too, Lucinda did not have the same standing with the Japanese that she had earlier enjoyed. Illness had changed her. The outgoing Nebraska girl had turned cool and remote. Although everyone was polite, William knew that she often seemed "like an aristocrat who might feel herself superior." Maids found her irritating because of the high standard of housekeeping which she demanded, and habits such as spending hours over a meal. What would happen if he were not with her?

Slowly, William walked over to Loue and held her hand. "You are a great Christian woman," he said, simply. "I sometimes feel I have not kept my wedding vows to cherish you as I should."

But, of course, he went. He could not turn down what might be a last chance. To the diary he confided: "Tomorrow I sail, leave Loue behind. The hardest decision of my life. War would separate us for years."

Hardly anyone expected the venture to succeed, and many were derisive. Axling commented: "At sea I feel as Henry Ford and Jane Addams must have felt in 1914 when they sailed on the 'ship of peace' for Europe, trying to stem the onrushing storm. They were criticized and laughed at. So are we. They were opposed, and obstacles put in their way. So with us."

In spite of misgivings, however, the little band stuck tenaciously to their task. The reception given to them by Christians in Hawaii was heartening. Axling's spirits were lifted. "Christians are the salt of the earth. They are leavening for the lump." This contact also gave the deputation some experience in carrying out their task and reaching their objectives.

Before leaving Japan they defined these objectives under six points, as follows:

1. To explore the distinctive contributions which the Christians of both nations should make toward the betterment of Japanese-American relations.

2. To strengthen the bond between the Christians of Japan and the Christians of the United States.

3. To convey the greetings of the newly established United Church of Japan and to make clear the purpose of its establishment.

4. To give expression to the gratitude of the Christians of Japan for all that American mission boards and American Christians have done, for furthering of the Christian movement in Japan during the past eighty years.

5. To discuss further policies of cooperation between the United Church of Japan and the mission boards of the churches of the United States.

6. To confer regarding the re-orientation and reconstruction of the Christian mission in Eastern Asia and its relation to the Christian churches of Japan and the United States.

The first major conference was held at the Mission Inn, Riverside, California, April 20-26, 1941. Here eighteen leading American churchmen, under the sponsorship of the Federal Council of Churches, met with the deputation. By previous agreement there was no debating, but an honest sharing of Japanese and American Christian concerns. This conference focused on such questions as those raised by the Chinese war, the tensions between Japan and America, and the nature of the new United Church of Christ in Japan.

The second major conference was held in Atlantic City, New Jersey, May 9-12. Here the deputation met with forty-five mission administrators to discuss in specific terms what the developing changes in Asia would mean for missionary endeavor, how mission boards could cooperate with the United Church of Christ in Japan, what functions missionaries could continue to perform, and how Christians could deal with mounting government pressures. In many ways this was the most productive of the meetings.

The last major conference was held in Chicago, May 29-31. This was a small gathering designed to follow up the Riverside conclave. An attempt was made to carry forward the same questions discussed by that conference.

Between these conferences, the deputation broke into teams of two or three and met with Christian groups in thirty of the larger American cities. Representatives were also able to address national conventions of the Presbyterians, American Baptists, Disciples of Christ, and United Brethren communions. They spoke at a number of universities and theological seminaries.

Few actions were taken, but one conference did issue a statement which summed up the feelings of Christians from both Japan and America: "We have met under the cloud of conflict, destruction and fear that darkens the world. With heavy and humble hearts we have constantly been aware of the sorrow and suffering that afflicts men everywhere. We have sought forgiveness for our share of responsibility for the tragedy of the world and have implored divine light and strength that we may know and do the will of God."

They were unsuccessful, but did they entirely fail? Was this another step toward a Christian understanding of world problems? Did they and others of like mind help mold the attitude which made it possible for the United States to rebuild her former enemies rather than seek vengeance? The cynical can argue that the rebuilding of Japan and Germany was motivated by the fear of communism. This is true. Nevertheless, part of the public opinion which made this remarkable change of policy from vengeance to rehabilitation possible may well have come from Christian motivation. Certainly, it was easier for Christian groups to reestablish fellowship after the second than after the first world war. Actions like this Christian deputation certainly prepared the way.

From Axling's point of view:

> The Christian fellowship deputation was the offspring of a dream. A great dream born in the minds and hearts of key leaders of the Japanese Christian Church. They dreamed that, as in the early Christian centuries, so today, Christians should serve as the mystic bond holding our shattered world together. Impelled by that dream and motivated by an unspeakable faith in the God of the impossible this deputation set forth on a high spiritual adventure.

What the deputation attempted in the emergency was what Axling had been trying to do for almost forty years in Japan. In 1941 it seemed that both had failed. We shall never know whether Axling was right or wrong. What could have happened had America encouraged Japanese control of the East, and had at the same time moved to support the more liberal factions within the country? Would Japan have been on our side during World War II? Would communism have been stopped in China? Would Russia have been on the opposite side, and communism crushed as an imperialistic world power? Possibly Japan would have turned fascist, anyway. In any event, it is difficult to think of Asia as being in worse circumstances than it is today as a result of the policy which the United States did follow.

In the face of mounting obstacles Axling stuck with characteristic determination and vigor to his ideals throughout the troubled years.

8. THE WAR YEARS

WILLIAM AXLING was at his office in the Tabernacle when word came of war between the United States and Japan. Unable to sit still, he shuffled from room to room and moved aimlessly through his beloved halls. "A dark day, a dark day," he kept saying to no one in particular. "Eighty years of peace shattered. I never thought I would live to see this day."

On one level of his consciousness, Axling had expected war to come and was making preparation. On another, he had held stubbornly to his hope that God would save his two beloved nations from this catastrophe. He had trouble understanding how two great nations could turn from solving human need to such madness as war. They needed each other. The East needed them both. Christ had shown the way so simply. Why could not men walk in that way?

On his "practical" level, Axling was aware of the great possibility of war when he left San Francisco on September 6, 1940, to return to Japan. At every turn he had felt a hardening of American attitude toward Japan. Two days earlier he had written to Dr. Decker acknowledging that the Japanese cabinet was then dominated by the Manchurian clique who had manipulated the nation into the struggle with China. This group, composed of young army officers and young capitalists, would stop at nothing to attain their ends. Their purpose was to strengthen Japan by way of state socialism at home and military domination abroad.

The always optimistic Axling still hoped that war might be averted and that justice might come to the Pacific. In the meantime, he instructed the mission treasurer to bank his pay in America. He would live on assets already in Japan—funds which would likely be confiscated if war came.

Arrival in Japan was a new shock. Missionaries and Japanese friends who came to meet the Axlings wore sober faces. In hushed tones they spoke of change. Their very demeanor spoke of fear and uncertainty. At once he sensed that this was not the Japan he had left in June, 1939.

Evidence for this observation piled up quickly. His neighbors in Fukagawa turned away when he came down the street. It had become impossible to strike up a casual conversation in a public place. Within a month, he had the upsetting experience of being sharply questioned by a detective. Axling could hardly believe how quickly war propaganda had poisoned the minds of a polite and courteous people and left them suspicious and full of fear.

After several weeks of this treatment, Axling remarked to a colleague: "For the first time I know the bitterness that Christ experienced when he came unto his own and his own folk received him not."

Although the change made it impossible for Axling to carry on his usual evangelistic work and curtailed many other missionany activities, he found plenty to do. His reelection as honorary secretary of the National Christian Council during these days when the United Church of Christ in Japan was in process of formation took much of this time. The word "honorary" in the title did not designate inactivity as it would in America. Even though he turned down a request that he give his full time to the council, he did contribute generously of his time. Many Baptists, who had felt for some years that Axling should spend more time building the Baptist structures, complained that he gave too generously.

Axling now spent a major portion of his time in personal counseling and giving much-sought advice. Long before counseling became a profession, he did it. In normal social contacts he seemed friendly but distant. He came alive under two quite opposite circumstances—in the pulpit, and in what we would now call the counseling situation. Any person in trouble found in Axling a sympathetic listener who neither condemned nor condoned. He seldom gave concrete advice, but as a remarkably balanced, concerned individual he enabled a disturbed person to find a way out of his trouble.

In the spring of 1941, Axling had accompanied the heroic but fruitless Christian peace delegation to the United States. Unfortunately, the time for reconciliation had passed.

By the summer of 1941, the Japanese were facing a hard choice. The United States was fully aroused. Economic sanctions against Japan were beginning to cut off vital supplies of scrap iron, oil, and rubber. Although an ally of Germany and Italy, she could expect no aid from Europe. Neither did she have time to wait for China's collapse. She must either withdraw from China and accept what economic privileges she might negotiate, or move forward on a course which would end in war against the United States.

The stakes were high, but from the Japanese Fascist view the possibilities were good. England was struggling for her very existence against Germany. Russia at the time was expected to collapse. The United States was weak in the Pacific and would not dare throw her full strength into the East while Germany was threatening Europe. With her advanced military technology, Japan expected to sweep easily through Southeast Asia and there obtain the raw materials which she needed to become the greatest industrial empire in the world. As Japan saw it, one well-planned attack on Pearl Harbor would destroy the United States' power in the Pacific. It was believed that a decadent United States would soon sue for peace.

In the autumn of 1941, the few moderates left in the government were pushed aside. Prince Konoye resigned from the Premiership and General Tojo became head of the war cabinet. We now know how greatly Japan miscalculated. The "Japanese spirit" was strong, Japanese soldiers were capable, and the sacrifices of her people were heroic. All of these together were not enough. The mere possibility of becoming the greatest industrial power was not sufficient—the United States already held that position. Russia did not collapse and Germany did not win. Asians, rather than welcoming the liberator who promised to secure Asia for Asians, offered stubborn resistance which bogged down the long, inadequate Japanese supply lines. Finally, the Pearl Harbor attack, far from demoralizing the United States, solidified public opinion behind a war in the East. America's mighty industrial power surged forward and a far from decadent spirit met the challenge.

As signs of war multiplied, missionary agencies began making plans to protect their personnel. Early in 1941 a delegation of the Methodist denomination was so shaken by an interview with Foreign Minister Matsuoka that they advised an immediate evacuation of their missionary personnel. Most boards, however, did not take such radical action. The Presbyterians encouraged missionaries to stay, but offered evacuation for those that wanted it.

The Baptists did not withdraw missionaries, but stood ready to do so. In the meantime, they sought to ascertain what policy would be the best for the security of those under their care and for the future of the Christian cause in Japan. Finally, each missionary was allowed to decide, though all were strongly advised to return home. Dr. Decker wrote to Axling, March 6, 1941: "You are in a position of great difficulty. The most that we can do is assure you of our sympathetic support and of our confidence that your decision, whatever it may be, will be an honorable one—a Christian one, arrived at after much prayer and agony of spirit."

The decision caused much agony on the part of all missionaries —Axling included. At the September, 1941, meeting of the National Christian Council, the Japanese Christians passed a resolution stating: "If any missionaries feel that they must return home, they will go with our blessing and our hearty effort to help find permanent work for them in their homeland. If they desire to stay, we shall welcome their services, and pledge them our best efforts toward protection and necessary assistance." By the fall of 1941, only about 140 of over 800 missionaries were still on the field.

After a long struggle, and with continuing anxiety and uncertainty, Axling decided to stay. Probably he did not really know why. Although he was unquestionably courageous, he avoided unpleasant situations whenever possible. Even though he obviously enjoyed his reputation as a self-sacrificing missionary, he did not desire martyrdom.

His internal battle went on for a year before hostilities broke out, and continued through two refusals to evacuate after the war began and until final repatriation in September, 1943.

Axling knew and weighed all the arguments. What could enemy aliens, restricted in their movements, possibly accomplish by staying? The Axlings, in their late sixties, were more likely to become a burden than a help. Many feared that the presence of American missionaries could only embarrass the Japanese church. Sometimes Axling saw the withdrawal of all missionaries as positively helpful for the church. He reasoned that withdrawal would give the Japanese church a chance to start afresh and work out cooperative relationships with the West in its own way.

Most often, however, the missionary withdrawal seemed to Axling like a cowardly betrayal. "The diplomat and businessman stayed by his post. How dare we think of doing less?" When he heard of missionaries leaving, he fretted: "Where is our sense of being sent by God? Are we so lightly rooted in the soil and soul of this land?"

Although no definite reason can be given, the decision to remain in Japan in the face of war was characteristic of Axling. He always placed far more importance on action than on words, more on example than on speech. The gospel, he believed, could be much more fully and effectively communicated by the Christian presence—the Christian life lived—than by all the theologies ever written. This conviction lay behind the work at the Tabernacle. He had moved to Fukagawa for this reason. This was his understanding of the Christian faith.

An entry in his diary, September 24, 1941, expresses why he stayed: "Our remaining . . . will at least demonstrate that the Christian bond holds even across barriers of national tension and friction. In this day of ultranationalism this demonstration is desperately needed."

In a statement to the Japanese press published in the United States four days before the Pearl Harbor attack, he declared his intention to remain in Japan, whatever might happen—because "our lives are solidly connected with Japan." His decision may have been wrong, but he made it honestly.

Many of his colleagues believed he was mistaken. Once again

his statements had a way of reflecting on their dedication to the task. Realizing this disagreement, Axling felt that some thought the mission board would have been wiser not to extend his active service beyond the 1938 retirement date. When he shared this thought with Dr. Decker, the latter assured him that the members of the board had no reason to feel that they had been mistaken in extending his term of service.

After many missionaries had left, the board asked the Axlings to live in the missionary residence at Waseda in order to help protect the property. They went reluctantly. William, especially, preferred to stay in Fukagawa—in part to protect his own home, but more to stand by his principles that missionaries should live in small houses among the common people.

They went, but William fretted: "Here we are living in the kind of house that in all my forty years of missionary life I have felt was wrong for us who profess to be followers of the Christ." Or, again: "In Fukagawa we were in the mainstream of the Japanese workaday world. Here we are out on the fringes." He seemed to forget that war propaganda had placed an effective wall of fear and suspicion around him wherever he was.

A few days after Pearl Harbor, the Axlings were placed under a loose house arrest. After the first air raid on Japan, April 18, 1942, the rules were made more stringent. Special police permission was granted for an occasional visit to the bank, two trips to the hospital, and to answer an occasional summons to a government office. Eventually, however, the Axlings were confined to a prison camp.

The great respect with which Axling was held was proved by those official summonses to ask his advice. Usually the summons was by a local officer who had known Axling in the old days. Occasionally, however, inquiries came from a higher level, as when persons from the Department of Education called to get his opinion about what could be done to assist missionaries who were marooned in Japan without funds.

The war brought intense suffering to Axling—a suffering which went much deeper and reached far wider than confinement, physical discomfort, and the prison camp. His abhorrence of the insane waste and human misery of any war was heightened by this war between his two homelands. In a very real sense, Axling's home was the world. He affirmed the European roots of his par-

ents, the America of his boyhood and early manhood, and the
Japan of his mature years. His commitment was to humanity—a
humanity which he saw as God's creation, redeemed by Christ,
called to live as brothers under the rule of God. War was a
demonic denial of all of these.

His indomitable idealism was never so nearly conquered as by
the outbreak of the war. All his life he had worked to Christianize Japan. His confidence had been placed in the hope that
Christians in America and Japan could influence their nations to
give the world an example of justice and brotherhood. Together
these nations could lead the East into peace and progress for
human good. As his dream had faded through that last year, he
prayed almost constantly: "O God of the nations, restrain, restrain. Let not the peace of the Pacific be broken."

As Axling prepared to write in his diary the day after hostilities erupted, he was startled by what he had entered one year
before. Slowly he reread: "This is not a chaotic universe. God
keeps the calendar and orders events." Then, after sitting in turbulent meditation for some time, he wrote: "In the light of today's tragedy, is what I wrote above one year ago true? Can God
be in a tragedy so dark and terrible?"

The testing of his personal faith was real. Over a month later
he wrote: "My faith has been in the throes of facing a mass of
unanswerable questions and dark doubts since the war spread
to the Pacific and the United States." He went on to confess: "I
have been forced to rediscover God, to find a God big enough
to deal with the present tragedy, a God equal to the titanic task
of building his kingdom in the ruins of the present man-built and
man-destroyed militaristic world civilization."

Nevertheless, Axling's faith never utterly crumbled. He was
sure that God reigned. "I still believe this, although the signs
are all against it. The whole world seems to be carried forward
by demonic forces or a blind force. O God, speedily reveal thy
right hand and save mankind from its madness."

Axling could readily understand the war in terms of judgment.
The social and political systems which had been developed de-
served God's wrath. "The old world could not go on. It was too
unfair to too large a number." But why such radical surgery?
Possibly, God was forced to "use pagan dictators of today to
work his will because we Christians have failed him." As he

looked to the future, the pessimism which had gripped many after World War I finally seemed to be reaching him. "Will the new world order be any fairer? Can unredeemed man build a better world?"

His inner spiritual battle was made more difficult by being separated from his work and cut off from his Japanese friends. As opportunities to speak became fewer, each one was savored. "My first message of the new year. What an unspeakable privilege to point hungry-hearted, sin-sick men and women to Christ!"

The house arrest denied Axling of almost all contacts with non-Christians. Unlike the apostle Paul, he was not allowed even the privilege of witnessing in his bonds. Not only were his own activities curtailed, but he was forced to watch what appeared to be the disintegration of the mission enterprise and the decline of the Japanese church. Even though he was correctly confident that most Japanese Christians were remaining faithful, the external signs of church activity were suffering seriously. "The church is having a difficult time," he worried. "Attendance dropped. Members tied up in urgent tasks, Sunday school attendance greatly reduced. A time of testing."

Finally, Axling was denied most of the rich personal contact which he had enjoyed with his beloved Japanese Christians. Many continued to run serious risks in order to supply the Axlings' needs, and to assure them of their continued good will. By necessity, however, the contacts were short and furtive. Even before the arrest, a friend who saw Axling off at the train was taken to the police station and questioned. Axling recognized the necessity of this separation. "It is hard when we make our friends suffer."

Two months before the war started, the Axlings stopped corresponding with "their Japanese daughter" whom they had raised and educated as their own child. Haruko's husband was an army officer and they did not wish to bring suspicion on the couple.

The very idea of confinement was unbelievably irksome to an activist like Axling. Mrs. Matsudiara, a former member of the Tabernacle staff, stopped by one day with some oranges. This sacrificial gesture pleased Axling very much, but it was difficult to lift his spirits. As conversation lagged, the only sound was the singing of a canary. Axling turned to Mrs. Matsudiara's son and said, "My boy, our only pleasure and consolation is this bird."

In the midst of his activity, Axling often reflected on the past. "A year ago, life appeared like a long-distance run. Now it has become a long-drawn-out wait, and this is infinitely more trying and tiring." Again: "It is easy to work for God. It carries one along on its own momentum. To wait is difficult. This requires poise and inward peace and faith."

The Axlings were allowed to attend chapel services, and some support came from sermons which proclaimed "God's providential direction of the life of individuals, nations, and the world." Finally, after six months of internment, Axling settled into an uneasy acceptance. He wrote: "Another month has dragged its weary way across our cloistered life. The month seemed unbearably long, but our lot is a happy one compared with the millions in concentration camps and prisons throughout the world. God have mercy on them and give them early relief."

In the spring of 1942, Axling made an unsuccessful attempt at gardening. Very little of the farm boy remained in him. The green thumb had disappeared in the forty years since he had last tried to grow a few vegetables in Morioka. When Lucinda affirmed, "We both enjoyed working out-of-doors," apparently she had not consulted William before making that statement.

The endeavor did absorb some time, but in general added to already existing frustrations. As supplies became more difficult to buy, the Axlings were dependent upon Japanese friends who shared their meager store. After the air raids began, few visitors came, but they continued to send "reminders of their love."

One result of the house arrest was to bring William and Lucinda together for hours at a time without the buffer of a mutual task. This was a new experience. In the early days, they spent many hours in common work. Later William was gone a great deal. Somewhat aware of his neglect, Axling had often commented: "Loue is a trump the way she puts up with being left alone so much."

The result of being constantly together, however, was not always harmonious. According to the diary: "It takes a lot of grace and forbearance for two people to be confined in a second-story apartment day after day, month after month. I and Loue certainly had a bad time of it today."

There was one task which the Axlings shared—housework. It was impossible to get a maid, both because of the scarcity of labor and because of the danger to any Japanese person who would accept a job with an enemy alien. William worked into his new role gradually. When Lucinda was in bed with a cold, he prepared the meals. "The first time in forty-one years of married life. I have scarcely known where the kitchen was."

As time went on, a division of labor was arranged. According to Lucinda: "He made the fires and cared for them and also made our bed and swept and dusted. I did the cooking and other kitchen and dining-room duties, laundry, and extra cleaning, such as window glass, kitchen floors, etc."

The arrangement accomplished its purpose. When the Japanese pastor called, he remarked, "Why, it is just as clean as if you had a maid!" The Japanese are a courteous people.

The treatment of the Axlings during this period was much kinder than that which Japanese nationals in the United States received after relocation began in March, 1942. Winifred Acock, who came to live with them several weeks before internment, felt that Axling's overly conscientious temperament caused him to interpret Japanese orders too strictly, and restrained him more than was necessary. About two months after the arrest, a friendly policeman returned their radio, explaining, "because you must be lonesome without it."

Shortly before the Axlings were interned, rumors spread that internment might happen. Throwing all caution to the wind, a large group of Japanese Christians came, practically filling the downstairs of the house. They stayed for hours, talking, reading the Bible, praying, and singing hymns. In the midst of the celebration Haruko and her husband also came. Miss Acock remained upstairs, fearful of the results.

A few days later, September 16, 1942, the Axlings were taken from the home and placed in a concentration camp. Miss Acock remained in the house until she was repatriated. During the first three weeks, William and Lucinda were in different sections of the same camp. Afterward, they were placed in separate camps about fifty miles apart. For some time after this separation neither had any word from the other. Then, until their repatriation in September, 1943, they were able once a month to send a note of one hundred words, containing only personal chit-chat.

Mrs. Axling was held at a confiscated Roman Catholic school with 116 other women. All but five were directly connected with

Christian missionary work. The rest, except for one Russian woman and her two small children, were teachers. The only other Baptist was Miss Thomasine Allen. Lucinda and Tommy, who had much in common, were a great comfort to each other.

Conditions were crowded and food was scarce. Mrs. Axling shared a room with twelve others. There was hardly room for the beds. Except for some heavy work which they were allowed to hire done, the women cared for their own needs. During the hot and humid summer months, tempers became short and relations strained, but "in the main we were a happy family," stated Mrs. Axling, "striving to serve instead of being served. All duties were proportioned out according to the monitor system by our member leaders, so that each one had her fair share of labor." Concern was given to the older and the weaker. Mrs. Axling profited from this arrangement. "Otherwise," she said, "I fear I should not have come through with flying colors as I did."

The Catholics maintained their devotional life in the school chapel. They also allowed the thirty-four Protestant women to hold services there. The Protestants began with a service every morning. Later they added a Wednesday prayer service and a Saturday evening service.

In order to fill with some profit and interest the long hours, one teacher, Miss Eleanor Potter, gave music lessons and formed a choir. Others put their skills to work offering Spanish, French, and Japanese languages. The Catholic teaching sisters taught courses in algebra, geometry, and philosophy.

Reflecting on the experience, Mrs. Axling later wrote:

And so we passed the year, learning to cooperate; to share what we had with those who were in need; to accept gracefully things which we needed; to bear and forbear; and to forgive and ask to be forgiven when wrong was done—in short, learning to be Christlike. And I think there is not one of us who does not feel that she is a better woman for the experiences of that year. Religious tolerance also came in and many new friendships were formed not only in our own group but among our Catholic sisters, friendships which will last a lifetime.

One source of satisfaction for the adults was found in making the lives of the children—a four-year-old boy and a six-year-old girl—as pleasant as possible. Apparently they succeeded, for one day little Millie exclaimed, "Mama, I'd like to live here always. Can't we?"

Dr. Axling's camp was more heterogeneous, both nationally and occupationally. Besides forty-two Catholic priests and two Protestant missionaries, there were college professors, businessmen, ships' officers, and newspaper reporters. They suffered the indignity of forced labor as well as overcrowding and food shortages. Characteristically, however, Axling's spirit rebounded. Actual suffering was much easier than inactivity. Even a measure of his optimism returned, and hope for man and the world was reestablished. The prison society could be a model for the future:

> Some of the men failed to measure up, but the majority met this challenge head on and played the game like men. We shared our work, our places to sleep, our bedding, our clothing, our food, our drink, our sorrows, our joys, our hunger, the cold—in fact we shared everything. My camp experience gave me a new hope for humanity, for here is the pattern for the kind of world that we have got to build when this tragic war is over and our experiment proved that it can be done. God has planted that possibility in Christ-redeemed personalities and we must not fail him if he gives us a second chance.

Of course, camp life offered little opportunity for Christian service. The Catholics held mass, and William and the other Protestants took turns conducting Protestant services. The only book he was allowed to retain was the Bible, which he read and reread.

Cut off from more active opportunities of Christian work, Axling developed a ministry of intercession. He had tried before. He was always a deeply spiritual man who prayed earnestly and took his devotional life seriously. On each birthday, he disappeared to spend the day alone in prayer and meditation. But never before had this activist been able to convince himself that intercession was his proper ministry. During periods of illness he had been too weak. During the house arrest he had fretted too much. In the concentration camp, however, he had the right mix of confinement and challenge to carry it through—temporarily, at least.

After returning to the States, he wrote a moving description of this aspect of his prison experience:

> Every day that dawned, prayer made it possible for me to take my place by the side of Christian colleagues all over Japan, colleagues in broken China, colleagues in restless India, colleagues in bleeding Europe, as well as Christian colleagues all over the beloved land of mine, and hold up

their hearts and hands as they carried on their God-given tasks. . . .
Prayer opened the way for a creative world-wide service with the place
of confinement as the base of operations.

Life is not simply action, motion, doing things. Life at its best is the
enrichment of the mind, the culture and discipline of the soul, the
building of a character with a likeness to Christ, giving the Spirit of
God a real chance to round out our personalities, and going the second
mile of service for our fellow men. In these terms, confinement in a concentration camp, the difficulties, the tragedies, the sufferings that come
our way, cannot stop life nor rob it of its meaning. Rather, they point
the way to a richer and fuller life.

On weekdays Axling spent two or three hours in manual labor.
cleaning up roads, cultivating and fertilizing land, and digging
tree stumps for fuel to heat water for the camp. One morning
during the winter a young policeman approached him and said:
"Yesterday when you were cutting wood I noticed that your
hands were swollen from chilblains. I wanted to give you gloves
at that time, but because of the situation here in Japan I could
not. These gloves were given me by the army. I have my own,
and so I will give these to you. Of course, you should be treated
the same as the others, but please warm your hands when you
are alone in your room."

After the war Axling used this incident to encourage Americans to send gloves and other clothing to Japan. He also searched
out the officer, Mr. Toda. The reunion was dramatic. This story
has grown and changed and become one of the Axling legends.
Yet, like a true legend, it illustrates the relationship between
Axling and the Japanese.

Through the good offices of the Swiss delegation, arrangements
were made for a prisoner exchange in the fall of 1943. Dr. and
Mrs. Axling were among the number of persons from Japan
and China who were included. With no opportunities for good-
byes to old friends, the Axlings were taken directly from their
camps to Yokohama. There they boarded a former French vessel,
rechristened *Teia Maru*. After picking up other prisoners in
China, the boat made its way to the tiny, then Portuguese, colony
of Goa, on the coast of India. The boat was crowded and uncom-
fortable, but the food was better than most had experienced in
their respective camps.

The first Sunday on board was an unforgettable experience for
all the missionaries. How thrilling the humble sound of a piano,

the mingled voices of men and women, and words of familiar hymns can be to those long denied such simple pleasures! Dr. Axling was the preacher.

In Goa, the *Gripsholm* came, carrying the Japanese nationals to be exchanged. The Japanese and Western prisoners were each arranged in long lines. As the actual exchange began, the lines filed by a checkpoint going in opposite directions—each experiencing the thrill of freedom for the first time in months or years. The *Gripsholm* seemed like a bit of heaven—adequate rooms, comfortable quarters, abundant food, reunion with old friends, and the opportunity to form new acquaintances with persons of similar experiences. Everyone was in a festive mood.

During the first days of the trip, Dr. and Mrs. Axling were like two young lovers, always walking arm in arm—often oblivious of the other passengers. William remarked to a friend, "Second honeymoon!" A few days later, however, the friend happened upon the Axlings and heard Loue roundly scolding William! Axling winked at his friend and remarked, "Honeymoon is over!" Such is often the course of true love.

Port Elizabeth, South Africa, gave the repatriates a heroes' welcome. Rio de Janeiro, Brazil, was not far behind. Finally, December 1, 1943, the Statue of Liberty broke through the fog. These seasoned and experienced travelers burst spontaneously into the national anthem.

When they landed, Axling discovered that he was in trouble with the American authorities. All returnees were routinely checked by the FBI. His strong pro-Japanese stand made Axling especially suspect. Also during the war he had appeared with Kagawa on a radio broadcast which was beamed at America. The content was a harmless Christmas program, but the Japanese had used it to imply that a famous missionary and peace lover was still ministering and presumably still holding his pro-Japanese opinion.

Fulton Oursler, substituting for Walter Winchell, picked up this incident and used it on a broadcast on August 15, 1943:

OMAHA, NEBRASKA. Agents of the FBI have been in this city secretly checking on William Axling, Nebraska-born Baptist missionary now in Tokyo, all because of short-wave broadcasts recently beamed by Axling from Japan to America. It is known that some years ago Axling adopted a Japanese girl and she was married to a young Japanese official just before Pearl Harbor. It is not known whether Axling is being held as a hostage or is acting as a free agent in his broadcasts.

When FBI agents also checked Axling's connection in Gothenburg, they caused a considerable stir in the small town. His friends were both shocked and worried. There is no reason, however, to believe that more than a routine check was involved. Axling was soon cleared and had no further trouble with authorities. Some naval officials, presumably on their own initiative, kept him under surveillance for awhile. In a letter to Home Secretary Jesse R. Wilson, Axling wrote: "While I was in Chicago, Palmer told me that Navy men kept calling up the Baptist headquarters there inquiring about me."

Axling's spirit was nearly as burdened in wartime America as in Japanese confinement. Daily, news came of Japanese atrocities. In America, Axling saw the steady poisoning of the human spirit by the vengeful savagery always set loose by war. He loved the people of both nations. He wanted America to defeat the militarists, but not to crush the Japanese people. How could he express himself, so that a war-crazed nation could hear his concern without doubting his loyalty?

The situation for Axling became more painful because of his desire to be liked. The opinions of others caused him either great sorrow or great satisfaction, but did not sway him on points where his integrity was involved.

In this case Axling realized that he had given cause for apprehension. His strong defense of the Japanese seemed unjustified in the face of Pearl Harbor. It was pointless for him to say that American foreign policy could have been changed in the 1930's or earlier to prevent the war; the Japanese sneak attack had destroyed any willingness of Americans to listen to such reasoning. Furthermore, for him to criticize America seemed improper in view of the support America had given him, even to the extent of repatriation, when he had ignored the warnings to return home.

Because Axling had been a recent occupant of a concentration camp, and because he was Axling, he received many invitations to speak. Audiences were surprised, however, when his "personal experiences" did not contain the expected atrocity stories. Without denying the scarcity of food, he stated that the Japanese were suffering shortages. He acknowledged that some guards expressed sadism, but said that others made life as bearable as possible. When it came to the Japanese Christians and their loyalty to Christ, he spoke in unqualified and glowing terms.

Whether correctly or not, Axling felt that "the powers that be" wished him to soft-pedal the positive and make Japan's sins more glaringly prominent. In most audiences, he sensed a strain of hostility. Gothenburg was no exception. "People of my own home town silently questioned my loyalty as an American citizen." In a thousand ways he discovered: "It is a tragedy to love two peoples that are at war with each other."

Despite all difficulties, however, Axling's personal warmth and sincerity came through. His positive, courageous words struck a spark which rekindled goodwill in many a person who had been almost overcome by corroding hate. After Axling had spoken in Lansing, Michigan, the president of the Baptist state convention commented: "Well, we did not get what we expected, but we got something of far more importance and what we needed."

Some, of course, rejected Axling's message and continued to doubt his loyalty. Others, like the Michigan Baptist leader, were refreshed and expressed their pleasure through a growing stream of congratulatory letters to the American Baptist Foreign Mission Society.

In June, 1944, the mission board officially acted on the Axlings' retirement. In a resolution of gratitude, the board expressed their appreciation for the years of service which the Axlings had given. The resolution made a special note of Axling's role in founding the Misaki Tabernacle and the Fukagawa Christian Center and his part in the growing ecumenical movement. Mrs. Axling was commended for her Christian influence upon all with whom she came in contact.

In response to the resolution of gratitude, Dr. Axling expressed his thanks to the board and his fellow missionaries for their cooperation and understanding. Typical of his continued eagerness to serve, Dr. Axling added, "We willingly step into the background and yield the field to younger men. If, however, as retired missionaries, there is any voluntary service that we can still render, we shall be glad to do so."

Not only did Axling express this desire to serve, but he let all who might be interested know of his plans to settle somewhere near New York where he would be available for deputation work

by the foreign board and for special assignments by international
and interdenominational organizations. (See Appendix A for the
full text of the resolution and the response made by Dr. Axling.)

In the same month in which his retirement took place, a report issued by a group of Protestant leaders upset Axling deeply.
Fifteen men, each connected with some Christian organization
with an interest in the Far East, but meeting as individuals and
calling themselves the Far East Settlement Group, issued a statement on postwar policy toward Japan. After reading the report
Axling wrote a letter to a member of that group, his old Presbyterian colleague A. K. Reischauer, taking strong exception to the
statement. His first objection was based on the practical grounds
that it would encourage the Japanese militarists to fight on and
give them opportunity to galvanize support under the slogan,
"This war is terrible, but peace will be worse." He also objected
on the grounds that it was wrong to condemn Japanese imperialism without at the same time condemning Western imperialism.
From Axling's perspective:

> If the statement had courageously made the stripping of Japan to be
> definitely followed by Great Britain's withdrawal from India and Burma,
> Holland's withdrawal from Java, France's from Indochina, and the United
> States' from the Philippines, thus giving the people of the Orient a chance
> to work out their destiny unhampered by Western imperialism and ex-
> ploitation, it would have given a fair and much needed Christian lead.

Axling, apparently, missed the intent of the group. It is true
that Article III, to which Axling took exception, does mention
favorably the statement of the Cairo Conference. At that conference, Roosevelt, Churchill, and Chiang Kai-shek issued a statement of typical wartime absolutism. It declared as the policy of
the free nations the intention to strip Japan of all the possessions
which she had acquired since 1914.

The Protestant statement was more specific: ". . . in accordance
with the declaration made at the Cairo Conference, Japan should
return Manchuria, Formosa, and the Pescadores to China and
give up all territory seized by her since July, 1937. Japan should
also relinquish control of all the islands of the Pacific which she
has occupied since 1914. Moreover, Korea should be liberated."
It then went on: "Other territorial readjustments of the Far East,
in justice to the populations concerned, should also be made, but
these lie outside the scope of this memorandum."

The document fully recognized that the economic necessities of the Japanese must be carefully protected. Though the country should be demilitarized, an adequate merchant fleet should be continued. Some reparations might be in order, but probably it would be better for world peace to forgo all except a minimal payment to China and the return of art treasures and cultural objects which had been removed from the mainland. The document warned against the indiscriminate punishment of the Japanese as war criminals and stressed the need of relief for the Japanese people as soon as the war was over. It also pleaded that Japan should be left free to develop its own form of government in the future. In other words, while Japan was to be stripped of many of its territorial acquisitions, the Protestant statement was a strong plea for moderation. It held up the ideal that Japan should be restored as a strong, self-sufficient member of the family of nations.

Axling, however, did not read the document that way. He was thoroughly convinced of the evil consequences which would flow from Article III. His displeasure was expressed in what for him was very strong language:

Article 3 of your statement is tragic for the Christian cause in Japan. To have that group of fifteen front-line American, Protestant leaders take up the Cairo refrain and unequivocably endorse it, makes the situation for our Japanese Christians absolutely impossible. It also spells doom—I fear—for any cooperation with the Christian forces in Japan for long, long years to come. . . .

This disagreement placed a severe strain on his friendship with Dr. Reischauer.

Retirement, disagreements with fellow missionaries, and the mistrust of some of his countrymen did little to slow Axling down. Lucinda engaged in some speaking, but mostly, as in the latter years in Japan, she was left alone. On January 15, 1945, Axling wrote in his diary: "New York enroute to Cleveland for the Second National Study Conference. Parted with Loue at the Forty-third Street Bus Terminal. In how many different places we have said 'good-byes' to each other!"

In 1945 the Council of Finance and Promotion of the Northern Baptist Convention published a brochure featuring Axling as the statesman missionary. Besides summarizing his attainments, listing possible lecture topics, and including numerous complimentary quotes from those who had heard him, the leaflet listed four purposes which Axling hoped to accomplish by the lectures.

1. Through them it is hoped to create a more Christian understanding of the race problem, particularly in its relationship to the Oriental.

2. Through first-hand experience he demonstrates that the Christian mission in Eastern Asia has not gone into eclipse. In spite of the war, it is an ongoing movement.

3. He interprets the value of Christian missions in broad outline and stimulates understanding, interest, and support for the world Christian program.

4. Out of his own experience he graphically pictures the part that the Christian church must play in the postwar world.

One of the most demanding of many speaking tours took Axling to the West Coast during February and March, 1945. He covered the states of Wyoming, Washington, Oregon, California, Arizona, and Colorado. He spoke in churches and before student groups, service clubs, high school assemblies, and college and seminary audiences. He also visited the Japanese relocation centers at Tule Lake, California; Poston, Arizona; and Amache, Colorado. Axling was especially grateful for this opportunity to chip away at the anti-Japanese feeling on the West Coast. Already some agitators were busy inflaming the populace against the return of Japanese-Americans to their homes. Frequently he found that "the hatred of all Japanese is terrible and terrifying."

Faithful pastors, standing in some cases almost alone against the forces of monstrous bigotry, were humbly grateful for his support. Axling wrote: "We have a right to be proud of them for their courageous stand."

Axling encountered his most unhappy experience in Auburn, California. One Japanese family already had returned to this community, only to have their property burned by a drunken mob. A record Sunday evening group of 140 gathered to hear Axling speak. Either they did not know his position or they came only to hear what a "traitor" would say. In any event, the audience sat in stony, sullen silence and then bolted for the doors as soon as the service was over. Only a few young people and one serviceman came forward to express appreciation.

Increasingly, Axling, who had always given priority to young people, placed his hope in the youth. He discovered that servicemen often were receptive. This fact thrilled him. "In their training they are taught to hate, but a good number of them in their heart of hearts hate to hate. They know it poisons their souls."

As might be expected, Axling was well received at the relocation centers. In most he spoke in both Japanese and English. Probably these meetings were more difficult for Axling than those in which he had opposition. As he wrote: "Their hearts are so hungry and so lonely and their outlook so hopeless."

Throughout the war Axling took every possible opportunity to further his four goals—increasing racial understanding, building confidence in the mission task, expanding the concept of the gospel, and calling men to work for God in the world. For a man in his seventies, he got about. Many days were like the one that he described in a letter:

> Yesterday was a strenuous day, but one of high privilege. From 10:00 to 11:00 addressed high school assembly (special assembly), 11:00 to 12:00 spoke to the students and faculty at Linfield College, 12:30 to 1:15 spoke to the Rotary Club, 2:00 to 3:15 conducted forum for teachers and students at Linfield College, 3:15 to 5:00 individual interviews with students, 6:00 to 8:30 dinner at home of one of the faculty members with other guests. It was really a day of unusual opportunities.

As the war pursued its relentless course, the horror was seldom far from Axling's mind. A diary comment of March 24, 1945, is typical: "Enroute to Long Beach. Drove from Santa Barbara to Long Beach. A scenic route along the sea. How peaceful! Yet on the other side of that peaceful sea there is a carnival of mass murder and large-scale destruction."

By the middle of 1945 it was evident to all that Japan would be defeated. After the fall of Okinawa, General Tojo was replaced by Admiral Koiso. There was still fear that Tojo's party would initiate a coup d'etat and stage a suicide stand. Then came the atom bomb. The first was dropped at Hiroshima on August 6, Loue's seventy-second birthday. The second was at Nagasaki three days later. By August 14 Japan had announced her willingness to surrender on the basis of the Potsdam Declaration. Axling wrote in his diary: "Japan's surrender reply reached Washington, and World War II officially declared at an end. Cease-fire orders go out to all fronts. God forgive all of us for what we have done to each other in this war."

9. INDIAN SUMMER

WITH FORCIBLY SUPPRESSED EXCITEMENT, Dr. William Axling read the letter brought from Japan by the Christian delegation which had visited that country in the fall of 1945. It was from an old friend and fellow secretary of the National Christian Conference, Rev. Tsunetaro Miyakoda. In his letter he described the eagerness of the Japanese people to hear the gospel and the pleas of Dr. Kagawa and others for evangelistic campaigns. He continued:

> We talked about inviting missionaries with deputation. We are waiting for the missionaries to come back to Japan and work for the evangelization of our country. We are waiting for *your help*, especially in this time.
>
> A month ago there came suggestion from Allied Headquarters to give a list of names of Advisers for the Church of Christ in Japan if we needed. We answered immediately and put the name of Dr. Axling at the top of the three we asked.

Here was tangible evidence that he was wanted and needed back in postwar Japan. Without hesitation he sat down and wrote the board of managers of the American Baptist Foreign Mission Society. He included relevant quotations from the letter and asked to be approved as a missionary of the society, so that he might get a passport to return.

Realizing that priorities should go to younger men, he did not ask for an ordinary appointment. All he needed was authorization so that he might get a passport. He was quite willing to continue on his retirement allowance, "unless inflation in Japan makes that absolutely impossible for me." His task as he saw it would be primarily evangelistic and at the service of the United Church of Christ in Japan.

The board's response was entirely predictable. At the moment it was impossible to accept the request. As soon as missionaries could go, they were not likely to approve a man approaching his seventy-third birthday. Their reply explained that arrangements had been completed for only a few missionaries to return. The board urged Axling to wait for more settled conditions before he attempted to return.

No one really expected Axling to be easily deterred. Already he had declared himself in print in an article in the *Christian Herald*. A condensation of this statement, "I Am Going Back to Japan," appeared in the Baptist periodical *Crusader* in April, 1946.

This article clearly reflects the new hope kindled in Axling's heart. After a decade of discouragement his life goal might yet be accomplished. The Christianization of Japan was again a possibility. The church alone had weathered the storm, as he stated it:

The clock has struck the midnight hour in Japan: midnight of the darkest night in the history of that nation. But the Christian scene is not a blackout. The church has not gone into eclipse. When the Fascist revolution broke out in Japan in 1939, the first casualties were agencies and organizations international in character. . . . The only internationally minded organization that weathered the storm was the Church of the living Christ. The only world-encircling bond that did not snap in the face of that crisis was the bond in Christ that bound Christian heart to Christian heart.

Although the church was the only institution that did not "go to smash," the job was far from done. The ground had been cleared of many obstacles, but building lay ahead. All of his dreams of the 1920's seemed to come back as Axling finished his article:

. . . . A new Japan can only come through an inner renewal. And an inner renewal can only come from Japan's soul. The battle for Japan's soul cannot be won by bombs and bayonets. The battle can only be won by spiritual forces.

Only the Christian gospel and its redemptive Christ can build a basically new Japan, and it alone can build a basically new world. It cannot evade the high and sacred task of giving it to the last man, woman, and child in every corner of God's world. . . .

Yes, I am going back! The clearing of the ground was complete. Japan's defeat was devastating. Although large armies were intact, and vast land areas were still under Japanese control, the home front was completely shattered. Months before the war ended, the destruction of Japan's merchant fleet had dried up supplies and forced most of her industries to grind to a halt. The fire bombs, later followed by two atomic explosions, had left every major city devastated. About two and one-quarter million buildings were totally destroyed, and well over one-half a million persons had been killed in air raids. Another million and a quarter had died in various ways as a result of the war. Japan's military leadership had bet everything on conquest and lost. Her homeland was in ruins, her empire tottering, and every adequate economic base destroyed. A proud and capable people who had been convinced of their superiority were now trembling before a conqueror about to send an army of occupation.

Defeat was traumatic. It swept away the validity of Japan's national symbols centering in the Emperor. When a centralized, hierarchical, authoritarian culture like Japan's cracks, it breaks wide open. The great respect for military and police personnel disappeared as postwar conditions forced people to improvise and to deal with a black market in order to exist. A naturally law-abiding people lost respect for law and order. Etiquette—which had been the basis of morality—was pushed aside in a desperate struggle to keep alive. An overly self-assured people suddenly lost all confidence in themselves. The physical suffering was severe, but the collapse of morale was yet more serious.

At the end of the war the Japanese church, like every other segment of society, was in a state of physical ruin and organizational disintegration. Christians, as others, were uncertain about whether and how to reinstate relationships with the West. Their problem was especially acute. No segment of Japanese society had been tied so closely with the West as the church. What attitude would Western Christians now take if the Japanese Christians reestablished contact with missionaries from the same country as the occupational forces? Would the Japanese Christians be further alienated from their own people?

Fortunately for all concerned, the occupation policy was enlightened. The response of the Japanese to occupation was equally remarkable. While some cooperated out of sheer expediency, many saw the occupation as an opportunity to rebuild Japanese society upon the democratic lines hoped for by the liberals in the 1920's. The facing of many national catastrophes had through the centuries developed in the Japanese character a stoic acceptance of whatever came. Unlike the German people, the Japanese were willing to accept responsibility for the war and move on. They realized they had been led astray by wartime propaganda. At the time they had believed and acted upon these statements. After peace came, however, they saw their mistake and were willing to act upon a new understanding. Although many feared the coming of the GI's, most did not hate them— any more than they would have hated an earthquake. When the occupation proved to be milder than they had expected, the Japanese people were pleasantly surprised and ashamed. It was more humane than their own occupation of other areas.

General Douglas MacArthur, with his dramatic interpretation of events, and his firm domination of the situation as a benevolent but absolute ruler, was the kind of person with whom the Japanese could identify. Finally, when the great general was dismissed by a civilian President, they understood that American democracy was genuine.

When Baron Shidehara, a 1920's liberal, became the first Premier of the government under occupation, he asked Dr. Toyohiko Kagawa to assist him in charting a new spiritual course for the nation by filling the role of a moral prophet. Kagawa reluctantly accepted. Even more than Axling, this internationalist Christian had been caught in the crossfire of the war. American propagandists at one point broadcast that America was going to defeat Japan and establish Kagawa as ruler! In rebuttal, Kagawa protested that he was a loyal citizen of his own country. When his statement was monitored in the United States, many construed it to be a repudiation of his Christian commitment. Such is the fate of true internationalists.

The first specific appeal for reestablishing contact with Christians of United States came from Rev. Tsunetaro Miyakoda, an assistant to Kagawa. Mr. Miyakoda, who had been a member of the Christian Fellowship delegation to the United States in 1941, now invited his American counterparts to return the visit. The Americans, since then loosely organized into the Riverside Fellowship, met September 11, 1945, at Buck Hill Falls, Pennsylvania, and decided to accept the invitation. Axling, as the only available member of the group from Japan, was present.

Within a few days arrangements were made for four prominent Protestants from United States, all of whom had attended the Riverside Conference, to go to Japan. They arrived in Tokyo, October 23, 1945—the first private individuals allowed into the country after the war. From that beginning wounds began to be healed. It was through that group that Axling received his invitation to return.

The actual flow of missionaries back to Japan was facilitated by the appointment of a commission of six representative and experienced missionaries whose duty it was to make preliminary arrangements. Since General MacArthur openly encouraged the sending of both missionaries and Christian literature to Japan, the task was comparatively easy. The authorities, however, were scrupulously careful not to favor any religious group.

Housing was a major problem. Missionary property was either destroyed or confiscated. Private missionary holdings, such as the Axling house, also had been confiscated. Army facilities could not be used for this purpose, nor could the missionaries be allowed to impose upon the impoverished Japanese. In early 1946 two members of the commission were allowed into Japan. In June, the other four went. Since there were no Baptists on the commission, Paul S. Mayer, of the Evangelical Association, served as the Baptist agent. As rapidly as arrangements for housing could be made, missionaries began to return. The priority list for Northern Baptists included R. H. Fisher, J. A. Foote, Marlin D. Farnum, William Axling, and Miss Thomasine Allen. Dr. Axling left for Japan in December, 1946. At seventy-three years of age, he had been granted a two-year term for special service.

Returning to Japan brought a generous mix of pleasure and pain to Axling. He docked at 3:00 P.M. and was taken to the home of J. A. Foote, in Yokohama. There he was met by a large

number of Japanese friends who could not get passes to the dock.
Tasuku Sakata spoke for many when he said: "I knew that Axling
Sensei would come back. I said all the time that he would."

Axling, who had read every available scrap of news, was prepared for the worst. At this first meeting, however, he was pleasantly surprised that his friends were not as thin as he feared. The
new rice crop had eased the food crisis somewhat. He was
startled by the overall toll that the war had taken: "My, how old
they have all grown!" he kept saying to himself.

As he began to move about Japan, his worst fears were confirmed. Ten years later he could still vividly describe the
situation!

> Ruins, ruins, unending acres of ruins! Here and there a naked chimney
> or a concrete gatepost lifted itself out of the ashes in mute appeal.
> Shanties thrown together of pieces of burned, blackened sheet iron were
> scattered among the wreckage. These teemed with men, women, and
> children, half starved and in rags. The biting winter winds and driving
> rains beat through these shelters day and night.
>
> So deadly was the devastation that often it was difficult to find even
> the debris-covered site where the churches and Christian schools had
> stood. The remnant of church members and students who survived the
> bombings and the flames was scattered to the four winds. This was
> Tokyo. This was Japan, when the war clouds cleared away.

What always impressed Axling most was the impact of the war
on the people, and it was to this need that he addressed himself.
That need, both physical and spiritual, was everywhere. Again
from his descriptions ten years later:

> They came empty-handed. Everything was gone. Their businesses and
> places of employment were gone. Just two empty hands. But with an
> indomitable will to begin anew and press on.
>
> An empty stomach and rags, however, play havoc with a person's will
> and morale. Our first task, therefore, was that of undergirding their will
> and buttressing their marvelous morale by helping to provide for their
> elemental physical needs. Christ in a similar situation often began there.
> Clothing, food, vitamins, temporary church buildings, the rebuilding of
> school buildings, physical and material reconstruction became the impera-
> tive order of the day.
>
> They came not only empty handed, but often empty hearted. This was
> especially true of the youth. Youth came out of the war and its inglorious
> defeat disillusioned and stunned. The State had let them down. Emperor
> worship was gone. Their dreams of spearheading a crusade for the libera-
> tion of Asia from the exploiting West had gone up in smoke. Everything

they had lived by and lived for was gone. Groping in a mental and spiritual vacuum they were on an eager, agonizing quest for a new way of life.

For the last of many times during his long life, Axling's sensitive spirit was exposed to massive human deprivation and suffering. As always, he suffered with the people. Long after the emergency was past, he could effectively squelch a festive gathering of missionaries by reciting some tragedy he had observed and commenting: "I am bleeding at every pore."

In every way possible, Axling identified with the people of broken Japan. Often he would stand by a bombed-out church building and say, with tears filling his eyes: "Please forgive America." When he arrived it was still customary for Americans to ride free on the trolleys. Axling always paid. Americans never were expected to wait for service. Axling always got in line. Occasionally, in order not to miss a speaking engagement, he would exercise his privilege and take a place on the train, but never for his personal comfort. His usual frugality now became more extreme, so that he might not appear to have more than his Japanese friends. His clothes were more worn than usual, and on his many travels he carried a battered old suitcase.

As late as 1949, when B. L. Hinchman arrived, Axling was noticeably embarrassed by the house furnishings Hinchman had brought at the advice of the mission board. A new refrigerator, which was still far too expensive for the Japanese, seemed especially inappropriate. Axling urged the newcomers to get the things out of sight as quickly as possible.

When Axling first arrived, he lived in a mission house which had been rented to two Japanese families. These families had been served legal notice to vacate, but since there was no place to go, the mission would not pursue the matter. Axling was given two rooms, one for a bedroom and the other for a study. He also preempted a corner of the kitchen.

For the first time in his life, Axling was forced to prepare all his own meals and do his own housework. The results were mixed. His observation that he let the oatmeal cook too long, and without enough water was typical.

Although the house was standing, repairs had been neglected since the beginning of the war. During a storm a section of the roof over his bedroom blew off, allowing the rain to soak the contents. Because of its southeast exposure the bedroom was fairly warm. The study, however, on the northwest corner, was always cold. Finally Axling used his connections to acquire an army stove for that room.

Axling's special appointment carried three major responsibilities. First, he was correspondent for the Baptist group and chairman of its committee on relations. This made him, in fact, the field secretary. It was his responsibility to coordinate Baptist interests with other Christian groups on the field, and to keep the line of communication open between the home board and the field.

His second responsibility was as missionary counselor and helper to those churches which before the merger had been Baptist in Central and Northern Japan. In this capacity he also helped in the reconstruction of a number of churches. At first rebuilding was impossible because of the scarcity of materials. The Kyodan, however, was able to secure a number of Quonset huts which were made available to various churches. Axling saw to it that his churches got their share!

The Tabernacle, which represented the center of Axling's work in Japan, had been sold during the war and the money used to save Kanto Gakuin. By mid-April, 1947, Axling had learned that the building could be regained for about $20,000. He immediately wrote to the mission board, urging that action be taken while recovery of the building for Baptist use was still possible. In spite of delays because some questioned the strategic importance of the Tabernacle and the availability of funds, the building was eventually regained for the Baptists. It is now the headquarters of Baptist work in Japan and the home of the Misaki-Cho Church.

Axling, always convinced of the value of a united church, was confirmed in this opinion by his observations after the war. He found the former Baptists maintaining their old fellowship, but organizationally integrated into the Kyodan. As he saw it, the only factor which would tempt them to leave would be the hope of greater financial aid from American Baptists.

Perhaps there was an economic factor in the minds of some who feared that the small Baptist groups would be forgotten or left unsupported by the Baptist Board in America if they remained in a large United Church. Others, however, motivated by theological concerns were reluctant to endanger what they held to be important Baptist distinctives by participation in the United Church. The Boards in America were not much help to those who were faced with the decision in Japan. The Woman's Foreign Board voted to support the United Church, but the General Society could not agree to take a similar action. Thus the lack of a positive step by the American Baptist Foreign Mission Boards left its missionaries outside the Kyodan, working with Baptist churches within the Kyodan. This reluctance resulted in a feeling of uncertainty on the part of both missionaries and Japanese churches that led ultimately in 1958 to the withdrawal of approximately twenty of the sixty-four Baptist churches from the Kyodan to form the Japan Baptist Union.

Axling, however, was so committed to a single Japanese church that he ignored the tremendous difficulties of the Kyodan. Put together under pressure and forced to live its early life fighting to keep its Christian faith pure and to improve its Japanese loyalty during all-out war, the Kyodan had not been able to resolve some important problems. Many feared that its centralized structure would prevent the rich heritage of the various Christian bodies from being adequately expressed. In spite of his commitment to Christian unity, Axling must have been aware of these difficulties. One suspects that his characteristic long-range view led him to expect changes for the better within the Kyodan.

Axling's own breadth of Christian feeling was illustrated by the reconstruction of one of the many churches which he made possible. Mr. Nobuo Tokita had taken his church out of the Kyodan and helped to reorganize the Baptist Convention. A major reason for this action was his opposition to the presbyterian polity of the United Church. His disagreements with Dr. Axling were of long standing, for he had been on the opposite side of the dispute over the administration of the Tabernacle. Nevertheless, Axling visited Mr. Tokita's church and offered to help in reconstruction. At the time, the First Baptist Church of Washington, D.C., was building an educational building. The pastor, Dr. Edward H. Pruden, had written to Axling, asking for a project which would help keep his people's minds on others as well as on themselves. Axling suggested Mr. Tokita's church, and the project was accepted. Mr. Tokita was deeply moved. As he expressed it: "I was against him, but his love caught me up."

Axling's third responsibility was with the evangelistic campaign conceived by Kagawa and sponsored by the Kyodan. This movement had various names, such as the "Japan for Christ" movement and the "Three Million Souls" movement. Later, the objective was raised to five million conversions.

Between April, 1947, and May, 1948, Axling spoke 174 times in eighty different villages, towns, and cities to a total of over 35,000 people. This movement was an all-out attempt to reach the masses of Japan with the Christian message. The meetings were held in schools, factories, public buildings, social clubs, and private homes, as well as churches. The response in terms of hands raised and cards signed was unexpectedly large. At one meeting in the Shigei Church, where Captain Luke Bickel had pioneered with his Gospel Ship, Axling reported that all of the 340 non-Christians in the meeting raised their hands. "During my ministry of fifty years," Axling wrote, "I have seen many minority votes, some majority votes, but this is the first time that I have witnessed a unanimous vote for Christ by a non-Christian audience."

Axling was too realistic to presume that everyone who raised a hand became a Christian. Nevertheless, if Japan, especially the Japanese youth, would listen, Axling would speak as long as his strength held out. Some who responded would be transformed into God's agents in the world. Others might be completely unaffected. In between, however, would be many who, while never joining the church, would be in some way changed by the Christian gospel. These, too, would help to form the context in which Japan would someday become a Christian nation.

Axling's mature understanding of these facts was revealed in an address which he delivered in 1948. He acknowledged that many Christian people, in America in particular, were unconvinced of the success of an enterprise until they could see statistical results. While recognizing the necessity of building Christian institutions, he pointed out that the richest and most redemptive results of the Christian movement cannot be tabulated. (For a fuller text of these remarks, see Appendix B.)

In these times following the war, Axling saw all of his work, especially the evangelistic campaign, as an answer to the aggressive thrust of communism. Fascism was no longer the enemy. He understood very well how communism could grow in the soil of economic distress and loss of morale which followed the war.

Writing in *Missions*, January, 1949, Axling used this threat to stir the American church to greater effort. "The Communists," he wrote, "are high-speeding an intensive campaign to win Japan's youth to their ideology and way of life. The Japanese Christian church through the 'Japan for Christ Movement' is pressing the battle for Japan's soul but she is woefully underequipped and undermanned. Which will win?"

In September, 1947, after Axling had acquired a house, Mrs. Axling returned. Once again they were at home in their beloved Japan. Although Lucinda's health kept her from regular duties, their home became a gathering place for both missionaries and Japanese seeking advice and encouragement.

Limited outside activities secluded Lucinda from some of the postwar suffering. Yet she faced her own problems. Her health remained precarious. The hours when William was gone were long and lonely. When he was home, age had added to his characteristic fatigue-induced withdrawal. Also, as Lucinda's deafness increased, conversation became more difficult.

The consequence of these conditions was often the loss of domestic tranquillity. The young Hinchmans, who for two years lived downstairs from the Axling apartment, were embarrassed by the "all-out family fight in the apartment of the saints above."

And yet, this couple were ever in love. William never left the house without kissing Loue good-bye. No matter how busy, he wrote every day when he was away. After the war, when travel was difficult and dangerous, he always telegraphed "arrived safely" as soon as he had reached his destination. On one occasion, this custom backfired. Unusually hurried, he wired only one word "arrived." Loue was beside herself until he finally returned safely. These returns were what she lived for. As soon as she knew the date when he would be back, she would hurry to tell whoever was within reach about the good news.

Loue had a right to worry about William. He worked incredibly hard for a man of his age. He also traveled constantly on the "murder trains," so called because of the danger caused by overcrowding and overtaxed equipment. In an article entitled "Hungry and Weary, but Fresh as a Cherry Blossom," published in *Missions*, November, 1947, he described one of these trips taken the summer before Loue returned:

For my trip to Mito, where I had promised to preach, I had to get up at six o'clock, prepare my breakfast, put my room and bed in order, make some sandwiches for my lunch, and leave the house at seven o'clock for Tokyo's Uena Station. Having to wait at numerous corners for cars, it took me two hours to cross the city.

Upon arrival at the station, I immediately shoved my way to the train for Mito. It was still an hour before train departure and the train was already overcrowded. By the time the train started at ten o'clock, my car was so crowded that I could scarcely breathe. For two hours I stood packed in so tight that it was almost impossible to move my hands or feet. During the final hour of the trip, however, I managed to get a seat, such as it was, for the seats on trains and electric cars in Japan now are all in rags and tatters. Moreover the trip to Mito was like riding in a prison. The glass in the car windows had been smashed and the windows are boarded up.

The city of Mito is flat. Scarcely a house remains unburned. All of the churches were destroyed in the air raids. Our meeting was held in the home of one of the members who has managed to build a barrack for his home and office. It was a fine meeting. There was no place for me to stay overnight, so I had to take the 5:30 train back to Tokyo. When it arrived it was absolutely impossible to get on it. The people were hanging on to the last step of every entrance, sitting in the openings which had served as windows and even standing on the couplings between cars. The platform of the Mito station was packed with people who wanted to get on. That was the condition at every station we afterward passed through. Fortunately for me one of the Mito church deacons had come to the station with me, so he rushed to the station master's office and secured permission for me to ride in the baggage car.

I reached my home at 10:45 P.M., having had nothing but a sandwich to eat since my 6:30 breakfast. Fortunately the electricity was still on and I soon made a bowl of Betty Crocker's split pea soup and toasted some bread. It tasted like a feast fit for a king. Then, in case the electricity might be off in the morning, I cooked my oatmeal for breakfast and got to bed at midnight, exactly an *eighteen hour day!*

After travel became more normal, Mrs. Axling occasionally visited Haruko and the children. This relationship, too, brought pain as well as pleasure. Haruko's marriage was a casualty of the troubled times which followed the war. Later she remarried, but her life was far from easy. Many of the same factors which kept the Axlings from being ideal parents kept them from being as helpful as they might have been in this difficult circumstance.

As the end of the two-year special term approached, Axling and his Japanese colleagues began a campaign to have it extended. The officers' council of the board was reluctant. The age of the Axlings plus the necessity of getting new missionaries accustomed to responsibility were probably major concerns. The reason given for not extending his service was the strong desire of the board to have Dr. Axling in America to help with the promotion of the Advance Program of the Foreign Missions Conference.

The Japanese sent several letters and petitions asking that the mission society leave the Axlings in Japan. Their reasons were moving and revealing. Love and respect for the Axlings was clearly expressed. The Japanese regard for age was emphasized: "To our thinking the last few years of missionary life count more than the early long years." They stated that the most highly esteemed missionaries were those who ". . . left to us not only their works but also their bodies." Also, the Axlings should be allowed to complete fifty years of service, ". . . which will be not only for his honor, but for the glory of God."

Axling pleaded his own case by listing reasons for staying and explaining how it could be done. The reasons, five in number, were the unprecedented evangelistic opportunity, the scarcity of evangelistic missionaries to meet that need, the desire of the Japanese for him to "finish our days here," the fact that many of the new missionaries were still learning the language, and the Axlings' personal desire to be near Haruko and the grandchildren a little longer.

After giving his reasons for staying, Axling listed ways and means by which this could be done. He would accept retirement from the American Baptist Foreign Mission Society and resign all Baptist responsibilities. He would make no further financial demands on the board, since his travel allowance was already budgeted, and he would live on his retirement pay. He would be an evangelist for Kagawa's movement, a trustee for the Japan Bible Society, a trustee for the Japan Christian Peace Association, an adviser of the Tokyo School for the Japanese Language, a member of the editorial board of the *Japan Christian Quarterly,* and so forth.

He went on to make it clear that if he should return to help in the Advance Program, it should not prejudice his return to Japan. Even though it was true that much pressure was being brought to bear on him to retire in Japan, the board need not worry, since "we doubt the wisdom of our doing this." He did, however, desire very much to finish fifty years.

The last paragraph of the letter condensed the reasons and

restated the appeal:

> I suppose it is unreasonable to expect anyone not on the ground here to feel the pull and the urge of the call to carry on for the salvation of Japan until the last ounce of energy has been expended. Especially now that the day of opportunity for which we have prayed and agonized has finally dawned.

The immediate solution was to accept a recommendation of the committee on relations in Japan, that Axling be continued six months, specifically for evangelistic campaigning. According to this arrangement, his closing date would be June 30, 1949. Later the officers' council of the board decided on an extension of one more year, to June 30, 1950. In doing so, they made it clear that the reference committee should use the intervening time to make plans for carrying on the work of the mission secretary beyond June 30, 1950, and to present to the home board a suitable recommendation.

In the spring of 1950, before this extension expired, William returned alone to the United States to promote the Japan Opportunity Program—a campaign to raise funds for the rebuilding and advancement of the Japanese mission. In four months he traveled seventeen thousand miles and gave 106 addresses to sixteen thousand people. Besides these activities, he made four radio broadcasts and appeared on his first television show.

At every opportunity Axling used all of his persuasive power to stir Americans to action. Reminding them that General Mac-Arthur had declared, "The battle for Japan has neither been won nor lost," he urged his hearers to provide the resources to win. "The hour for this advance has struck." Earlier opportunities to capture Japan for Christ had passed unrealized, because of small resources. Must this chance too, go by default?

As he had done before, Axling used the communist threat to stir American Christians. He vividly described the efforts of this group:

> Just before I left Tokyo one day, I stood and watched a parade of three thousand red students and their fellow travelers. Block after block, battalion after battalion, marching four abreast with arms interlocked. Flags flying, banners waving, shouting slogans, singing their crusading songs, with faces aglow, their whole personalities possessed with a crusader's zeal and determination to win.
>
> Compared with them our Christian life and service is tame and timid and tepid. It is neutral and negative and spineless.

Axling reminded his audiences that during the war Americans had risen to heroic heights and had sacrificed much for a military victory. Now with the soul of Japan, the cause of Christ, the future of mankind at stake, "are we doing it today?"

Some of his hearers were stirred, even deeply moved, but few acted significantly.

By the fall of 1950, physical conditions were greatly improved in Japan. The Japanese church and missionary organizations were again stabilized. Among the Baptists, B. L. Hinchman, who had arrived in Japan January 19, 1949, assumed the responsibility of missionary secretary. Other missionaries had arrived on the field and some had acquired the language. The need for Axling was not so great. These same more-settled conditions, however, removed many of the reasons against Axling's return. Why not allow him to continue his work as an evangelist at large with the Kyodan? Besides, the board had about given up trying to determine his course. The Axlings again owned their own home in Japan, and their health was quite good.

In November, 1950, Axling returned to Japan and began what proved to be his last tour of duty. During this time he had no official connection with the Baptists. He also began resigning from the boards of trustees of numerous organizations and institutions. Most of his time was given to evangelistic preaching.

Also during this last tour Axling spent much time helping American army personnel, and especially their wives, adjust to a strange land. Among these was his grandniece, Mildred Westen.

Axling's unusual physical stamina, which had failed him only at times of extreme stress, seemed as robust as ever. He could still handle the heavy oil drums containing the household fuel, and walk at a rapid pace. That year at the Baptist missionary retreat his active participation in running games worried everyone. Yet no one was quite willing to ask the seventy-seven-year-old missionary to sit down.

Reports and letters during the last five years in Japan bristled with statistics—with miles traveled, sermons preached, size of audience, and number of commitments made. A description of a twenty-two-day campaign in Nagano province in 1951 is typical —he preached forty-four times "in nineteen villages and towns and three cities." The response was 4,249 first decisions and 1,043 rededications.

By 1954, the crowds had dwindled and the response was smaller. In March, Axling wrote Dr. Elmer A. Fridell: "There are reactionary trends and the crowding of people to the churches that characterized the early years of peace no longer obtains." The dwindling of crowds, however, did not reduce the number of engagements or the energy expended. In September Axling wrote to Gordon H. Schroeder, then pastor of his home church in Lincoln, Nebraska: "Mrs. Axling and I have passed our eightieth milestones, and still the opportunities for service keep coming."

In addition to preaching, these opportunities came by way of personal counseling. Although these contacts are more difficult to document, they may well have been more influential. People came for all kinds of reasons. Axling was never too busy or too tired from his travels to spend hours with a humble Japanese woman who came because of a death in the family, or a laborer who had been dismissed from a job. One day his secretary, Mariya Takahashi, was startled to see a certain man walk into the office. Axling, who was standing there, smiled and extended his hand.

"Well, well, it has been a long time since I saw you last. How have you been?"

The man bowed his head and replied, "I must ask your kind help."

"Let us talk in the other room," suggested Axling.

After some time the two emerged and the man said, "If you could do this for me, I would be very much indebted to you."

After the man had gone, Axling turned to his secretary and said, with a smile, "That man is my friend. Before the war he followed me wherever I went. In the street car or the train he was there to protect me."

The fact was that the man had been a secret policeman assigned to Axling, and Miss Takahashi remembered him as an "altogether repulsive person." After the war the department was dissolved and the agent was down and out. Something in the man he had harassed convinced the policeman that Axling could and would help him. He was right.

This compassionate, forgiving man was the same Axling who would often come downstairs when he was living over the Hinchmans and say, gravely, "Bill, may I see you outside?" Then would follow a hushed conversation in which he would describe a footprint he had discovered or a strange man he had seen passing the house several times. His fear of burglars led frequently to calling the police. Fear and trust, suspicion and confidence were well mixed in William Axling.

Much of the last five years was occupied with the receiving of honors from missionaries, his Japanese colleagues, and civil authorities. In 1951 the fiftieth anniversary of his coming to Japan was celebrated. During his last year, 1954, public honor followed public honor.

The timing of these recognitions was determined by the fact that Mrs. Axling's health made it necessary for them to plan to return to the United States. In January, 1950, she fell and broke her leg. In the hospital she developed pneumonia. The doctor gave little hope for recovery. Dr. Axling stayed in his room and prayed for hours. Even when she had overcome the pneumonia, the doctor said she would not walk again. By summer, however, she was walking, shopping, and running with her grandchildren. Everyone except Uncle Billy was surprised. By 1954, however, Loue's reserve seemed entirely gone.

Two of the honors came from the Japanese Government. The first, on May 14, 1954, was in recognition of his work to further the goodwill and friendly relationships between Japan and the United States. He became the first missionary to be awarded the Second Order of Merit of the Order of the Sacred Treasury by the Japanese National Government. In October of the same year, in recognition of his outstanding social work, he was made an honorary citizen of Tokyo. This was a first for a non-Japanese. Through the years, the Axlings had received many invitations to take part in Imperial ceremonial affairs, and William was often invited to socialize with prominent persons of the Empire. On July 13, however, he received the unusual invitation for a personal audience with the Emperor. At the time the Axlings were living in a humble three-room house in Shin-okubo in Tokyo.

As would be expected, he was honored on many occasions by various church groups in Japan. In July, the United Church held a congratulatory reception in honor of his singular recognition by the Government. On December 12, the Baptists of Japan had a farewell reception. Rev. Isamu Chiba, principal of Soshin Girls' School in Yokohama, was chairman. The chief speaker was Rev.

Hajine Watanabe, one of the founders of Kanto Gakuin, who said simply, "We feel lonely and sad because we are parting with our elderly father and mother; and yet we are in high spirits."

After the Axlings were presented with beautiful Japanese costumes, William responded: "Mrs. Axling and I are now filled with immense thanks. Everywhere and always we have been received not as missionaries but as a brother and sister, for which we feel wholly unable to express our gratitude." Then, after the speeches and a closing prayer, the Axlings dressed in their costumes and posed for pictures.

The next day a farewell gathering was held by the National Council of Churches in the Christian Center in the Ginza, Tokyo. Rev. Michio Kozaki, president of the council, gave the major address, in which he thus characterized the honored guests:

> Today we rarely have a witness for Christ with such a genuine Christian character as Dr. Axling. . . . As we advance in our age, the sense of our evangelistic mission is apt to become weak. But it is entirely different with Dr. Axling. With the increase of his years, he devoted himself all the more for the work of evangelism.

Rev. Ken Muto, head of the United Church of Christ in Japan, added these words:

> I was always impressed by the fact that he really knew Japanese people and respected them. He knew absolutely no racial discrimination for the Japanese people. Because of this we all had our respect and love for him. One other thing I wish to say is with regard to our appreciation for his special cooperation with the work of the United Church of Christ. There have been many difficulties since its organization, and Dr. Axling, as a distinguished pioneer Baptist, has always given his invaluable advice and support for its development, for which I cannot fully express our gratitude and appreciation.

The American Baptist missionaries in Japan paid their formal respects to the Axlings by dedicating the book *Out of the Ashes* to them. In this statement of appreciation they expressed their thanks for the understanding of the gospel, the vision, the ministry of love, and the patience demonstrated by William, and the "perpetual cheerfulness" of Lucinda. "And so, to you, Aunt Lu and Uncle Billy, we gratefully dedicate this little volume." (For the full text of the dedication, see Appendix C.)

The last months in Japan were even busier than usual. Besides the meetings, visitors came from all over the Empire. The Axlings were also invited into many homes. In spite of all this, Axling continued to speak throughout the country. Miss Ada Nelson, with whom they spent the last four months before sailing home, remembers:

> He would always come back with glowing reports about how many people he had spoken to, how many first decisions and rededications had taken place. In spite of his age, few churches offered to provide transportation for him. He would start out early, walking up the ninety-two steps which led to the street car line from our house, and would come back late at night, coming down the steps and through the dark tunnel and to the house.

And so in an almost miraculous way, William Axling was granted a glorious Indian summer at the end of his ministry in Japan. As throughout his life, his victories were darkened by defeat. As fruitful as the last years were, it became increasingly evident that Axling's ministry was drawing to an end. The greatest of men cannot serve far beyond his own generation. Axling's grasp on the language was as good as ever, but his speech was now old-fashioned. Even though his major concern was youth, he was identifying with the past generation. Such an alert, open, sensitive person as Axling never gets completely out of touch, but he was slipping. He had done much to bridge the gap between the pioneer and the modern missionary. Now the modern missionary must take over. In the last years Axling did all he could to pass on his vision, which would never be out of date—the vision of "a new Japan, a bright Japan, a glorious Japan" made possible by the gospel of Christ.

By January 18, 1955, after a sukiyaki dinner with the Sakatas, the Axlings boarded the steamship *President Cleveland* for their last crossing of the Pacific and their final return to America.

10. NO EAST—NO WEST

As IN THE CASE of all his previous residences, William Axling looked upon Atherton Baptist Homes in Alhambra, California, as a base of operation, rather than as a place to live. With characteristic prudence, he had made all the arrangements for occupancy before leaving Japan. He was delighted with a "beautiful place and the community of some eighty-five fine people, most of whom have spent their lives in direct Christian work."

Axling had no intention of sinking into inactivity in this "final" retirement. On the way from Japan the couple spent three weeks in Honolulu, "which turned out to be a speaking fest instead of a rest." Between February 22, when they settled at Atherton, and October 1, William traveled sixteen thousand miles within the United States and delivered seventy lectures. The months of May and June took him to Washington, Oregon, Indiana, Michigan, New York, Pennsylvania, North and South Dakota, and Nebraska.

This pace kept up almost unabated for the next five years. National and state conventions, association gatherings, seminary chapels and lecture series, councils of churches programs, meetings of service clubs and civic organizations, all responded to his open optimism and earnest sincerity. Gene E. Bartlett, then pas-

183

tor of the First Baptist Church of Los Angeles, was among many who expressed insightful appreciation:

> When you were speaking I couldn't help thinking of two things: first, of the changes that have come to our world in the fifty years of your service. That's a miracle in itself. But equally, is the fact that you have kept pace with that change! Your whole approach is as fresh and contemporary as though you were just starting your work in Japan. That's a great tribute to you, and I am grateful for your coming.

Just before leaving Japan, Axling finished his last full-length book, *Japan at the Midcentury.* It appeared in Japan in the spring of 1955 and was published by the Judson Press in the United States in 1957. Most of this book had been written in 1946, much of it at the missionary residence at Andover Newton Theological School while he was waiting to return to Japan after the war. He was then unable to find a publisher. Finally, after revisions, made largely while riding Japanese trains, he and some of his friends underwrote publication, with the understanding that all royalties would be used to begin a fund for the building of a chapel at Kanto Gakuin. Completion of this chapel was one of the objectives of the World Mission Campaign, launched in 1965 by the American Baptist Convention.

Japan at the Midcentury, with its subtitle "Leaves from Life," is an interweaving of Axling's life with an interpretative history of Japan. The Foreword states: "The contents of this volume were gleaned from the laboratory of life. They are the saga of the pilgrimage of the Japanese people from the hedged-in frozen life-patterns of Feudalism to the freer expansive ways of nascent democracy."

The book also restates the purpose of Axling's life and work. He was more convinced than ever that Japan was the best place to begin building socialized democracy in Asia because of the compactness of her territory, the high literacy rate of her people, and her tradition of stable government. Her war experience had left feelings of resentment toward dictators and disillusion with the promise of imperialism. Axling added that, in postwar Japan, politics, education, and industry were in the hands of leading liberals.

In order for Japan to fulfill her high place in the East for the good of the world, two things must happen. First, Japan must establish economic justice for every last man, woman, and child.

Second, and even more basic, Japan must have a soul—a soul which only Christianity could supply. "It has the redemptive Gospel that can lift the Japanese people out of their present spiritual vacuum." As Axling saw it, unless what he called a "full-orbed" Christian faith captured the nation, "a new Japan is an empty dream." Without a new Japan, Axling feared chaos in Asia which would drag down the whole world toward destruction in another war.

In every way possible, Axling endeavored to kindle in the heart of American Christendom his vision of what must be done in Japan. Nowhere did he make his case more powerfully than in the script that he wrote for a pictorial brochure produced by the Friendship Press in 1959. This attractive twenty-four-page booklet, *This Is Japan*, gave a good summary of Japan's land and people, educational advance, industrialization, postwar conditions, the status of the Christian movement, and the importance of Japan in an awakened Asia.

Axling's description of the Christian movement in Japan, although comprehensive, fair and positive, left no doubt that current efforts would not accomplish the needed task. He perceptively grouped Japanese Christian efforts into four classifications.

First, was the United Church, in which at that time thirty-four denominations were "pooling their spiritual and material resources in a flexible but united effort to bring the redemptive impact of the Gospel to bear upon the nation."

Second, was the National Christian Council of Japan, which included the work of such major denominations as Anglican, Lutheran, and Southern Baptist, as well as the United Church.

Third, was a large NonChurch Christian Fellowship which had "grown spontaneously out of the nation's rice roots." Axling had high words of praise for this movement:

> It makes a study of the Bible a major purpose of its existence. Christ is the divine magnet that holds the fellowship together. As in the early church, the torch is carried from person to person, heart to heart, home to home. Its potentialities are great, and it challenges the church to make the Bible itself the core and center of her message and to revitalize her inner life through exalting Christ as the church's rallying center.

Fourth, were the missions and Japanese organizations working outside the National Christian Council but cooperating in the Evangelical Missionary Association of Japan. They had established their own institutions and were producing their own literature.

Long experience had led Axling to believe that the fragmented methods being followed would never accomplish the task of Christianizing Japan. In a key paragraph he stated:

> This all adds up to the disturbing fact that postwar Protestantism in Japan with a total of only 322,707 adherents still presents a blurred picture of over one hundred different denominations and groupings. An evangelistic front broken into innumerable fragments! This at a time when the nation is responsive and the hour has struck for a great Christian crusade centered in Him, who with such pathos and passion prayed that all may be one and that the world may believe.

Gradually Axling's opportunities to proclaim his message began to decline. First to diminish were invitations to distant places. For awhile local speaking engagements filled the gap. By 1960, most people who were interested had heard him. Whenever a month went by without an opportunity to speak, Axling was likely to write to the mission board inquiring if he were out of favor.

His interest and involvement with the Japanese people never waned. Shortly after settling in Los Angeles, the Axlings transferred their membership from the First Baptist Church of Lincoln, Nebraska, to the Los Angeles Japanese Baptist Church. William also asked the pastor, his long-time friend, Rev. K. T. Shiraishi, to acquire a resting place for himself and Mrs. Axling among the Japanese people.

Since Rose Hills Memorial Park had recently established the "Cherry Blossom" section for the Japanese, Mr. Shiraishi bought four lots, two for the Axlings and two for himself. The next day, a somewhat embarrassed salesman returned half of the money and explained that the site was for Japanese only. Once again, racial segregation had raised its head. Against Dr. Axling's urgings, Mr. Shiraishi canceled the total sale, because he "had no desire to remain there alone without the Axlings."

Until the end of his life Axling's friendship and counsel was sought by Japanese Christians. The Axling apartment in Alhambra was a stopping place for many Japanese who visited the United States. Axling also kept in touch with many of the Japanese who were studying in this country. In 1957, one of these who was studying at the University of California, Los Angeles, wrote a typical letter:

The first experienced life in a new strange society was throwing my spirit into confusion. Naturally, there had been a lot of dissatisfaction in my mind. However, the God-fearing atmosphere in your home reminded me of what I should have been. I am really grateful now to be able to get my spirit again. How much I appreciate your splendid guidance. I am solicitous of your further assistance and encouragement.

Many students through the years received helpful recommendations, encouragement, and scholarship assistance. The monetary value of the scholarship usually was small, but often much appreciated by young Japanese students struggling to make their way in a strange land. Many responded in a way similar to the following: "A couple of days ago I received your gift, $25.00, from the Baptist office in New York. Thank you very much, Dr. Axling, for your kindness and encouragement for my study. I will stay another year here at Chicago Divinity School."

The Axlings were also active participants in the Atherton community. Uncle Billy's good humor, boundless optimism, enormous goodwill, and tireless energy enabled him to become one of the leaders among the notable residents. Besides his contribution to the general atmosphere, he is remembered for the establishment of a weekly missionary prayer meeting. All in all, he was a valued member of the community.

Mrs. Axling's health continued to decline. Serious illness, broken limbs, and finally a stroke strictly limited her activities. William's frequent absences, her deafness, and the difficulty he had with conversational speech left her very lonely. Yet William remained the center of her life. One day when he was away she was walking home from the nearby Baptist church with Miss Winifred Acock. Suddenly she said, "You know, that's just like Will."

"What's just like Will?" asked Miss Acock.

"The song we just sang, 'Just When I Need Him Most,'" Lucinda replied. "He's away so much and I wish he were here, and he's away. But just when I need him most, he's always there."

No sooner had she finished speaking than a car drove up and Dr. Axling got out. They walked off together.

Finally in 1959 Lucinda suffered a complete nervous breakdown. Few if any of the many heartbreaking experiences of Axling's long career outranked his beloved Loue's illness. A letter written June 9, 1959, best expresses his feeling:

There is no change in Loue's condition. Her mental break shifted the scene for her from the present to the far past. I can only see her once a week. Sometimes she is at Morioka making preparations for the workers' Christmas. Or she is taking a group of Japanese young people to the sea shore for a fish bake. Or helping a Japanese couple get ready for their wedding. She pointed to one of the nurses standing near and said, "That's the bride." Always concerned about someone else. So her soul breaks through her shattered mind and continues to shine. This helps to put the stars back in my sky.

January 7, 1960, "just as the sun was rising in the East," Lucinda was mercifully relieved by death. Those who attended the funeral, held in Merrian Chapel at Atherton Baptist Homes, were deeply moved when Dr. Axling rose and asked permission to give a final tribute:

Mrs. Axling's health began to break the last year that we were in Japan. Our friends here in Atherton Court, therefore, never had an opportunity to know her real stature or the full-orbed life of service that she lived.

I have, therefore, asked for the privilege of saying a few words about Mrs. Axling, whom I knew as we lived and labored together almost fifty-nine years.

Then, in a firm and tender voice, he reviewed Lucinda's accomplishments. He characterized her as a person absolutely without racial prejudice, as a true spiritual pioneer, a faithful homemaker, and a valuable fellow worker. He concluded:

If under God I have been able to accomplish anything during the past fifty-nine years, much of the credit goes to Mrs. Axling, the other member of the team.

Those who knew Axling well, observed a noticeable difference soon after Lucinda's death. Age, which had begun to take its toll, now advanced rapidly. He still took many speaking engagements. As soon as he was behind the pulpit, much of the old vigor returned and audiences still thrilled to his earnest preaching.

As in the last days of Japan, so in the last days of Alhambra, many honors were bestowed upon William Axling by both civil and religious groups. The most outstanding was the gift of a *hato-tsue* cane, sent by the governor of Tokyo in recognition of one of its honorary citizens who had reached eighty-eight years of age. This "pigeon cane" was sort of a key to the city, granting its possessor, like a pigeon, permission to go at will to any part of the city.

By the spring of 1962, William Axling's robust strength was fading. In May he attended, in full Japanese dress, a dramatic presentation of his life, written by Mr. Louis Wilson, of the drama department of the California Baptist Theological Seminary, and performed in the First Baptist Church of Alhambra by seminary students. Afterward he wrote to Mr. Wilson: "Pardon this late note, but typing is very difficult for me these days, and I am miles behind in my correspondence. I think that you and the seminary students did a wonderful job with the drama, considering the material you had to work with. Frankly, I was afraid it would play me up. On the contrary, it was very factual."

What is factual about a man like William Axling? He was a rather ordinary little man, who through driving dedication made an extraordinary contribution to the cause of God among men. He was not an intellectual, but he had keen insight. He was a great preacher, but of rather limited scope. He was a poor administrator, but began several movements and contributed to the organizational development of many others. He was loved and respected by multitudes, but intimately known by very few. The closer one came to him, the more reserved he seemed. Yet he was most effective as a counselor.

When asked in the last months of his life to evaluate his work, he replied: "My name has figured with a great many movements, but the main strength of all of these was the Japanese Christians themselves." In another context he might well have replied with his favorite verse of Scripture: "I can do all things through Christ which strengtheneth me" (Philippians 4:13, KJV).

His physical strength declined rapidly through the summer and fall of 1962. Miss Alice Bixby, herself a resident of Atherton Homes, and a long-time missionary to Japan, added her personal care to the ministry of the staff. As he passed his eighty-ninth birthday, for the first time he began to lose interest in life.

Even then, when aroused, there was an awesome continuity in his life. Local Japanese Christian women, hoping to revive his appetite, offered to bring him Japanese food. "Yes, I would like to have some," replied Axling.

They prepared his favorite food, *unagimeshi* (boiled eel and rice). He tried to eat, but his stomach had for some time refused to accept solid food.

After the women had gone, Miss Bixby scolded him, "Why did

you say such a foolish thing to those Japanese ladies? You knew that you could not eat it."

"Out of courtesy," he replied, heavily. "I like no food now." Such was his Japanese-like response.

One of the last things he wrote was likewise in character. He had begun an autobiography, but completed only a few pages. In it he stated, "As I look back over these almost eighty-nine years, guidance at every turn of the road is so evident that all the praise belongs to him and to him alone."

On February 24, 1963, just as the sun was setting, the man called Axling slipped quietly into what he would have called "the realm of higher service."

His pastor, Rev. K. T. Shiraishi, led the memorial service, in which several others participated, for Los Angeles friends and relatives. He was then placed beside Mrs. Axling, not in the Cherry Blossom section, but in an integrated plot near by. In death as in life, he stood by principles which he never quite attained, but toward which he made progress.

Other services were held in Japan. Haruko attended the one at the Tabernacle. The building was "decorated with pure flowers and brightly lighted" as befitted the memory of "our teacher." One of his favorite hymns was sung:

> "O Jesus, I have promised
> To serve Thee to the end."

Many persons, most of them friends of Axling, and leaders in Japanese religious and civil affairs, gave testimonials concerning his work.

If Axling had chosen what should be said at his graveside, it probably would have been a sermon which he used often during the Alhambra years. He called it "No East, No West." In this sermon he reminded his audience that physically the world was now one. "For the first time in history we are living in God's kind of world, a world in which there is no East and no West." After making this point he would illustrate ways in which mankind had not yet responded to the possibilities of this fact. "Where spiritual and human values are concerned, we have not yet attained God's kind of world." The one way to bring the two together was through the "redemptive Christ of today."

Dr. Takaaki Aikawa, speaking at the memorial service at the Tabernacle, responded to Axling's life and testimony for all Christians: "I, representing all the Japanese and all Japanese Christians, offer here the deepest thanksgiving and hearty gratitude for what he has done for the Japanese in the Glory of God. And the sincerity of our gratitude will be proved in our effort in completing his dreams about churches, about Christian education, and about social work."

ACKNOWLEDGMENTS

Grateful acknowledgment is hereby made for permission to quote from the following copyrighted material:

On page 32, *A Theology of the Social Gospel* by Walter Rauschenbusch, by The Macmillan Company, 1917, pp. 6-7.

On pages 65-66, *Christianity and the Social Crisis* by Walter Rauschenbusch, Torch Book edition by Harper & Row, Publishers, 1964, p. 412.

On pages 135 and 136, *A History of the Ecumenical Movement, 1517-1948*, edited by Ruth Rouse and Stephen Charles Neill, published in the U.S.A. by The Westminster Press, 1954, reprinted 1967, pp. 461-462. © The Trustees of the Society for Promoting Christian Knowledge, 1953. Used by permission.

On pages 185 and 186, *This Is Japan* by William Axling, by Friendship Press, New York, 1959, p. 21. Used by permission.

Permission has also been received to quote from the writings of Axling published in the *Christian Herald*, November, 1945, several issues of *Mission Magazine*, and several issues of *The Baptist*, copyright held by *The Christian Century*.

Also, a portion of the script of a radio broadcast by Fulton Oursler, substituting for Walter Winchell on August 15, 1943 (American Broadcasting Company), has been used.

APPENDIX A

The resolution of the Board of the American Baptist Foreign Mission Society, on the occasion of the retirement of Dr. and Mrs. Axling in June, 1944.

In December, 1900, two young people, the Reverend and Mrs. Axling, were appointed to foreign mission service in Japan. In December, 1943, they arrived in the homeland, wartime repatriates, from the land to which they had given more than forty-three years of outstanding Christian witness.

The Misaki Tabernacle and the Fukagawa Christian Center in Tokyo stand as a memorial to the devotion of Rev. and Mrs. Axling. In addition to his responsibilities directly related to Baptist mission work, Dr. Axling made important contributions to the total Christian cause in Japan. He was Secretary of the National Christian Council, President of the Conference of Federated Missions of Japan, a delegate to the International Missionary Council in Jerusalem in 1928, and to the Madras Conference in 1938. He served for many years as the Secretary of the Kingdom of God Movement, an interfaith, all-Christian evangelistic crusade, and was associated with Dr. Kagawa in the work of the United Evangelistic Movement.

Mrs. Axling's influence on students, through her Bible classes, and her wide personal contacts, has been an outstanding contribution. Mothers' groups were a definite responsibility and joy to her. The Axling home was always open to strangers and friends alike who knew they were welcome there. Their sympathetic hearts made them always responsive to situations of need. Following the great earthquake in 1923, Dr. and Mrs. Axling adopted a little Japanese girl, Haruko, who has grown up to be their pride and joy.

Dr. Axling known as an exceptional linguist, has a command of the Japanese language such as few foreigners possess. This fact, coupled with his wide acquaintance among prominent Japanese business and professional men, gave him many opportunities to present Christ. He has always been in great demand for special evangelistic meetings by Christian groups throughout the Empire. He was looked to for advice and counsel, a veteran missionary who knew and loved the Japanese. Author of *On the Trail of Truth about Japan, Japan Wonders Why,* and a biography entitled *Kagawa,* he is himself known and loved by both Japanese and American Baptists.

Therefore be it resolved that the Board records with appreciation its gratitude for these distinguished missionaries and disciples of Christ; and that this action be made known to Dr. and Mrs. Axling with our best wishes for God's continued guidance and protection of their lives for the years ahead.

The written response made by Dr. Axling to this resolution:

In accordance with your action, Mrs. Axling and I today step out of the ranks as active missionaries of the American Baptist Foreign Mission Society. This relationship has covered a period of forty-three years and eight months. I cannot let the day pass without expressing our profound gratitude to God and to you for the high privilege of these years.

As we come to the close of this relationship and look back over the years, we are mightily moved. As far as we are concerned, not a single cloud has drifted across this relationship. The Society's officers and Board of Managers have invariably shown us the finest courtesy, heart-cheering understanding, and every Christian consideration.

We also wish to express our deep sense of gratitude to the missionaries of the Society with whom it has been our privilege to labor and fellowship during these long years. We owe them much, very much, for their unfailing love and fine spirit of cooperation. Their undying loyalty to Christ and their devotion to His cause has been a constant inspiration to us.

We have had our day. We have had our chance. We praise God, and thank you most sincerely for this long, long day and for this wonderful chance. We are keenly conscious of the many shortcomings and failures which have characterized the years. Most earnestly do we crave both God's and your forgiveness.

We willingly step into the background and yield the field to younger men. If, however, as retired missionaries, there is any voluntary service that we can still render, we shall be glad to do so.

Praying that God's blessing may continue to rest in rich measure upon the Society, upon its secretaries, upon its Board of Managers, and upon its world-wide work, believe me.

Yours in the bonds of Christian service,

William Axling

APPENDIX B

(From an address delivered by Dr. William Axling in
1948, revealing some of his philosophy of missions.)

In the minds of most people, the worthwhileness of the Christian mission in a given area, stands or falls on a number of converts won, on the number of churches organized, and the number and size of Christian institutions established. The materialistic American mind is unconvinced until it can get its hand on a counting machine and tabulate. It wants figures, and it wants them to pile up fast.

We must win converts, and we must organize them into churches if we are going to build on a permanent basis. We must establish Christian institutions if we are going to penetrate communities with Christian ideals and Christian influence.

But we must not forget or fail to realize that the Christian moves and works in a realm of the imponderable, and many of its richest and most redemptive results cannot be tabulated. Like all definite values they are intangible.

By what yard stick can you measure and tabulate the creative and curative, the saving and sweetening influences of Christ on human history? All you can say is that he deflected the whole course of that history from a pagan pattern to one in which God and man joined firm forces in building new men and new women, and building a spiritual community, and in building a new heaven and a new earth. But when you have said that, you have only touched the fringe of that influence. What is true of Christ, is true in a larger measure of the Christian mission.

197

APPENDIX C

(The Dedication of the book *Out of the Ashes, the Post War Decade in Japan,* published by the Japan Missionary Fellowship of the American Baptist Foreign Missionary Society and the Women's American Baptist Foreign Mission Society, 1955, pp. 7-8.)

To the Axlings, as you return to America:

For your fifty-three years of unswerving obedience to the "High calling of God in Christ Jesus" as you have served Him in Japan . . .

For your penetrating understanding of the full meaning of the Gospel, and for your fearless proclamation of that Gospel . . .

For your vision—enriched rather than dimmed by the years—which imparts to all you meet your confidence in God's promises . . .

For your ministry of loving statesmanship which has helped Christians of many backgrounds recognize their spiritual unity . . .

For the example you have shown to us of the meaning of Paul's words, "Woe be unto me if I do not preach" the message of the cross . . .

For your patience in dealing with green young missionaries . . .

For the countless evidences we have seen of the love you two have, one for the other, which serves as striking examples to all young homemakers . . .

For your perpetual cheerfulness, Aunt Lu, in spite of being left alone so often; and for the wonderful things which come out of your oven . . .

For all these reasons and many more we young missionaries are "thankful for every remembrance of you."

The Japanese government, too, has shown its appreciation for your service. Although unable to publicly recognize your *real* work, that of evangelism, the government has greatly honored you for some of the fruits of your evangelistic work: education, social welfare, and international understanding. You have received the highest decoration ever given a missionary: the Second Order of the Sacred Treasure. You have been received in audience by H.I.H. the Emperor. You are the first foreigner to be made an Honorary Citizen of Tokyo.

But we rejoice that there awaits for you a far greater honor than the passing plaudits of men. Because you have fought the good fight and have indeed kept the faith, there awaits for you a crown of righteousness which God the righteous judge shall give you. And we know what you will do with that crown: you will lay it at the feet of Him who saved you, called you, upheld you, and did His work through you.

And so, to you, Aunt Lu and Uncle Billy, we gratefully dedicate this little volume.

INDEX